80-1595

Arming America

How the U.S. Buys Weapons

Arming America
How the U.S. Buys Weapons

J. RONALD FOX
Formerly Associate Professor of Business Administration
Harvard University

DIVISION OF RESEARCH
GRADUATE SCHOOL OF BUSINESS ADMINISTRATION
HARVARD UNIVERSITY

Boston · 1974

Distributed by
Harvard University Press
Cambridge, Massachusetts
1974

PRINTED IN THE UNITED STATES OF AMERICA

Foreword

THIS STUDY REPRESENTS the culmination of a three-year research project conducted by Dr. J. Ronald Fox. The project began in 1968 while I was the Director of the Division of Research at the Harvard Business School and Dr. Fox was Associate Professor. In 1969 Dr. Fox was granted a two-year leave of absence from Harvard to accept a presidential appointment as Assistant Secretary of the Army. During those two years the research project benefited from the numerous project management activities and Congressional hearings in which Dr. Fox participated. The project also benefited during that time from Assistant Professor James S. Reece's continuing research on contract changes.

The budget for the United States Department of Defense will approach $90 billion for the fiscal year 1975. This event, in the context of unprecedented inflation, requires renewed effort to provide for the defense needs of the United States at the lowest reasonable cost. I believe this book contributes to that effort.

Financial support for this project was administered by the Division of Research at the Harvard Business School. We are deeply indebted to The Associates of the School for their financial support of research by Dr. Fox and many other members of this Faculty.

Soldiers Field
Boston, Massachusetts
February 1974

LAWRENCE E. FOURAKER
Dean

Acknowledgments

ARVA ROSENFELD CLARK edited the drafts of this text and brought to bear her very considerable talents in helping to bring this volume to its present form. Rarely is an author fortunate enough to find an editor with the analytic and communications skills of Ms. Clark. To her I am very grateful.

Many individuals contributed to the research that resulted in this volume. They include civilians and military officers of the United States Department of Defense, concerned employees and officers of defense contractor organizations, Assistant Professor James S. Reece of the Harvard Business School, Army General Nikitas Manitsas, Army Colonel Nevin L. McCartney (retired), Chief Warrant Officer William Scott, and Air Force Colonels Richard J. Lorette and James D. Suver. These individuals, along with Army, Navy, and Air Force officers who have been graduate students at the Harvard Business School over the past five years have made significant contributions to this work.

Henry Paulson, John Ramsey, and Lee Gladden provided major contributions to the information pertaining to defense contractor profits and contractor financing.

Considerable thanks are also due to Dean Lawrence E. Fouraker of the Harvard Business School, and to Professor Richard E. Walton (who succeeded Dean Fouraker as Director of the Division of Research), for their continuing support and encouragement over the three years I worked on this project.

I wish to express my thanks to Frederic M. Scherer, Jonathan F. Swain, and Colonel John Bennett (retired) for their many thoughtful comments and suggestions on earlier drafts of this volume.

Ms. Joan Scribner and Ms. Shirley McNerney each spent a year at the Harvard Business School employing their considerable administrative skills in gathering research materials and organizing them. Ms. Ellen Perry deserves considerable credit for typing substantial parts of the manuscript and arranging for drafts of chapters to be used as discussion papers in courses conducted at the Harvard Business School during 1972 and 1973.

Although many persons have contributed significantly to this work, the author has enjoyed complete freedom on what is said and left unsaid. For that, too, I am grateful. I alone am responsible for any mistakes of fact or judgment which this volume may contain.

Newton, Massachusetts   J. RONALD FOX
February 1974

Table of Contents

List of Tables

List of Figures

CHAPTER I

Introduction

IN 1962 AND 1964 TWO BOOKS published by the Harvard University Graduate School of Business Administration identified a number of profound and debilitating problems in the management of the weapons acquisition process. The books were *The Weapons Acquisition Process: An Economic Analysis,* by Merton J. Peck and Frederic M. Scherer, and *The Weapons Acquisition Process: Economic Incentives,* by Frederic M. Scherer.[1] Their appearance coincided with the beginning of a decade of attempted reforms in management training, performance, and accountability within the Department of Defense. These efforts were encouraged by the Government, business, and academic communities. Congress, the press, and informed citizens demanded change; administrations promised change. But in the 1970s there are few indications of health in the vital life signs of the industry. At the juncture where the Federal Government and private industry meet in common enterprise, a profound flaw sends tremors throughout the national economy. Dedicated and honest men and women have tried to institute and direct meaningful change within the Pentagon and its defense and aerospace programs. Yet during the last ten years, even the heartiest reformers have been discouraged. In short, a vital restructuring of the process of defense management has yet to be accomplished.

This book is designed as a follow-on to the earlier studies cited above. The first volume of *The Weapons Acquisition Process* described the basic structure of the process and presented an economic analysis. The second volume built on the first but was limited to a study of economic incentives. The current study of the weapons acquisition process is designed to deal with the management of the process, a topic discussed in only a peripheral way in the earlier volumes. A reader interested in the economics of acquisition would be well

NOTE: Footnotes appear at the end of each chapter.

advised to read the earlier Peck and Scherer books as well as the other works cited throughout the following chapters.

Peck and Scherer focused on six specific problems in the management of research, development, and production programs conducted by industry and the Department of Defense: (1) schedule slippage, (2) cost growth, (3) lack of qualified Government personnel, (4) high frequency of personnel turnover, (5) inadequate methods of cost estimation, and (6) insufficient training in the measurement and control of contractor performance. To correct these weaknesses, administrators introduced innovations in three areas during the 1960s: program planning and selection, source selection and contracting, and the management of ongoing programs.

To improve program planning and selection, a strong Systems Analysis group was installed in the Office of the Secretary of Defense, and a Planning, Programming, and Budgeting System was introduced. To improve source selection and contracting, several innovations were attempted: formal source selection procedures; contractor performance evaluation procedures; total package procurement; contract definition; and incentive contracting. In the management of ongoing programs, innovations included: the adoption of the program manager concept; the consolidation of contract administration; the Program Evaluation and Review Technique (PERT); PERT/Cost; cost and schedule control system criteria; systems engineering; cost information reports; contractor funds status reporting; configuration management; and technical performance measurement.

New planning and control techniques for streamlining the acquisition process were taught to potential Army, Navy, and Air Force program managers at a school established by the Office of the Secretary of Defense at Wright-Patterson Air Force Base in Dayton, Ohio. Several consulting firms were organized in the private sector for the purpose of training personnel within Government and industry in these new techniques. They prospered.

Perhaps the single most important element in the new approach to management was the commitment to centralized decision making. The new Planning, Programming, and Budgeting System (PPB) correlated resource inputs with categories of performance (e.g., strategic retaliatory forces, tactical air forces, general purpose forces, and research and development). The Office of Assistant Secretary of Defense for Systems Analysis was established. Here, the Assistant Secretary and a staff of more than 100 professional personnel provided cost/benefit analyses for the use of the Secretary of Defense and other decision makers in the Pentagon.

After several years of sustained effort, however, serious cost, schedule, and technical performance problems continued to disrupt the acquisition process. Defense officials made continual allusions to the costly discrepancies between projected and actual performance by defense contractors. In 1968 Robert Charles, Assistant Secretary of the Air Force, told an audience at George Washington University: "A review of six recent contracts indicates that actual technical performance of the operational equipment came to less than 86% of the contractor's proposed performance on which the decision to proceed was based." [2] In 1969 Robert Benson, who had just completed two years as an analyst in the Office of the Secretary of Defense, testified during Government hearings that "about 90% of the major weapon systems that the Defense Department procures end up costing at least twice as much as was originally estimated." [3] Also in 1969 Richard Stubbing, an analyst in the Bureau of the Budget, told the same Congressional committee: "Of eleven major weapon systems begun during the 1960's, only two of them had electronic components that performed up to standard. One performed at a 75% level and two at a 50% level. But six—a majority—of the eleven performed at a level 25%, or less than the standards and specifications set for them." [4] In that year, too, the U.S. General Accounting Office performed a survey of 38 ongoing major weapon systems programs and found cost estimates already 50% higher than the original contract figures.[5]

In 1970 a general responsible for defense procurement activities in his service mentioned several ongoing programs in a letter to his Chief of Staff. One weapon system then in production he called "a marvelous gadget [but] too rich for our blood, and we are busily and hopefully 'scrubbing it down.' " A second development program had run into trouble primarily because "the contractor selected and his peculiar subsystems were not ready." A third development program had been "bungled by the developer. When the military staff realized the size of the bungling, the program was suspended."

In 1971 the Assistant Secretary of Defense for Financial Management (Comptroller) conducted a survey of 35 major development and production programs. He found that only two were on, or ahead of, schedule. In the same year the General Accounting Office made a survey of 61 weapon systems and found that estimates for development and production programs had increased $33.4 billion over initial estimates.[6]

Although the general public was unaware of most of these problems, by 1971 cost and schedule mismanagement of two programs—the F-111 and the C-5A—were common knowledge. As the price of the F-111 increased, the Air Force reduced from 1,726 to 519 the number of aircraft it planned to buy. The cost of the plane had increased from the original estimate of $2.8 million in 1962 to an estimated $14.7 million per unit by 1970. Cost was but one problem. The Navy version of the aircraft was ultimately canceled in the late 1960s when it was found to be too heavy for carrier landings. The C-5A development program was burdened with major financial and technical diffi-

culties. Lockheed's costs as producer of the C-5A increased so drastically that
the company faced a potential loss of more than $500 million if the fixed-price
contract for the aircraft was not amended to provide relief. Cost problems
were overshadowed by technical difficulties when cracks were found in the
wing of the aircraft in 1970. In 1971 cracks were reported in the engine
mountings. By mid-October 1971 one engine had fallen from the wing of a
C-5A and the entire fleet of C-5A aircraft had been grounded pending further
investigation. In 1971 the Navy's MK 48 torpedo program, the Army's Cheyenne Helicopter program, and the Main Battle Tank program were experiencing major cost problems and were all three years behind schedule.

Cases of financial mismanagement and technical failure were becoming too
frequent to hide. As the 1970s began, critics of the Defense Department
within Congress and the media became more vocal and more persistent. In
March 1970 the Logistics Management Institute prepared a preliminary report
on Government-contractor relationships in the defense industry. The report
summarized the most common criticisms of the Defense Department management of the acquisition process:

> *First* is the observation that the weapon systems acquisition process
> apparently is out of control. Initial time and cost estimates—and even
> updated estimates—cannot be depended upon. Mandatory engineering
> changes arise continually throughout the process. Management infor-
> mation and control systems do not identify impending problems in time
> for preventive action to be taken.
>
> *Second* is the claim that bargaining positions are unbalanced; first one
> side, then the other has the advantage. The theory of countervailing
> pressures acting to produce fair and realistic contract terms does not
> hold. With emphasis on economies of scale and series production there
> are only a small number of weapon systems competitions each year
> and prospective contractors believe that their very existence may be
> jeopardized by failure to win. Hence the Department of Defense
> (DOD) is in the dominant position and can compel an unreasonable
> bargain. Following award of the contract, the DOD, committed to the
> timely success of the program, is in the weaker position as the sole
> source contractor negotiates for contract changes, product acceptance,
> and follow-on business.
>
> *Third* is that incentives both for efficient operation and for candor about
> expectations are lacking. Heavy reliance on historical costs in pricing,
> lack of adequate consideration of capital required in negotiating profit
> rates, and the high risk of low future utilization of contractor-owned
> facilities impede investment and modernization of plant. The hazard
> to program survival, of high cost, long duration, or looming technical

difficulties, as each program competes with others in and out of the DOD, motivates extreme optimism by DOD and contractor personnel alike.

Fourth are allegations of confusion, connivance, and deception by the DOD-contractor combination. Close cooperation and common interest are held in contrast to the arm's length relationship preferred by much of regulation and policy. Policy notwithstanding, the military departments receive advice and assistance from prospective contractors in preparation of requests for proposals. Contractors receive aid from Government personnel in performance of contracts. Contracts fail as instruments of control.[7]

In 1970 these indictments were repeated in study after study. The President's Blue Ribbon Panel, the National Security Industrial Association, the Defense Science Board Task Force on Research and Development Management, the Aerospace Industries Association, and the General Accounting Office all found serious flaws in the current management of the systems acquisition process. Criticism of the industry intensified as Congress investigated not only the F-14 and C-5A aircraft, but the Cheyenne helicopter, the Main Battle tank, the TOW missile, the Sheridan armored vehicle, and the SRAM missile. During the 1950s and 1960s Congressional interest in the weapons acquisition process had been limited largely to the House and Senate Armed Services Committees. By 1970 and 1971 the U.S. Congress Joint Economic Committee and the House Committee on Government Operations, as well as the House and Senate Armed Services and Appropriations Committees, conducted extensive hearings on defense procurement.

Many critics offered sweeping explanations for the failure of the system. Congressman Henry B. Gonzales of Texas was one of several who believed that mismanagement resulted from conscious and willful acts that are tantamount to sabotage. His accusation was quoted in the April 1968 issue of *Air Force Magazine*:

The profiteers who intentionally gouge the Government for excessive profits during a time of war are also guilty of consciously withdrawing efficiency from our industrial capacity. These private businessmen profiteers are in reality guilty of sabotage. Our history has been one of rampant war profiteering, and I am convinced that even the limited annual reports of the Renegotiation Board reveal that profiteering is going on now, is increasing, and will continue to increase unless something more realistic is done to stop it.

Arthur E. Fitzgerald, a former Deputy Assistant Secretary of the Air Force, attributed breakdowns to an irresponsible labor movement. Testifying before the Government Procurement Commission in March 1971 he stated:

> Labor takes advantage of the soft approach to business in the environment without profit motivation. In this environment, labor is able to increase wages and at a more rapid rate than in commercial fields. There has never been a strike over work standards in the aerospace industry. Major system managers usually give the union what is demanded. Since union contracts are not negotiated prior to systems contracts, quite often, newly negotiated union contracts increase the costs of all systems contracts long after the systems contracts are awarded. It would be wise to tie the union contract to a life of the systems contract so that labor cost growth would be known in advance.

In testimony before the Joint Economic Committee, Fitzgerald extended his theories to include a vast interlocking national conspiracy that sought to increase military power and to force the country to overspend on defense.

Some critics turned their attention to the defense procurement system itself to find causes for failure and remedies. Senator William Proxmire, chairman of the Joint Economic Committee, singled out the practice of "rewarding" failures by relieving contractors from their contractual commitments. The late Congressman L. Mendel Rivers, chairman of the House Armed Services Committee and a long-time friend of the Defense Department, insisted that if he were Secretary of the Army, he would deal with cost growth and performance degradation by reorganizing the entire procurement system. Former Deputy Secretary of Defense David Packard (the senior official responsible to the Secretary of Defense and the President for the conduct of defense research, development, and procurement), speaking at the annual meeting of the Armed Forces Management Association in 1970, referred to the current state of defense procurement as "a mess":

> . . . I suppose that some of our critics will call this a meeting of the military-industrial complex. So be it. I am not embarrassed by the fact that we need industry to help the Department of Defense. I am only embarrassed that we haven't done a better job. Many of you, and certainly those *not* in the industry, may expect me to talk about what a grand job we have all done and how necessary we are for one another. I am not going to do that. I am going to talk about the things we do wrong and the things we have to do better.
>
> Let's face it—the fact is that there has been bad management of many defense programs in the past. We spent billions of the taxpayers' dollars;

sometimes we spent it badly. Part of this is due to basic uncertainties in the defense business. Some uncertainties will always exist. However, most of it has been due to bad management, both in the Department of Defense and in the defense industry. We can and are doing something about that. I am not talking just about cost overruns as so many of our critics do. Overruns are the end product of our mistakes rather than the key issue to be addressed. I am surprised that our critics took so long to discover cost overruns. They have been around a long time, and many of the cost overruns that receive the most publicity were organized by defense and industry years ago. We are now paying the price for mistakes in contracting, in development, and in management.

Frankly, gentlemen, in defense procurement, we have a real mess on our hands, and the question you and I have to face up to is what are we going to do to clean it up.[8]

The Current Study

In response to the serious and persistent problems in the management of defense procurement, the Director of Research at the Harvard Graduate School of Business Administration encouraged me, in 1968, to initiate a research project designed to identify the underlying causes of the problems of cost growth, schedule slippage, and technical performance shortfalls.

My interest in the field of defense procurement began in 1959 when I was a research associate with Professor J. Sterling Livingston at the Harvard Business School. During the following year Professor Livingston was awarded a contract to design and pilot-test a cost planning and control system for the Navy's Polaris project. I spent the following two years as project manager for that effort, conducting field research which resulted in the design of the PERT/Cost Planning and Control System for the Polaris project. In 1962 the PERT/Cost System was adopted by the Department of Defense and NASA as a standard planning and control system for large development projects.

In 1962 and 1963 I was a consultant to a number of defense contractors, reviewing their internal cost planning and control systems and assisting them in responding to Government requirements. During the period of 1963–1965 I accepted an appointment as Deputy to the Assistant Secretary of the Air Force for Management Systems. In that capacity, I visited numerous Air Force program offices and contractor facilities to identify problems in the management of the acquisition process and to make recommendations for improvements.

In 1965 I returned to Harvard to conduct a course entitled Project Management and Defense and Aerospace Marketing. In 1969 Harvard granted me a two-year leave of absence to accept an appointment as Assistant Secretary of the Army, responsible for Army installations, logistics, and procurement. As a final project for the Secretary of Defense before returning to Harvard in 1971, I spent six months as chairman of a joint Government-industry group conducting an analysis of defense contract financing and profit policy.[9] The Government and industry personnel associated with that study interviewed representatives of 12 contractor organizations and collected data on 166 Army, Navy, and Air Force programs in various stages of completion. These programs accounted for nearly $10 billion in fixed-price and cost-reimbursement contracts with 45 defense contractors.

Upon returning to Harvard in the summer of 1971, I assembled information and observations from my experiences with the planning and control of large development and production programs. In addition, I had the opportunity to supervise, for several years, the research of three Harvard doctoral candidates—James Reece, James Suver, and Richard Lorette—and more than 25 master's degree candidates who prepared reports on various aspects of the management of the acquisition process. Each of these individuals contributed to the data collection and analysis involved in the preparation of this report.

Much of the documentation supporting this report comes from interviews with several hundred military and civilian personnel working in the various stages of the acquisition process, including more than 25 Government program managers and representatives of more than 25 defense contractors. The situations cited in this report are drawn from more than 35 Army, Navy, and Air Force program offices.

The portions of this report pertaining to the role of the Congress are based largely on my own observations and experiences as Assistant Secretary of the Army (Installation and Logistics) from 1969 to 1971. During that period I testified as the Army's principal witness in 14 separate House and Senate hearings on the authorization, appropriation, and management of procurement and construction funds.

Major credit for the sections of this report pertaining to contract changes belongs to Professor James Reece of the Harvard Business School.

In several chapters of this report I have compared the European approach to weapons acquisition with our own. In 1970 I assembled a small group of Defense Department personnel to conduct a brief study on planning and control techniques in several European countries which produce highly developed weapon systems. Our visits were limited to eight defense contractor firms and three defense ministries. The information we gathered provides the basis for the comparisons drawn in this study.

Research Goals and Methods

Since the publication of the Peck and Scherer studies, the magnitude of the defense acquisition process as a factor in the U.S. economy has continued to be major. Each year the Department of Defense spends a total of more than $20 to $30 billion for the development and production of complex weapon systems. This investment represents a major commitment of the nation's resources and involves substantial long-range commitment of future Federal expenditures. The fact that the defense and aerospace industry is one of the largest industrial employers in the United States is sufficient reason to seek solutions to the costly problems which, despite their recurrence, only sporadically engage public concern. For every individual case of mismanagement and technical failure, critics and proponents within Congress, industry, and the Pentagon propound theories and recommendations. Independent and comprehensive research and analysis may provide the fundamental insights and solutions which as yet have failed to materialize.

The defense systems developed and produced by the Department of Defense are grouped into categories such as aircraft, communications, electronics, ships, missiles, tanks, and satellites. Most of the actual work on these systems is accomplished by U.S. industrial firms under contract with the Department of Defense. As was the case in the earlier Harvard study, I have devoted little attention to the acquisition of items available in commercial markets, or items which flow from a well-established technology (i.e., desks, trucks, conventional cargo ships, etc.). Buying such commodities is largely an application of conventional production management and purchasing practices. The development of each major defense and aerospace system, on the other hand, requires extended negotiation between Government and industry personnel. The scarcity of useful information upon which to base estimates of schedules, costs, and technical performance makes each negotiation a complex and, at this time, an inefficient procedure. In examining the manner in which large development and production programs are conducted, I have sought to identify and test the assumptions on which existing Government regulations, controls, and management techniques are based. In addition, I have described and attempted to explain patterns of behavior that accompany the development and production of complex weapon systems.

The research supporting this book is not simply a collection of statistics from a large number of defense and aerospace programs. Rather, my analyses are based on:

1. An examination of procurement regulations and practices;
2. An examination of contractor bids and proposals to perform work for the Government;
3. An examination of records of actual performance by contractors on large development and production programs;
4. Interviews with Government and industry personnel directly involved in the defense and aerospace business.

I believe that instances of cost growth, schedule slippage, and technical performance degradation will continue to inundate the weapons acquisition process until we look beyond statistics to the structure of the system itself. More than a decade after the publication of *The Weapons Acquisition Process,* the problems cited by Peck and Scherer are still with us. Failures occur despite continued Congressional pressure for reform and the innovations introduced by Secretary of Defense Robert S. McNamara and others. Indeed, many critics allege that today's decision makers in the Pentagon repeat most of the mistakes of the 1950s. If this is true, more than ten years of reorganization have produced few workable solutions.

What in the nature of the relationship between Government and private industry makes the management process impervious to reform? Are there realistic solutions for the problems which confound the industry? In this study I have tried to answer these questions.

Since the purpose of this study is to identify and analyze recurrent patterns of unproductive and inefficient management, I have not cited individual programs, persons, and organizations by name, except in those instances where the information is already in the public domain. This study is not an exposé. It is an attempt to pinpoint the most fundamental reasons for breakdowns in the acquisition process. As outlined above, I have concentrated especially on those aspects of the present system of rewards and penalties which undermine the goals of the acquisition process. I do not believe that weapons acquisition management can function responsibly unless this system is restructured. A piecemeal approach to reform will not revive the industry. I have tried to give form to this restructuring in the last chapter of this book. Much of the analysis in this report also applies to the contracting and program management activities of the National Aeronautics and Space Administration (NASA), the Atomic Energy Commission (AEC), the Federal Aviation Agency (FAA), and, increasingly, to the Department of Health, Education, and Welfare (HEW), the Department of Transportation (DOT), and the Department of Housing and Urban Affairs (HUD). Officials within these departments and companies working for them may find this report useful.

Unlike research projects dealing with a specific functional area of business operations, this study is multidisciplinary, involving the fields of production, operations management, marketing, control, finance, and human behavior. It is intended for use by policy makers, management personnel within Government and industry, and students of business administration and public policy.

SUGGESTIONS FOR READING THIS BOOK

There are two ways to approach the material in this book. The reader who is directly involved in the weapons acquisition process will probably wish to read consecutive chapters. Other readers may prefer to separate the technical chapters from those describing the more general problems that afflict the acquisition process. All readers are advised to begin with Chapter II in order to gain an overview of the total system. Readers in the second category may then wish to proceed to the following chapters:

NOTES TO CHAPTER I

1. Merton J. Peck and Frederic M. Scherer, *The Weapons Acquisition Process: An Economic Analysis* (Boston: Division of Research, Harvard Business School, 1962) and Frederic M. Scherer, *The Weapons Acquisition Process: Economic Incentives* (Boston: Division of Research, Harvard Business School, 1964).
2. Address by the Honorable Robert Charles, Assistant Secretary of the Air Force (Installations and Logistics), to the George Washington University R&D Contracts Conference, Washington, D.C., November 7, 1968.
3. Testimony of Mr. Robert S. Benson before the U.S. Congress Joint Economic Committee during hearings on defense procurement, Washington, D.C., March 10, 1969.
4. Testimony of Mr. Richard Stubbing, U.S. Bureau of the Budget, before the U.S. Congress Joint Economic Committee during hearings on defense procurement, Washington, D.C., March 10, 1969.
5. Comptroller General of the United States, *Report to the Congress on Major Weapons Programs*, 1969.
6. Comptroller General of the United States, *Report to the Congress on the Acquisition of Major Weapon Systems*, B-163058, March 18, 1971.
7. Logistics Management Institute, report on *The DOD-Contractor Relationship—Preliminary Review*, Task 69-21, March 1970, pp. 8–10.
8. Address by the Honorable David Packard, Deputy Secretary of Defense, at the annual meeting of the Armed Forces Management Association, Los Angeles, August 20, 1970.
9. Industry Advisory Council, Report to the Secretary of Defense by the Subcommittee to consider *Defense Industry Contract Financing*, June 11, 1971.

"Weapon systems now in development or procurement will cost at least $104.6 billion before procurement is completed."
Report of the Blue Ribbon Panel to the President and the Secretary of Defense, July 1, 1970

CHAPTER II

The Acquisition of a Major Weapon System: An Overview

TO MOST AMERICANS the term "defense industry" means the manufacturing of weapons. During World War II this simple definition was accurate. The weapons acquisitions process was comparatively uncomplicated. Several manufacturers often produced the same weapon system—aircraft, tanks, guns—all using the same design. Mass production was swift and dependable. Once production began, there were seldom any interruptions.

As weapons have become more complex, so, too, has the process by which they are produced. The classic commercial manufacturing cycle (planning, designing, tooling, producing, and distributing) served the defense business well during World War II, but today it is no longer adequate. And no workable replacement has yet been found. Recent defense programs have bogged down in endless series of costly stops, starts, and changes.

Before and during World War II the defense industry was usually compared to a manufacturing industry, such as automobile production. More recently, the housing industry—a contracting industry—provides a more accurate analogy.

The housing contractor hires his architect and before the first board is cut, unless he has another development down the road, the contractor has to let the architect go. The same thing follows with the carpenters, electricians, plumbers and roofers. In the aerospace contracting business, a hard drive is made for a defense program. Some preliminary design is accomplished, some computer modeling, some independent research and development (R&D). Usually a large engineering team is amassed to demonstrate to the military buyers that the company has the capability "in being" to do the job. If contract award is delayed, as is too often the case, this high-cost team stands virtually idle for months. Costs to the company and to the Government are astronomical. . . .[1]

The purpose of defense procurement is to develop and supply the weapons, equipment, and services required to meet U.S. national defense objectives. To meet this goal, the Department of Defense executes more than ten million procurement actions (contracts and contract modifications) per year, which obligate more than $30 billion in funds. Ninety-nine percent of the procurement actions, however, account for only 40% of the funds, and nearly 90% of these actions involve less than $10,000 each. In this book we shall analyze contracts (and contract modifications) for *major* systems development and production. Major contracts amount to less than 1% of all procurement actions, but they represent more than 50% of defense procurement dollars.

As defense procurement has emerged from the era of mass production, the skills required for handling major programs have changed. The regulations that govern the business operations of the Defense Department and industry have also changed. In 1947 the Armed Services Procurement Regulation (ASPR) was a slim volume of 100 to 125 pages; in 1973 the ASPR consisted of several large volumes, totaling approximately 3,000 pages, with new pages added each month. In April 1971 an officer in the Program Control Division of the Air Force F-15 project reported: "There are 1,282 directives affecting the systems management process during the concept formulation phase of a major defense program." In other words, a team planning a weapon system must conform to directives concerning all phases of the acquisition process, including, for example, integrated logistics support, reliability, configuration management, parts numbering, milestone reporting, cost estimating, monthly budgeting, performance measurement, training, maintenance, and more than 1,200 other matters of varying importance.

In the absence of relevant management training, these directives were intended to provide helpful guidelines for the acquisition process. In practice, they often inhibit and restrict the process. Although Secretary of Defense Melvin Laird reduced the number of these directives, they still comprised more than 1,000 pages. The National Aeronautics and Space Administration has a separate set of procurement regulations which closely parallel the ASPR.

At the time of the Peck and Scherer studies (1962–1964), the major products of the defense industry were described as "weapon systems." The term remains in use and still refers to technically complex items such as planes, missiles, ships, tanks, and electronics. The term includes not only the major item of equipment itself but the techniques, hardware, subsystems, and all personnel needed to operate and support the major item. Subsystems may include power plants, electronics gear, armaments, guidance and navigation equipment, ground support equipment, test and checkout equipment, maintenance facilities and equipment, spare parts, communication equipment, training equipment, and technical data (including operating and maintenance handbooks and parts catalogs). In addition, documentation for technical manuals and supply manuals is a significant part of a weapon system. For example, in the Department of the Army publications library, there are 98,916 pages for the Hercules missile system, 55,927 pages for the Hawk missile system, and 45,063 pages for the Pershing missile system.

One result of the amorphous nature of the term "weapon system" is that there are no commonly accepted limits for the preparation of cost estimates. Two or more people preparing separate cost estimates for the same weapon system may include, or exclude, such items as spare parts, development costs, personnel costs, supplies, maintenance, or any of a variety of associated hardware and services. Hence, the same weapon system may be identified with widely differing cost estimates at different times.

"Systems program management" is the name given to the process by which weapon systems are acquired. The term includes the entire spectrum of management activity which enables governmental agencies and their contractors to accomplish a program's objectives.

The remainder of this chapter provides a brief introduction to the acquisition process. Each topic is covered in greater detail in subsequent chapters.

THE ACQUISITION PROCESS

The acquisition of a weapon system is a two-stage process. The first stage includes planning, research, development, testing, and evaluation. The second stage is production. Stage one is summarized below in the general order in which it occurs.

1. The Department of Defense identifies a security threat or defense need.
2. The Department designs an engineering development program to meet the need and draws up a budget.
3. Congress authorizes and appropriates funds for the engineering development program.
4. The administration releases funds for the program.
5. The Department and interested contractors develop technical approaches to the program (often occurs in conjunction with steps 1–4).
6. The Department prepares a statement of work.

7. Requests for proposals (RFP's) are issued by the Department to interested contractors. Conferences are held for interested bidders.
8. Contractors submit proposals to the Department, where they are evaluated.
9. One contractor (or more) is selected and a contract for development of the weapon system is negotiated.
10. The contractor performs work under the contract and negotiates modifications where required or where desirable.
11. The contractor delivers items for Government testing.

In the earliest stages of developing a defense system, conceptual effort is carried on at the discretion of individual military services, until such time as a service determines that a system should be acquired. Since the decision to develop a major defense system is a crucial commitment, the Office of the Secretary of Defense must approve such a decision. Each service designates a single individual (usually the Assistant Secretary for Research and Development) to assume responsibility for conceptual effort on major new programs.

The considerations which determine the need for a new weapon system program, together with a plan for that program, are recorded in a document called the Decision Coordinating Paper (DCP). The DCP defines program issues, including: special logistics problems; program objectives; program plans; performance parameters; areas of major risk; system alternatives; and acquisition strategy. The DCP is prepared by a military service after agreement on an outline has been reached with the Office of the Secretary of Defense. The Director of Defense Research and Engineering (DDR&E) in the Office of the Secretary of Defense has the primary responsibility for review of the DCP and recommendation of its approval, or disapproval, to the Secretary or Deputy Secretary of Defense.

When a military service is sufficiently confident that a program is ready for full-scale engineering development, the Secretary of the service requests approval of the DCP. The formal prerequisites for obtaining a decision to proceed into engineering development are:

1. Primarily engineering, rather than experimental, effort is required.
2. The misson and performance envelopes are defined.
3. The best perceived technical approaches have been selected.
4. A thorough trade-off analysis has been made.
5. Cost effectiveness for the proposed weapon system and competing systems within the Defense Department have been compared, and the proposal is considered feasible.
6. Cost and schedule estimates are credible and acceptable.

In actual practice these prerequisites are often ignored. In recent years, paper studies and analyses have often been substituted for essential system development and testing. As a result, uncertainties which could have been eliminated or reduced in the research and exploratory development phases were carried over into advanced engineering development or operational systems development, where unresolved technical problems are significantly more expensive and troublesome to remedy. In addition, when exploratory development and testing do not take place, the new technology that could improve weapon capability is often lost. Were all six prerequisites conscientiously fulfilled, the acquisition process would suffer fewer false starts. In the name of military urgency, however, a blanket approval has often been requested and granted.

In selecting weapon systems for development, the Defense Department receives specific requests from each military service and often responds to them individually. This diversity of independent requests often leads to an unnecessary duplication in the capabilities of major weapon systems; e.g., an overlap between land-based missiles of various ranges, or between aircraft of various capabilities, or between land-based and sea-based aircraft.

Once approval has been granted to proceed with engineering development, a program moves into the Contract Definition phase. There is a fundamental difference between defense contracts and commercial contracts: buyers and sellers of commercial systems do not usually arrive at a purchase and sale agreement until at least one unit of the item has been developed; buyers and sellers of defense programs agree upon the purchase price and a firm estimate of the cost before the product exists. As the product is being designed and produced, the concomitant management process involves trade-off decisions regarding schedules, costs, and technical performance.

In 1971 the Office of the Secretary of Defense rescinded the formal directives regulating Contract Definition in an effort to reduce unnecessary rigidity. Military services were encouraged to design new Contract Definition methodology for each new program, tailored to the needs of that program. In fact, however, most of the basic steps of Contract Definition remained intact. The Report of the Blue Ribbon Panel to the President and Secretary of Defense outlined the basic steps of the Contract Definition phase of the acquisition process:

> Contract Definition is itself divided into three phases. The first of these is the preparation and issuance of a Request for Proposal (RFP), and the selection of contractors for Contract Definition. The RFP is the document that solicits the first formal response from industry connected with the acquisition of a new weapon system. It calls for sufficient information

needed for selection of the contractors who are to undertake the detailed competition. The time and effort spent in this phase vary widely, but a period of four-to-six months is average.

Following the selection of contractors to participate in Contract Definition, the second phase begins with the award of fixed-price type contracts, under which each contractor prepares proposals for the engineering development effort. These proposals are detailed and voluminous, and one copy of a proposal may weigh as much as one ton.

The third and final step in the Contract Definition phase is that of source selection. In current practice, the contractor's proposals for development of complex systems are broken down into a large number of technical and management considerations. Each of these items is then assigned for evaluation to a small number of technical or management experts who in the aggregate comprise an evaluation team which may number several hundred. Prior to the evaluation of each element, weight factors have been assigned but not disclosed to the small groups evaluating the many compartmented factors. These weight factors are predetermined by a small team of experts primarily on the basis of value judgments. After the evaluation is made of each individual element, the scores assigned to each element of the proposal are summed up and the raw data are forwarded to a selection board, usually comprised of general or flag officers. The selection board then applies the predetermined weights and recommends the selection of a contractor based on these weighted scores plus other factors such as price and past performance, which are not given preassigned weights.

Concurrent with the evaluation and selection process, each of the contractors who participates in Contract Definition, and who submits a proposal, is engaged in contract negotiations. The negotiations are conducted by personnel not involved in the evaluation and selection. Prior to the completion of the evaluation process, the negotiators have each of the participating contractors sign a contract. When the selection of the contractor is finally made, the contract previously signed by the selected contractor is executed.

During the Contract Definition phase, the technical and design approaches to the systems development contained in the proposal of a prospective contractor are often exposed to other prospective contractors, so that potentially better and/or less costly features of each proposal can be considered by other prospective contractors for incorporation in or adaptation to their own proposals. Industry generally considers this practice to constitute unethical conduct on the part of the Government, particularly since it has no counterpart in non-government business transactions. The potential inherent in this practice for its use by Government personnel to influence the ultimate selection of a contractor is obvious.[2]

Theoretically, if a weapon system developed by a contractor is not satisfactory in terms of performance or cost, it will not go into production. The Department could reject the system and negotiate a contract with another company to develop a replacement system. Then the second company would negotiate contracts and contract modifications, develop a system, and deliver it for Government testing. When a weapon system performs unsatisfactorily, however, the Department of Defense works out an accommodation with the company under contract. This occurred in the case of the F-111 fighter aircraft—General Dynamics Corporation; the C-5A giant transport aircraft—Lockheed Aircraft Company; the Mk 48 torpedo—Westinghouse Electric Company; the AH-56A Cheyenne Helicopter—Lockheed Aircraft Company; the Short Range Attack Missile (SRAM) and the TACFIRE battlefield electronic control system—Litton Industries.

Since then senior defense officials have favored the development of two or more prototypes for each mission. They would then select a system on the basis of proven performance before going into production. Kelly Johnson, a widely respected aircraft designer at Lockheed Aircraft Company, cited one of the principal advantages of prototype development in a report to the Senate Armed Services Committee: "If a prototype fighter in which you have invested $50 million doesn't work out, you can run a bulldozer over it without too great a loss. But when you build a new fighter only once every 15 years, as we have been doing, you're locked into a multibillion dollar program." [3]

In authorizing appropriations for fiscal 1972 the Senate Armed Services Committee discussed the prototype strategy:

At the present time, Department of Defense development procedures are so structured that in each area there is only a single weapon system available to modernize the forces—and this system is often a very costly one. This means that Congress is faced with the decision of approving the procurement of that system or denying modern weapons to our armed forces. The Department of Defense has recently announced certain steps that would begin to correct this tendency, but until it is corrected modernization must go forward with those systems available. It would be far more desirable for the nation to be able to have alternative weapon systems and technical approaches from which to choose those systems best designed to accomplish the most important military missions before a large financial commitment has been made. In this context it is encouraging that the Department of Defense has announced an intention to develop experimental prototypes of new aircraft and other weapon systems and components without a prior commitment to production. This can help provide testable hardware at a lower cost, since an experimental prototype aircraft, for example, need not contain many of the costly electronics and other sub-systems which increase the cost of weapon system development under current procedures.[4]

Despite this encouragement, however, most Pentagon officials doubt that Congress will officially adopt a policy whereby funds for prototype development are appropriated for each major defense program.

When a weapon system tests successfully, the second stage begins. In theory, steps two to eleven of the development phase are repeated for the production phase, since a contractor other than the initial development firm might submit a more feasible bid and win the production contract. Does this competitive approach actually function in the Pentagon? During the decade of the 1960s, the company awarded the first production contract for each major weapon system has always developed the system. Cost management concerns are inevitably overwhelmed by the military's sense of urgency. In addition, companies, and the military services, often argue that the expertise required for the first production contract cannot realistically be transferred from one contractor to another, since so many modifications in design are made during initial production engineering. The policy of awarding production contracts before prototypes are completely tested adds strength to this argument. For obvious reasons, the developing contractor encourages this overlap between development and production.

There is good reason for military impatience to move into production. The beginning of the acquisition process—Department of Defense planning sessions and Congressional budget hearings—lasts from 18 to 24 months or longer. And, according to a report from the Office of the Secretary of Defense in August 1971, over half the service procurement account (for items other than ammunition) is spent three years or more after the funds are finally appropriated by Congress. From initial planning to actual expenditure of funds for production, there might be a time span of eight years.

The focus of most major defense systems is on research and development in areas which extend the frontiers of scientific knowledge and engineering capability. A typical defense system is technologically advanced and complex. Production is characteristically low volume, with the final costs of the acquisition process frequently running into billions of dollars. Even after a great expenditure of time and money, however, rapidly evolving technology and unexpected changes in defense priorities contribute to a high rate of obsolescence. This creates an environment of uncertainty and risk for buyer and seller, exacerbated by the unpredictability of technical performance, development time, and cost.

Examples of major hardware systems that entered the defense inventory during the 1960s are: the AH-1 Cobra armed helicopter, with a unit cost of $12 million; the UH-1 troop carrier helicopter, with a unit cost of $300,000; and the M60A1 tank, with a unit cost of $250,000.

In 1973 the following weapon systems were in various stages of initiation or development, with production planned for the next several years:

1. The Air Force manned B-1 bomber, intended to replace the present B-52's; more than $350 million planned for research and development.
2. The ULMS-Trident, underwater long-range missile system. A completely new, enlarged submarine, intended to double the 2,500-mile missile range of the current Poseidon; more than $100 million estimated for research and development.
3. The Army's new surface-to-air SAM-D missile system; an initial $110.5 million estimated for research and development.
4. The F-15-Eagle, a new Air Force advanced intercepter-fighter aircraft system; more than $400 million estimated for research and development.
5. The F-14A-Tomcat, a new Navy intercepter aircraft system; $128 million estimated for research and development and approximately $700 million estimated for production.
6. The AWACS, airborne warning and control system; $145.1 million estimated for research and development.

These programs are typical of the major defense/aerospace development programs, and they differ from commercial development programs in at least one respect. A private company seldom undertakes a project which requires the expenditure of hundreds of millions of dollars and five to ten years to complete. The Government does it routinely, several times a year.

From World War II until the 1970s, military research and development comprised by far the largest single share of the total U.S. technological effort. In 1960, for example, the defense R&D budget was $5.6 billion of a total U.S. Federal R&D budget of $8.7 billion. The space program, together with expanding defense research, brought Federal research and development expenditures to a peak of $13 billion in 1966 and 1967, with defense accounting for approximately half of that amount. By 1970, however, Federal defense and space research and development expenditures were down to approximately $11 billion, where they remained during 1971 and 1972.[5]

DEPARTMENT OF DEFENSE BUDGET CATEGORIES

The Department of Defense divides its total budget into categories defined by activity. Defense Budget Category VI is allocated to research and development. This category is further divided into six classifications, as follows.

Defense Budget Category VI: Research and Development
1. *Research:* includes all basic research and any applied research that is directed toward the expansion of scientific knowledge.
2. *Exploratory Development:* includes studies, investigations, and development efforts ranging from applied research to development of sophisticated weapons; oriented toward specific areas of military need.
3. *Advanced Development:* includes all programs for development of weapons for experimental testing. This is the essential link between Research (1) and Exploratory Development (2), on the one hand, and the incorporation of improved capabilities into new weapon systems in Engineering Development (4). As noted earlier, however, the Research and Exploratory Development steps often occur on paper only.
4. *Engineering Development:* includes development of items for military use which have not yet been approved for procurement or operation. At any given time, there are between 70 and 80 systems in this category. These represent a research and development budget of more than $25 million, or a total production investment of more than $100 million.
5. *Management and Support:* includes the overhead expense for categories 1–4.
6. *Emergency Fund:* available for use in any category at the discretion of the Secretary of Defense.

In the 1972 Senate Report, *Authorizing Defense Appropriations for Fiscal Year 1972,* the Senate Armed Services Committee expressed concern over the increasing cost of defense systems. The report compared the cost of major systems in the 1970s with those of earlier years.

Weapon systems now in development or procurement will cost at least $104.6 billion before procurement is completed. This cost does not include the funds necessary for operation and maintenance of these systems. The purchase cost of modern weapon systems has increased by many times even with the last few years. It was to be expected that a new fighter aircraft for the mid-1970s would cost considerably more than the fighters of World War II vintage. It is striking, however, that fighter aircraft now being developed for procurement in the mid-1970s will cost five to six times more than comparable aircraft at the beginning of the 1960s. The cost of tanks is increasing over fourfold during the 1965–1975 decade. A burst of .50-caliber machinegun fire, our primary air-to-air munition until the end of the Korean War, costs about $20; we are now developing tactical air-to-air munitions costing several hundred thousand dollars per round—an increase by a factor of tens of thousands. The avionics package in some types of new military aircraft will alone weigh two or more tons and cost several million dollars. At over $1,000 per pound this is about twice as costly as gold.[6]

The House Armed Services Committee also cited the increase cost of weapon systems in its 1972 Defense Authorization Report, and gave the following examples:[7]

TANKS

Weapon	Date	Amount
M-3	Early 1940s	$125,000
M-48	Early 1950s	175,000
M-60	Early 1960s	200,000
M-60A1E2	Early 1970s	500,000
MBT-70	Middle 1970s	900,000

FIGHTER AIRCRAFT

Weapon	Date	Amount
P-51	Early 1940s	$ 200,000
F-86	Late 1940s	400,000
F-100C	Middle 1950s	1,100,000
F-104C	Late 1950s	1,600,000
F-4B	Early 1960s	3,500,000
F-15	Middle 1970s	9,000,000

An example of the continuing increase in the costs of a single unit of a weapon system was announced in 1971: on November 3 the Secretary of the Navy revealed that his service was planning to build a single aircraft carrier that might cost more than $1 billion.

Technical complexity is one reason for the rising cost of defense systems. The Lockheed C-141 jet cargo aircraft, for example, includes 250,000 parts and requires some 20,000 engineering drawings to manufacture. A space assembly of a booster and capsule may contain 300,000 parts. (By comparison, a 1972 automobile had 3,000 parts.) The Army's Nike-Hercules system consists of more than one million parts, ranging in weight from a small fraction of an ounce to hundreds of pounds. It uses one quarter of a million feet of wire, 2,000 vacuum tubes, 12,000 resistors, thousands of capacitors, relays, and other electronic devices, and a host of functional components such as gyroscopes, servomechanisms, and electronic computers. In addition, approximately 80,000 ordnance engineering drawings are required to document the Nike-Hercules.

Accompanying the complexity in defense systems are increased demands for reliability during performance. For an automobile driven continuously for 1,000 hours at 50 miles/hour, the average mean time between failures is 90 hours. For fighter aircraft in operation in the early 1970s, the average mean time between failures is 150 hours. In contrast to these, the Apollo command and service modules developed a reliability measured in terms of 9,700 hours between failures; i.e., more than 100 times greater than the mean time between failures for the automobile.

The management of business operations and of technical development programs also increases in complexity as technology advances. It is virtually impossible for any one individual to comprehend every aspect of the research, engineering design, and production stages of a major acquisition program, as well as the system's operational characteristics. Programs are not usually completed for several years, and during those years the performance of thousands of components of a weapon system must be designed and manufactured to work together as a unit. Individuals and firms involved in defense work become increasingly specialized, as do program facilities. Coordination of the manifold operations of procurement is itself a major Defense Department activity.

Most major development and production programs experience repeated setbacks before a final breakthrough is achieved. How does a defense manager accommodate himself to a job that has so much built-in frustration? Most of those who choose to remain in the Department of Defense are, by temperament or design, unfailingly optimistic. In dealing with observers from Congress, the press, or the public, most Government (and industry) managers minimize the importance of cost overruns, schedule changes, and performance failures. Their progress reports and predictions are invariably enthusiastic, no matter what setbacks their programs actually experience. The gap between prediction and performance engages public attention only when major programs flounder. It is, however, a daily fact of life in the defense industry.

With this brief overview of the acquisition process, we will begin an examination of the major elements of the process and their interactions.

NOTES TO CHAPTER II

1. R. Jameson, *Armed Forces Journal,* January 6, 1969.
2. Report of the Blue Ribbon Panel to the President and the Secretary of Defense on the Department of Defense, July 1, 1970.
3. Interview with Kelly Johnson cited in "Why Prototyping Is Making a Comeback," *Business Week,* August 14, 1971, p. 103.
4. U.S. Senate, Armed Services Committee, Report 92-359, *Authorizing Defense Appropriations for Fiscal Year 1972,* "The Cost of Modern Weapon Systems."
5. *Special Analyses of the Budget of the U.S. Government, Fiscal Year 1972* (Washington: Government Printing Office), p. 273.
6. U.S. Senate, Armed Services Committee, Report 92-359, op. cit.
7. Ibid.

CHAPTER III

The Defense Market

IN THE DEFENSE INDUSTRY there is little that resembles the free market. In 1962 Peck and Scherer stated: "A market system does not now exist in the weapons acquisition process. We can state the proposition more strongly. A market system in its entirety can never exist for the acquisition of weapons." [1] In the 1970s the situation has not changed.

At the end of the Revolutionary War, George Washington dissolved the Army and sent the soldiers home. Later, Washington requested Congress to appropriate money for a small regular army but was denied the funds. In June 1784 Congress passed a resolution expressing the view that "standing armies in time of peace are inconsistent with the principles of republican governments, dangerous to the liberties of a free people, and generally converted into destructive engines for establishing despotism."

By the middle of the nineteenth century, however, just before the Mexican War, the United States military services included 9,000 officers and men. Immediately prior to World War II, the military services numbered 139,000. In 1973 more than 3 million men and women were serving in the United States military. They were stationed at 470 bases, camps, and installations within the country and in 3,372 bases around the world.

Figure III-1 depicts the steady rise in the defense budget after 1940, with pronounced increases for World War II, the Korean War, and the Vietnam War. After World War II and the Korean War, the defense budget was reduced, but only to a point substantially higher than the level immediately preceding the conflicts. Military manpower levels were also higher following these two wars than immediately before.

Although defense procurement and research and development budgets increased 25% after 1964, almost all of this increase can be accounted for by

FIGURE III-1. U.S. DEFENSE BUDGET: 1940–1972

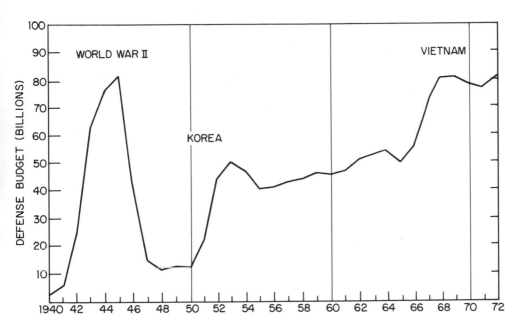

SOURCE: See Table III-3.

inflation. Table III-1 illustrates that in constant 1972 dollars, the defense budget in 1972 was close to the 1964 level.

TABLE III-1. DEFENSE R&D AND PROCUREMENT BUDGET: 1964–1972
(in billions of dollars)

	1964	1968	1971	1972
In current dollars	$24.3	$32.5	$28.2	$30.6
In constant 1972 dollars	$31.5	$38.2	$29.3	$30.6

SOURCE: Office of Statistical Services, Office of the Assistant Secretary of Defense (Comptroller), 1971.

A table released by the Office of the Assistant Secretary of Defense (Comptroller), on January 28, 1971, compared peak and postwar defense budget trends for World War II and the Korean War with expenditures for the war in Vietnam through 1972, with the index of changes expressed in terms of constant prices (see Table III-2).

TABLE III-2. DEFENSE WARTIME BUDGET TRENDS:
INDEX OF CHANGES, IN CONSTANT PRICES

	Index		
	Prewar	*Peak*	*Postwar*
World War II	100	3,839	405
(1940–45–48)			
Korea	100	290	219
(1950–53–56)			
Southeast Asia	100	132	100
(1964–68–72)			

SOURCE: Office of the Assistant Secretary of Defense (Comptroller), January 28, 1971.

During World War II and the Korean War rising military expenditures were partially offset by reductions in other Federal programs. Military expenditures accounted for 16.3% of the Federal budget in 1940. In 1945 the war effort took 83.9% of the budget (Table III-3). This pattern was repeated during the Korean War: military expenses received 27.7% of the Federal budget in 1950 and 62.1% in 1953. During these war years, funds for Federally sponsored domestic programs were reduced or kept stable. During the Vietnam War, however, a different pattern emerged. Military expenditures actually declined slightly as a percentage of the total Federal budget—from 41.8% in 1964 to 41.5% in 1969. Meanwhile, the domestic budget increased at a greater rate than the defense budget (Figure III-2).

Between 1960 and 1970 the Federal Budget grew more than 100%, from $92 billion to $198 billion. More was added to Federal spending in this single decade than in the previous two centuries. During this period the United States spent approximately $670 billion on defense,[2] an increase of 61%. At the same time, domestic programs increased by more than $80 billion, or 143% (see Figure III-3).

Defense spending is frequently measured as a percentage of the Gross National Product. Figure III-4 shows that by this measure, defense spending remained relatively constant after 1956, and even experienced a small decline between 1968 and 1970. In its report on the 1972 Defense Authorization Bill, the Senate Armed Services Committee stated:

> It is important to realize that there have been significant reductions in the share of our national resources taken by defense over the last 5 years. Due to both inflation and real growth, the Gross National Product has increased significantly since fiscal year 1968, while defense outlays have not varied greatly. Thus, defense spending since fiscal year 1968 has

TABLE III-3. UNITED STATES DEFENSE BUDGETS: 1940–1972
(in billions of dollars)

Year	Defense	Federal Budget	Defense/ Federal	GNP	Defense/ GNP
1940	$ 1.5	$ 9.1	16%	$100.6	1.5%
1941	6.0	13.3	45	125.8	4.8
1942	23.9	34.0	70	159.1	15.0
1943	63.2	79.4	80	192.5	32.8
1944	76.7	95.0	80	211.4	36.3
1945	81.2	98.4	83	213.6	38.0
1946	43.2	60.4	71	210.7	20.5
1947	14.4	39.0	37	234.3	6.2
1948	11.8	33.0	36	259.4	4.5
1949	13.0	39.5	33	258.1	5.0
1950	13.1	39.6	33	284.6	4.6
1951	22.5	44.0	51	329.0	6.8
1952	44.1	65.4	67	342.0	12.9
1953	50.5	74.2	68	365.4	13.8
1954	47.0	67.8	69	363.1	12.9
1955	40.7	64.6	63	397.5	10.2
1956	40.7	66.5	61	419.2	9.7
1957	43.4	69.4	62	442.8	9.8
1958	44.2	71.9	62	444.2	10.0
1959	46.6	92.1	51	482.1	9.7
1960	45.7	92.2	49	503.8	9.1
1961	47.5	97.8	48	520.1	9.2
1962	51.1	106.8	48	560.3	9.2
1963	52.8	111.3	47	589.2	9.0
1964	54.2	118.6	46	628.7	8.7
1965	50.2	118.4	42	676.3	7.4
1966	56.8	134.6	41	721.2	7.8
1967	70.0	158.3	45	793.9	8.8
1968	80.5	178.8	45	865.0	9.3
1969	81.2	184.5	44	931.4	8.7
1970	77.8	197.9	39	976.5	8.0
1971	76.4	212.7	36	998.5	7.7
1972 (est)	72.0	229.2	35	1040.0	7.7

SOURCE: U.S. Council of Economic Advisers, *Economic Indicators*, June 1971 (for all data subsequent to 1959). *Statistical Abstract of the United States*, 1970 (for all data prior to 1960).

fallen from 9.5% of Gross National Product to 6.8%. The Federal Budget has grown during the same period so that the proportion of Federal outlays taken by defense has shrunk from 42.5% of the overall Federal Budget to 32.1%. Inflation has been severe during these 5 years—although defense outlays were about the same in current dollars in fiscal year 1968 as they are in fiscal year 1972 ($76–$78 billion), the fiscal year 1972 budget buys about $20 billion less.[3]

FIGURE III-2. U.S. DEFENSE AND NONDEFENSE BUDGET TRENDS:
1940–1972

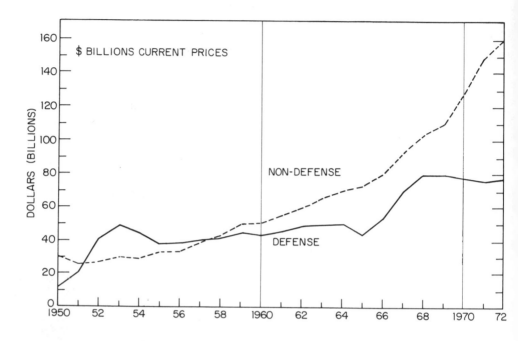

SOURCE: See Table III-3.

An analysis of defense spending as a percentage of Gross National Product for 1971 and 1972 indicates that the ratio was approximately 6.8/7.0%, the lowest since the 6.7% ratio of 1951.

Although Defense Department officials and other statisticians use this ratio extensively, a number of economists question its relevance. If the purpose of defense spending is solely to ensure national security, there is no reason for it to increase or decrease in direct proportion to the Gross National Product. According to Arthur F. Burns, a senior advisor to President Nixon on domestic affairs in 1970, the appropriate measures of defense costs are the opportunities foregone by diverting national resources to defense. Senator William Proxmire, Chairman of the U.S. Congress Joint Economic Committee, shared this point of view. He stated that the true cost of defense to the nation includes the civilian goods and services that are never realized because of defense spending, as well as the growth that could have been achieved through larger investments in human and business resources.

In 1972 the defense business was still the largest industry in the United States. The Defense Department's annual purchases from American business

FIGURE III-3. DEFENSE SPENDING AS A PERCENTAGE OF THE TOTAL
U.S. BUDGET: 1940–1972

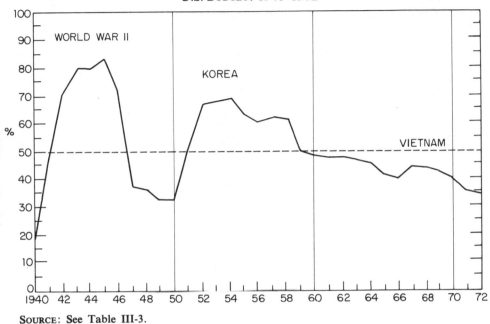

SOURCE: See Table III-3.

FIGURE III-4. U.S. DEFENSE SPENDING AS A PERCENTAGE OF GROSS
NATIONAL PRODUCT: 1940–1972

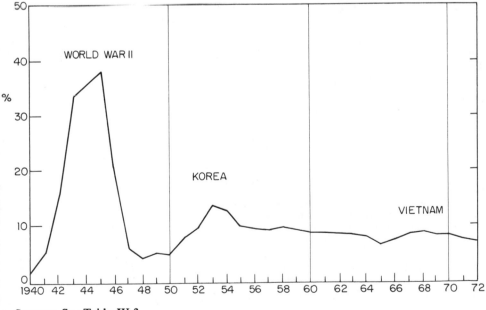

SOURCE: See Table III-3.

cost more than $36 billion. These included aircraft ($8 billion); missiles ($5 billion); ships ($4 billion); ordnance, vehicles, and related equipment ($3 billion); electronics and communications ($1 billion); and a variety of other items, ranging from battery chargers to musical instruments.[4] The Defense Acquisition Process cost more than $80 million per working day throughout the year. The total estimated cost of completing the 61 weapon systems under development by the Defense Department in 1971 was $150 billion. Of this amount, only $55 billion had been committed through the 1971 budget.[5]

Approximately one-half of all the Government-supported research and development programs in the United States are sponsored by the Department of Defense (Table III-4). Although total Government funding for research

TABLE III-4. GOVERNMENT-SUPPORTED RESEARCH
AND DEVELOPMENT: 1970–1972
(in millions of dollars)

	Obligations			Expenditures		
	1970	*1971*	*1972*	*1970*	*1971*	*1972*
		Esti-	*Esti-*		*Esti-*	*Esti-*
Department or Agency	*Actual*	*mate*	*mate*	*Actual*	*mate*	*mate*
Defense-Military Functions	7,338	7,400	8,309	7,424	7,543	7,734
National Aeronautics & Space Administration	3,825	3,382	3,215	3,699	3,319	3,109
Health, Education & Welfare	1,251	1,506	1,637	1,235	1,359	1,477
Atomic Energy Commission*	1,346	1,307	1,251	1,346	1,307	1,251
Transportation	315	468	566	246	414	543
National Science Foundation	288	343	495	293	330	403
Agriculture	289	312	321	288	309	314
Interior	160	188	213	153	188	207
Commerce	124	157	181	118	133	151
Environmental Protection Agency**	75	118	132	38	82	96
Office of Economic Opportunity	101	116	100	76	88	94
Veterans Administration	59	62	62	58	61	62
Housing & Urban Development	30	52	49	14	55	50
Smithsonian Institution	20	22	31	20	24	31
Justice	10	11	25	5	14	21
Labor	21	24	25	20	24	25
All Other	79	87	125	64	82	98
Total	15,331	15,555	16,737	15,098	15,332	15,666

* In this table, both obligations and expenditures for AEC are accrued costs, approximated for purposes of analysis. Details do not always add up to totals, due to rounding.

** The obligations and expenditures reported for Commerce and the Environmental Protection Agency include a portion, but not all, of the research and development activities conducted by other agencies in these years and transferred to the National Oceanic and Atmospheric Administration of Commerce in October 1970 under Reorganization Plan No. 4 of 1970, or to the Environmental Protection Agency in December 1970 under Reorganization Plan No. 3 of 1970. Therefore, the 1970 and 1971 figures for these agencies do not reflect the full level of the activities transferred to the new agencies. Figures for the other agencies are adjusted to avoid duplication or omission.

SOURCE: *Special Analyses of the Budget of the United States Government, Fiscal Year 1972* (Washington: U.S. Government Printing Office), p. 273.

and development doubled in the 1960s, most of the growth occurred before the end of 1966. After 1966, the Federal growth rate dropped from an average of 9% per year to 1% per year. Meanwhile, the growth rate in non-Federal (primarily industrial) funding for research and development remained fairly constant.[6]

The Army, Navy, Air Force, and the Office of the Secretary of Defense, and the National Aeronautics and Space Administration (NASA) have each been assigned specific roles. They are the major customers for goods produced by the defense industry. (NASA's budget peaked at $6 billion in 1966. By 1972 the level had been reduced to slightly more than $3 billion.)

Defense spending in the United States is concentrated in five major industry groupings. These are shown in Table III-5. The industries included in each

TABLE III-5. DEFENSE SPENDING BY MAJOR INDUSTRY
GROUPINGS: FEBRUARY 1970

Industry Grouping	Proportion of Output Purchased by Defense	Employment (in thousands)
Ordnance and Accessories	76.8%	322
Radio, TV, and Communications Equipment	38.6	666
Aircraft and Parts	72.4	851
Other Transportation Equipment	26.4	300
Electronic Components and Accessories	33.8	374
Total		2,513

SOURCE: Bureau of Labor Statistics, Department of Labor, *Monthly Labor Review*, February 1970, and Office of the Secretary of Defense, *Report on DOD Regional Employment Problems*, August 1971.

group sell at least 25% of their products to the Defense Department and NASA. The defense output of the aircraft and ordnance industries, respectively, reached as high as 72.4% and 76.8% in 1970.[7]

In 1970 one out of every five electrical and mechanical engineers employed in private industry worked on a defense-related contract. The same is true for two out of every five airplane mechanics, two out of every five physicists (not including teachers), and three out of every five aeronautical engineers.[8] From the start of the Vietnam build-up in 1964 to the peak year of 1968, defense-related industrial employment rose 52%, to a total of 3.5 million. In 1968, the country also supported 3.5 million active military personnel, as well as 1.3 million civilians working for the Defense Department. This means that the number of people directly and indirectly involved in the defense effort in 1968 was 8.3 million—10% of the nation's work force.[9]

Between 1968 and 1971 these employment figures dropped. Total defense manpower in all three categories was cut by over 2.2 million. Military personnel were reduced by 848,000; Defense Department civilian employees, by 138,000; employees in the defense industry, by 1.2 million.

Each of the military services, and NASA, has an independent buying organization, although the four organizations purchase a number of similar systems. For example, each purchases aircraft, missiles, electronics equipment, communications equipment, test equipment, and vehicles. The Navy is the major customer for ships, but small numbers are also purchased by the buying organizations of the Army and Air Force.

BUYING ORGANIZATIONS

Since the publication of *The Weapons Acquisition Process* by Peck and Scherer in 1962, each of the military services has reorganized its buying commands. The budgets and buying organizations in 1970–1972 are described below.

Army

The total research, development, and procurement budget for the Army changed only slightly during the 1970–1972 period. In 1970, the budget was $6.31 billion; in 1971, $5.17 billion; in 1972, $5.75 billion. Research and development accounted for approximately 30% of these amounts. Procurement activities utilized the remainder.[10]

The Army Materiel Command is in charge of all Army development, and procurement activity. The command employs approximately 10,000 military and civilian personnel. They are responsible for: preparing contractor work statements and issuing requests for proposals; selecting contractors; administering contracts; evaluating progress; testing products; and handling all other management tasks associated with the acquisition process. The headquarters for the Army Materiel Command are in Arlington, Virginia. Seven subordinate commodity buying organizations (Electronics; Missiles; Mobility Equipment; Munitions; Tank-Automotive; Test and Evaluation; and Weapons) are scattered throughout the United States. Figure III-5 illustrates the organizational structure of the command and its relationship to the Secretary of the Army, and identifies the major programs assigned to the various commodity commands.

FIGURE III-5. ARMY BUYING ORGANIZATION CHART

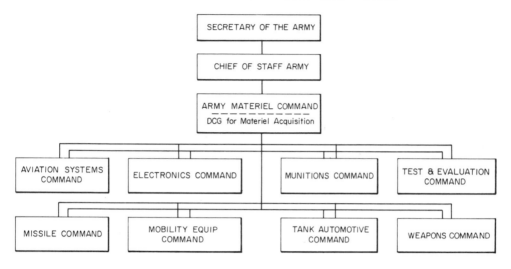

Navy

The research, development, and procurement budget for the Navy is substantially larger than the Army's. Within the 1970–1972 period, the budget varied only moderately from year to year. In 1970 total expenditures were $10.11 billion; in 1971, $9.93 billion; and in 1972, $11.75 billion. Of these amounts, 20% to 22% was devoted to research and development, with the remainder for procurement. The Navy spent $16.2 billion for the procurement of ships and aircraft during this period.

The organization responsible for development and procurement for the Navy is the Navy Material Command. Approximately 10,000 military and civilian personnel within this command have the responsibility for managing the acquisition process. The headquarters of the Navy Material Command and its six subordinate commodity buying organizations—Air Systems; Electronic Systems; Facilities Engineering; Ordnance Systems; Ship Systems; and Supply Systems—are located in Arlington, Virginia. Figure III-6 illustrates the organizational structure for the command and its relationship to the Secretary of the Navy, and identifies the major programs assigned to the commodity commands.

Air Force

The research, development, and procurement budget for the Air Force is approximately the same as that for the Navy. In 1970 total expenditures were

FIGURE III-6. NAVY BUYING ORGANIZATION CHART

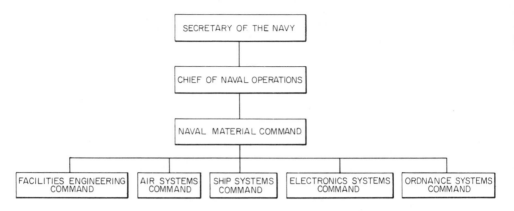

$10.35 billion; in 1971, $9.44 billion; and in 1972, $9.49 billion. Research and development accounted for 30% to 32% of these amounts, with the remainder for procurement. During this period, the Air Force spent $10.4 billion for the procurement of aircraft.

The Air Force organization responsible for development and procurement is the Air Force Systems Command, which employs approximately 10,000 military and civilian personnel. Its headquarters are located in Camp Springs, Maryland. Three subordinate commodity buying organizations (Aeronautical Systems; Electronic Systems; Space and Missile Systems) are located elsewhere. Figure III-7 illustrates the organizational structure for the

FIGURE III-7. AIR FORCE ORGANIZATION CHART

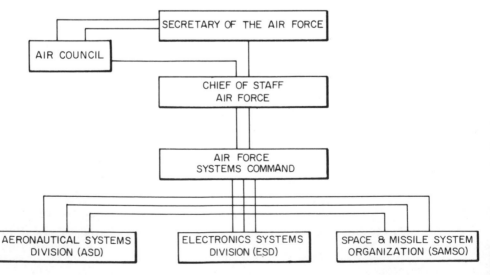

command and its relationship to the Secretary of the Air Force, and identifies the major programs assigned to the three commodity commands.

NASA

The research and development budget for NASA decreased steadily during the 1970–1972 period. In 1970 the budget was $3.8 billion; in 1971, $3.4 billion; and in 1972, $3.2 billion.[11]

Eleven field installations manage the acquisition process for NASA, all under the direct supervision of the NASA Administrator. NASA's headquarters are located in Washington, D.C. Figure III-8 gives the names and loca-

FIGURE III-8. NATIONAL AERONAUTICS AND SPACE ADMINISTRATION
BUYING ORGANIZATION CHART

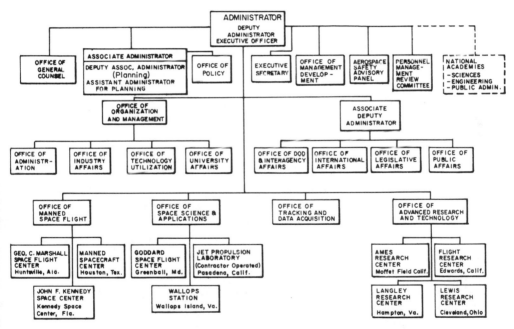

tions of ten of the installations. The eleventh is a joint AEC-NASA installation devoted to space nuclear propulsion, located in Germantown, Maryland.

THE DEFENSE MARKET

As Peck and Scherer pointed out in 1962, the defense market differs from the commercial market in several crucial ways. First, it is not determined by supply and demand. Instead, Congress determines annually how much the Defense Department will spend for research, development, and production. The size of the defense budget for each fiscal year is determined by domestic political and economic conditions, by international events, and by the interests of the Congressmen and Senators who serve on defense, space, and appropriations committees and subcommittees.

Secondly, the price of a weapon system is not determined by market competition. Under a cost-reimbursement contract, the price depends on costs actually experienced, plus a profit, or fee, negotiated separately and in advance. Fixed-price and incentive contract prices also depend on costs actually experienced in that they are renegotiated each time a contract change occurs (on large contracts once a month or more frequently). Under all three types of contract, the contractor's profit is largely determined by the level of costs planned when the contract was initially negotiated.

Without the multiplicity of buyers that are present in the commercial market, the defense and aerospace industry must cope with the built-in instability of its one-customer market. An unexpected rise or fall in the level of Congressional appropriations for defense spending can alter the industry's profit picture radically. The Defense Department and NASA plan on the basis of their short-term and long-term goals, on the one hand, and the limits of their annual budget appropriations, on the other. Defense contractors may be severely damaged financially if such plans are unrealistic.

In the defense and aerospace industry, major acquisition programs are usually long-lived, and weapon systems are not delivered to the buyer until years after contracts are negotiated. Under these circumstances, private firms cannot afford the large initial investments required for research, capital equipment, and test facilities. In recognition of the unique problems of the industry, the Government underwrites a sizable share of the contractors' financial investment. In addition, the Government provides industrial facilities, makes advance and progress payments, and assists in strategic material acquisition.[12] The present Government-defense industry relationship is called a "bilateral monopoly." The term is used to describe a market in which a single buyer and a single seller exist interdependently: neither can survive without the other.[13]

A summary of the differences between the defense market and the industrial market is given below.

Following this description of Government buyers and the defense market we will now examine the characteristics of defense contractors.

Market Characteristics[14]

Industrial Market	Defense Market
The seller initiates new product innovations, based on analyses of potential markets. He has no certain knowledge of a product's saleability.	The buyer establishes the requirements for a product. The producer then begins development and production.
The buyer has a wide range of choice between products in the same category that have real or advertised differences.	Relatively few products are produced simultaneously for the same mission. Although the buyer sometimes has the option to choose among prototypes, the time and cost of producing new systems once production has begun discourages replacement.
Price is a dominant factor in a buyer's choice because adequate substitutes for a product are often available.	Price is only one of the factors that govern a customer's choice. It may be far less important than quality, availability, or the technology required to realize a specific program objective.
The market tends to be impersonal. Buyers and sellers act independently.	The market is highly personal. The buyer has constant contact with the seller's organization.
The producer finances the development-production effort.	The buyer bears most of the development cost and may provide equipment and facilities for the use of the producer.
The market usually contains several, or many, customers for each product.	The market is essentially one-customer (monopsonistic).
Prices are primarily determined by competition.	Price is determined by an evaluation of anticipated and actual costs.
Demand is either relatively constant (e.g., for staples), or tends to be a function of disposable income (e.g., for nonessentials).	Demand is a function of the technology available, or of estimates of a potential enemy's technological resources.
The basic design of the product changes slowly and requirements for a given model are relatively stable.	The product may be technologically obsolete before production is completed.

NOTES TO CHAPTER III

1. Merton J. Peck and Frederic M. Scherer, *The Weapons Acquisition Process: An Economic Analysis* (Boston: Division of Research, Harvard Business School, 1962), p. 57.
2. *The U.S. Federal Budget, 1971* (Washington: Government Printing Office).
3. U.S. Senate, Armed Services Committee, Report 92-359, *Authorizing Defense Appropriations for Fiscal Year 1972*, p. 273.
4. Office of the Secretary of Defense, *The Defense Budget, 1971*.
5. *The Military Balance, 1970–71* (London: The Institute for Strategic Studies, 1970).
6. *Special Analyses of the Budget of the United States Government, Fiscal Year 1972* (Washington: Government Printing Office), p. 273.
7. Report of the U.S. Congress Joint Economic Committee, March 10, 1969.
8. National Science Foundation, *Federal Funds for Research, Development and Other Scientific Activities,* Annual Report, 1970.
9. Ibid.
10. Office of Statistical Services, Office of the Assistant Secretary of Defense (Comptroller), 1971.
11. *Special Analyses of the Budget of the United States Government, Fiscal Year 1972*, p. 273.
12. Lt. Col. David I. Cleland and First Lt. William R. King, "The Defense Market System," *Defense Industry Bulletin,* January 1968, p. 7.
13. Peck and Scherer, op. cit., p. 60.
14. Adapted from Cleland and King, op. cit., p. 8.

CHAPTER IV

Defense Contractors

UNTIL WORLD WAR II Government arsenals produced almost all Army ordnance equipment and a major part of Navy ordnance and ships. The technology of pre-World War II weapons and equipment was relatively easy to understand, and the Government was well equipped to handle manufacturing. The emergence of the airplane as a major weapon system marked a turning point: its technology was beyond the capability of most Government arsenals. With the exception of work done at the Naval aircraft factory at Philadelphia and the Army Air Corps engine laboratory at McCook Field, aviation development was turned over to private industry. During World War II the Government again depended on private industry to supplement its arsenal production. By 1958 only 10% of the appropriations for weapons production was earmarked for arsenals. Private industry received the rest.

More than 20,000 contractors are involved in prime defense and aerospace research, development, and production programs. These 20,000 select more than 100,000 subcontractors. (Fifty percent of a prime contract for a major weapon or space program is usually subcontracted.) The 120,000 prime contractors and subcontractors are located in every state of the Union, and in 363 of the nation's 435 Congressional Districts. The Office of the Assistant Secretary of Defense (Comptroller) identifies five major centers of defense activity within the United States:

1. A southern California complex
2. A San Francisco Bay area complex
3. A New York City-northern New Jersey complex
4. A Boston-centered complex
5. A Washington, D.C.-centered complex

Defense contractors located in these centers and throughout the country fall into five categories, described by Peck and Scherer in *The Weapons Acquisition Process*:

(1) *The weapon systems firms.* These firms contract to deliver a fairly complete weapon system such as an aircraft or a missile. They undertake a great deal of the development work and are responsible, either contractually or informally, for the delivery of the complete weapon system. Sometimes the contractor is formally designated as the system prime contractor and most of the various elements are developed under subcontract to this firm. In the other cases, some major elements such as the engine or the radar are developed under prime contracts with the service and are "integrated" by the major contractor. Even in the latter case, the major contractor furnishes much of the weapon system and places subcontracts for some major subsystems, and is in practice regarded as "the" contractor of the weapons program.

Traditionally the airframe companies have regarded themselves as the "systems" firms in aircraft and missiles. But for missiles, we also find electronic firms assuming this role, as electronics have become an increasingly large proportion of some weapon systems. Furthermore, the systems firms in the large ground electronics installations for radar warning or communications are drawn primarily from the electronic industry. In tanks, the systems firms were the automotive companies, while for ships, the shipyards have had this role. But in the last two cases the services tended to retain most of the integrating and coordinating function.

(2) *The subsystem firms.* These firms provide major subsystems such as the fire control system, the engine, and the warhead that make up a weapon system. Depending upon the organizational pattern, such firms may or may not be subcontractors to the weapon system firms. Even though the term subsystems suggests a minor role, such subsystems in aggregate account for a substantial part of the expenditures in a weapons project. Some weapon system firms also perform subsystem roles, just as some firms predominantly engaged in subsystem activities occasionally act as weapon system managers.

(3) *The overflow producers.* Such firms receive parts of the weapons project from the weapon system firms, usually on subcontract. They differ from the subsystem firms in that their assignments lie within the traditional areas of competence of the weapon system firm. The use of overflow production is largely an aircraft industry phenomenon, although in World War II it existed throughout the weapons industry.

The rationale of such parceling out of a weapons program is usually the lack of capacity in the weapon system firm, although upon occasion it may be the existence of specialized skills in another firm.

There are three types of firms in this category: the major weapon systems firms themselves; a few specialized and fairly sizable "overflow" companies that make their living by producing wings, tail assemblies, and so forth; and finally small machine shops, contract drafting, and engineering service firms that have grown up in the immediate neighborhood of the large companies.

(4) *The parts firms.* These firms supply the tubes, gauges, valves, instruments, and so forth for subsystems. Although the contributions of such firms to weapon systems are not widely publicized, advances here have made possible much of the technical progress in weaponry. Some parts are used in both weapons and commercial products, others are used in many weapon systems, and a few are developed for specific weapon systems.

(5) *The materials makers.* These firms supply the materials for weapons: aluminum, titanium, high quality steel, fiberglass, electrical cable, etc., as well as such chemicals as liquid oxygen, boron, and so forth. Some materials such as standard aluminum alloys are essentially civilian products, but to an increasing extent others such as the special ceramics and beryllium have been developed largely for use in weapons.[1]

THE TOP DEFENSE CONTRACTORS

Of the 20,000 prime defense contractors, a relatively small number receive the majority of the procurement dollars. During World War II, 100 defense contractors accounted for 67.2% of the dollar value of defense spending, while the top 25 accounted for 46.5%.[2] During the Korean War this pattern was repeated: the top 100 contractors accounted for 64% of the total, the top 25 contractors for 45.5%.[3] As the United States moved closer to a peacetime economy in the 1953–1960 time frame, however, the top 100 defense contractors captured 73.7% of the major contract awards. The share of the top 25 contractors climbed to 55.3%. By 1970 the top 100 defense contractors still received 69.7% of all defense spending; the top 25, 46%.[4] Despite the general slowdown in defense procurement in 1970 the top 100 companies continued to receive more than two-thirds of the defense procurement dollar. As seen in Figure IV-1, the percentage-of-procurement trend for the top 100 contractors during the 35-year period ending in 1970 was largely determined by the trend of the top 25.

The list of the leading defense contractors showed substantial stability in the 1960s. All but 13 of the top 50 contractors in the 1958–1960 time frame

FIGURE IV-1. TOP 100 AND TOP 25 DEFENSE CONTRACTORS:
1940–1970

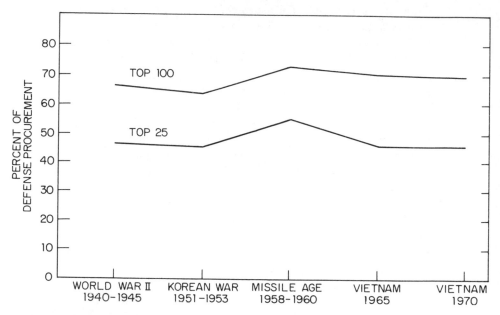

were listed among the top 50 in 1970. Of the 13 not making the list, seven were listed among the top 75. Only six were no longer among the top 100.

Table IV-1 lists the top 100 defense contractors in 1970 and shows their relative position for the 1958–1960 period. While the turnover among the top 50 defense firms was relatively minor during the decade of the 1960s, the same cannot be said for other firms on the list. Of the top 100 firms appearing in 1958–1960, only 63 appeared in 1970. The stability of the top 50 firms is far more significant, however, in appraising concentration within the industry. In 1970 the top 50 firms received 60% of all prime defense contract awards. The second 50 firms accounted for only 6% of the total.

As defense spending began to slow down toward the end of the 1960s, a number of indices suggested that significant changes were taking place in the defense and aerospace industry. Each year *Forbes* publishes a list of the 100 most profitable companies in the United States. In 1965, 27 defense contractors were listed among their "top 100." The number remained constant in 1966 and then declined sharply in each of the three subsequent years. By 1970 only 12 defense contractors appeared on the list (Table IV-2).

Another sign of declining fortunes among defense contractors appeared in *Forbes* annual listing of the 100 U.S. companies leading in growth in earnings (Table IV-3). In 1967, 29 defense contractors were among this group. In 1968, there were only 20; in 1969, 17; and by 1970, only 11.

TABLE IV-1. 100 COMPANIES RECEIVING THE LARGEST DOLLAR VOLUME OF
DOD PRIME CONTRACT AWARDS: 1970
(in millions of dollars)

Company	DOD Total	1958–60 Rank
1. Lockheed Aircraft Corp.	$1,848	3
2. General Dynamics Corp.	1,183	2
3. General Electric Company	1,000	4
4. American Telephone and Telegraph Company	931	7
5. McDonnell Douglas Corp.	883	8
6. United Aircraft Corp.	874	6
7. North American Rockwell Corp.	707	5
8. Grumman Corp.	661	17
9. Litton Industries	543	0
10. Hughes Aircraft Company	497	10
11. Ling Temco Vought, Inc.	479	25 and 61*
12. Boeing Company	475	1
13. Textron Inc.	431	45
14. Westinghouse Electric Corp.	418	19
15. Sperry Rand Corp.	399	11
16. Honeywell, Inc.	398	37
17. General Motors Corp.	386	21
18. Raytheon Company	380	12
19. Ford Motor Company	346	35 and 36*
20. Avco Corp.	270	26
21. American Motors Corp.	266	0
22. RCA Corp.	263	14
23. General Tire & Rubber Company	262	22
24. International Business Machines Corp.	256	15
25. Raymond Morrison Knudsen	256	65
26. Martin Marietta Corp.	251	9
27. Tenneco, Inc.	249	28
28. Olin Corp.	248	53
29. Teledyne Inc.	238	59 and 43*
30. Standard Oil Company (New Jersey)	229	24
31. International Telephone and Telegraph Corp.	217	27
32. Texas Instruments Inc.	191	0
33. Northrop Corp.	184	23
34. TRW Inc.	179	33
35. Bendix Corp.	168	20
36. Mobil Oil Corp.	166	44
37. du Pont (E. I.) de Nemours & Company	162	86
38. Singer Company	154	46
39. Collins Radio Company	146	34
40. Pan American World Airways Inc.	143	39
41. FMC Corp.	141	55
42. Standard Oil Company (California)	140	29
43. Morrison-Knudsen Company	138	65

TABLE IV-1 *(continued)*

Company	DOD Total	1958–60 Rank
44. National Presto Industries Inc.	$133	0
45. Hercules, Inc.	127	51
46. Asiatic Petroleum Corp.	126	96
47. Pacific Architects and Engineers, Inc.	116	0
48. Uniroyal, Inc.	115	0
49. General Telephone and Electronics Corp.	108	62
50. Reynolds (RJ) Industries, Inc.	107	0
51. Goodyear Tire and Rubber Company	104	40
52. Chamberlain Mfg. Company	102	0
53. States Marine Lines, Inc.	99	71
54. Massachusetts Institute of Technology	96	47
55. Day and Zimmerman, Inc.	96	0
56. Magnavox Company	95	84
57. City Investing Company	93	0
58. Chrysler Corp.	92	18
59. Thiokol Chemical Corp.	92	32
60. Texaco, Inc.	86	41
61. Norris Industries	84	0
62. Eastman Kodak Company	83	0
63. Control Data Corp.	81	0
64. Harris-Intertype Corp.	79	0
65. Sanders Associates Inc.	76	0
66. Curtiss-Wright Corp.	76	30
67. Aerospace Corp.	73	0
68. Lear Siegler Inc.	71	64
69. Automation Industries, Inc.	71	0
70. Colt Industries, Inc.	69	0
71. Signal Companies, Inc.	68	48
72. Federal Cartridge Corp.	68	0
73. United States Steel Corp.	66	0
74. Gulf and Western Industries	65	0
75. Mason & Hanger—Silas Mason Company	63	91
76. Condec Corp.	62	0
77. White Motor Corp.	61	0
78. Johns Hopkins University	61	76
79. Fairchild Hiller Corp.	59	52
80. Western Union Telegraph Company	58	0
81. Moore and McCormack Company Inc.	57	0
82. Sverdrup and Parcel and Associates, Inc.	53	0
83. Page Aircraft Maintenance Inc.	53	0
84. AMF, Inc.	52	0
85. Whittaker Corp.	52	0
86. International Harvester Company	47	85
87. Motorola, Inc.	47	89
88. Gulf Oil Corp.	46	90

TABLE IV-1 (*continued*)

Company	DOD Total	1958–60 Rank
89. Atlantic Richfield Company	$46	77
90. Lykes-Youngstown Corp.	46	0
91. Dynalectron Corp.	44	0
92. Walter Kidde and Company, Inc.	43	0
93. Gould, Inc.	41	0
94. Seatrain Lines Inc.	41	0
95. Seaboard World Airlines Inc.	41	0
96. Caterpillar Tractor Company	40	0
97. Flying Tiger Line, Inc.	40	0
98. Dynamics Corp. of America	39	0
99. Cessna Aircraft Company	39	0
100. Fairchild Camera and Instrument Company	39	0

* Merger company

SOURCE: Office of the Assistant Secretary of Defense (Comptroller), Directorate for Information Operations, *100 Companies Receiving the Largest Dollar Volume of Prime Contract Awards, Fiscal Year 1970.*

Merton J. Peck and Frederic M. Scherer, *The Weapons Acquisition Process: An Economic Analysis,* (Boston: Division of Research, Harvard Business School, 1962), Appendix 5A.

During the same period a number of leading defense contractors began to seek out business in the private sector. Table IV-4 shows that 17 of the leading 23 defense contractors reduced their dependence on defense business. While several contractors received less defense work because of the phasedown in spending, their increased sales indicate that they were consciously seeking new markets.

In a 1967 paper dealing with the intersection of the public and private sectors, Professor Murray Weidenbaum of Washington University commented on the attempts of the defense and aerospace industry to diversify:

> These companies have attempted to utilize the technological capabilities developed in the course of their military and space work to design and produce a great variety of commercial items. These have included aluminum sports boats, prosthetic devices, heavy duty land vehicles, adhesives, wall panels, welding equipment, and gas turbine engines—items in a wide variety of industry and market areas.
>
> With one major exception, these internal product diversification attempts by the specialized defense/space firms have each been relatively small in comparison with military or space work. The exception, of course, is transport aircraft for the commercial airlines. The large jetliners—the DC-8's, the 707's, and the 880's—each have involved large numbers of scientists, engineers and other employees; the resultant unit

TABLE IV-2. MAJOR DEFENSE CONTRACTORS AMONG THE TOP 100 U.S. FIRMS
IN PROFITABILITY: 1965–1970

1965	*1966*	*1967*
Magnavox (8)	Magnavox (3)	Ling Temco Vought (4)
Caterpillar Tractor (9)	Ling Temco Vought (4)	Eastman Kodak (18)
General Motors (12)	Grumman (9)	Gulf & Western Ind. (20)
Eastman Kodak (15)	TRW (20)	TRW (24)
McDonnell Douglas (21)	McDonnell Douglas (21)	RCA (30)
Litton (25)	Eastman Kodak (25)	Litton (31)
Boeing (28)	Gulf & Western Ind. (26)	Textron (33)
Grumman (34)	Pan American (30)	R. J. Reynolds Ind. (37)
IBM (36)	Texas Instruments (31)	General Dynamics (40)
Ling Temco Vought (37)	General Motors (38)	Control Data (43)
Dupont (38)	Caterpillar Tractor (39)	General Motors (45)
Lockheed (41)	Litton (49)	Grumman (47)
General Dynamics (43)	Boeing (50)	Moore & McCormack (52)
Texas Instruments (44)	Textron (51)	Avco (55)
Motorola (47)	General Dynamics (54)	IBM (57)
FMC (51)	RCA (55)	Lockheed (58)
TRW (52)	Lockheed (58)	Caterpillar Tractor (64)
Chrysler (53)	Dupont (60)	Pan American (68)
General Electric (55)	IBM (63)	Magnavox (74)
R. J. Reynolds Ind. (57)	R. J. Reynolds Ind. (68)	Texaco (76)
Ford (65)	Avco (69)	Hercules (94)
RCA (66)	White Motor (70)	White Motor (100)
Moore & McCormack (67)	FMC (72)	
Textron (70)	General Electric (74)	
General Tire & Rubber (73)	Moore & McCormack (76)	
Texaco (78)	Hercules (79)	
Hercules (79)	General Tire & Rubber (87)	

1968	*1969*	*1970*
Norris (5)	McDonnell Douglas (9)	Magnavox (13)
Magnavox (8)	Magnavox (15)	Norris (16)
Eastman Kodak (25)	Norris (22)	Eastman Kodak (21)
IBM (37)	Eastman Kodak (37)	Gulf & Western Ind. (24)
Gulf & Western Ind. (44)	IBM (52)	Whittaker (47)
McDonnell Douglas (49)	Cessna (60)	IBM (65)
City Investing (54)	General Telephone & Elec. (66)	TRW (74)
General Motors (55)	Caterpillar Tractor (69)	Litton (78)
RCA (66)	AMF (73)	R. J. Reynolds Ind. (84)
Walter Kidde (68)	Moore & McCormack (79)	Textron (91)
Whittaker (69)	Walter Kidde (79)	General Motors (92)
Cessna (72)	Fairchild Hiller (88)	Grumman (100)
Avco (76)	RCA (91)	
R. J. Reynolds Ind. (80)	Textron (94)	
Textron (87)	R. J. Reynolds Ind. (98)	
Texaco (96)		
TRW (97)		

SOURCE: Compiled from the January 1 issues of *Forbes* for 1965 through 1970. Number in parentheses is growth-in-earnings ranking based on the five-year annual increase in per-share earnings.

TABLE IV-3. MAJOR DEFENSE CONTRACTORS AMONG THE TOP 100 U.S. FIRMS
IN EARNINGS GROWTH: 1967–1970

1967	*1968*	*1969*
Teledyne (1)	Whittaker (1)	City Investing (4)
Gulf & Western Ind. (2)	Teledyne (9)	Teledyne (9)
Ling Temco Vought (5)	Gulf & Western Ind. (10)	Norris (13)
Control Data (13)	City Investing (11)	Whittaker (17)
Litton (27)	Norris (16)	Walter Kidde (23)
Grumman (32)	Control Data (17)	Gulf & Western Ind. (25)
Collins Radio (34)	Walter Kidde (20)	Colt Ind. (30)
Textron (45)	Ling Temco Vought (21)	McDonnell Douglas (33)
Pan American (47)	Collins Radio (33)	Sperry Rand (40)
United Aircraft (48)	Sperry Rand (37)	Raytheon (45)
TRW (48)	Magnavox (47)	Magnavox (46)
RCA (49)	Eastman Kodak (59)	Lear Siegler (56)
Magnavox (52)	United Aircraft (60)	IBM (78)
Sperry Rand (55)	Grumman (64)	Eastman Kodak (80)
Texas Instruments (57)	Textron (70)	Textron (87)
White Motor (64)	Uniroyal (75)	Northrop (94)
Eastman Kodak (65)	Raytheon (82)	Litton (98)
Westinghouse (71)	Boeing (93)	
Boeing (71)	RCA (95)	*1970*
Signal Companies (80)	Cessna (98)	City Investing (2)
Fairchild Camera & Instr. (82)		Teledyne (10)
Olin (87)		Whittaker (23)
FMC (92)		Norris (24)
Moore & McCormack (92)		McDonnell Douglas (43)
Raytheon (96)		Gulf & Western Ind. (49)
General Telephone & Elec. (97)		Sperry Rand (53)
Caterpillar Tractor (98)		Raytheon (55)
IBM (99)		IBM (59)
ITT (100)		Lear Siegler (62)
		Northrop (95)

SOURCE: Compiled from the January 1 issues of *Forbes* for 1967 through 1970. Number in parentheses is growth-in-earnings ranking based on the five-year annual increase in per-share earnings.

sales prices are comparable with those of many military products. However, with the exception of Boeing, the profit performance on these jet programs has been extremely poor. The losses incurred both depleted the venture capital of several key aerospace companies and reduced the enthusiasm for diversification of others. . . .

A variety of reasons is usually given for the inability of the large specialized defense/space contractors to utilize their resources profitably in commercial endeavors: concentration of management interest on defense

TABLE IV-4. SALES OF MAJOR DEFENSE CONTRACTORS TO THE DEPARTMENT OF DEFENSE
AS A PERCENTAGE OF TOTAL SALES: 1965–1969
(in millions of dollars)

	1965	1966	1967	1968	1969
Lockheed					
Total	$ 1,814	$ 2,085	$ 2,336	$ 2,217	$ 2,075
% to DOD	95%	73%	77%	84%	98%
General Dynamics					
Total	1,473	1,797	2,253	2,662	2,509
% to DOD	80%	63%	81%	84%	50%
McDonnell Douglas					
Total	1,762	2,239	2,934	3,609	3,024
% to DOD	58%	45%	72%	42%	35%
General Electric					
Total	6,213	7,176	7,737	8,380	8,447
% to DOD	13%	17%	17%	18%	19%
Boeing					
Total	2,023	2,357	2,880	3,274	2,835
% to DOD	29%	39%	32%	23%	23%
North American Rockwell					
Total	2,625	2,754	2,516	2,803	2,667
% to DOD	28%	21%	27%	24%	25%
United Aircraft					
Total	1,430	1,663	2,212	2,408	2,350
% to DOD	44%	69%	50%	55%	42%
AT&T					
Total	2,194	2,404	2,550	2,618	2,895
% to DOD	29%	28%	26%	30%	32%
Martin Marietta					
Total	603	670	696	682	981
% to DOD	52%	50%	42%	58%	27%
General Motors					
Total	20,734	20,209	20,026	22,755	24,295
% to DOD	1%	3%	3%	3%	2%
Sperry Rand					
Total	1,248	1,280	1,487	1,563	1,607
% to DOD	26%	33%	33%	29%	29%
Grumman Aircraft					
Total	852	1,059	969	1,153	1,180
% to DOD	41%	31%	50%	55%	35%
Avco					
Total	443	617	756	866	817
% to DOD	53%	82%	59%	67%	56%
Raytheon					
Total	488	709	1,106	1,158	1,285
% to DOD	60%	52%	36%	39%	43%

TABLE IV-4 (*continued*)

	1965	1966	1967	1968	1969
General Tire					
Total	$ 950	$ 1,002	$ 955	$ 1,039	$ 1,088
% to DOD	32%	33%	29%	24%	24%
LTV					
Total	1,304	1,631	1,872	2,770	3,750
% to DOD	20%	19%	29%	27%	24%
Ford					
Total	11,537	12,240	10,516	14,075	14,756
% to DOD	3%	4%	4%	3%	3%
Westinghouse Electric					
Total	2,390	2,581	2,901	3,296	3,509
% to DOD	11%	14%	16%	8%	12%
Textron					
Total	851	1,132	1,446	1,704	1,682
% to DOD	23%	49%	34%	29%	25%
RCA					
Total	2,042	2,549	3,014	3,106	3,188
% to DOD	11%	10%	9%	8%	9%
Bendix					
Total	754	1,052	1,274	1,389	1,468
% to DOD	31%	27%	23%	16%	13%
ITT					
Total	423	500	492	542	602
% to DOD	49%	44%	52%	45%	40%
IBM					
Total	969	1,342	1,869	2,876	2,580
% to DOD	19%	14%	10%	9%	10%
TOTAL SALES	$65,122	$71,048	$74,797	$86,945	$89,590
% TO DOD	17%	19%	22%	19%	17%

SOURCE: Total sales (or a comparable figure when these were not available) were taken from the 1970 *Moody's Industrial Manual*, published by Moody's Investor's Service, Inc.

and space business, limited marketing and distribution capability, lack of mass production experience, low capitalization in relation to sales, lack of experience in designing, producing and servicing consumer and industrial products, and very specialized equipment.[5]

In an analysis of defense contractors it is essential to recognize their involvement in the NASA market. In 1970 NASA contractors received $2.76 billion in prime contract awards—less than 10% of the amount ($38.9 billion) spent on prime defense contracts during the same year.[6] The top 100 NASA contractors received 91.5% of all prime contract awards.[7] Forty-one of the top 100 NASA contractors were among the top 100 defense contractors. Even these figures, however, understate the degree of overlap among leading NASA contractors and contractors for the Defense Department. In 1970, 20 of the leading NASA contractors (Table IV-5) received $2,163

TABLE IV-5. 20 LEADING NASA PRIME CONTRACTORS: 1970
(in millions of dollars)

	NASA Sales	DOD Sales	DOD Rank
1. North American Rockwell	$ 531	$ 707	7
2. Grumman Aerospace	284	661	8
3. McDonnell Douglas	236	883	5
4. Boeing	158	475	12
5. International Business Machines	133	256	24
6. General Electric	132	1,000	3
7. Bendix	110	168	35
8. Martin Marietta	108	251	26
9. Aerojet-General	72	262	23
10. TRW	58	179	34
11. RCA	54	263	22
12. Sperry Rand	48	399	15
13. Lockheed Aircraft	41	1,848	1
14. General Dynamics	38	1,183	2
15. Trans World Airlines	36	—	—
16. Service Technology	27	—	—
17. United Aircraft	27	874	6
18. Federal Electric	26	—	—
19. Philco-Ford	24	346	19
20. General Motors	20	386	17
	$2,163	$10,141	

SOURCE: NASA, *Annual Procurement Report, Fiscal Year 1970.*

billion in prime NASA contract awards (nearly 80% of the total) and $10,-141 billion in prime defense contract awards (almost 25% of the total).[8] All but three of these top 20 NASA contractors were among the top 100 defense contractors.

Companies are drawn into defense work for a variety of reasons. One of the more important has been a rapidly changing technology—solid-state, cryogenics, lasers, and new materials. With each major advance, firms familiar with the new techonology bid for defense contracts. Sometimes a new company is formed by a group of specialists within a larger firm who wish to capitalize on their knowledge of the emerging technology.

Once a company is an established defense contractor, there are several reasons for its continuing interest in defense business. The senior executive of a large commercial firm doing business worth several tens of millions of dollars with the Defense Department mentioned four:

1. Members of the company involved in defense business gain valuable training in the technical and managerial skills needed for commercial business.
2. Defense work has a favorable influence on investment analysts and some segments of the American public.
3. The firm wants to devote part of its industrial capacity to national defense as an expression of patriotism.
4. Pressures to continue come from company personnel currently employed on defense programs.

Most of the firm's commercial products are far less complex than systems developed or produced for the Defense Department. Management realized that their employees enjoyed the prestige associated with space-age technology.

When the major share of a company's business is defense work, the drive for new contracts becomes compelling. One reason is that technical and management personnel who have worked on defense programs are now geared for advanced technology and complex equipment. Also, since the Department of Defense handles its own distribution, defense contractors do not develop a phase of their operations vital for commercial business. By the time a firm has developed the personnel, facilities, and equipment to handle programs budgeted for hundreds of millions, or billions, of dollars, management must keep the company operating at or near full strength or risk serious financial losses. During our interviews with industry managers, this concern seemed to outweigh all others. The fact that profits in the defense industry are almost solely a function of the level of costs seemed of secondary importance.

THE DEFENSE INDUSTRY AND PRIVATE INDUSTRY: A FINANCIAL COMPARISON

Peck and Scherer observed in 1962 that there was a substantial overlap between the 100 largest defense contractors and the 100 largest U.S. industrial corporations (Table IV-6). By 1970 this overlap had increased. Table IV-6 shows that, in 1970, 40 of the 100 largest commercial industrial corporations were among the 100 largest defense contractors.

In Professor Weidenbaum's study, six firms whose defense and aerospace orders exceeded three-quarters of their total sales volume are compared with

TABLE IV-6. OVERLAP BETWEEN THE 100 LARGEST DEFENSE CONTRACTORS
AND THE 100 LARGEST INDUSTRIAL CORPORATIONS: 1939–1970

Period	*Number of Firms on Both Lists*
World War II Defense Contractors and 1939 Industrial Ranks	29
World War II Defense Contractors and 1945 Industrial Ranks	53
Korea Defense and Industrial Ranks	41
"Missile Age" Defense and Industrial Ranks	40
1970 Defense and Industrial Ranks	43

SOURCES: Office of the Assistant Secretary of Defense (Comptroller), *100 Companies Receiving the Largest Dollar Volume of Prime Contract Awards, Fiscal Year 1970.*

Fortune list of the largest U.S. industrial corporations, 1970.

Merton J. Peck and Frederic M. Scherer, *The Weapons Acquisition Process: An Economic Analysis* (Division of Research, Harvard Business School, 1962), p. 120.

six commercial firms adjacent to them on the *Fortune* list of the 500 largest industrial corporations.[9] Using information in *Moody's Industrials,* Weidenbaum drew a number of financial comparisons. He found that with respect to profit margin on sales, defense and areospace companies operate on much smaller after-tax profit margins than do typical industrial corporations.

FIGURE IV-2. INDUSTRY COMPARISON—1

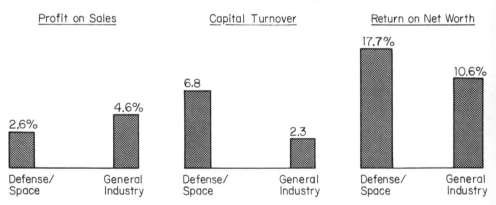

The Government provides its major contractors with progress payments monthly, or more frequently, and at a rate of 70% to 90% of costs incurred. Some contractors are also provided with substantial amounts of plant space and equipment. As a result, defense and areospace contractors report a far higher ratio of capital turnover (i.e., dollars of sales per dollar of invested capital).

To some extent, the lower profit margins and higher turnover rates for defense and aerospace companies tend to offset each other. However, the return on net worth (net profits as a percentage of stockholders' investment) for the six major defense firms in the Weidenbaum study was considerably higher than the return on net worth for the sample of commercially oriented firms.

The stock market's evaluation of defense and aerospace contractors has been less favorable than for other business firms. Weidenbaum points out that this results, in part, from the inherent instability of the Government market and the historical volatility of the fortunes of individual contractors. The relatively low dividend-payout ratio (the proportion of net income which is disbursed to stockholders in the form of cash dividends) may also have an adverse effect. Reflecting these factors, earnings of defense and aerospace companies tend to be more fully discounted, as shown by lower price/earnings multiples.

FIGURE IV-3. INDUSTRY COMPARISON—2

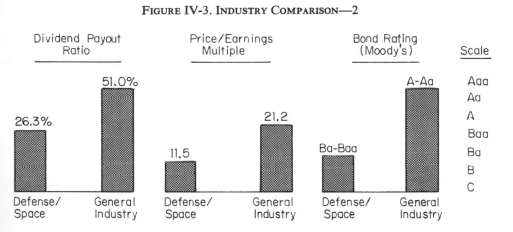

Of the six firms which composed the Weidenbaum general industry sample, four were able to issue bonds with a rating of either A or Aa; one chose not to issue bonds at all; the last placed its bonds privately. Of the six companies in the defense and aerospace sample, only one issued bonds on the market and these had the relatively low rating of Ba-Baa; one placed its bonds privately; the last four did not issue bonds. It is apparently easier for large commercially oriented firms to enter the bond market.

Weidenbaum's study included an analysis of the capital structure of defense and aerospace vs. general industry firms. Large defense contractors have a far lower ratio of company-owned plant and equipment to sales, relying to a relatively small degree on their own physical assets. Similar relationships hold when the dollar volume of plant and equipment per employee is examined, and when crude capital-to-output ratios are prepared (the ratio of plant and equipment depreciation, as carried on the company books, to "value added," or in-house effort). Indirectly, of course, these calculations emphasize the importance of Government-supplied capital. Weidenbaum compared the proportion of sales volume which represents such in-house effort ("value added") with purchased materials, subcontracts, and the work of supplier firms generally. In his sample, defense and aerospace companies subcontract less than the remaining corporations.

FIGURE IV-4. INDUSTRY COMPARISON—3

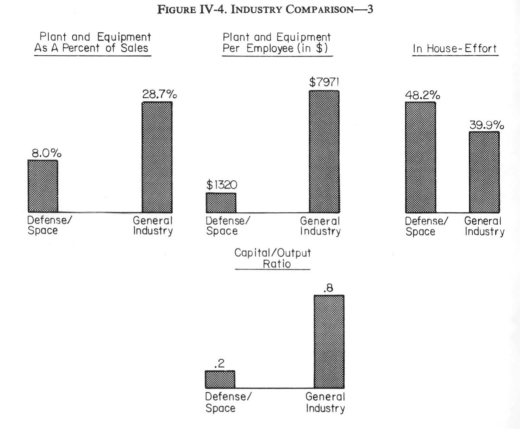

As shown in Figure IV-5, the Weidenbaum study yielded a number of interesting manpower statistics. The high proportion of engineers and other professionals in defense and aerospace work is reflected in the greater payroll cost per employee. Sales per employee are much lower for the defense and aerospace group, reflecting the greater labor requirements of Government work. To explain these statistics, Weidenbaum compared the defense industry's emphasis on research and development with the mass production techniques (requiring a smaller labor force) of other industries.

Weidenbaum's observations are supported by a separate study of the financial condition of 28 defense contractors conducted in early 1971 by a joint

FIGURE IV-5. INDUSTRY COMPARISON—4

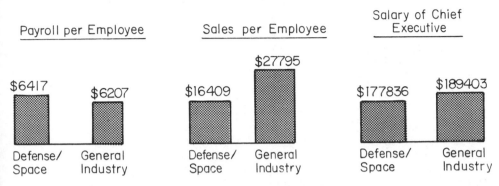

Defense Department/industry group working under the direction of the Office of the Secretary of Defense. This second study revealed that, from 1965 to 1969, the debt/equity ratios of 28 contracting companies (Table IV-7) rose from .28 to .40, an increase of 46%. In a composite of most of the major defense contractors, the increase was even more pronounced: a 54% rise, from .55 in 1965 to .83 in 1969.[10] The defense industry debt/equity ratio was 99% greater than that of general industry in 1965, and 102% greater than general industry in 1969.

In the aerospace segment of defense contracting, the growth in debt/equity ratios has been even more pronounced. In a sample of 65 aerospace companies, long-term debt increased by a factor of 5 from 1964 through 1970 ($816 million in 1964, $4.1 billion in 1970).[11] Over the same period, equity did little more than double, increasing from $3.2 billion in 1964 to $7.2 billion in 1970. Thus, the debt/equity ratios of the aerospace industry increased from .25 in 1964 to .57 in 1970—an increase of 128%.

A comparison of the total debt-to-net-worth ratio for the aerospace industry and selected general industries using similar production techniques reveals that despite unstable sales patterns, aerospace led the list, and exceeded the second highest leveraged industry by approximately 15 percentage points (Table IV-8). However, the Office of the Secretary of Defense (Directorate for Information Operations) showed that aerospace sales were projected downward. If sales do drop, the high debt-to-net-worth ratios will be a serious financial burden for some contractors.

Financial leverage involves the use of debt to generate increased sales and profits, thereby increasing return on an equity base which, because of the use of debt, need not grow as rapidly as sales and earnings. The risk of using leverage is that, beyond an optimum mix of debt and equity in a firm's capital structure, the fixed costs of the debt may become too great. In a period of declining sales, earnings may be insufficient to cover these fixed

TABLE IV-7. LONG-TERM DEBT AS A PERCENTAGE OF TOTAL EQUITY PLUS
LONG-TERM DEBT OF 28 DEFENSE CONTRACTORS: 1961–1970

	1961	1962	1963	1964	1965	1966	1967	1968	1969	1970
Teledyne, Inc.	21.28	40.60	43.42	47.37	33.36	26.96	43.75	34.43	30.00	26.55
LTV Aerospace Corporation	NA	NA	NA	NA	0.00	51.37	44.40	45.48	33.50	34.68
Ling Temco Vought, Inc.	80.90	73.22	53.62	59.53	59.66	63.57	49.18	92.23	97.63	101.95
Aerojet General Corporation	18.07	16.49	25.91	22.87	20.33	18.10	21.52	19.98	18.79	17.66
Avco Corporation	18.47	14.69	11.88	10.12	27.34	34.88	44.87	45.20	49.66	61.66
Bendix Corporation	0.35	0.30	0.25	0.17	0.97	0.41	2.45	23.89	26.08	27.06
Boeing Company	19.94	19.38	29.40	26.36	20.91	45.28	39.00	36.73	44.28	43.52
General Dynamics Corporation	56.01	46.55	32.88	23.65	28.00	31.44	27.25	17.64	27.94	29.51
General Electric Company	12.48	11.44	9.91	14.16	14.98	18.18	24.23	23.10	20.95	17.71
General Telephone & Electronics	52.27	53.64	54.77	55.41	57.18	57.97	60.98	59.96	59.56	58.96
Grumman Corporation	17.36	13.15	23.43	20.98	22.47	20.78	37.36	34.58	31.86	33.87
Honeywell, Inc.	22.62	21.41	26.38	23.11	30.19	31.70	37.23	37.73	35.98	46.58
Litton Industries, Inc.	42.84	42.50	47.59	47.40	46.28	41.97	38.28	29.73	36.94	46.15
Lockheed Aircraft Corporation	20.00	13.81	10.65	8.73	5.74	5.05	28.58	27.14	51.16	NA
Magnavox Company	25.04	20.59	10.03	8.20	25.57	20.46	17.40	15.25	14.41	12.88
Martin Marietta Corporation	20.08	16.50	13.78	12.97	18.88	17.69	29.42	37.15	44.60	42.73
McDonnell Douglas Corporation	0.00	0.00	0.00	0.00	0.00	0.00	30.94	26.50	21.25	19.73
No. American Rockwell Corporation	0.00	0.00	0.00	0.00	0.00	0.00	15.37	29.49	31.53	30.90
Northrop Corporation	13.42	11.26	19.51	19.68	25.54	24.64	39.19	49.47	47.31	45.20
Raytheon Company	30.74	28.05	27.93	27.35	25.44	21.18	17.69	14.96	11.46	12.03
Sanders Associates, Inc., Del.	2.52	1.02	0.81	0.00	0.00	0.00	0.00	43.04	44.54	65.45
Singer Company	9.01	8.59	9.54	9.06	8.86	19.61	20.80	27.63	26.80	26.77
Sperry Rand Corporation	38.16	45.91	41.04	39.69	36.76	32.76	23.41	23.44	26.28	NA
Texas Instruments, Inc.	10.04	7.30	5.51	3.39	26.86	19.20	18.83	17.27	25.15	22.25
Textron, Inc.	43.44	37.01	20.04	27.22	20.52	20.89	15.83	26.41	23.84	29.28
Thiokol Chemical Corporation	14.75	11.04	8.19	6.06	3.98	2.89	2.83	17.34	20.39	12.63
United Aircraft Corporation	20.84	20.53	28.37	26.73	21.07	24.32	34.89	32.54	30.89	29.52
Westinghouse Electric Corporation	24.25	23.19	22.35	21.02	19.11	18.21	27.19	24.75	22.28	30.55
Composite of above 28 companies	NA	NA	NA	NA	27.89	30.91	35.33	38.46	40.06	NA

SOURCE: *Standard and Poor's.*

costs and losses will be magnified. The principle of leverage will then work
in reverse. For debt leverage to work successfully, it is vital that earning
levels remain stable and earning growth is predictable.

Defense and aerospace firms have not been alone in their increasing use
of debt financing. During the decade of the 1960s most large U.S. corporations came to rely on this practice. As shown in Table IV-9, 83 of the top
500 corporations listed in *Fortune* in 1960 had no debt. In 1970 the number
of debt-free corporations was 19, a reduction of 77%. In the 1970 *Fortune*
list,[12] 106 companies had debt-to-total-capital ratios of more than 40%; in
1960 only 24 companies had shown such a high ratio. The increased use of
leverage during the 1960s grew out of optimistic growth expectations, coupled

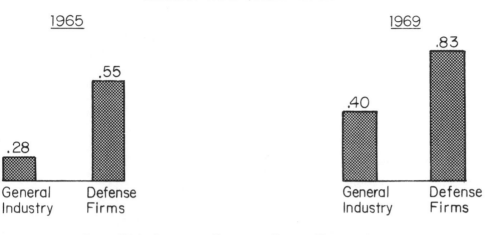

FIGURE IV-6. DEBT/EQUITY RATIOS

TABLE IV-8. AEROSPACE LEVERAGE RATIOS COMPARED WITH
SELECTED MANUFACTURING INDUSTRIES: 1969

	Total Debt to Net Worth
Aerospace*	112.0%
Communication Equipment**	64.0
Electrical Lighting & Wiring Equip.	76.6
Electrical Components & Accessories	97.0
Engineering Laboratory & Scientific Equipment	76.1
Fabricated Structural Products	93.0
Genl. Indus. Machy & Equip.	81.9
Instruments, Measuring & Controlling	82.7
Metalworking Machy & Equip.	72.9
Special Industry Machinery	81.6

* Aerospace data include 65 companies reported by AIA.
** Selected manufacturing data are the median ratio for that industry as reported by Dun and Bradstreet.
SOURCE: Industry Advisory Council, Report to the Secretary of Defense by the Subcommittee to consider *Defense Industry Contract Financing*, June 11, 1971, Appendix L.

with the widespread belief that Government would manage the economy to avoid recessions. The general upward movement of the stock market also may have encouraged the shift by placing a greater premium on higher earnings per share.

The *Standard and Poor's* earnings-per-share statistics for 28 major defense firms (Table IV-10) indicate that the high aerospace debt leverage might already have been having adverse effects. Avco, for example, dropped from a high of $3.71 per share in 1967 to $.40 per share in 1970. LTV, Bendix, and Boeing experienced similar declines. During the same period defense

TABLE IV-9. CHANGES IN THE RATIO OF DEBT TO TOTAL CAPITAL
FOR LARGE U.S. COMPANIES: 1960 AND 1970

Percent	No. of Firms in 1960	No. of Firms in 1970
0	83	19
1–20	199	132
21–40	190	241
41–60	20	90
61–80	4	13
81–100	0	3

NOTE: Debt Ratio = $\dfrac{\text{Long-Term Debt}}{\text{Long-Term Debt} + \text{Equity}}$

SOURCE: *Fortune* 500 listing for 1960 and 1970.

firms experienced a general decline in price/earnings ratios. Between 1967 and 1970, the year-end multiples for Teledyne dropped from 52 to 13; for Honeywell, from 38 to 24; for Litton, from 41 to 11; for Raytheon, from 27 to 12; and for Thiokol, from 18 to 12 (Table IV-11). This decline reflects investors' unwillingness to pay 1967 prices for a dollar of defense industry earnings-per-share in 1970: investors do not have confidence in industry growth in sales or in earnings.

INSTABILITY IN THE DEFENSE AND AEROSPACE INDUSTRY

High financial leverage in the defense and aerospace industry has produced two unwelcome side effects: financial stress and a loss of flexibility in management decisions. To assess the extent of the financial burden, pretax fixed-charge coverage ratios were calculated for 28 major defense firms (Table IV-12). New income plus income taxes and fixed charges were divided by fixed charges. The numerator represents the earnings available to pay interest and other fixed charges. Although this ratio is commonly used to test the safety of bond investment, it can also gauge the liquidity and margins of safety associated with financial leverage. The ratios become particularly meaningful when related to standards of financial stability.

Graham, Dodd, and Cottle state that in manufacturing industries, the average earnings before interest and taxes for a seven-to-ten year period should be sufficient to cover fixed charges at least seven times.[13] They further stipulate that earnings during the poorest year should cover fixed charges at least five times. If these criteria are applied to the firms listed in Table IV-12, approximately 16 of the 28 firms would fail to meet the minimum standard. Seventeen of the 28 firms did not meet the "poorest year" requirement in

TABLE IV-10. EARNINGS PER SHARE (ADJUSTED) FOR 28 MAJOR
DEFENSE CONTRACTORS: 1961–1970

	1961	1962	1963	1964	1965	1966	1967	1968	1969	1970
Teledyne, Inc.	0.05	0.11	0.30	0.28	0.42	0.79	1.18	1.51	1.89	1.91
LTV Aerospace Corporation	NA	NA	NA	NA	1.18	1.67	2.63	2.27	2.51	1.66
Ling Temco Vought, Inc.	−3.33	2.02	1.63	1.54	1.92	4.34	7.11	4.72	−0.05	−12.79
Aerojet General Corporation	2.47	2.80	3.59	3.36	3.18	3.13	−2.17	1.58	0.66	0.85
Avco Corporation	1.24	1.70	2.00	2.05	1.78	2.30	3.71	3.76	3.12	0.40
Bendix Corporation	2.22	2.08	2.04	2.17	2.50	3.28	3.33	3.30	3.71	1.76
Boeing Company	2.23	1.70	1.35	2.82	4.78	4.13	4.10	3.84	0.47	1.02
General Dynamics Corporation	−14.32	5.29	4.97	3.77	4.48	5.16	4.91	2.83	0.24	−0.62
General Electric Company	2.72	2.97	3.00	3.24	3.90	3.75	4.01	3.95	3.07	3.63
General Telephone & Electronics	1.00	1.15	1.38	1.57	1.87	2.16	2.12	2.10	2.23	2.02
Grumman Corporation	0.90	0.92	1.11	1.59	3.01	3.95	3.04	2.68	3.06	2.90
Honeywell, Inc.	1.74	1.86	2.41	2.89	2.61	3.07	2.85	3.41	4.15	3.34
Litton Industries, Inc.	0.45	0.67	0.92	1.17	1.49	1.99	2.36	1.70	2.31	1.85
Lockheed Aircraft Corporation	2.60	3.57	4.06	4.18	4.69	5.29	4.86	3.96	−2.90	NA
Magnavox Company	0.63	0.86	0.77	0.94	1.50	2.25	2.00	2.56	2.38	1.56
Martin Marietta Corporation	1.91	1.93	1.54	1.35	1.49	1.92	1.64	2.08	2.21	1.75
McDonnell Douglas Corporation	0.68	0.77	0.94	1.35	1.74	2.31	0.03	3.20	3.94	3.16
No. American Rockwell Corporation	2.41	2.91	3.51	4.19	3.88	4.11	2.76	2.83	2.20	2.27
Northrop Corporation	2.11	2.16	2.16	1.66	2.10	2.49	2.86	3.33	3.80	4.06
Raytheon Company	0.80	1.12	0.73	0.98	1.12	1.45	1.97	2.10	2.35	2.32
Sanders Associates, Inc. Del.	0.25	0.56	0.70	0.72	0.69	0.68	1.23	1.39	−0.43	0.17
Singer Company	2.66	3.29	3.75	4.19	4.03	4.44	4.71	4.53	4.85	4.25
Sperry Rand Corporation	0.78	0.43	0.85	0.70	1.02	1.73	1.94	2.26	2.37	NA
Texas Instruments, Inc.	0.94	0.85	1.20	1.79	2.46	3.14	2.10	2.41	3.06	2.71
Textron, Inc.	0.51	0.74	0.85	1.02	1.31	1.76	2.09	2.10	2.14	1.90
Thiokol Chemical Corporation	0.98	1.14	1.08	0.75	1.04	1.35	1.08	1.19	1.20	0.72
United Aircraft Corporation	0.90	1.73	2.08	2.82	4.33	3.93	4.73	5.10	4.21	3.74
Westinghouse Electric Corporation	1.23	1.56	1.28	2.05	2.86	3.16	3.21	3.49	3.76	3.06
Composite of above 28 companies	NA	NA	NA	NA	2.54	2.82	2.72	2.86	2.52	NA

SOURCE: *Standard and Poor's.*

TABLE IV-11. PRICE-EARNINGS RATIOS—CLOSE OF YEAR FOR
28 MAJOR DEFENSE CONTRACTORS: 1961–1970

	1961	1962	1963	1964	1965	1966	1967	1968	1969	1970
Teledyne, Inc.	NA	NA	16.07	24.23	33.21	23.33	52.35	33.31	19.50	12.74
LTV Aerospace Corporation	NA	NA	NA	NA	NA	16.32	17.06	18.39	6.13	4.44
Ling Temco Vought, Inc.	−5.04	5.32	6.66	7.58	16.75	11.44	17.58	20.13	−507.50	−0.81
Aerojet General Corporation	29.57	15.91	11.25	7.18	10.53	9.94	−12.44	20.33	20.45	22.06
Avco Corporation	19.46	14.78	11.12	10.49	13.90	9.51	17.52	12.97	7.37	31.25
Bendix Corporation	14.89	13.16	11.49	10.17	13.27	10.52	16.25	14.85	8.96	14.99
Boeing Company	11.21	10.92	13.24	12.21	13.68	15.89	22.07	14.81	59.84	13.97
General Dynamics Corporation	−1.94	5.36	4.78	9.28	12.67	9.33	13.49	16.30	115.62	−30.85
General Electric Company	27.67	25.84	29.04	28.78	30.26	23.60	23.94	23.77	25.24	25.86
General Telephone & Electronics	29.00	19.57	22.92	24.04	24.60	20.95	19.75	18.99	13.45	15.10
Grumman Corporation	13.41	15.84	11.80	11.47	10.28	8.74	12.25	14.79	8.17	6.90
Honeywell, Inc.	37.50	22.75	30.69	20.89	28.54	21.62	38.20	33.43	34.10	24.85
Litton Industries, Inc.	67.72	38.99	36.27	21.71	41.30	36.17	41.30	40.30	15.38	11.33
Lockheed Aircraft Corporation	13.22	11.34	8.77	9.15	12.47	12.52	11.11	12.03	−5.95	NA
Magnavox Company	33.63	21.24	28.41	16.56	27.29	16.39	19.81	21.78	15.55	24.52
Martin Marietta Corporation	14.07	11.08	12.91	13.33	14.68	11.00	12.50	13.58	9.16	9.93
McDonnell Douglas Corporation	12.64	14.68	11.42	10.43	14.28	11.33	NA	15.00	6.47	6.46
No. American Rockwell Corporation	18.05	16.37	9.78	9.24	10.87	8.35	14.49	15.02	9.77	8.81
Northrop Corporation	14.07	10.76	9.14	12.58	13.15	10.94	14.90	16.18	9.34	5.79
Raytheon Company	22.26	12.07	13.96	10.97	17.33	18.28	26.65	23.75	13.94	11.85
Sanders Associates, Inc. Del.	48.40	27.05	19.91	11.64	28.21	41.54	52.85	42.45	−62.79	75.74
Singer Company	22.05	19.22	22.80	18.97	15.63	10.36	14.62	17.55	17.29	15.29
Sperry Rand Corporation	29.48	31.69	25.00	19.82	21.57	17.20	32.93	20.52	15.66	NA
Texas Instruments, Inc.	51.69	29.81	27.6.	26.39	35.16	31.81	51.37	42.95	40.77	29.70
Textron, Inc.	12.80	10.05	11.66	13.05	16.32	14.66	24.82	21.49	12.21	12.96
Thiokol Chemical Corporation	33.90	22.50	16.52	16.00	18.99	13.06	18.40	16.91	9.06	12.33
United Aircraft Corporation	31.20	19.95	13.70	15.48	18.97	20.77	17.23	12.92	9.32	9.02
Westinghouse Electric Corporation	31.50	20.51	26.46	20.73	21.77	14.99	21.81	19.56	15.46	21.81
Composite of above 28 companies	NA	NA	NA	NA	NA	18.09	23.78	20.57	17.43	NA

SOURCE: *Standard & Poor's.*

TABLE IV-12. FIXED CHARGES COVERAGE—PRETAX—FOR
28 MAJOR DEFENSE CONTRACTORS: 1961–1970

	1961	1962	1963	1964	1965	1966	1967	1968	1969	1970
Teledyne, Inc.	7.50	3.83	3.65	5.03	7.25	10.21	9.23	11.70	10.44	13.21
LTV Aerospace Corporation	NA	NA	NA	NA	6.20	7.32	7.21	7.33	4.15	2.38
Ling Temco Vought, Inc.	−2.90	2.51	3.23	3.86	3.94	6.03	4.93	1.63	1.14	0.64
Aerojet General Corporation	18.93	17.94	16.46	14.72	12.88	13.22	−6.55	4.65	2.33	3.54
Avco Corporation	15.49	29.72	39.67	47.40	16.78	9.19	6.30	5.40	3.11	1.24
Bendix Corporation	19.52	21.89	16.30	15.31	25.22	24.25	13.49	8.20	7.39	3.56
Boeing Company	19.75	9.94	7.88	30.29	21.02	14.51	5.48	5.47	0.71	1.12
General Dynamics Corporation	NA	4.50	6.66	11.09	11.91	10.67	9.39	4.84	0.30	0.70
General Electric Company	56.38	63.12	69.21	29.47	26.81	18.19	11.85	10.50	7.52	6.42
General Telephone & Electronics	4.36	4.41	4.69	4.71	4.74	4.89	3.93	3.65	3.29	2.89
Grumman Corporation	15.20	10.01	8.93	7.60	13.16	18.65	8.82	9.35	9.53	5.56
Honeywell, Inc.	18.54	17.26	20.79	21.27	10.72	8.71	6.16	6.93	5.96	3.64
Litton Industries, Inc.	9.95	11.46	9.92	10.10	10.43	10.90	12.67	8.07	6.36	3.71
Lockheed Aircraft Corporation	13.48	18.18	29.95	61.01	67.83	43.91	15.60	12.39	−4.84	NA
Magnavox Company	19.36	26.03	20.59	18.32	24.44	22.23	21.14	26.39	19.00	12.67
Martin Marietta Corporation	14.10	19.64	21.51	20.74	19.30	14.06	8.58	7.84	5.25	4.49
McDonnell Douglas Corporation	26.89	NA	NA	NA	NA	NA	0.71	10.21	23.90	13.74
No. American Rockwell Corporation	12.78	9.43	10.25	16.24	29.40	147.56	12.01	9.48	6.05	4.84
Northrop Corporation	12.72	17.58	10.60	6.05	7.48	8.53	5.33	7.06	6.96	5.26
Raytheon Company	4.41	5.22	4.06	5.18	5.48	7.26	6.03	5.76	6.38	6.27
Sanders Associates, Inc., Del.	188.00	148.00	60.44	287.50	236.50	23.50	13.78	9.22	−0.63	1.22
Singer Company	7.19	8.15	9.51	7.82	6.18	5.11	4.71	4.49	4.00	3.21
Sperry Rand Corporation	3.77	2.88	4.01	4.15	3.96	6.02	9.92	10.58	6.26	NA
Texas Instruments, Inc.	29.03	30.25	51.18	65.56	44.24	23.20	14.70	16.69	12.02	8.42
Textron, Inc.	3.26	5.72	9.04	13.63	15.76	20.47	23.44	19.20	14.98	11.60
Thiokol Chemical Corporation	13.56	19.13	22.08	11.75	15.80	64.65	25.75	22.22	8.31	4.89
United Aircraft Corporation	3.95	6.57	7.71	8.16	13.46	7.64	6.13	5.87	4.94	3.63
Westinghouse Electric Corporation	9.06	10.19	9.70	15.29	22.27	27.15	15.94	11.80	10.63	4.89
Composite of above 28 companies	NA	NA	NA	NA	11.74	10.86	7.17	6.54	4.60	NA

SOURCE: *Standard & Poor's.*

1970, and 11 failed the test in 1969. In 1968, the year of highest defense earnings, four firms still failed to generate sufficient earnings to cover fixed charges five times.

Many defense firms now consider cash flow a primary factor in their decision making; thus, their increasing use of long-term debt to finance working capital requirements. Table IV-13 shows that for eight major defense

TABLE IV-13. LONG-TERM DEBT AS A PERCENTAGE OF WORKING CAPITAL FOR EIGHT MAJOR DEFENSE AND AEROSPACE COMPANIES: 1960–1969

	1960	1961	1962	1963	1964	1965	1966	1967	1968	1969
Boeing Company	35.0%	36.0%	33.0%	47.2%	43.3%	36.8%	107.3%	133.2%	100.0%	104.2%
Northrop Corporation	27.6	24.9	23.1	43.1	49.5	52.4	48.3	80.7	72.0	74.0
Lockheed Aircraft Corporation	69.4	40.6	23.5	17.8	14.2	9.2	9.9	48.0	58.8	107.5
McDonnell Douglas Corporation	52.5	59.0	45.3	56.9	56.9	58.2	113.5	*232.0*	*133.5*	91.0
No. American Rockwell Corporation	0	0	0	0	0	0	0	29.7	50.0	61.4
Fairchild-Hiller	0	0	0	0	0	0	0	59.2	89.3	65.8
General Dynamics Corporation	69.5	*303.0*	*113.5*	66.7	45.2	60.0	83.4	76.4	50.2	78.8
Grumman Corporation	10.6	27.5	22.0	42.2	40.0	40.2	44.3	67.5	72.5	71.4
Total	264.7%	491.0%	260.4%	273.9%	249.1%	346.8%	406.7%	726.7%	576.3%	654.1%
Average	33.1	61.4	32.6	34.2	31.1	30.8	50.8	91.0	72.0	81.7
Adjusted Average*	27.9	26.9	32.6	34.2	31.1	30.8	50.8	70.5	63.2	81.7

* Adjusted to eliminate peak impact of temporary financial problems as follows:
  Lockheed—1960 problem with Electra.
  General Dynamics—1961 problem with 880.
  McDonnell Douglas—1967 and 1968 problem with DC-9.
SOURCE: *Standard & Poor's.*

and aerospace firms the ratio of long-term debt to working capital roughly tripled between 1960 and 1969, rising from a level of approximately 28% in 1960 to almost 82% in 1969. Most of the increase occurred after 1966.

The defense and aerospace industry experienced a sharp increase in sales during the 1965–1968 period. To respond to the increased demand for defense products, the industry expanded its capabilities. By 1971, however, production for the Vietnam War had dropped back sharply. The Department of Commerce projected that in 1971 shipments of complete aerospace vehicles would total $10.3 billion—a 17% decrease from the $12.4 billion shipped in 1970, and a 30% drop from the amount shipped in the peak year of 1968.[14] The Department of Commerce forecast through 1980 projected a decline of up to 4% (in the 1970s) in the value of shipments, in each of four Selected Industry Code (SIC) classifications: guided missiles, aircraft, aircraft engines and engine parts, and aircraft equipment.

The Commerce publication further stated:

> The U.S. aerospace industry is faced with the phasing out of the F-111, F-4, and A-7 aircraft. The major portion of the C-5 military transport program will be completed in 1971, and military helicopter procurement is being severely curtailed. New programs, such as the F-14, F-15, and B-1 are just getting started, while the S-3A, AWACS, and International Fighter will not have an immediate effect in bolstering the declining industry.

Aerospace sales may also be affected by competition from foreign firms. Great Britain and continental European countries are meeting their military and commercial requirements by forming consortiums. The Department of Commerce reported:

> The British-French "Concorde" supersonic airliners and "Jaguar" strike trainer; the Franco-German "A 300B" airbus and "Transall" military transport; the NATO-produced "Atlantic" maritime patrol aircraft; the Dutch-German-Northern Ireland F-28 short-range jet airliner; the French-Italian-Spanish-Belgian "Mercuri" short-haul jet airliner; and the British-German-Italian "MRCA" multi-role combat aircraft make it clear that an intra-European aerospace industry is in existence.

If forecasts for continued decline in the sales volume of defense firms are correct, the problem of excess capacity may become urgent. Overcapacity leads to an increase in fixed charges, followed by an increase in the cost of weapon systems. Declining sales volume inhibits contractor investment in labor-saving capital equipment and also discourages the flow of capital to defense firms.

The simultaneous decline in defense, NASA, and commercial business in 1970 and 1971 had an immediate effect on defense-related industry. Overall employment was down by about 30%. Despite the adverse economic situation, however, all major contractors remained in business.

The situation at the beginning of the 1970s dramatized a condition which existed for many years without recognition—low utilization of plant and equipment throughout the industry. Low activity levels lead to unabsorbed overhead expenses, which is passed on to remaining customers. Overcapacity, then, contributes to increasing unit prices for all production items.

Despite this overcapacity, many aerospace contractors try to maintain their engineering manpower levels in order to remain competitive for future defense programs. Aerospace Industries Association figures show that the nonproduction-to-production worker ratio increased from .83 in 1960 to 1.04 in 1971. The increase is passed on to the Government in the form of higher overhead charges.

The industry is not unaware of the problem. Thomas G. Pownall, president of the Martin Marietta Corporation Aerospace Group, commented on overcapacity to a gathering of businessmen on May 18, 1971:

> It was natural, then, that we would become a bit complacent. We were riding high; we were optimistic about continued business prosperity. I think, in all candor, we must admit that the aerospace industry built a serious overcapacity, which has highlighted and exacerbated the downturn. From a peak of 1.4 million workers in 1968, the industry has dropped nearly a third—some 400,000! It has been particularly dramatic among the ranks of the engineers and scientists: it was reliably reported recently [*Business Week,* March 27, 1971] that 100,000 of them are jobless; among engineers alone, the rate rose to almost 10%.[15]

Among defense and aerospace groups seriously affected by cutbacks in Government spending were the helicopter manufacturers. Helicopter production, which began with prototypes in the early 1940s, climbed to more than 3,300 aircraft in 1966, but dropped through the 1,000 mark on the way back down in 1971. The data in Table IV-14 compare peak deliveries during

TABLE IV-14. HELICOPTER DELIVERIES: PEAK AND 1970

Manufacturer	Peak	1970
A	90	6
B	390	24
C	2,485	985
D	1,129	0

1964–1969 with 1970 deliveries. One manufacturer accounted for 98% of the helicopters delivered in 1971; two manufacturers accounted for nearly 100%—a graphic example of overcapacity. Employment in the helicopter industry began with a handful of visionaries in the 1940s. It rose to a 1968 peak of over 40,000, dropped to 22,000 in 1970, and was significantly lower in 1971.[16] From 1965 to 1971 there was only one developmental helicopter program—the Cheyenne AH-56A, developed by Lockheed for the Army. At the close of 1971, Lockheed had not yet completed the Cheyenne program. It had been scheduled for completion in 1969.

Despite the decline in defense budgets, the defense and aerospace industry remained, in 1970, the nation's largest manufacturing employer, with more than one million workers. The Aerospace Industries Association projected that employment in the industry would decline an additional 6.3% between December 1970 and December 1971, from 1,067,000 to 1,000,000. Nevertheless, the space industry was expected to remain the nation's number one manufacturing employer.

The cutback in defense spending between 1969 and 1971 affected thousands of small and intermediate firms as well as the defense giants. The phasedown was especially difficult, however, for the four firms listed in Table IV-14.

THE DEPARTMENT OF DEFENSE AND DEFENSE CONTRACTORS: GIANTS ON A TIGHTROPE

The immense size and complexity of defense and aerospace programs, the need for negotiation on thousands of contract changes, and the Government's emphasis on timely completion, all contribute to a relationship of mutual dependence between the Defense Department and its prime contractors. Stress develops among Government and industry personnel during negotiations on contract incentives, prices for individual changes, schedules, and the technical acceptability of finished products. On the other hand, warm personal relationships develop among technical personnel in Government and industry who work together for years.

In March 1970 the Department of Defense's Logistics Management Institute, in a preliminary report prepared for the Office of the Secretary of Defense, made the following observations concerning the Defense Department/ defense industry relationship:

> The period since World War II has witnessed a substantial change in the relationship between DOD and that segment of the private economic sector called "defense industry." These changes have been caused primarily by the great technological innovations in weapons and methods of waging war. The relationship, in many respects, has become more intimate. And here we come face to face with the dilemma which disturbs and confuses many who adopt the simplistic view of complete separation of the public and private sectors, with free enterprise arrayed on one side and the DOD on the other side. The fact is that, in the development and production of major weapon systems, a substantial portion of the defense industry does

not operate as free enterprise in its prime contractual relationship with the Department of Defense. Because the Government, in its role as buyer, and industry, in its role as seller, do not interact in a free and open market, it is considered by some that the relationship is counter to the principles of free enterprise and thus is inherently bad and unethical. Perhaps this attitude has resulted in a concerted effort to cling to features of a free enterprise relationship, even when those features may not be suitable in development and production of modern weapons. . . .[17]

Over the two decades 1950–1970 the Defense Department/defense contractor relationship was marked by erratic shifts in policy and points of view. For example, cost-reimbursement contracts were initially favored over fixed-price contracts, but were later considered one major reason for program management difficulties. More recently, fixed-price contracts have fallen out of favor. In similar fashion, Government preference for hardware prototype vs. paper design competition wavers back and forth. Shifts have also occurred over the years in the degree of Defense Department involvement in contractors' internal operations.

In this unstable and artificial market environment, business terms like "progress payments," "buyer," "seller," "profit," "competition," and "financial control" lose their conventional meanings. Scherer commented on the dilemma in the second volume of *The Weapons Acquisition Process: Economic Incentives:*

> Private enterprise, in the strict sense, has not been employed for at least two decades to develop and produce advanced weapon systems nor is it likely that true private enterprise is possible at all in the non-market environment of weapon acquisition. A substantial degree of Government intervention—socialism if you like—is inescapable.[18]

Senior executives in the industry recognize this ambiguity and admit to dissatisfaction. Jackson R. McGowan, President of the Douglas Aircraft Division of McDonnell Douglas Corporation, was quoted in an October 1, 1971, edition of the *Los Angeles Times*: "We need a gender for our industry. At present we arc neither fish nor fowl; neither private industry nor Government."

Harvard economist John Kenneth Galbraith was quoted in *The New York Times,* November 1968, as proposing that major defense suppliers be nationalized through Government acquisition of their shares and assumption of their debts. In his view, this would merely constitute recognition of the reality of those companies' roles as public firms. He contended that they were already public because (1) most of their working capital was supplied by the Government; (2) procurement of their products and services was not price competitive; and (3) they were sustained by the Government despite their faults and failings in performance.

Subsequent sections of this report will explore this relationship further and seek to develop recommendations for solving these problems.

NOTES TO CHAPTER IV

1. Merton J. Peck and Frederic M. Scherer, *The Weapons Acquisition Process: An Economic Analysis* (Boston: Division of Research, Harvard Business School, 1962), pp. 114–116.
2. Ibid., p. 117.
3. *Army, Navy, Air Force Journal,* April 16, 1960, p. 11.
4. Office of the Assistant Secretary of Defense (Comptroller), *Military Prime Contract Awards, Fiscal Year 1970.*
5. W. L. Weidenbaum, *The Military/Space Market: The Intersection of the Public and Private Sectors* (St. Louis: Department of Economics, Washington University, 1967).
6. National Aeronautics and Space Administration, *Annual Procurement Report, Fiscal Year 1970.*
7. Ibid.
8. Ibid.
9. Weidenbaum, op. cit., pp. 52–57.
10. Industry Advisory Council, Report to the Secretary of Defense by the Subcommittee to consider *Defense Industry Contract Financing,* June 11, 1971.
11. Aerospace Industries Association, *Facts and Figures, 1971.*
12. *Fortune,* May 1971.
13. Benjamin Graham, David L. Dodd, and Sidney Cottle, *Security Analysis: Principles and Techniques* (New York: McGraw-Hill Book Company, 1962), p. 348.
14. U.S. Department of Commerce, *Aerospace Trends and Projections, 1965–1980.*
15. Thomas G. Pownall, "The Challenge of Changing Defense Markets," an address delivered to a national meeting of the Small Business Administration, Washington, D.C., May 18, 1971.
16. Aerospace Industries Association, op. cit.
17. Logistics Management Institute, report on *The DOD-Contractor Relationship—Preliminary Review,* Task 69-21, March 1970, p. A-1.
18. Frederic M. Scherer, *The Weapons Acquisition Process: Economic Incentives* (Boston: Division of Research, Harvard Business School, 1964).

"The most frustrating thing is that we know how we
ought to manage . . . and we refuse to change. . . ."
THE HONORABLE DAVID PACKARD
Deputy Director of Defense, 1970

CHAPTER V

The Pentagon

TO UNDERSTAND DEFENSE PROCUREMENT, an observer must understand the
environment in which procurement decisions are made. New defense officials
often take from six to twelve months to master the intricacies of Department
policy and protocol—e.g., how information is channeled and/or suppressed;
how decisions are affected by conflicting military-civilian priorities; how the
Defense Department and defense contractors interact; how the Department
is influenced by Congress and by the press; which management techniques
are officially sanctioned; how cost controls are applied or avoided; and,
finally, how change can be effected. Some senior officials function comfortably
within the system and introduce innovations which facilitate the procurement
process. Others never find their way through the maze of ritual and tradition.

In this chapter an attempt is made to analyze the decision makers: their
concept of their roles; their motivations; and their responses to pressure,
criticism, and conflict. Future chapters will analyze in greater detail their
continuing roles in the initiation, funding, development, administration, and
completion of weapon acquisition programs.

DEPARTMENT OF DEFENSE PERSONNEL

More than two million people are employed by the Department of Defense. It is the largest single-unit bureaucracy in the world. The men and
women who govern this bureaucracy and are responsible for the nation's
defense capabilities are divided among three categories: (1) civilians nominated by the President and approved by the Senate; (2) senior career military officers (Army and Air Force generals and Navy admirals); and (3)
senior career civil service personnel.

The Secretary of Defense, a civilian appointee, is the highest ranking official in the Department. The Secretary's immediate staff consists of fifteen civilians, nominated by the President with the Secretary's counsel: two Deputy Secretaries of Defense, the Director of Defense Research and Engineering, eight Assistant Secretaries of Defense, and four Assistants to the Secretary.[1]

The President also appoints Secretaries of the Army, the Navy, and the Air Force. Each service Secretary reports directly to the Secretary of Defense. Each has a chief assistant, called the Undersecretary of the Army, Navy, or Air Force, and four Assistant Secretaries. Each of the Assistant Secretaries directs one of the following areas within his service: (1) financial management; (2) installations and logistics; (3) manpower and reserve affairs; (4) research and development. These five civilian officials are nominated by the President with the advice of the Secretary of Defense. Each service Secretary has a staff of several hundred military and civilian personnel.

Also reporting to the civilian Secretary of each service is the military Chief of Staff of the service. Each Chief of Staff is appointed by the President and becomes the senior military officer in his branch of the armed services. The President also appoints a Chairman of the Joint Chiefs of Staff from one of the services. The individual Chiefs of Staff are directly responsible to the Secretary of Defense as well as to the Secretaries of their respective services. The Chairman of the Joint Chiefs of Staff reports to the Secretary of Defense. The Office of the Joint Chiefs of Staff employs approximately 2,000 military and civilian personnel. In addition, each Chief of Staff is served by several thousand military and civilian personnel. A military officer working for a Chief of Staff also serves the Secretary of his service. Although the Secretary is the senior official within the Pentagon, officers receive their military promotions on the basis of evaluations from their military superiors, including their Chiefs of Staff. This fact is especially significant during periods of controversy between Secretaries or Assistant Secretaries of a service and the Chief of Staff.

Most senior defense officials and their staffs—about 26,000 people in all —work in the Pentagon. The division of civilian and military personnel within the Pentagon is about even.

Civilian control of all United States military activity is prescribed by the Constitution. The effectiveness of this policy is considerably diminished by the fact that most civilian appointees serve brief terms of office. The range is from a few months to seven years; the average, less than three years. Appointees come from a wide variety of backgrounds. Among them have been lawyers, businessmen, bankers, public accountants, engineers, and teachers. In reviewing nominees, the Senate conducts hearings to examine their training, experience, reasons for accepting nomination, and administrative plans if confirmed. Most nominees have had no previous Pentagon experience. The basis for their selection varies. Some are thoroughly trained and experienced in the field they will oversee within the Department of Defense: procurement, personnel, research and development, financial management, etc. Some have had no relevant experience but have been loyal to the President's political party.

The Secretary of Defense and Secretaries of the Army, Navy, and Air Force select individuals to fill senior positions on their staffs. They are usually under considerable pressure from White House staffs (of either party) to base their selections on political rather than professional credentials. In the last decade, according to most Government and industry observers, the Defense Department has had fewer "political" Secretaries and Assistant Secretaries than other Federal departments. These appointees, in turn, have achieved some success in limiting the number of unqualified personnel on their staffs. At any one time within the past number of years, perhaps 10 or fewer of the 35 senior civilians within the Pentagon have been strictly political appointees. Nevertheless, at least one service Secretary stated that he resented the amount of time and effort he had to expend to resist White House pressure for appointments of party favorites.

Federal regulations require that senior appointees divest themselves of all stocks, bonds, and interests in profit-sharing plans of any firm doing more than $10,000 of defense business. Although there are many managers in private industry who are well qualified for defense positions, many are either unwilling or unable to forego financial gains resulting from the sale of their holdings and/or loss of stock options. Consequently, Assistant Secretary positions are sometimes vacant for several months.

Senior military positions within the Department are held by career officers, most of whom have served in combat assignments (e.g., Korea or Vietnam). The total number of generals and admirals serving in the United States military throughout the world is more than 1,800. All of them, including Pentagon staff, are rotated among assignments that usually last less than three years, coincidentally about the average term of office for civilian appointees. There is at least one significant difference between civilian and military staff, however. When military officers leave the Pentagon, they remain in the service. Secretaries and Assistant Secretaries return to positions outside the Federal Government. The long-term commitment of the career officer is to his service and to military values. Civilian appointees, who are to be the source of authority amidst conflicting service rivalries or military-civilian priorities, assume this responsibility for a relatively short time. Perhaps of more importance, career officers are promoted on the basis of performance ratings prepared by their military superiors, not their civilian supervisors within the Pentagon. These evaluations naturally include considerations of service loyalty. And although individual officers may rotate after two or three years, the military point of view remains relatively stable, while political administrations change and civilian appointees come and go.

An extreme example of the conflict between Pentagon civilian and military loyalties was described by a colonel who had been assigned to the staff of an Assistant Secretary in order to develop a military personnel information system. With this system, the Assistant Secretary felt he would be able to take a more active role in the assignment of career officers within his area. Just before the colonel began his new assignment, the Deputy Chief of Staff of his service informed him that "the Chief of Staff does not want to see this information system developed," and instructed him to work so slowly that the Assistant Secretary would not realize his objective. The colonel was reminded by the Deputy Chief of Staff that his future depended on his military superiors, not the civilian Secretariat. At the end of a year and a half the Assistant Secretary left the Pentagon to return to a position in industry. The project was then placed directly under the control of the Deputy Chief and was completed without providing information that could affect assignments and promotions.

Another group of career officials with vested interests that sometimes conflict with those of Presidential appointees are the senior civil servants. They holds ranks of GS-16, -17, and -18, comparable to military generals and admirals. They work in the offices of the Secretary of Defense, the Secretaries of the services, the Assistant Secretaries, and the Chiefs of Staff. Unlike military officers or civilian appointees, they often remain in the Pentagon for ten to fifteen years. They are therefore an important source of continuity within the Defense Department.

RESPONSIBILITY FOR WEAPONS ACQUISITION

The overall management of weapons acquisition is the responsibility of three of the nine Assistant Secretaries in the Office of the Secretary of Defense.

1. The Assistant Secretary for Financial Management (Comptroller) directs cost estimating, budgeting, and some cost control activities.
2. The Assistant Secretary for Installations and Logistics determines procurement policy and the quantities of each weapon to be purchased. He also directs contract administration and program management.

3. The Assistant Secretary for Research and Development directs ongoing research and development programs and the initiation of new programs.

Although all three Assistant Secretaries are involved to some degree in all
phases of the acquisition process, the Assistant Secretary for Installations and
Logistics has primary responsibility for policies governing contract negotiation and administration throughout the duration of development and production programs.

Within the Office of each service Secretary, there are also Assistant Secretaries of Financial Management, Installations and Logistics, and Research
and Development. Each of these Assistant Secretaries reports to his counterpart in the Office of the Secretary of Defense, as well as to the Secretary of
his own service. The latter has the immediate responsibility for directing his
work. Since both of his superiors report to, and are directed by, the Secretary
of Defense, an Assistant Secretary may seek the support of the Secretary of
his service when conflicts arise with his opposite number in the Office of the
Secretary of Defense.

For any given program, the responsibility for Government and contractor
cost control is shared by three Assistant Secretaries in the buying service
and three Assistant Secretaries in the Office of the Secretary of Defense. This
means that either (1) one or more Assistant Secretaries direct cost control
activities for the program and work with the military buying organizations
and defense contractors; or (2) no Assistant Secretary takes responsibility,
each hoping that one of the others has done the necessary work. All twelve
Assistant Secretaries of Financial Management, Installations and Logistics,
and Research and Development frequently make public statements about the
need for cost accountability in defense programs. Most of them, however, are
reluctant to institute stringent cost control procedures. There are at least
four reasons for their ambivalence.

1. Every Assistant Secretary, within a service or working with all three
services, wants to acquire the weapons and equipment needed by the
services, on schedule and for the lowest reasonable cost. At the same
time, each is directed to build and/or maintain an industrial base that
will meet tomorrow's uncertain defense needs. Lowering contractor
costs means reducing the number of employees in a contractor's plant.
This supports the first objective but endangers the second. Indeed,
during periods of declining defense spending (e.g., 1970 and 1971),
defense contractors constantly visited Pentagon officials to plead for
additional business, on the grounds that the capability of their plants
was vital to the needs of national defense. Some military officers sup-

ported this contention, as did Senators and Congressmen within whose districts employment was being affected.

2. An Assistant Secretary considers himself as the chief spokesman for his service's program or his own area of responsibility. The military services expect an Assistant Secretary to champion their programs before Congress and to obtain as much financial support as possible. If an Assistant Secretary frequently fails to obtain the level of funding requested, he will lose the support of senior military officers. He will then find it almost impossible to gain access to important information known to military personnel. (Within the Pentagon, the withholding of information is probably the most effective weapon in any official's arsenal.)

   Even the Secretary of Defense may subscribe to the point of view that civilian appointees are spokesmen for the military. Lieutenant Commander Lawrence J. Korb, a faculty member at the United States Coast Guard Academy, conducted an extensive study of the role of the Secretary of Defense and his relationship to the military staff. In an article in the December 1971 issue of the *Naval War College Review,* Commander Korb reported: "Secretary Laird also sees himself as the Department of Defense advocate before the Congress and the public. His public statements do not emphasize the waste and inefficiency in the Pentagon. Rather, Laird points out that present defense spending is at 'rockbottom.' . . . The Chiefs see the Secretary as the 'defender of Defense.' They expect him to protect their services from the onslaughts of those who want to reduce defense spending drastically. . . ."

3. An Assistant Secretary has such a large area of responsibility that he can concentrate on a number of challenging and important tasks while avoiding the unpopular job of reducing costs. (One Assistant Secretary commented that his job was not to improve efficiency, but to keep his service out of trouble.)

4. An Assistant Secretary who has no experience in industrial practices and business management may not know how to begin to control costs.

Senior research and development officials have somewhat different responsibilities and priorities from their counterparts in other areas of defense management. They advocate new technology, initiate new development programs, and petition the Office of the Secretary of Defense and the Congress for program funds. Most of them have excellent technical backgrounds, but few have any training in business management. Nevertheless, in addition to their other duties, they are responsible for the efficient management of their programs. In fact, however, cost-versus-effectiveness analyses and periodic cost-performance correlations are far less important to them than the advancement of weapons technology. Periodic status reports that are prepared for senior research and development officials seldom contain any appreciable information on cost performance. According to one official, cost performance measurement problems are seldom considered during program evaluation sessions:

> Practically all of the discussion centers around challenging technical problems. The question of whether the level of direct or indirect costs is appropriate, or excessive, is simply not a consideration until the program is threatened by higher levels in the Government or the Congress concerned with providing additional funds to cover cost growth.

Senior staff from a variety of Pentagon offices try to motivate research and development officials to utilize effective management techniques, but they are often frustrated. During the course of a program which was experiencing substantial cost growth, for example, a military research and development official visited the president of the contracting firm expressly to tell him not to worry about costs. The program was of major importance to the service, according to the officer, and therefore all necessary funds would be made available if the weapon system met performance standards. His attitude was not atypical.

Since research and development officials work every day with programs that cost hundreds of millions, or even billions, of dollars, they sometimes become insensitive to smaller sums of money. During a meeting called to discuss a major contract change in a system under development, several staff members asked the briefer whether the new feature was worth the cost—approximately $200 million. An Assistant Secretary for Research and Development was obviously disturbed at the implied opposition to the proposal. In an outburst of exasperation, he snapped: "Hell, we spill $100 to $200 million per year. That amount of money is peanuts compared to the size of the program."

In 1970 one military service initiated a major effort to improve procurement management. Senior research and development officials, together with staff from financial management, procurement, and other offices, held progress review meetings at monthly or bimonthly intervals. During these meetings, the research and development people joined in discussions on the initiation of new development programs, the selection of program managers, the reduction of paperwork, improved training for Government personnel, and a variety of other topics. In over half the meetings, however, as soon as the discussion turned to methods of improving incentives to contractors for controlling costs, research and development officials left the meetings.

In another situation a meeting had been called to discuss a major new development program. The briefer reported that all prospective contractors had agreed to implement a relatively new cost control technique supported by an Assistant Secretary of Defense. To this, an Assistant Secretary for Research and Development retorted: "That's a shame!" When questioned later, he commented that budgets, performance measures, and periodic cost estimates were "all activities that the comptrollers and procurement people are trying to use to limit research and development activities." He believed that measuring performance against a cost plan imposed harmful restraints on creativity.

Of all senior Pentagon appointees, those assigned to research and development positions most frequently identify with the point of view of the contractor. Most of them come to the Department from defense-oriented laboratories or companies and return to those employers when they leave Government service. The Report of the Blue Ribbon Panel to the President and the Secretary of Defense on the Department of Defense included an analysis of the careers of 124 Secretaries, Undersecretaries and Assistant Secretaries who had served in the Pentagon since 1958.[2] Of these 124, only 10, or 8%, accepted a position with one of the 100 largest defense contractors upon their departure. A comparable analysis was made for directors, assistant directors, and other professional personnel in the Office of the Director of Defense Research and Engineering. Out of a total of 101 officials, 31 (30%) accepted employment with one of the top 100 defense contractors, and 16 of these 31 were merely returning to their previous employers. From these figures the Panel concluded:

> It should be emphasized that there is no record or evidence of attempts by former Presidential appointees or former officials in DDR&E to exercise influence in the award or administration of contracts. DDR&E is a focal point in determining what kinds of weapons systems are developed, and, therefore, to a certain extent, by what contractors. Familiarity with this process would provide an insight into the direction of future weapons requirements which could be of value to a defense contractor. If the dominant consideration is avoiding any potential use of influence, or the appearance of influence, there is no justification for treating former high-level civilian employees any less restrictively than retired senior military officers.[3]

It is always difficult within any bureaucracy to measure the effectiveness of specific management practices. This is particularly true in the Department of Defense, which operates without the profit incentive and which, even in peacetime, does not use any of the normal commercial techniques for measur-

ing adequacy or efficiency. In most small and medium-sized commercial
business operations, the effectiveness and efficiency of an operation can be
measured annually, and sometimes monthly. In large business organizations,
the full effect of top-level decisions may not be fully observed for a number
of years. But even in these organizations, cost effectiveness is measured regularly, in order to analyze the impact of management decisions on long-term
profits and the efficiency of ongoing operations.

In the absence of normal business incentives, top-level defense officials
adopt a variety of management styles. A few managers, military and civilian,
come to the Pentagon with an understanding of its size and complexity and
the ways in which any large bureaucracy resists change. These individuals
select areas in which they wish to make improvements. They often try to
implement their plans in the following four steps:

1. They communicate plans for a change in management policy to all
   concerned personnel throughout the organization and institute a training program.
2. They try to win the support of the career military and civilian personnel who will continue to operate the Department after the change
   is instituted.
3. At frequent intervals they measure progress toward achieving the
   change.
4. They try to adjust the bureaucracy's system of rewards and penalties
   so that use of the improved procedures will be effectively rewarded.

When these reforms go counter to established priorities of a segment of
the Defense Department, there are several ways to subvert them. For example:

1. Directives are sent to field organizations establishing a new management policy, but training programs are not instituted to develop the
   appropriate management skills.
2. The directives are sent to the field but rewards continue to be provided for following older management policies. Rewards are not provided for following the new policy.
3. Support is quietly solicited from members of Congress, industry, industry associations, and military service associations, who then voice
   strong public opposition to the new policy.
4. Long-term study groups are formed to analyze the impact of the new
   policy and to outline a comprehensive method of implementation.
   After several months, the reports are completed. Pages of evidence
   attest to the difficulty of implementing the new policy.

Executives in private industry who contract with more than one Defense Department buying organization repeatedly express amazement at the variety of interpretations applied by different Government organizations to Pentagon policy statements. Government managers at each level interpret directives to conform to their own management methods. Since few intermediate-level Government managers receive adequate training, however, it is not surprising that policy directives are not uniformly implemented.

Some Defense Department managers attempt no changes in the status quo during their terms of office. They read the hundreds of letters and documents which arrive at their offices every day, attend the numerous briefings that are scheduled within the Pentagon, and maintain a low visibility. Mediocre managers in industry do the same. In the Defense Department, however, the recent upswing of attention from the Congress and the press requires that even the most passive managers support reform, though this support may be limited to public statements.

In the mid-1960s a senior partner from a leading management consulting firm conducted an extensive study of major problems in the management of the defense procurement process. The study cost several hundred thousand dollars. At its conclusion he made a number of definite recommendations for reform. These were accepted and approved, and the firm received warm praise from many sources within the Pentagon. Several months elapsed and virtually no action was taken to implement the recommendations. Finally the consultant voiced his disappointment: "I'm fed up! I hear lots of nice words from all the senior officials, but no line executive will stand up and say what he is going to do."

Some top-level managers who come to the Pentagon from small and medium-sized businesses have for years been successful in making spot decisions with a minimum of analysis. In their companies, they were a major source of rewards and penalties for their employees. Unfortunately, many of them try to apply the same management style to their new activities in the Pentagon. Here, however, they control few of the rewards, and the size of defense operations makes formal analyses, detailed planning, and thorough follow-up mandatory. After these managers have been in the Department for one or two years, they become disheartened by their failure to effect change, usually without understanding the reasons for their failure.

Between 1964 and 1972 there were at least two service Secretaries who were particularly effective in introducing major reforms. During the same period there were also at least two service Secretaries with reputations for exercising very great caution in dealing with the military. The latter two

Secretaries delegated authority to the Chiefs of Staff of their services for promotions, personnel assignments, the development of major programs, and the number of weapons to be purchased. They then devoted their own efforts to issues that did not interest the Chiefs of Staff.

Although some ranking officials concede that the acquisition process within the Defense Department does not function at top efficiency, they fear that the institution of new management policies will arouse Congressional and public indictment of past policies. If program costs are reduced, according to this rationale, critics will complain that past program costs should have been lower, too. So they are reluctant to "risk" reform.

Many examples of this kind of reasoning were found. An industrial engineering study was planned for a program experiencing unexpected cost increases. An Assistant Secretary vetoed the study: "If you conduct the study and the price comes out lower, people will say that you have been doing a bad job. I don't believe that you have, do you?" It was a convincing argument. The study was dropped.

Some Pentagon officials interpret criticism of their programs as personal attacks. One Assistant Secretary steadfastly refused to investigate serious cost increases in a major program under his jurisdiction. He was incensed at the implied slur on his competence. In a similar situation, a formal management survey of the weapons acquisition process in one military branch was prepared by a senior Pentagon analyst and submitted to the service Secretary and one of his Assistant Secretaries in 1965. The report cited a number of serious problems: (1) lack of trained civilian personnel, (2) too frequent turnover of military personnel, (3) undermanning of program offices, and (4) ineffective cost control efforts from program office staff, both military and civilian. The senior military commander of the buying organization was outraged at the implication that his command did not consist of well-trained, well-supervised, and highly efficient personnel. In an angry letter to the Assistant Secretary, he censured the report and insisted that the situation was completely under control:

> Many of the alleged deficiencies noted by [name] have been recognized previously and corrective actions have been initiated or accomplished. Certain findings and proposals of the report, I consider either unrealistic or beyond our control. . . . We can ill afford to expend our resources correcting false impressions.

During the next four years, however, a number of military and civilian personnel from the same buying organization stated informally that the problems cited in the report still permeated the command. During that four-year period problems of cost growth and technical performance shortfall cropped up repeatedly. And in 1971 the Comptroller General issued reports to the Congress citing turnover of military personnel, lack of training for procurement personnel, and other management problems responsible for poor program performance within the service. All the recommendations included in the 1965 report were repeated in 1971.[4]

In August 1969 a senior military official discussed the problem of overruns:

> These increases do not necessarily reflect mismanagement or bungling, but the simple fact of rising costs of doing business or just the cost of doing more than was originally contemplated. We in the defense business are no more immune from such forces than any other segment of society.

Some officials, however, were bluntly critical. At the annual meeting of the Armed Forces Management Association in August 1970, Deputy Secretary of Defense David Packard spoke plainly about mismanagement:

> Let's face it—the fact is that there has been bad management of many defense programs in the past. We spend billions of the taxpayer's dollars, sometimes we spend it badly. Part of this is due to basic uncertainties in the defense business. Some uncertainties will always exist. However, most of it has been due to bad management, both in the Department of Defense and in the defense industry. . . .
>
> . . . . .
>
> I have been in this job now for 19 months. Frankly, I am ashamed I have not been able to do very many of the things that need to be done to improve the situation I found here in January 1969. The most frustrating thing is that we know how we ought to manage—you, me, all of us—and we refuse to change based on what we know. . . .

Not everyone agreed. At the same meeting an Assistant Secretary and a senior military officer voiced opposing opinions. Neither saw any outstanding problems in Government procurement, certainly nothing to indicate that criticism of the Department was anything more than an overreaction to "routine" problems of cost overruns and schedule slippages. Secretary Packard was not in attendance at either of the panel meetings where their views were expressed.

A surprising number of defense officials, both military and civilian, believe that development programs will cost a fixed amount no matter what management policies are followed. The cost estimates prepared for programs during the budget cycle each year are treated as minimum amounts that must be approved in full if a program is to begin or continue. Often, the only method considered for cutting program costs is a reduction in the number of weapon systems produced. Improvement of production or management efficiency is rarely even considered as an alternative. The remarks of a senior official concerning a development program experiencing sizable cost growth are typical: "The high cost of the program is simply a fact of life, and if we want the program, we'll have to live with it."

One deterrent to the institution of improved cost-control management is constant military pressure on Pentagon decision makers to ignore costs, or to handle cost overruns by petitioning Congress for more money. All senior military officers want to strengthen their services in order to minimize chances of failure in the event of international conflict. Each believes that national safety depends on acquiring more and more armed forces and more and more advanced weapons, and that total preparedness for all-out conflict is the only sane policy. Admiral Thomas Moorer, Chairman of the Joint Chiefs of Staff, was quoted in the November 1970 issue of *Fortune*:

> The threat is there and we get paid to tell Americans it is there. If we get caught with insufficient forces, we're also blamed for saying a threat exists. It all boils down to whether or not the U.S. is going to protect and maintain its interests as a world power.

Senior military officers are given no incentives to trim the size of their organizations, or to cancel or cut back programs that experience sizable cost increases. Rather, they are motivated to work for continual increases in appropriations for new weapons and equipment. Former President Eisenhower took note of this preoccupation: "The military services, traditionally concerned with 100% security, are rarely satisfied with the amounts allocated to them out of an ever generous budget." [5] Given the military commitment to ever-expanding arsenals, arguments for sufficiency in defense must come from the Congress or from Government officials who are not overly dependent on military personnel for information or political support. Civilians in charge of setting policy and priorities within the Department, from the Secretary of Defense down, should be ready to judge between military single-mindedness and the nation's actual defense needs.

In this context, the nature of the working relationships between civilian appointees and military officers is not reassuring. Pentagon Secretaries and Assistant Secretaries are eager to cultivate the friendship of their military subordinates in order to facilitate information flow and insure cooperation. After hearing repeated references to so-called civilian leadership in the Pentagon, one Assistant Secretary voiced his surprise at the amount of effort expended by senior civilians to win and retain the allegiance of the Chiefs of Staff and their military assistants. Another Assistant Secretary commented: "If you start asking probing questions around here, the sources of information soon begin to dry up. The attitude of the career personnel seems to be, 'what's the matter, don't you trust us?' " On most issues, when a general or admiral tells a Secretary or Assistant Secretary that the military staff does not wish to change a particular course of action, the pronouncement is not usually challenged. One Assistant Secretary observed:

> The difficult part of the current military/civilian appointee relationship is that the civilians have to play a humoring role and a soft role, selecting very carefully those points to challenge. To challenge too many points is to cut off your sources of information.

A senior appointee in another service made a similar comment:

> One of our problems in the Secretariat is that we have to take actions that are perceived as being loyal to the team, and when the military staff puts its prestige on the line, it is very, very difficult to override them.

While working hard to strengthen their individual services, military officers are happy to underscore so-called civilian control of the Defense Department when they are under attack from critics. In an address to an influential industry group, one general stated: "Remember, we don't make national policy or military policy, we simply execute it." An article appearing in *The New York Times* on May 23, 1970, quoted General Thomas S. Power (USAF retired), former head of the Strategic Air Command:

> Let us look at the Pentagon. At the top is a large group of civilians appointed by the President and the Secretary of Defense. These men are in complete charge of all military operations. They exercise this authority through the Joint Chiefs of Staff. . . . I do not think it is widely understood that there is not a single military man in this country who has any authority to do anything given to him by law by the people of this country. The authority is held entirely by civilians and is only delegated to the military at their discretion and subject to their veto. Keep this in mind when inclined to raise a fuss about too much military influence.

In addition to pressures from the military, high-ranking defense officials are subject to demands from Congressmen and Senators. To avoid unwelcome Congressional attention, many Secretaries and Assistant Secretaries stay out of the public eye as much as possible. Despite the notorious complexity of Defense Department procedures, they feel they will be subject to unreasonable attack if they take a strong position on any controversial subject. They choose to follow the advice given by a ranking staff member on a major Congressional committee to a group of senior military and civilian defense personnel: "The fastest way to succeed in Washington is to avoid making decisions. That way, you do nothing that anyone can criticize."

Members of Congress keep track of Defense Department programs that affect their constituents. They often act as unofficial lobbyists at the Pentagon for defense contractors within their districts. Some Congressmen and Senators are partisans of one or more branches of the armed forces. Some are zealous about the effective use of defense appropriations. A number of defense officials are sufficiently self-confident to receive inquiries and complaints from Senators and Congressmen with equanimity. Others experience intense anxiety at the slightest hint of criticism. One Assistant Secretary was known to receive an unusually large number of telephone calls from members of Congress. No matter what the complaint, he attempted to modify the offending practice or to soften its impact. His subordinates felt that the merits of the cases involved were rarely the issue.

Since the Defense Department is dependent on the Congress for appropriations, most Pentagon Secretaries and Assistant Secretaries are eager to project an unblemished image of management efficiency. When management problems are cited by Congress, or the press, officials often blame them on a particular type of contract or the mistakes of an earlier administration. A common Pentagon response to Congressional or media criticism of defense management is: the *critic* is the problem. Antagonism toward the press is fed by any exaggeration or error that is printed. Although press reports are usually reasonably well documented, Defense Department staff try to invalidate them by focusing on even minute inaccuracies. Officials convinced of the value of a program naturally minimize its shortcomings. They fear that any proof of program mismanagement will undermine public and Congressional confidence and lead to cutbacks or cancelations.

Defense officials are also the focus of pressure, both subtle and overt, from defense contractors. Executives from the industry visit military and civilian officials in the Pentagon several times a year. An Assistant Secretary may see representatives from the 10 to 20 largest contractors for his service every few months. Pleasantries are exchanged; the visitor mentions his company's progress on various programs. Sometimes a low-key sales talk is delivered: the service should buy additional quantities of a weapon system or should undertake a new development program in order to capitalize on technological advancements or to preserve the firm's defense capabilities. Sometimes the contractor mentions problems his company is having with Defense Department contract administrators. Soon, these senior executives are on a first-name basis with the Assistant Secretary. At the same time, the Assistant Secretary's military and civilian staff—some of whom are involved in contract negotiations with the visiting executives—address him as "Mr. Secretary" as a matter of protocol.

Senior defense officials are on the regular guest lists for industry cocktail parties in Washington. Here they discuss development and production problems informally with senior representatives of major contractors. When the companies have complaints about program administration, they voice them at the highest level of the Pentagon. Officials from smaller contracting or subcontracting companies cannot afford these social amenities. When they do visit the Pentagon, they are often surprised at the "open door policy" of generals, admirals, and Assistant Secretaries. Despite this, and because they do not have frequent social contacts with senior officials, they feel that their grievances are not treated with the same deference as is accorded the largest contractors.

When a senior Defense Department official visits a defense plant, the Government program manager or plant representative is present for all formal meetings with top contracting executives. Toward the end of the visit, however, the visiting official is usually invited to a private meeting with company executives. This custom is severely criticized by field procurement and program management personnel. They know that during the private meetings matters relevant to their programs are often discussed. Although most Pentagon officials will take time to listen to their version of any controversial issues, the exclusiveness of these private discussions suggests to field personnel that senior defense officials are more sympathetic to industry executives than to those responsible for protecting Government interests in the field. This weakens the authority of Government program staff who try to monitor contractor performance and administer contracts effectively.

Several Pentagon officials have expressed surprise and disappointment at the poor performance of many major defense contractors. One Assistant Secretary, formerly employed by a defense contractor, made the following comment after a year and a half in the Pentagon:

> One of the metamorphoses I have gone through down here is to change my view of the condition of American business. I came to this place thinking they were the greatest. Now I think that even among some of the giants, there are serious problems that need to be corrected.

Other officials have reached the same conclusion. A former Secretary of a military service commented:

> I was very surprised at the poor contractual performance of many con-
> tractors, and was equally surprised to see these firms by-pass the chain
> of command and come to the top of the organization seeking to have their
> case supported on the basis of their comments. Time after time, when
> they came to us with problems, I would look into the situation and then
> find that, if anything, the field personnel had been lenient in dealing with
> the contractor on the problem that had arisen.

Program managers and management personnel at all levels often express
uncertainty about the Government-contractor relationship. Since so many
divergent views are expressed by Pentagon officials, this is not surprising.
The relationship is sometimes referred to as "a partnership between Government and industry." Others call it "an adversary relationship," in which
two parties with some identical and some conflicting objectives meet to carry
out a continuing arm's-length negotiation of contracts, contract changes,
and material acceptance criteria. A great many senior officials support the
partnership theory. A recently retired general officer, formerly in chage of
purchasing for his service and now an industry consultant, stated: "The
team approach instead of the adversary approach cannot be emphasized too
much. We must get back to the team approach between the Defense Department and the defense industry."

General Thomas P. Gerrity, former Commander of the Air Force Logistics
Command, gave his opinion in an address before the National Security Industrial Association on January 25, 1968: "If anybody thinks that we are less
than a partnership, they are fundamentally wrong."

A different observation was made by Robert N. Anthony during his tenure
as Assistant Secretary of Defense (Comptroller):

> The interests of the Government are basically different from those of
> the contractor. The contractor wants as much profit as he can get, but the
> Government wants to pay only a fair price. We should not ignore this
> basic difference. In particular, I think it is softheaded to talk about a
> "partnership between Government and industry." We are partners when
> it comes to performance and delivery, but are *not* partners on price. On
> matters relating to price, we are on opposite sides of the fence, and we
> should face this frankly.

REPORTING PROGRESS TO THE PENTAGON

To gain perspective on Pentagon attitudes toward management problems
and their causes, we conducted a series of interviews in September 1971
with personnel from major Army, Navy, and Air Force program offices. We

wanted to learn how information is transmitted from these program offices to decision makers in the Pentagon. Several program office staff members described what they believed to be a serious breakdown in the reporting system. Somewhere between the program office and the Congress, evaluations of program performance and expectations underwent radical alterations. On reading Congressional testimony regarding their programs, they often discovered that cost status or technical capabilities were described as far more favorable than the facts would warrant. No such assessment had been passed from their program office to the next higher management level.

An Air Force officer assigned to the program control division of a major Air Force development program described the following incident. His office had prepared a quarterly progress report on the program for the Office of the Secretary of Defense. When this report was passed up to the next management level, it included information on 14 serious problems. The progress report was evaluated at each level of Government management between the program office and the Office of the Secretary of Defense. Each level earmarked certain funds for the program and eliminated from the report all mention of one, or more, of the 14 problems. Three days later, when the report reached the Secretary of Defense, it indicated that the program was in excellent condition, with no significant problems. The Air Force officer who discussed the incident did not know whether the 14 problems had actually been solved or whether they were simply "postponed." In any event, there was obviously strong motivation at every management level to keep controversial information from reaching the Secretary of Defense.

In a separate incident that occurred in early 1971, representatives of the General Accounting Office met with Deputy Secretary of Defense David Packard to brief him on their independent analysis of several major defense programs. They cited major problems that they had found in all the programs. It was reported that Secretary Packard was profoundly disturbed by the report, since prior to the GAO study he had been assured by his military staff that all the problems later found by the study team had been observed and corrected. At those briefings, current program status had obviously been misrepresented.

Middle-level managers fear that if higher-level officials in the Department or the Congress know what is really happening on some programs, they will make the "wrong" decision; that is, they will cut back or cancel programs. These middle-level managers are convinced that Pentagon and Congressional officials have neither the background nor the training to understand the need for additional funds. Therefore, they invariably pass along more positive evaluations than were prepared for them by managers closer to the programs. They regard ranking Defense Department officials in much the same way that management executives in private corporations regard their boards of directors. And, like most corporate board members, most senior Pentagon officials accept management decisions at face value. Myles L. Mace, in *Directors: Myth and Reality,*[6] quoted a board member who explained why he never asked critical questions at board meetings:

> I, as an outside director, am unwilling to show my lack of grasp of understanding of the problem or to display my ignorance. To be able to challenge the management with a discerning question, you've got to know enough really to be on fairly sound ground. Part of the problem is that you don't want to look like an idiot. And it's very easy to look like an idiot, unless you spend enough time getting your facts in line, and, you know, understanding what you're talking about.

Assistant Secretaries in the Pentagon often find themselves in the same position. They realize that their knowledge about defense systems is limited. Development and production of large weapon and equipment systems are so complex that independent analysis by untrained outsiders is not feasible. An Assistant Secretary faced with program decisions often asks a few superficial questions and then approves the recommendations of his military staff.

Congressman William S. Moorhead cited an example of this problem in an address to the Armed Services Procurement Regulation Institute, September 29, 1969:

> In the C-5A case, I came across two memoranda. . . . The first memo quotes Air Force Secretary Brown. . . . "The overhead rates are Lockheed's problem, aren't they? Can they increase our price beyond the ceiling? I don't think so. Up to that price, we do pay part of the overrun."
>
> The memorandum replying to that comment said: "You are correct in your statement that Lockheed cannot increase our price of the current C-5A contract beyond the contract ceiling—providing we introduce no changes to that contract. However, the Air Force's share of the overrun above the target price could amount to more than a quarter of a billion dollars."
>
> These memos indicate that the Secretary of the Air Force was not aware of the pricing formula which would increase the Air Force's price, not by a quarter of a billion dollars, but in the neighborhood of two billion dollars.

In any complex decision-making process the individuals who most significantly affect the process are those who control the sources of information. In the Pentagon, part, or all, of the information on which a decision should be based may not be transmitted to a senior official until the time at which the decision must be made if it is transmitted at all. This means that the senior official may come to a meeting with little or no understanding of the issues to be discussed. When he hears "the facts" and a recommended course of action, he frequently accepts the recommendation without question, since the case as presented is credible.

Several "games" are played in the Defense Department, as in other bureaucracies, to affect the decision-making process. A standard practice is to present a top official with two alternative solutions to a problem. The official believes he has the evidence on which to base an objective choice. Usually, however, the favored alternative is attractively presented and the other is made to seem untenable. Another game is called "decision briefing." The official is invited to a meeting with all other interested principals. He is told that this is a decision briefing (not an "information briefing," during which no decisions are made). The game is to convince the official that he must make an immediate decision and then to present him only with facts that support the course of action favored by the military staff.

In one instance a military officer was in the process of preparing a $45 million budget request for a major program. A briefing on the request was to be made to the Office of the Secretary of Defense. In his proposal the officer also described a $13 million alternative, and an analysis of the impact of both proposals. When the senior military advocates of the program learned that the briefing would include a description of the $13 million alternative, they demanded its deletion—even though they agreed that the presentation was accurate. They argued that presenting an alternative would weaken the opportunity for the service to obtain the full $45 million. No alternative was discussed when the formal briefing was conducted.

A seasoned bureaucrat will listen to a briefing, ask questions, and then, despite pressure for an immediate decision, will confer with his staff and attempt to gather more information. A newcomer, on the other hand, may play the game as directed.

Program advocates occasionally anticipate delaying tactics on the part of a Secretary or Assistant Secretary and do not schedule briefings until 24 hours before a decision is due. In the absence of any conflicting information, an official often accepts whatever recommendations are put before him.

Another useful game is called "the decision has already been made." In this game the official is informed that events have taken the military staff by surprise, that he would surely have been informed earlier had his interest in the program been known, but that at the moment a particular course of action is well under way, and any change would cost taxpayers millions of dollars.

If a Secretary or an Assistant Secretary requests information about a controversial program, he may be provided with the fewest possible data. If even this does not support earlier staff decisions, the requested information may take a long time to reach the official. As it passes through various management levels, changes in wording or presentation will gradually diminish the controversial nature of the material.

One former Assistant Secretary summarized his views on the decision-making process succinctly: "It was my experience that adequate, reliable information usually did not exist for decision making on major issues." Three other Assistant Secretaries stated that before they arrived at the Pentagon, they believed that major defense decisions were based on careful analyses of all relevant facts. They were soon convinced that decisions were often based on information that was carefully screened before being presented to the nominal decision maker. In another conversation, an Assistant Secretary commented: "If the events presented as facts around here actually turned out to be facts, most of our problems would disappear." One official commented that he had learned that the only way to control the development of new programs was to enter the decision-making process long before the senior military officers had taken a strong position on individual programs. "Once a formal position is announced, it is very difficult to bring about any change without endangering your resources of information on future programs."

In every large organization senior officials are unable to keep in constant contact with multiple sources of information. The Pentagon is no exception. Large corporations deal with this problem by creating semi-autonomous divisions whose presidents are responsible for profit and loss and other measures of accomplishment. In the Pentagon several factors discourage this approach: the variety and complexity of the work; the absence of profit and loss indicators; and unreliable measures of effectiveness and efficiency. In addition, the size and duration of major development and production programs give lower-level managers leeway to make optimistic forecasts of time, costs, and technical performance. "There is simply no need to lie," according to one program manager, "one only has to be optimistic."

The Report of the Blue Ribbon Panel to the President and the Secretary of Defense on the Department of Defense was devoted in part to the role of the Secretariat and its relationship to inside management.

> The President and the Secretary of Defense do not presently have the opportunity to consider all viable options as background for making major decisions because differences of opinion are submerged or compromised at lower levels of the Department of Defense.[7]

> • • • • •

> The hierarchical structure of the Services is necessary to the discipline and the coordinated control of large numbers of men, but it is not neces-

sary to stimulate innovations in techniques nor is it even favorable to civilian review and control of the military establishment. To these ends it is essential that the Secretary of Defense be advised and informed by a civilian staff capable of discovering the real controversies within a Service and of advising on the division of functions and resources among Services. This civilian staff, largely concentrated in Systems Analysis, simply cannot be taken out of the main center of decision making without depriving the Secretary of Defense of the capacity for independent decision making. The Secretary will not turn over the direction of military forces to this civilian group (if he did, they would have to be put in uniform). But the Services have no right to reject independent review of their top-level decisions, and the nation cannot afford to give final power to them.[8]

There is ample evidence to support the conclusions of the Blue Ribbon Panel. In one case, a service Secretary decided to delay a decision to allow a weapon system to enter production until additional information was collected. Within two weeks, however, a senior military officer, about to retire from the service and aware of the Secretary's plan to withhold a decision, announced that his service "intends to issue a production contract on the [weapon system] early in fiscal year 1972." He was further quoted in a national journal as saying that he "had confidence that Congress would be convinced the weapon was essential." This particular weapon system was, as the military Chief of Staff indicated, "important to the service." The military assistant to the Chief of Staff described the program as "cost effective at any price."

In another case, an Assistant Secretary sent a letter to a senior military officer, classified "secret," in which he raised questions about a program on which the service was spending several hundred million dollars a year. In the letter he asked the officer to consider changes in the manner in which funds were being spent (not a reduction in funds) so that the program might be more effective. Within days, the Assistant Secretary received several calls from Congressmen and heads of outside associations supporting the program, and even a call from the governor of a state affected by the program. Although the Assistant Secretary had specific evidence of ineffective use of funds, his letter received only a cursory response from those in charge of the program. No action was taken to correct the problems to which he referred.

Pentagon officials do not usually discuss the need for basic changes in the defense procurement system during their terms of office, or even later. Sometimes they do not want to endanger subsequent career development by making enemies of private contractors. Nor do they wish to offend career Government personnel who have become personal friends. One former Assistant Secretary, for example, was privy to several intelligence reports on United States weapon capability. These analyses suggested that several of the development programs within his service were unnecessary. But he did not make any public statements because, in his words, "the Chief (of Staff) has taken a strong position on the need for these items, and this means that the service has to fall in line behind him." He believed that a public statement would not change priorities and, furthermore, would endanger his friendships with many of his former Pentagon colleagues.

The system for dividing responsibility and authority between civilian appointees and military officers in the Pentagon seriously hampers the weapons acquisition process. If sufficient defense capability is to be maintained efficiently and effectively, civilian control of defense activities must become a working reality. Civilian appointees control few of the incentives or penalties for personnel performance. They have as much, or less, authority in the Defense Department as the board of directors in a private corporation. To achieve a more appropriate balance of power, personnel assignments and promotions—military and civil service—must be directed by civilian appointees rather than Chiefs of Staff. Civilians must, in fact as well as intent, define defense priorities and control information channels. And finally, to achieve stability within the Department, it is imperative that Secretaries and Assistant Secretaries serve, at the minimum, four-year terms of office. Fundamental reform in the weapons acquisition process must begin in the Congress and in the Pentagon.

NOTES TO CHAPTER V

1. *U.S. Government Organization Manual* (Washington: Government Printing Office, 1970–71), pp. 112–192.
2. Report of the Blue Ribbon Panel to the President and the Secretary of Defense on the Department of Defense, July 1, 1970, p. 187.
3. Ibid.
4. Comptroller General of the United States, *Report to the Congress on the Acquisition of Major Weapon Systems*, B-163058, March 18, 1971.
5. Dwight David Eisenhower, *The White House Years*, Volume II, *Waging Peace 1956–61* (New York: Doubleday, 1965), p. 615.
6. Myles L. Mace, *Directors: Myth and Reality* (Boston: Division of Research, Harvard Business School, 1971).
7. Report of the Blue Ribbon Panel, p. 1. Statement by Dr. George J. Stigler, Member of the Blue Ribbon Panel and Professor of American Institutions, University of Chicago.
8. Ibid., p. 198.

CHAPTER VI

Planning for Major Development and Production Programs

ALTHOUGH WEAPONS ACQUISITION nominally originates with the Congress of the United States, a broad outline of the planning process within the Defense Department will help the reader to understand the role and responsibilities of the various Congressional committees to be discussed in Chapter VII.

Before the mid-1950s most new weapons acquisition programs were initiated independently by the individual branches of the military. The services made little attempt to coordinate their acquisition policies or planning. Each developed and produced those systems which it believed would strengthen its own capabilities. As a result, the Army might be preparing for a long war of attrition, the Navy for amphibious operations around the world, and the Air Force for a nuclear war of short duration. Occasionally, individual service strategies did complement each other, but this was by coincidence rather than design.[1]

Defense procurement policy and procedures were relatively simple and flexible before the mid-1950s. Since the technology required for most weapon systems was not highly innovative, development costs were relatively low. New programs proliferated. Between 1945 and 1955, 22 bomber prototypes and 33 fighter aircraft prototypes were built.[2] This expansiveness was not discouraged by Congress. Once a program had received initial authorization, its continued funding was virtually guaranteed, however inadequate the information on its cost or capability. The Defense Department made no attempt to develop or coordinate control systems for cost, schedule, or technical performance. Each contractor and military program manager simply developed his own management techniques.

In the late 1950s the "missile gap crisis" produced an even stronger emphasis on the accumulation of new weapon systems. Duplication of programs among the military services continued unchecked. Eventually, however, the increasing cost and complexity of new systems—e.g., the B-70 bomber, the Atlas missile, the Titan missile, the Polaris submarine—forced the Defense Department to contemplate reform in the selection and the management of its acquisition programs.

In 1961 President John F. Kennedy chose Robert S. McNamara to be his Secretary of Defense. McNamara understood the urgent need to coordinate the services' unilaterally developed acquisition programs and to link procurement directly to national security objectives. As a first step in this direction, he introduced a Five-Year Defense Force Structure plan, to be prepared annually by the Office of the Secretary of Defense. In the preparation of this plan, trade-off decisions were to be made among competing weapon systems, regardless of the service originating the programs, and unnecessary duplication was to be eliminated.

By 1970 the annual Five-Year Force Structure plan had become the Five-Year Defense Plan. Although the planning and programming techniques developed under McNamara's direction have been modified over the years since his administration, the basic system remains the same.

FIVE-YEAR DEFENSE PLAN

A new Five-Year Defense Plan is prepared annually. It takes shape during a period of approximately fifteen months, and involves nine phases of planning activity, described below.

Step 1 (October)	*The Joint Chiefs of Staff issue the Joint Strategic Objectives Plan (JSOP), Volume I.* The JSOP-Vol. I is the Joint Chiefs' official statement on national security objectives, and is based on their evaluation of military intelligence information, Presidential policy, and national defense needs. Its strategic concepts and objectives are developed on a world-wide basis. The JSOP-Vol. I is issued each year in October and is distributed to the Office of the Secretary of Defense and to all service Secretaries and Assistant Secretaries, as a guide in their planning activities.
Step 2 (January)	*The Secretary of Defense issues the Strategy Guidance Memorandum* The Office of the Secretary of Defense begins a comprehensive analysis of the JSOP-Vol. I as soon as it is received. The Secretary of Defense then prepares a tentative Strategy Guidance Memo-

randum and sends it to the Joint Chiefs of Staff for review and comment. Like JSOP-Vol. I, this memorandum deals with national security goals. Changes in JSOP-Vol. I are usually based on changes in defense policies or priorities and on commitments made by the President.

After the tentative Strategy Guidance Memorandum is reviewed by the Joint Chiefs of Staff, the Secretary of Defense prepares a final version. The purpose of this document is to present a coordinated, complete, and current strategic plan that will serve as a guide for the entire defense community.

The final Strategy Guidance Memorandum is issued each year in January as a part of the Five-Year Defense Plan.

Step 3
(January)

The Secretary of Defense issues the Tentative Fiscal Guidance Memorandum.

Also in January the Secretary of Defense issues the document which sets the budget limits for the defense programs of each service. The Tentative Fiscal Guidance Memorandum is a five-year plan. For each branch of the armed forces, it covers major mission and support categories individually; e.g., strategic forces, land forces, intelligence and communications, training.

The Tentative Fiscal Guidance Memorandum is sent to all military departments (Chiefs of Staff, service Secretaries and Assistant Secretaries, and their staffs) for review and comment.

Step 4
(February)

The Joint Chiefs of Staff issue the Joint Strategic Objectives Plan (JSOP), Volume II.

While the Tentative Fiscal Guidance Memorandum is under review, the Joint Chiefs of Staff are completing JSOP-Vol. II. This document describes the required force levels (manpower and weapon system), and related costs, necessary to fulfill the national security objectives described in JSOP-Vol. I (and the Strategy Guidance Memorandum). It is prepared without regard to the fiscal limits outlined in the Tentative Fiscal Guidance Memorandum.

JSOP-Vol. II is published in February and is sent to the Secretary of Defense.

Step 5
(March)

The Secretary of Defense issues the final Fiscal Guidance Memorandum.

After reviewing JSOP-Vol. II and the comments received from the Joint Chiefs and service Secretaries on the Tentative Fiscal Guidance Memorandum, the Secretary of Defense issues a reserve Fiscal Guidance Memorandum. Like the tentative version, it forecasts spending for five years and gives funding breakdowns by category for each service. Only two aspects of the final Fiscal Guidance Memorandum are completely firm, however: totals by program year and totals by military service. Unless specifically prohibited in the Fiscal Guidance Memorandum, each service may reallocate its funds among major mission and support categories. This gives the services enough flexibility to balance program costs for personnel, equipment, construction, and other operating expenses.

The final Fiscal Guidance Memorandum is issued each year in March and is sent to all military departments for use in planning.

Step 6
(April)

The Joint Chiefs of Staff issue the Joint Force Memorandum

In April the Joint Chiefs of Staff issue a Joint Force Memorandum, similar in subject matter to JSOP-Vol. II but revised on the basis of the budget figures contained in the Fiscal Guidance Memorandum. (As noted above, JSOP-Vol. II does not take budget limits into account.) The Joint Force Memorandum assesses the risks involved in the reduced force levels (made necessary by limited funding), as measured against the objectives described in JSOP-Vol. I and the Strategy Guidance Memorandum. It also describes the major force level issues to be resolved during the upcoming fiscal year. In addition, the Joint Force Memorandum compares the costs of its recommendations with the costs approved in the Five-Year Defense Plan (as enunciated in the Fiscal Guidance Memorandum).

The Joint Force Memorandum is sent to the Office of the Secretary of Defense for review and to the service Secretaries and Assistant Secretaries and their military counterparts to provide further guidance in planning activities.

Step 7
(May)

Each military service issues a Program Objective Memorandum (POM).

In May of each year each military service submits a POM to the Secretary of Defense. These POM's, based on the strategy and fiscal guidance described in the preceding six steps, outline the services' total program requirements for weapon systems, manpower, and funding.

Step 8
(June–
August)

The Secretary of Defense issues Program Decision Memoranda (PDM's).

After a review of the POM's, the Secretary of Defense issues a series of PDM's. These contain funding decisions for each major defense program and identify the resources allocated for specific program components; e.g., bombers, tanks, fighter aircraft, missiles. The PDM's are sent to the Joint Chiefs of Staff and the service Secretaries for analysis and comment.

All PDM's are issued by the end of July. Comments must be submitted to the Secretary of Defense within the next two weeks. If service officials have dissenting views, they must submit to the

Secretary of Defense any relevant information that was not included in the original POM's, in order to facilitate a full re-evaluation of the issues involved.

The Secretary of Defense and his staff review all comments received from the Joint Chiefs of Staff and other military and civilian officials. To resolve major problems, the Joint Chiefs and/or the service Secretaries meet as often as necessary with the Secretary of Defense. Final PDM's are then issued, listing changes or modifications in the Secretary of Defense's original program decisions. These, together with the Fiscal Guidance Memorandum, form the new Five-Year Defense Plan.

Step 9
(September–
December)

Budget Estimates

On September 30 of each year, each military service submits an estimated budget for the next fiscal year (July 1 to June 30) to the Secretary of Defense, based on the new Five-Year Defense Plan. The Secretary of Defense directs a review of these estimates by his staff, who are assisted by members of the President's Office of Management and Budget. At the conclusion of this review, the Secretary of Defense issues a series of Program/Budget Decisions (PBD's).

The complete defense budget for the next fiscal year is sent to the President's Office of Management and Budget for approval late in December. Once approved, it becomes part of the total Federal budget submitted by the President to the Congress early in January. The Congressional review of the defense budget is described in Chapter VII.

SYSTEMS ANALYSIS

The preceding description of the defense planning, programming, and budgeting cycle understates the complexity of the process. As each military service prepares its recommendations for new or continuing weapons acquisition programs, it develops massive supportive documentation. In the Office of the Secretary of Defense, the Systems Analysis office plays a significant role in evaluating all recommendations and back-up material. The Systems Analysis office analyzes the cost estimates submitted to the Secretary of Defense by each branch of the military, and prepares independent cost estimates for recommended programs. Cost-versus-effectiveness ratios are made for major defense programs. In addition, the Systems Analysis office provides advice to the Secretary of Defense in the preparation of the Five-Year Defense Plan and the annual defense budgets.

The activities of the Systems Analysis organization have received both criticism and praise.[3] The outstanding virtues and limitations of systems analysis are listed below.

Advantages of Systems Analysis
1. A cost-effectiveness analysis of an acquisition program accomplishes at least three objectives: (a) it establishes a framework within which to identify those program activities which determine cost effectiveness; (b) it describes the interaction of the program activities which affect cost; and (c) it provides a basis for comparison and evaluation.
2. Systems analysis describes the inductive reasoning and numerical data that determine not only which program elements are relevant to cost analysis but the quantitative values to be assigned to each element.
3. A cost effectiveness analysis provides a model for comparing many alternative combinations of program variables, and for evaluating the interactions of program variables in alternative combinations. Once the model is established, new calculations can be made whenever estimates or assumptions are modified.

Disadvantages of Systems Analysis
1. There is no established body of theory to guide in the selection of reasonable criteria for cost effectiveness analysis. Many of the assumptions upon which analyses are based cannot be verified. Thus, the aura of scientific objectivity that surrounds systems analysis is not altogether warranted.
2. In any cost effectiveness analysis there is always the possibility that factors of major significance will not be properly accounted for or will be omitted entirely.
3. Alternative weapon systems sometimes have multiple missions that partially overlap. When cost effectiveness for competing alternatives is being measured, each system's missions are given values, or the cost effectiveness for only the systems' dominant function is analyzed. Such analyses have limited value, because they do not adequately describe the complexity of the systems they are comparing.

Since 1964 the Systems Analysis organization has been composed of several hundred specialists. Periodically, military officers or members of Congress suggest that the size and scope of this office be reduced. Whatever its shortcomings, however, the Systems Analysis organization provides the Secretary of Defense with the only reviews of defense programs that are not influenced by the military. Unless the Secretary of Defense supports this kind of independent study, he will have little chance of determining how to gain maximum efficiency from the defense funds appropriated by Congress.

The overriding concern of each military service is to win approval for programs that will enhance its prestige, and will allow it to continue its traditional functions. This was explained by an Assistant Secretary:

> As long as we have strong, capable aircraft-carrier personnel, tank personnel, manned bomber pilots, we will be deluged by proposals for new programs in those areas. No man is about to recommend the discontinuance or reduction in the branch that holds the key to his future advancement. There is nothing that stifles promotion opportunities quite like a major cutback in personnel or a reduction in equipment. If anyone is to place a lid on the number of new programs, it has to come from a strong Secretary of Defense or the Congress.

In an article in the April 1969 issue of *The Atlantic Monthly,* General David M. Shoup, commandant of the Marine Corps in the early 1960s, commented on the factors that influence military planning:

> At the senior command levels, parochial pride in the service, personal ambitions, and old Army-Navy game rivalry stemming back to academy loyalties can influence strategic planning far more than most civilians would care to believe. The game is to be ready for deployment sooner than the other elements of the joint task force and to be so disposed as to be the "first to fight". . . .

The Blue Ribbon Panel summarized the problem of service parochialism in its 1970 report:

> There is an apparent inability of service staff elements to divorce themselves from their own service interests in establishing priorities for requirements. It is evident that the needs of the user in the field often take second place to weapons developments considered most important to the particular service for the protection or expansion of its assigned roles and missions.[4]

For military planners, stepped-up concern about cost effectiveness on the part of the Secretary of Defense is taken as an unhappy omen. When systems analysis was introduced into the Defense Department, it was considered, by the military, a definite threat to service prestige and weapons development. One technical consultant who was employed by a military service in the mid-1960s observed that general officers frequently ordered changes in the briefings prepared for the Office of the Secretary of Defense. These changes were designed to give a favored program more credibility than the facts warranted. In most cases, the original briefing had indicated that the program's cost effectiveness was not as favorable as that of competing programs.

When a military Chief of Staff makes it known that he wants his service to undertake a weapons acquisition program, it is highly unlikely that unfavorable information about that program will ever reach the Secretary of Defense through official channels. As described in Chapter V, military officers are strongly motivated to achieve the objectives set by their superiors. Analysis and documentation prepared in support of a Chief of Staff's favorite programs will suppress relevant information, if necessary, rather than reveal any data likely to raise doubts in the Office of the Secretary of Defense or in Congress.

The Secretary of Defense himself works under considerable pressure from the military. Although the ultimate decisions affecting the acquisition of weapon systems are his responsibility, he does his work as a member of a team which includes the Joint Chiefs of Staff and the Secretaries of the military services. Decisions become particularly difficult for him when he must choose among systems promoted by competing services or when a system described as "essential" by a military Chief of Staff is not deemed cost effective by the Systems Analysis group. Most of the military officials who serve with the Secretary have considerable political "clout." To balance their demands with a broader concern for national security and economic stability, a Secretary of Defense must have unusual stamina, self-confidence, political acumen, and a gift for interpersonal relationships.

DEFINING NEW ACQUISITION PROGRAMS

In 1970 the National Security Industrial Association, an organization of defense contractors, conducted an extensive study of the weapons acquisition process. In their report, they commented on the competitive forces within Government and within the defense industry which affect the initiation and definition of new weapon programs.

> Within DOD itself, competition is a very active force. This is reflected in DOD's drive to stay ahead of our potential enemies by fielding weapons which incorporate the latest possible technology; in DOD's relationships with other governmental departments; in the efforts of the military services to protect and expand their respective roles and missions and to obtain a larger share of the defense budget; in the relationship between the military services and the Office of the Secretary of Defense; and in the competition among the branches, commands, arsenals, yards, centers, and laboratories of the military services.
>
> For industry, competition is keen because the overall total of defense business is seldom adequate to support the available capacity of even the

hard-core defense contractors, thus forcing companies into a continuous life and death struggle to obtain defense contracts. Defense programs often are of gigantic magnitude, which results in competition more intensely concentrated than is typically encountered in the commercial marketplace. The risk of losing the contract is matched only by winning the competition and signing a contract involving unreasonably high risk.[5]

Our discussions with Defense Department and industry personnel, and a review of the case histories of ten current defense programs, revealed that defense contractors are profoundly influential in the origination and development of new program ideas. Private firms often assist Government staffs in writing the Requests for Proposals for new systems that are eventually issued to potential contractors. Industry officials research areas to which their particular companies' skills might be applied and identify key Government offices that will welcome their proposals. They also attempt to find out what funds are actually or potentially available for particular programs. According to the industry executives we interviewed, intelligence information concerning defense funding is a major factor in the preparation of the cost estimates submitted to the Defense Department.

In 1962 Peck and Scherer described the initiation of defense programs in *The Weapons Acquisition Process*:

> Once the facilitating technology is available or can be foreseen, the eventual appearance of new weapon system program ideas is almost inevitable. . . .
> As long as major and minor advances in basic physical concepts and specific component performance continue to appear, new ideas for the development of weapon systems and major subsystems will be forthcoming in quantity. Defense firms in particular are prolific sources of evolutionary ideas.[6]

Peck and Scherer also noted that industry advocates for new program ideas are often responsible for major breakthroughs in technological development.

> It must be said in fairness that much of the advocacy surrounding U.S. weapons programs is not of a malicious mercenary sort. Both contractors and sponsoring agencies, which are often the contractors' allies, believe their weapons programs are essential to the national defense. If this belief does not come from pride in invention, it soon develops as a result of constantly living with the idea. This zeal serves a useful function, since it fortifies the participants in the difficult task of selling a program to the skeptics in a decision-making chain. Indeed, history shows that were it

not for zealous advocacy, many new military developments would never
have received approval until it was too late. . . .[7]

On the other hand, this professional zeal can also lead to unrealistic program definition. In its 1970 report entitled *Policy Changes in Weapon System Procurement,* the House Committee on Government Operations cited
several instances in which contractors influenced the definition of new defense programs.[8] Former Army Chief of Research and Development, General
A. W. Betts, discussing the "inordinate price" it would cost the Government
to fulfill the range specification of the Cheyenne helicopter, explained the
contractor's role in establishing the system's specifications.

> The original requirement specified a ferry range of 1,500 nautical
> miles, but when the response to the request for proposals came in from
> the several contractors involved, Lockheed was the only one that prom-
> ised 2,500 nautical miles range. Subsequent thereto, when we firmed up
> the total package-type procurement with Lockheed, that [a ferry range
> of 2,500 nautical miles] ended up as a requirement in the contract. Yet
> honestly, we did not know enough about the detailed technology with
> respect to the aircraft to know that it was not reasonable to expect that
> aircraft in its configuration to achieve that much ferry range.[9]

During the same hearings a senior naval officer described some of the problems of establishing performance requirements for new weapon systems.

> The operational people in the Navy Office of Chief of Naval Opera-
> tions define the operational requirements. They are familiar with opera-
> tional and combat situations. Then the people in the Naval Materiel
> Command ask contractors: "How can we meet the operational require-
> ments?" But the statements of operational requirements do not show the
> relative importance of various performance requirements or alternative
> combinations of range, speed, payload capability. Rather, the operational
> requirement contains a list of presumably independent technical perform-
> ance requirements to be met.

Defining new weapon systems may be almost as difficult as building them.
Those who specify operational requirements have an unenviable task: how to
develop weapon systems that will be effective against an unknown enemy
having unknown weapons, ten years in the future. To cope with the uncertainty inherent in the situation, those who define requirements "hedge their
bets." They recommend the acquisition of the most sophisticated systems attainable. Cost is, at best, a secondary consideration.

Intelligence estimates of the capabilities of potential enemies are used by military planners who prescribe operational requirements for new systems. These estimates vary widely, however. For example, some intelligence analysts believe that the Soviet Union and China pose no serious threat to the security of the United States. Others believe that the United States may some day face the threat of total extinction at the hands of either or both of these nations. A variety of international "threats" can be used to support a variety of proposals for new defense programs.

The definition of defense needs can also be affected by professional curiosity. Scherer observed:

> Much of the initial impetus for new weapons development comes, I think, from the fascination of scientists, engineers, and military planners with the technical challenges posed by new weapons concepts; from the urge to triumph over nature in solving a difficult technical problem; and from the desire to be recognized by one's peers for achieving a successful solution.[10]

A factor that cannot be overlooked in the conception of new defense programs is the overwhelming urge of all bureaucracies to perpetuate themselves. One defense industry executive told us that, in his experience, new programs are often designed because "large R&D organizations in the Department of Defense need to feed themselves." This motivation was expressed in different terms by a military officer who was involved in determining new program requirements: "R&D specialists want to acquire the best possible weapons and equipment that American technology can devise, whether or not there is actually any foreseeable military threat."

In some cases a military need precedes the development of a corresponding technical capability. In other cases a technical capability precedes the definition of a military need. In either situation defining a weapon system's operational requirements is a complex task. It may take two weeks or two years. The process by which an idea is turned into a full-scale acquisition program may be described in terms of the four types of work performed—research; exploratory development; advanced development; engineering development—or in terms of the four stages of acquisition: concept formulation; validation; full-scale development; and production.

Work designated as research is performed before the first stage of acquisition begins. The first stage, concept formulation, includes two kinds of work: exploratory development and advanced development. The second and third stages of acquisition, validation and full-scale development, depend on work known as engineering development. Figure VI-1 illustrates the relationship between the four types of work carried on during a defense program and the first three stages in the acquisition of a weapon system.

FIGURE VI-1. STAGES IN THE ACQUISITION OF A WEAPON SYSTEM

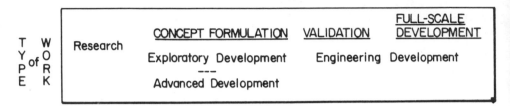

Following is a description of the four types of work:

1. *Research* includes all systematic effort by which data are gathered and examined, with the particular object of discovering something or understanding something. There are two types of research:
   A. *Basic Research* is directed toward an increase in scientific knowledge. The primary aim of the investigator is a broader knowledge or understanding of the subject under study, rather than its practical applications.
   B. *Applied Research* normally follows and is predicated upon basic research. It is concerned with the practical application of scientific knowledge, material, and/or techniques, and is directed toward the solution of an existing or anticipated military need.
2. *Exploratory Development* includes all effort (short of a full-scale development program) directed toward the solution of specific military problems. Such effort may range from fundamental applied research to the development of sophisticated "breadboard" hardware.* Solutions are evaluated in terms of performance feasibility and practicability. Examples of exploratory development projects include: the study of the "fatigue" characteristics of deep-diving submarines; a study of wind tunnel performance of newly designed aircraft.
3. *Advanced Development* includes experimental and operational testing. Technical feasibility and prototype studies are made to compare the cost of a new design with the cost of modifying equipment and systems presently in use. As an example of an advanced development project, air-cushion ships have been tested for use in such varied missions as amphibious, mine, strike, and antisubmarine warfare in order to determine their military usefulness, technical capability, and cost effectiveness.

---

* "*Breadboard*—(1) An assembly on any convenient mount of parts of circuits of a system, used to test or to demonstrate, without regard to the final configuration that such assembly will have in operation. (2) The mount on which this assembly is made." (From *Defense and Aerospace Glossary for Project Management,* compiled and edited by J. Ronald Fox, Hawthorne Publishing House, Washington, D.C., 1970, p. 46.)

4. *Engineering Development* includes all work necessary to prepare a system for use. This is done before a production program is (or is not) authorized.

These four types of work activity contribute to the first three stages in the acquisition of a weapon system. All four stages are described below.

I. *Concept Formulation*

During this stage, studies are made to determine how operational requirements for a new weapon system can best be realized. Preliminary designs are readied. Schedule, cost, and performance estimates are drawn up. Alternate management systems are evaluated. Before and during the concept formulation stage, Government and industry officials engage in lengthy discussions to determine operational dates, possible funding levels, and other program requirements. At the same time, Government laboratories seek to improve every aspect of system performance, striving for greater reliability, lighter weight, lower volume, etc. Repeated attempts are made to achieve the best balance of those operational requirements which have been specified by the Defense Department.

Before the concept formulation stage is over, seven tasks are accomplished.

1. The operational requirements for the new system are redefined.
2. Several designs are prepared that meet the operational specifications for the weapon system. The most satisfactory alternative is chosen and the rationale for its selection is described in detail.
3. Major areas of technical risk are identified and plans made to eliminate them.
4. A plan is drawn up which broadly defines and quantifies the performance, cost, and schedule objectives of the acquisition program.
5. Also prepared are system performance specifications, with major subsystems and their interrelationships identified.
6. Any special logistic support problems are identified.
7. A Decision Coordinating Paper (DCP) is prepared (described below).

A wide variety of organizations conduct studies designed to achieve these seven tasks. For small programs, studies are often conducted by organizations within the Defense Department. For large programs, private firms are chosen, and placed under contract, to conduct studies of specific problems; e.g., the technical feasibility of guidance subsystems or propulsion subsystems; development of cost-effectiveness models; threat analyses. For some large programs, several major contractors are funded to conduct all or part of the concept formulation studies in competition. Each of the competing contractors has the facilities to conduct follow-on development efforts.

A Decision Coordinating Paper is prepared by the Office of the Secretary of Defense for each major development and production program. Its purpose is to provide guidance to the service developing the new weapon system. It is also used as a basic reference document by the Secretary of Defense and other senior defense officials who review the program. It is usually no more than 20 pages long.

DCP's set review thresholds for costs, schedules, and technical performance. They also contain program justification statements, they list schedules and anticipated program performance, and they describe the alternative designs that were developed to meet operational requirements. Each DCP is prepared by the Director of Defense, Research, and Engineering. He works with the Assistant Secretaries of Defense for Installations and Logistics, and Financial Management (Comptroller); and with officials of the military service sponsoring the program.

II. *Validation*

During this stage of the acquisition schedule, the preliminary designs for the new weapon system are tested and verified. Final plans for the management of the program are made. Contractor proposals for engineering development are solicited and evaluated, and the development contractor is selected. The objective of this stage of program growth is to verify that the technical and economic bases for initiating a full-scale development program are valid. Advancement into the next stage of acquisition depends upon (1) establishment of performance specifications that can be realized, and (2) the choice of an acceptable proposal from a development contractor. Before a system moves into full-scale development, however, the Secretary of Defense must give his approval.

In the commerical market, design characteristics for a given product are relatively stable. In contrast, the operational requirements for defense systems may change one or more times a year. After each change, Government and industry managers must prepare new plans, new schedules, and new budgets. This process occurs repeatedly during the validation stage of an acquisition program and throughout the remainder of the life of the program.

III. *Full-Scale Development*

During a full-scale development program, final design, engineering, and manufacturing specifications for a weapon system must be prepared and a production model built. After the development contractor is selected and a contract negotiated, prototypes are developed, produced, and tested. The object of this phase of the acquisition process is to develop a weapon system that will be approved for production by the Secretary of Defense and authorized and funded by Congress.

IV. *Production*

During this stage of acquisition, a weapon system is produced in quantity for use in the field. The phase begins when a production contract is negotiated and awarded. Production acceptance tests are then conducted by the Government to validate the performance of the production model developed in the previous phase. The program ends when the number of weapon systems authorized by Congress are produced and ready for military deployment. The production phase includes production tests and user acceptance tests.

It has become the custom to initiate the production phase of the acquisition process before the development program is complete. Defense Department and contractor personnel give a number of reasons to support this practice.

1. The need for the weapon system is "urgent." There is no time to wait for the testing of the production model before undertaking the production program.
2. Some materials and components required for production require long ordering lead-time or long manufacturing cycles. If purchase orders are not placed while the development program is still under way, there may be a time lag between the end of development and the beginning of production.
3. Since the development contractor is usually awarded the production contract, many company personnel work on both programs. If a production commitment is not made before the end of the development program, specialists familiar with the system may be laid off or go into other programs.

Some Pentagon officials have tried to discourage this practice (called "concurrency"). But officials from military operational commands, as well as contractors and R&D managers within the Defense Department, continue to exert considerable pressure to have production contracts awarded before the production model is satisfactorily tested. There is at least one reason for this urgency that is not mentioned publicly: If the commitment to production is *not* made until the production model is approved, growth in R&D costs will be revealed tht could otherwise be charged to the production program. Contractors and R&D officials would prefer to keep these overruns hidden.

When a new weapon system is being acquired by a military service, the most technologically sophisticated components are usually incorporated into its design, whether or not they actually improve the system's performance. This is usually a matter of military pride and prestige rather than operational necessity. As a result, the Defense Department has traditionally emphasized major advances in total systems rather than incremental improvements in components and subsystems. According to one senior Pentagon officer, "We have been too slow in moving forward in the area of modifications and improvements and have tended to seek the ultimate instead." Another senior defense official commented: "A major problem that we have in the acquisition process is that when we have to design a new system as a total gestalt, all the guys down in the buying organization specify all the latest components from the brochures. The system then has all the now 'razmataz' and each one of these components ends up still having a number of problems that must be worked out."

During a 1970 hearing of the House Committee on Government Operations, David Packard, the Deputy Secretary of Defense, discussed the unnecessary complexity of some new weapon systems. He referred to the development of the MBT-70 tank as an example: "The boys wanted everything but the kitchen sink." [11] Speaking earlier, in 1969, to the Aerospace Industries Association, Mr. Packard discussed the same subject:

> The third problem in the management of the Department of Defense is to procure and operate Defense resources in the most efficient manner possible. This brings me to some observations about major weapons systems. I have reached the firm conclusion that we are designing and building weapons that are too complex, and therefore too costly. We further compound the problem by trying to produce hardware before it is fully developed.
>
> This means that we are going to take a very hard look at whether we need all this gadgetry when we go into a new development. A computerized fire control may increase the accuracy of tank gunnery, but so far it does not give evidence of increasing the reliability of gunnery. A tank with its gun out of order is no tank at all. [12]

The president of a large company which makes 35% of its sales to the Defense Department told us that his firm's approach to product development for its commercial business is very different from its approach to defense system development. In commerical business his firm has been able to maintain its position at the top of its field by developing its products incrementally; i.e., changing one component at a time as use and improved technology warrant. In the defense business each successive acquisition program for a particular weapon system involves major changes in most components of the system. The programs take a long time to complete, and the period between programs is also a long one. The result is that major improvements in defense systems are not as far-reaching as the steady incremental improvements undertaken in commercial programs over the same period. (The incremental approach is used in designing successive models of many commercial products; e.g., automobiles; television sets; large custom turbines; complex radio and electronics equipment.)

Since military using commands and R&D laboratories seek approval to incorporate as many new and sophisticated components as possible into new weapon systems, an unusual phenomenon occurs: all such components are labeled "low risk" or "moderate risk." In two years of reviewing more than 25 major development programs, I never encountered an official report in which a component, subsystem, or full-scale system was labeled "high risk." When a system component does not perform adequately, senior Pentagon officials do everything they can to avoid time-consuming reviews. In senior-level briefings, most functional problems are blamed on the need for "better integration," "better systems engineering," "better configuration management," or a "better interface." Unnecessary complexity of system components is rarely mentioned.

These "full-speed-ahead" tactics are a natural response to the inordinately long waiting period between program recommendation and program approval. As in most bureaucracies, a large number of officials have the power to delay or withhold approval, but few have the authority to make decisions on their own. There are at least six levels of management between a program manager and the Secretary of Defense. At each level, a program manager's written report is reviewed and usually modified. Some reports are reviewed, and changed, ten or more times before they reach the Secretary. At most review sessions, officials make changes that will increase the likelihood of approval for the recommended program. While their changes do not usually involve outright lies, sections of the briefing are often deleted or altered, or new sections added—whatever is deemed necessary to win approval at the next level of management.

The designation of a program as "urgent" is a common method used by the military to secure funding. Each defense program competes for Congressional appropriations against: (1) other programs recommended by the same military service; (2) programs recommended by other military services; and (3) nondefense programs. Since most major development and production programs are considered high-priority by the military service which initiates them, almost all are given an "urgent" label. Sometimes the label is assigned because of a genuine belief in the country's immediate need for additional defense capability. In many cases, however, the designation is simply inaccurate. In recommending one multimillion dollar production program to the Secretary of Defense, the Joint Chiefs of Staff indicated that there was an "urgent" requirement that several thousand units of the weapon system be produced for delivery to a particular ally. The program was approved. One month later the senior U.S. military commander assigned to the foreign country in question returned for a visit to the United States. He talked of his surprise at learning of the program's "urgent" label, since the need for the system in the designated country was not at all pressing. At some point between the initiation of the requirement in the field and the recommendation from the Joint Chiefs of Staff, someone had probably decided that the program was more likely to be authorized if it was considered indispensable.

Every step of the Defense procurement process, from the origin of a program to its completion, is governed by rules that are contained in the *Armed Services Procurement Regulation* (ASPR), a publication numbering 3,000 pages. The document was conceived when President Harry S. Truman expressed concern to his Secretary of Defense, James Forrestal, about the unprecedented freedom allowed in peacetime procurement after World War II:

> For these reasons, I am asking you to specify detailed standards to guide your procurement officers concerning the placing of business with small concerns and the circumstances under which they may waive the general policy of advertising for bids. It is of great importance in procurement matters to establish standards and definitions to guide all personnel who have authority to place contracts. Otherwise, differences in interpretation and policies may result in imprudent contracts and give rise to doubts about the wisdom of this new procurement system.[13]

Truman's request resulted in the passage of the Armed Services Procurement Act in 1947, establishing uniform contracting policies and procedures for all organizations within the Department of Defense. In 1960 the Secretary of Defense designated the Assistant Secretary of Defense (Installations and Logistics) as the official responsible for contracting policies and procedures.

For each edition of the ASPR, 54,000 copies are printed. Approximately half are distributed to Defense Department offices throughout the world. The remainder go to contractors, foreign governments, educational institutions, and other organizations. Revisions to the ASPR are published every six months by the Assistant Secretary of Defense for Installations and Logistics. Between these regular revisions, Defense Procurement Circulars are issued whenever important revisions or new directives go into effect. In 1970, for example, an Equal Opportunity ruling by the Secretary of Labor was communicated through a Defense Procurement Circular.

The Government and industry personnel who work on a defense program do not need to master the complete ASPR. What is essential to them is a thorough familiarity with regulations governing basic contracting practices; e.g., formal advertising *versus* negotiation; mandatory contract clauses; requirements for competition; types of contracts. Much of the ASPR is devoted to more specialized areas; e.g., contract terminations; patents and copyrights; bonds and insurance; foreign purchases.

In 1963 the Secretary of Defense ruled that the individual Army, Navy, and Air Force procurement publications should be codified into the ASPR. Until that time each military department had published its own detailed procurement regulation manual, which interpreted as well as supplemented the ASPR. The so-called "reduction-in-implementation" effort was designed to make regulations consistent throughout the Defense Department. The result was a tripling of the size of the ASPR and an elimination of more than 6,000 pages of separate Army, Navy, and Air Force regulations.

A second innovation in 1963 increased the size of the ASPR: the centralization of authority for defense contract administration in the newly created Defense Contract Administration Service (DCAS). This is described in more detail in Chapter X. Before 1963 each military service maintained a separate contract administration organization and periodically issued directives concerning the relationship between its purchasing and administration offices. When DCAS was established, regulations governing its authority and areas of responsibility were incorporated into the ASPR.

The length and detail of the ASPR is but one indication of the overwhelming complexity of the weapons acquisition process in the United States. In an effort to gain some insight into other modes of procurement, I organized a team of Defense Department personnel to study defense development and procurement programs in England, France, and Germany in 1970. During our visits to these three countries, we learned that their governmental agencies were far less involved in the development of specifications for new defense programs than was typical in the United States. Government specifications for a particular European defense program, for example, were contained in a document approximately one-eighth of an inch thick. Specifications for a similar American program filled a document more than ten times as large.

Government officials in all three countries told us that they resist any attempts, from within Government or from industry, to increase the detail in defense program specifications. They believe, in the words of one official, that "the more complicated and detailed a contract specification, the weaker the position of the government in controlling costs." In other words, when there are lengthy and detailed program specifications to begin with, government and industry managers have more opportunities to propose contract changes, thereby weakening the incentives provided in the initial contract agreement.

The weapons acquisition cycle in England was described to us by senior industry executives, as follows. (1) The government sponsors a project study; e.g., a small paper study devoted to general research, generally involving less than 10 designers. (2) The government sponsors a feasibility study. This results in a proposal for a development program at a specified cost. The study is usually made by 12 to 18 specialists. (3) The government provides a holding contract for approximately three months, during which a firm works with the government to prepare an incentive contract. In a few cases the three-month holding period is extended; on rare occasions for as long as two years. While schedule, cost, and technical requirements are being planned for the program, government personnel are also evaluating the feasibility of the weapon system. (4) A contractor is chosen and an incentive contract is negotiated and signed.

Current European development and production programs involve far fewer personnel than defense programs in the United States. Firms in France and Germany made their personnel records available to us, and we learned that they typically hire one-fifth to one-tenth the number of people engaged by American contractors to perform similar tasks. For one large European aircraft development program, the number of employees directly involved ranged from 100 to 300. For similar aircraft development programs in this country, at least 1,000 employees would be directly involved. We noted that the family of French-built Mirage aircraft required design teams ranging from 25 to 230 engineers. In the United States a team of this size is required simply to prepare an aircraft design proposal.

R&D specialists in the U.S. Department of Defense give several reasons for the lower number of personnel required on European programs. Some believe that our defense programs are so amorphous that they can be expanded indefinitely by defense contractors or Defense Department managers to consume whatever funds are available or attainable. In addition, European programs are smaller because they rely on steady incremental improvements in weapon systems rather than periodic programs of major proportions.

Government and contractor officials in England, France, and Germany cited the scarcity of government funds for defense as a major factor in limiting program costs. Still another factor is the importance of the export market: to win foreign customers, system designs are kept relatively simple and costs low.

In all three countries, and particularly in France, the government involves industry in the development of program requirements in order to make certain that specifications take into account the current technological state-of-the-art as well as the limit on available government funds. One French contractor described the process: "At the beginning of a program, the French government says, 'We have approximately X francs available. Now you, Mr. Contractor, tell us what you can give us for that.' "

In the United States the amount of funds available for specific programs each year is within the control of the Congress. The following chapter describes the manner in which the Congress exercises this control.

NOTES TO CHAPTER VI

1. Richard J. Lorette, "The Relationship Between the Pressures on the System Program Director and the Growth of Weapon System Cost Estimates" (Boston: unpublished doctoral dissertation, Harvard Business School, 1969), Chapter III.
2. James Fergusen, "New Trends in Weapon Systems Contract Development: Definition of Hardware—The Way To Go," *Government Executive*, May 1969, p. 54.
3. *Cost Effectiveness Concepts* (Part I), Department of Defense Weapons Systems Management Center, Ohio, 1965.
4. Report of the Blue Ribbon Panel to the President and the Secretary of Defense on the Department of Defense, July 1, 1970, p. 68.
5. National Security Industrial Association, *Defense Acquisition Study, Final Report,* Washington, D.C., July 1, 1970.
6. Merton J. Peck and Frederic M. Scherer, *The Weapons Acquisition Process: An Economic Analysis* (Boston: Division of Research, Harvard Business School, 1962), p. 236.
7. Ibid., p. 248.
8. U.S. House of Representatives, a report of hearings before a subcommittee of the Committee on Government Operations, *Policy Changes in Weapon System Procurement,* 1970.
9. Ibid., p. 120.
10. Frederic M. Scherer, *The Weapons Acquisition Process: Economic Incentives* (Boston: Division of Research, Harvard Business School, 1964), preface, p. x.
11. U.S. House, Committee on Government Operations, *Policy Changes in Weapon System Procurement.*
12. David Packard, Deputy Secretary of Defense, address to the Aerospace Industries Association, Williamsburg, Virginia, May 22, 1969.
13. Excerpt from a letter from President Harry S. Truman to Secretary of Defense James Forrestal, provided by the Office of the Assistant Secretary of Defense (Installations and Logistics), 1947.

CHAPTER VII

Congress and the Weapons Acquisition Process

ARTICLE II OF THE CONSTITUTION stipulates that "the President shall be Commander-in-Chief of the Army and Navy of the United States." The so-called "War Power" clauses of the Constitution (Clauses 11–14) of Section 8, Article I give to Congress the authority "to declare war," "to raise and support Armies," "to provide and maintain a Navy," and "to make rules for the government and regulation of the land and naval forces." To insure civilian control of all military activity, Congress has over the years maintained and strengthened its right to determine the size of the armed forces and the kind and number of weapons and equipment produced for their use.

Before the Department of Defense can spend money for research, development, or production of weapon systems, Congress must: (1) grant it authority to carry on specific programs, and (2) appropriate funds to pay for each authorized activity. Two separate pieces of legislation are required. In its annual Defense Authorization Bill, Congress states which new programs, from among those proposed by the Defense Department, will be initiated, and which ongoing programs will be continued. In its annual Defense Appropriations Bill, Congress grants "obligational authority" to the Defense Department; that is, the authority to pay out funds, or to contract ("obligate" funds) for each of the activities approved in the Authorization Bill. Although the funds allotted for individual weapon systems approved in the Authorization Bill may be reduced or increased in the Appropriations Bill, no money may be appropriated for unauthorized weapon systems. Nor may Defense Department officials, military or civilian, initiate or continue unauthorized programs. During the course of the fiscal year, the Defense Department may, however, request Congress to authorize new or lapsed programs and to increase appropriations for programs already authorized.

THE CONGRESSIONAL COMMITTEE SYSTEM

Since Congress fulfills most of its major Constitutional responsibilities through its standing (permanent) committees, a very brief outline of the committee system as it relates to the defense industry is included here.

There are 17 standing committees in the Senate and 21 in the House of Representatives.[1]

Senate	*House of Representatives*
Aeronautical and Space Sciences	Agriculture
Agriculture and Forestry	Appropriations
Appropriations	Armed Services
Armed Services	Banking and Currency
Banking, Housing and Urban Affairs	District of Columbia
Commerce	Education and Labor
District of Columbia	Foreign Affairs
Finance	Government Operations
Foreign Relations	House Administration
Government Operations	Interior and Insular Affairs
Interior and Insular Affairs	Internal Security
Judiciary	Interstate and Foreign Commerce
Labor and Public Welfare	Judiciary
Post Office and Civil Service	Merchant Marine and Fisheries
Public Works	Post Office and Civil Service
Rules and Administration	Public Works
Veterans' Affairs	Rules
	Science and Astronautics
	Standards of Official Conduct
	Veterans' Affairs
	Ways and Means

In addition, there are nine joint Senate-House committees:

Atomic Energy
Congressional Operations
Defense Production
Economic
Federal Expenditures
Internal Revenue Taxation
Library
Navajo-Hopi Indian Administration
Printing

Each committee studies its area of responsibility through research and investigation carried on by committee members and staff assistants, and by conducting hearings. At least once a year each committee prepares legislation or recommendations for consideration by the full membership of the House and/or Senate. Budgets proposed by Federal agencies are also reviewed by the Appropriations Committees and Subcommittees of the House and Senate (e.g., the Defense Appropriations Subcommittees).

In each branch of Congress the majority party is awarded a majority of the seats on each committee. The minority party is traditionally represented on committees in rough proportion to its numerical strength in the House or Senate. Each Senator usually serves on three or four joint and/or standing committees, although some belong to as many as six or seven.[2] Most Congressmen serve on only two joint and/or standing committees; in some cases, three.[3] Although responsibility for committee assignments belongs to the full House and Senate, actual membership is determined by special assignment committees appointed by the Congressional leaders of each party. Senators and Congressmen actively pursue assignment to powerful committees such as the Armed Services Committees and Defense Appropriations Subcommittees. When Senator Allen Ellender was chairman of the Senate Appropriations Committee, for example, he also chose to head the Defense Appropriations Subcommittee. Major committees receive enough attention from the media to insure some measure of public exposure for their members. This is one of the factors considered by many members of Congress when they indicate committee preference.

The chairman of each committee is chosen annually and is always the Congressman or Senator of the majority party who has had the longest uninterrupted service on the committee. The chairman exercises considerable power within his committee. He controls committee agenda; chooses the chairmen and members of each subcommittee from the membership of the parent committee; decides whether or not to hold hearings on particular issues; decides when hearings will be held; and determines the style and pace of individual hearings. The chairman also has the right to represent the whole committee on the floor of the House or Senate. Perhaps the clearest indication of the chairman's influence is the voting record of committee members. A staff member of the House Armed Services Committee revealed that no more than five of the 40 members of the committee ever voted against the late Congressman Mendel Rivers when he was its chairman.

Chairmen also exercise control over committee activity through appointment of committee (or subcommittee) staff. This usually means that other committee members have access to the information gathered by the staff at the discretion of the chairman.

As a result of the seniority system, 11 of the most powerful Congressional committees were chaired by legislators from *four* states in 1972.[4]

Committee	*Chairman*
Senate Appropriations	Sen. Allen J. Ellender, D., Louisiana (age 81)
Senate Finance	Sen. Russell B. Long, D., Louisiana (age 53)
House Armed Services	Cong. F. Edward Hebert, D., Louisiana (age 70)
Senate Armed Services	Sen. John Stennis, D., Mississippi (age 70)
Senate Judiciary	Sen. James O. Eastland, D., Mississippi (age 67)
House Rules	Cong. William M. Colmer, D., Mississippi (est. age 70+)
Senate Foreign Relations	Sen. J. William Fulbright, D., Arkansas (age 67)
Senate Government Operations	Sen. John L. McClellan, D., Arkansas (age 75)
House Ways and Means	Cong. Wilbur D. Mills, D., Arkansas (age 62)
House Appropriations	Cong. George H. Mahon, D., Texas (age 71)
House Banking and Currency	Cong. Wright Patman, D., Texas (age 78)

Like other men of advancing age, Senators and Congressmen often succumb to physical and mental infirmities. A committee system which awards positions of power primarily on the basis of party and seniority does not, of course, take into account the health or stamina of its members, and those legislators who benefit from the seniority system, and their supporters, have been powerful enough to cut off movements toward reform.

In 1970, while serving as Assistant Secretary of the Army, I was invited to a meeting in the office of the chairman of a major Senate committee. The Senator was over 70 years old at the time. I was asked to be prepared to discuss the problems which were affecting a defense program located in the home state of the chairman. Several Congressmen from the same state were also invited. When we had all gathered, the Senator made a few introductory comments and thanked me for coming to his office. He then asked me to discuss the problems affecting the program and what could be done to maintain defense employment in his state. Almost as soon as I began to speak, the Senator fell asleep. The meeting lasted for approximately one hour. I directed my comments to the Congressmen and to the Senator's staff. Toward the end of the hour, the Senator awoke with a start, listened to the close of the discussion, and thanked me at length. He closed by saying that he knew I would do whatever I could to help the people in his state. When I left the office, the Senator's administrative assistant followed me. He assured me that the Senator's behavior was not a sign of personal animosity or a lack of interest in the program. The Senator "simply had a problem." Subsequently, I learned that the Senator frequently slept during committee hearings and meetings. Despite these lapses, he maintained a rigid control of committee operations and decisions by virtue of his seniority.

The four committees through which annual Defense Department budget requests are filtered to Congress are the Armed Services Committees and the

Appropriations Committees of the Senate and House of Representatives. In early January the President submits his State of the Union message and Federal Budget to Congress. The end of the fiscal year occurs on June 30. Sometime between these two dates Congress must authorize and appropriate defense funds for the next fiscal year, July 1 to June 30.

Occasionally, the new fiscal year begins before defense bills are passed. Congress then passes a "continuing appropriations" bill, which allows the Department of Defense to spend funds at a rate equal to, or less than, (1) the rate most recently in effect, or (2) the rate under consideration—whichever is lower. Measures providing for continuing appropriations always have time limits, ranging from a few weeks to several months. These time limits may be extended several times. In 1970, for example, a continuing appropriations measure was extended twice.

Although authorization and appropriation of defense funds are closely allied, there is, in theory, a good reason for dealing with them in separate committees. Ideally, members of the committees which authorize defense expenditures, the House and Senate Armed Services Committees, have specialized knowledge and expertise in the area of national defense; military operations; weapon requirements, technology, and production; and the operations of the Department of Defense. They should therefore be able to evaluate Defense Department budget requests on the basis of their own in-depth understanding of defense needs, as well as the back-up work of an expert staff.

Defense Appropriations Committees of the House and Senate, on the other hand, must reconcile requests from all Federal agencies with actual tax monies that Congress will make available during the next fiscal year. Each appropriations subcommittee, then, must study those programs which have been authorized by Congress with an eye to the best possible use of tax money. Members of the Defense Appropriations Subcommittees have, in theory, not only a broad understanding of national defense needs, but are capable of analyzing the management of ongoing programs and the accuracy of current budget proposals.

After each subcommittee reports to the full House or Senate Appropriations Committee, members of the parent committees measure and compare the nation's health, education, defense, transportation, and all other needs and prepare a budget which will balance these combined needs. In actual fact, most bills reported out of the Defense Subcommittees are passed on intact to the floor of the House or Senate.

THE NATURE OF FEDERAL DEFENSE BUDGETING

Before examining the nature of the hearings conducted by the Armed Services and Appropriations Committees, it seems appropriate to consider the concept of budgeting as it applies to Federal agencies such as the Department of Defense. This is often misunderstood by people outside the Government. The layman uses the term "budget" to designate a plan or schedule for spending money that he already has, or has a commitment to receive. The Federal Government's use of the term refers not only to a plan or schedule to spend money, but also to annual requests to the Congress for funds by individual Federal agencies. During annual Congressional budget hearings, representatives of each Federal agency present and defend their funding requests; that is, they attempt to "sell" the Congress on the necessity for a specified amount of money for use in the following fiscal year. The budgeting function within Federal agencies is comparable to the marketing function in commercial firms. The success of the marketing/budgeting activity has a major impact on the amount of money that will be made available for the activities of the firm/ Federal agency. The Defense Department is naturally sensitive to the subtleties of the marketing/budgeting process and is engaged year round in some phase of preparation for budget hearings by the Congress.

At any given time the Defense Department is actually involved with three defense budgets. It is (1) spending, or obligating, the money appropriated by Congress for the current fiscal year; (2) preparing for Congressional hearings or presenting testimony before Congressional committees for the next fiscal year defense budget; and (3) planning and preparing a recommended budget for the fiscal year to begin two years hence. For example, in March 1972 the Department was using funds from the fiscal 1972 budget; presenting testimony to House and Senate committees for the recommended budget for fiscal 1973; and planning and preparing a recommended budget for fiscal 1974.

The annual defense budget that is presented and defended before Congressional committees takes shape during the 12 to 18 month period prior to the hearings. Involved in the planning and preparation are Army, Navy, and Air Force staffs; the Secretaries and Assistant Secretaries of the Army, Navy, and Air Force and their staffs; and the Secretary and Assistant Secretaries of Defense and their staffs. These officials determine defense needs in part on the basis of requests from field units. Since several years elapse before military field units actually acquire the weapons and equipment requested from the Defense Department and, two or three years later, authorized by Congress, these units must predict their needs several years in advance. This poses serious problems for military organizations whose needs change as weapons technology evolves.

Program requests prepared by field units are submitted for review and revision to successively higher levels of management within the military services before they reach the Office of the Secretary of Defense. During this refining process, competing requirements for funds must be evaluated, and cutbacks and cancellations of some programs are inevitable. Since there is always a limit on the amount of money Congress will appropriate, however generous their inclinations, the annual budget proposals for individual programs are often reduced in size by the military service headquarters so that as many programs as possible will be authorized and funded for each service. To get the most out of defense funding, this "foot in the door" technique has proven highly effective. For once any program is funded, history shows that Congress can usually be prevailed upon to keep it going—regardless of cost, schedule, or performance irregularities.

A major defense contractor discussed the side effects of the "foot in the door" policy.

> On the [name] program we had a seven-month gap in production caused by the failure of the service to budget funds for us in the 1971 budget. They told us that they wanted to continue our program but that they had to skip a year in the funding in order to introduce some other production program in the budget. This means that we have to stretch out the 1970 contract to make it last throughout the 1971 production period. That is going to cost the Government a lot of money in the long run.

In a March 15, 1971, edition of the *Washington Post,* Senator Thomas J. McIntyre (D., New Hampshire), Chairman of the Senate Subcommittee on Defense Research and Development, commented on the "foot in the door" approach.

> We had been unable either to eliminate or substantially affect a single program getting ready to emerge from the far end of the pipeline. I have discovered, much to my own frustration, that the present viewpoint seems to be that we are committed to a system's ultimate production as soon as we have sunk virtually any money into it. This is an attitude we will have to change.
>
> There is no way, even with the savings which an end to our involvement in Vietnam will produce, that we could avoid a substantial increase in the total defense budget if we went into production on all the major systems now in the R&D pipeline.

At the beginning of the calendar year, legislative liaison officers serving the military services attempt to determine the dates of authorization and appropriations hearings. Although hearings usually begin in March, actual dates are frequently changed as committee chairmen respond to events in their home districts and official business of the House and Senate.

AUTHORIZATION HEARINGS

The Armed Services Committees' hearings on authorization are divided into two parts. Initially, "posture hearings" are scheduled for each committee, during which military and civilian officials at the highest levels of the Pentagon set the stage for specific budget requests. Their statements include descriptions of past and present Defense Department performance, plans for the future, and general defense policies and goals. Congressional attendance for posture hearings is usually much higher than for any subsequent hearing. Testimony is given by the Secretary of Defense, the Chairman of the Joint Chiefs of Staff, the Director of Defense Research and Engineering, and the Secretaries and Chiefs of Staff for each military service. Although posture hearings are closed to the public, an unclassified version of the Secretary of Defense's statement is often available through the Government Printing Office.

During the second phase of authorization hearings, specific budget requests are presented and discussed. Testimony is given by Assistant Secretaries of Defense and of the Army, Navy, and Air Force, as well as their military counterparts and the Deputy Chiefs of Staff. During the authorization hearings, as well as later during the appropriations hearings, each service is considered separately, and research and development programs for each service are separated from procurement programs.

Civilian Pentagon officials who testify during committee hearings require three or more weeks of intensive preparation. An Assistant Secretary of Installations and Logistics, for example, will be expected to present budget proposals for his service's procurement programs. In preparation, he must review 25 to 50 major programs and be ready to discuss their current status, their importance to the service, their funding requirements, and the effects on the service if specific programs are not authorized. He is accompanied to the hearings by the procurement budget officer (a general or admiral) from his branch of the service. This budget officer spends most of his time during the year preparing for the hearings by keeping abreast of performance on all service programs. Assistant Secretaries are also accompanied by ten or more military and civilian specialists, who are ready to answer technical questions raised by Congressional committee members.

An Assistant Secretary's statement is in summary form. He will give total budget requests for aircraft, missiles, ships, ammunition, tactical vehicles, and/or combat vehicles, etc.; compare current estimates with previous budgets; explain budget needs; and may discuss controversial programs in some detail. The procurement budget officer will discuss budget requests item by item. This may take a few hours or a few days. During all testimony, witnesses may be questioned at any time by committee members.

Since 1959 Congress has broadened its authority over the acquisition process through the passage of seven laws:

> 1959—Public Law 86-149 requires authorization for the procurement of aircraft, missiles, and naval vessels.
> 1962—Public Law 87-436 requires authorization for all research development, testing, or evaluation of aircraft, missiles, and naval vessels.
> 1963—Public Law 88-174 requires authorization for all research, development, testing, or evaluation carried on by the Department of Defense.
> 1965—Public Law 89-37 requires authorization for the procurement of tracked combat vehicles.
> 1967—Public Law 90-168 requires annual authorization of the personnel strengths of each of the Reserve components as a prior condition for the appropriation of funds for the pay and allowances for the Reserve components.
> 1969—Public Law 91-121 requires authorization for the procurement of other weapons to or for the use of any armed force of the United States. (Essentially this covers heavy, medium, and light artillery; anti-aircraft artillery; rifles; machine guns; mortars; small arms weapons; and any crew-fired piece using fixed ammunition.)
> 1970—Public Law 91-441 requires authorization for the procurement of torpedoes and related support equipment; also requires authorization of the average annual active duty personnel strength for each component of the Armed Forces as a condition precedent to the appropriation of funds for this purpose.

Separate Defense Authorization Bills are passed by the House and Senate upon completion of the Armed Services Committees' hearings. A joint Senate-House conference committee, appointed by the respective committee chairmen, reconciles differences between the two bills and both houses then adopt the Compromise Defense Authorization Bill. The authorization process is sometimes amazingly brief. In 1970, for example, a $21.3 billion Defense Authorization Bill was released to the House by its Armed Services Committee two days before debate began. The House took only three days to debate and pass the bill.[5]

APPROPRIATION HEARINGS

Hearings by Defense Appropriations Subcommittees begin when the Authorization Bill is passed, occasionally before. The Defense Appropriations Bill is divided into 31 categories:

Army
 Military Personnel
 Reserve Personnel
 Operation and Maintenance
 Procurement of Equipment and Missiles
 Research, Development, Test and Evaluation
 Military Construction
 Military Construction, Army National Guard
 Military Construction, Army Reserve
Navy
 Military Personnel
 Reserve Personnel
 Operation and Maintenance
 Procurement of Aircraft and Missiles
 Shipbuilding and Conversion
 Other Procurement
 Research, Development, Test and Evaluation
 Military Construction
 Military Construction, Naval Reserve
Marine Corps
 Military Personnel
 Reserve Personnel
 Operation and Maintenance
 Procurement, Marines
Air Force
 Military Personnel
 Reserve Personnel
 Operation and Maintenance
 Aircraft Procurement
 Missile Procurement
 Other Procurement
 Research, Development, Test and Evaluation
 Military Construction
 Military Construction, Air National Guard
 Military Construction, Air Force Reserve

Research and development funds appropriated by Congress must be obligated within three years and procurement appropriations within two years.

"Procurement" and "research and development" are not mutually exclusive categories, however. At least 10% to 15% of the work on major programs can be defined in either category. Tasks such as tooling, building of prototypes, production engineering, testing, and a variety of others are periodically re-defined by the Defense Department and defense contractors. Their decisions are based on the availability of funds and the likelihood that Congress will appropriate funds in one category or the other. For many defense programs, funds in the gray area amount to more than $100 million.

Appropriations Subcommittee proceedings may last for weeks or months. The witnesses are, for the most part, the same officials who appeared before the Armed Services Committees, and they usually present the same testimony. This means that the Secretary of Defense, the Chairman of the Joint Chiefs of Staff, the Director of Defense Research and Engineering, the Assistant Secre-taries of Defense, Chiefs of Staff and their Deputies, Secretaries and Assistant Secretaries of individual military services, and other military and civilian officials within the Defense Department may give the same testimony before four separate committees. Despite this lengthy exposure to Congressional committees, Pentagon witnesses are seldom questioned in depth. The "hard" questions—questions which might help Congress to determine which new and ongoing defense programs are essential to national defense, which programs are redundant or nonessential, and which programs should be restructured, cut back, or canceled because of poor management or faulty performance—are rarely asked.

CONGRESSIONAL PREPARATION FOR HEARINGS

One reason for their superficial performance is the committee members' lack of preparation. Interviews with several Congressional staff persons re-vealed that the Congressmen and Senators serving on authorization and appro-priations committees rarely read the material gathered by their staffs in prepa-ration for the hearings. After one committee meeting a member of the com-mittee staff asked me:

> Did you see the members flipping through the pages of the back-up material while you were reading your statement? Well, that's because none of them had taken the time to read the material prior to this meet-ing. When you sent over that material two weeks ago, I tried to get the Congressmen to take the time to read it, in view of all the attention being given to defense this year. Hell, I struck out completely. It turns out to be a big enough job just to get a few of them to come to the hearings. They just aren't interested.

Another staff member told us that he "could not get the committee members interested in holding the line on unit costs of equipment, or encouraging the military to slow down the production decisions until R&D problems are solved. A general comes over here and they pat him on the shoulder and say, 'How are things going, General?' If the general says 'O.K.,' then they are relaxed. The committee members do no advance homework for these hearings. They seem to be more interested in other matters."

An illustration of this attitude occurred during the 1971 House Armed Services Committee hearings on Army procurement. Under discussion was the AH-1G Cobra helicopter program. In the five years preceding 1971, this committee had authorized several hundred million dollars for the Army to purchase Cobra helicopters from Bell Aircraft Company. Well in advance of the 1971 hearings, the Army had provided the committee with several pages of pictures and descriptive material on the Cobra. During the hearings, however, one Congressman appeared confused by the budget request. After indicating that he did not understand the discussion, he finally asked, "What is a Cobra?"

Upon completion of committee hearings and deliberation, Defense Appropriations Bills move from Defense Appropriations Subcommittees to their parent committees and thence to the floor of the House and Senate. Following debate, each body passes its own bill. If there is a difference between the two bills, as is usually the case, a joint Senate-House Conference Committee prepares a compromise bill. This is eventually passed by both houses, and the Department of Defense can make its plans for the fiscal year.

During the fiscal year, changes in specific program requirements sometimes make it necessary for the Defense Department to obtain additional funds, or to move existing funds from one program to another ("reprogramming"). At this point, the Department may request permission from Congress to reprogram funds, may request supplementary appropriations from Congress, or may make use of an Emergency Fund. When funds are reprogrammed, the size of the total budget does not change. Funds are merely shifted from one program to another. If reprogramming involves a relatively small amount of money, the Defense Department may notify Congress after the fact. In most instances, however, Congressional hearings are necessary. Occasionally, the reprogramming technique is used to obtain funds for a program which Congress has refused to authorize during the regular budgeting process. The supplementary appropriations process requires the same Congressional hearings and legislation as the annual authorization and appropriation process. Congress is strongly averse to the use of this procedure in peacetime. In times of international conflict or severe economic stress, however, it is common.

The Emergency Fund is included by Congress in its appropriations for research and development. It is under the direct control of the Secretary of Defense. He may use it in situations demanding immediate action when there is no time for consultation with Congress. The fund usually exceeds $100 million each year.

So much publicity surrounds House and Senate defense hearings that the casual observer might assume that Congress exercises considerable control over the final defense budget. In fact, however, the budget recommended by the Department of Defense is affected very slightly by Congressional debate. Congressional reductions in defense funding proposals over the two decades 1950–1970 often amounted to less than 2%. Between 1961 and 1971 the reduction was always less than 5%, with the exception of 1970 when it reached 7%. In 1970 lengthy hearings and debate in both chambers of Congress led to a reduction of only 3%.

An analysis of 75 defense programs for which authorization and appropriation of defense funds was requested in 1971 provides an illustration of Congressional impact on the budget. The 75 programs are listed in Table VII-1. Table VII-2 shows that in 1971 the Armed Services Committees reduced authorization requests by 2% in the House and by 9% in the Senate. The Conference Committee compromised with a reduction of 5%. This is a familiar pattern: the smaller reduction is usually made by the House and the Conference Committee usually splits the difference between the House and Senate bills. The appropriation process has a slightly greater impact on the final budget. In 1971 the House reduced the budget proposed by the Defense Department by 10%. The reduction made by the Senate was 11%. The Conference Committee settled on a 10% reduction (Table VII-2).

Of the 75 defense programs for which funds were requested in 1971, Congress approved 41 as requested or with increases. Seven programs received no funding. The remaining 27 programs (Table VII-3) experienced reductions ranging from 2% to 83%.

Most of the individual Senators and Congressmen who must each year define priorities in defense spending and translate defense policy into actual funding are men and women with good intentions. But to make effective analyses of multibillion dollar budget requests requires skill and time. It is easier to defer to the judgment of military "experts." The annual defense budget represents Federal expenditures of more than $80 million for each working day. Many Senators and Congressmen are overwhelmed, even intimidated, by the magnitude of the requests and by the confidence and apparent competence of Defense Department witnesses. Most ask as few questions as possible in order to hide their unfamiliarity with advanced technological and financial operations. When questions are prepared for them by their staffs, they often have trouble understanding the questions they find themselves read-

Table VII-1. 75 Defense Programs for Which Authorization and Appropriation of Defense Funds Were Requested in 1971

PROCUREMENT

Aircraft	*Missiles*	
Air Force	*Air Force*	*Other Army*
F-111F	Maverick	M60A1 tank
A-7D	Falcon	M60A1E2 tank
F-4E	SRAM	M561 Gamma Goat
RF-4C	Minuteman	M551 Sheridan ARAAV
UH-1H		M-16
C-9A	*Navy/Marine Corps*	*Ships*
C-5A	Condor	CVAN-70 Lead-time items
International Fighter	Sparrow	DLG Guided missile
	Hawk (MC)	Frigate conversions
		Poseidon conversions
Navy/Marine Corps	*Army*	DLGN-38
S-3A	Safeguard ABM	DD-963 Destroyer
E-2C	TOW	LHA
A-6A	HAWK	Nuclear Attack Subs
A-6E	LANCE	
EA-6B		*Other Navy*
A-7E		Sonobuoys:
F-4J		Julie/Jezebel
P-3C		SSQ-47
T-2C		DIFAR
TA-4E		Torpedoes:
F-14A		Mark 46
		Mark 48
Army		
CH-47		
UH-1H		
OH-58		
AH-1G		

RESEARCH AND DEVELOPMENT

Army	*Air Force*	*Navy/Marine Corps*
MBT-70	AWACS	F-14C
Cheyenne	B-1	HARPOON
SAM-D	F-15	Point Defense System
HAWK (improved)	AX	LAMPS
Advanced BMD	ABRES	Poseidon
LANCE	LIT	ULMS
HLH	SRAM-SCAD	AEGIS
	Minuteman III	
	CONUS interceptor	

Source: *Armed Forces Journal*, February 1, 1971.

TABLE VII-2. 75 R&D AND PROCUREMENT PROGRAMS: 1971

	Total in Millions	Percent
Administration Request	$9,435.1	100
Authorization		
House	$9,282.6	98
Senate	8,625.6	91
Conference Committee	8,968.1	95
Appropriations		
House	$8,542.0	90
Senate	8,452.9	89
Conference Committee	8,554.5	90

SOURCE: *Armed Forces Journal*, February 1, 1971.

TABLE VII-3. PERCENTAGE CONGRESSIONAL REDUCTION FOR
27 MAJOR DEFENSE PROGRAMS: 1971

Percent Reduction	No. of Programs
1–10%	8
11–30	8
31–50	6
51–70	3
71–90	2
91–99	0

SOURCE: *Armed Forces Journal*, February 1, 1971.

ing and the answers they receive. Called upon to evaluate issues beyond their comprehension, they rely on their superficial impressions of Pentagon witnesses, the advice of military and industry lobbyists, and the recommendations of their staffs.

During the 1970 debate on the C-5A program, several Congressmen and Senators openly admitted that they accepted the judgment of Air Force personnel uncritically, since their own knowledge was inadequate. Senator George Murphy (R., California) said: "I am relying on the judgment of the experts that this is a good airplane." [6] Senator Margaret Chase Smith (R., Maine) commented: "Of course, I can only take the word of those who know more about it than I do." [7] Congressman Richard Ichord (D., Missouri) pointed out that there were "so many variables involved here in making the computation that the final figures, to say the least, are quite confusing to me." At the close of the debate, Congressman Allard Lowenstein (D., New York) expressed his feelings:

> I speak with some sadness as this comes to a conclusion. I love this place. To be elected to it is easily the greatest honor I shall expect to attain. Yet much that happens here leaves me feeling that we are not

conducting ourselves as we should . . . we have greater obligations to the country than has been shown by our behavior today.[8]

In 1971 I asked several presidents and vice presidents of large defense firms to describe their attempts to discuss their programs with members of Congress. Industry representatives are often called upon to testify at formal committee hearings. In addition, they attempt to win support for their programs through informal contacts. Here are some typical comments:

> I briefed Senator [name] and Congressman [name] recently on some technical programs. When I finished, they thanked me very much but indicated that they did not understand what I was talking about, but thought it was nice that someone would take the time to tell them what was going on.

> * * * * *

> I went to see Senator [name] and talked to him about the need for him to support the introduction of [a new weapon system]. At the end of the meeting, the Senator said: "Bill, I really enjoyed the conversation. I didn't understand it, but I enjoyed it. This is the first time anyone has come to talk to me about possibilities for the future. I always find out about things after the fact—when they are already under way."

Congressional staff members experience many of the problems that frustrate the Congressmen and Senators they serve. They do not have ready access to sources of information used by the Pentagon.[9] They are usually incapable of determining whether Pentagon witnesses correctly assess security gaps. They are often not qualified to judge whether a proposed system will successfully fulfill its mission. They are unable to rule on the accuracy of costs estimated for new weapon systems, or the reasonableness of cost growth for ongoing programs. One defense company official made a complaint that was repeated by other industry executives:

> We find ourselves repeatedly trying to explain to Congressional staffs over and over what is happening. The Congressional staffs are inadequate—they often have little or no technical background. We often have to stop in the middle of a briefing and explain what an electro-optical system is. With their present level of knowledge, the Congress should not be faced with detailed technical problems such as whether to have Titanium fuel lines. As it is, they can be snowed by a good technical pitch.
> If Congress is going to get into the details of programs, then they should have adequate, capable staffs. When a Congressional staff member comes in to see us, we have to start from scratch. We say, "This is the end

where the radar is positioned," and they say, "What is radar?" The level
of sophistication is very low.

Size of committee staffs, rather than a lack of dedication or hard work,
is the fundamental problem. The Senate Armed Services Committee is currently limited by Congress to 14 staff members.[10] The House Armed Services
Committee is limited to a staff of 13.[11] In 1971 each of these committee staffs
was expected to analyze more than 75 major defense programs. Budget requests ranged from $3 million to hundreds of millions of dollars. A total of
more than $70 billion was at stake.

In an address to the Armed Services Procurement Regulations Institute on
September 29, 1969, Congressman William S. Moorhead (D., Pennsylvania)
analyzed the need for improved staff and back-up resources.

> Congress is inhibited in at least two ways from carrying out its Consti-
> tutional duties, but both of these could be overcome by an informed
> public.
>
> The first inhibition is the lack of adequate staff and supporting re-
> sources to examine the military budget properly. Second is the inherent
> problems of the committee system.
>
> Because Congress has the unpopular task of imposing taxes, Congress
> is reluctant to spend money on its own operations even when such ex-
> penditures could save the taxpayers money. The amount of justification
> that both of these staffs (House Armed Services Committee and Defense
> Appropriations Subcommittee) has to analyze is incredible. However,
> there is a professional staff of only nine in Armed Services and only six in
> Defense Appropriations that handles this task.
>
> Another example of inadequate back-up resources, the Congress has
> provided over 4,300 computers for the executive branch and none—ex-
> cept for housekeeping chores—for the legislative branch.
>
> Under these conditions, when the military budget—totaling over $80
> billion—comes before the Congress for authorization and appropriation,
> it can be readily seen that Congress is almost hopelessly handicapped in
> obtaining a thoroughgoing, independent analysis of the Pentagon's pro-
> posal.
>
> I propose that we in the Congress start considering seriously our own
> allocation of resources. I would contend that one of the best investments
> we could make is in the expansion and upgrading of our committee staffs
> and a substantial but reasoned investment in terms of back-up resources.
>
> Obviously, all of this is going to cost money, and it is the natural reac-
> tion of appropriations committees to be somewhat wary of new expendi-
> tures. But one systems analyst, or one budgetary expert, who draws a
> salary of $20,000 a year, may in the end save the Government a million

dollars. That is the kind of investment that all of us in Congress should be able to endorse.

Some committee chairmen have tried to improve their staff resources. Early in 1971 Senator Stennis reorganized the staff serving the Senate Armed Services Committee. When he proposed that $95,000 be added to the budget for the work of the committee's staff, he was strongly reprimanded by Senator Ellender, chairman of the Senate Appropriations Committee and the Defense Appropriations Subcommittee. Senator Ellender stated that too much money was already being spent for analysis and investigation. To support his argument, he cited the cost underrun experienced in the previous year by Senator Stennis' committee:

> Did the committee consider the fact that last year the Armed Services Committee was allotted $300,000 and used only $263,000 so that there was a balance of $37,000 remaining? The fact is, and I repeat, we are providing $80,000 more than was spent last year and that, it seems to me, is ample money to provide for those necessary to do the work.[12]

To lighten their work load and to give a semblance of expertise to committee hearings, committee staff often solicit questions from the Pentagon. These are then read by Congressmen or Senators during hearings. The Pentagon, of course, welcomes the opportunity to provide questions that will enable Pentagon witnesses to win favor for budget requests. Naturally, planted questions do not raise controversial issues. A military officer who had at one time been a legislative liaison officer commented on the pervasiveness of question-planting: "Much of my time in that job was spent writing questions and statements for the House and Senate members of the committees to use during hearings or to use in their public statements and speech making."

A committee staff member told me that members of his committee had requested that the Pentagon accompany prepared questions with their answers. In 1969, however, this practice lost favor. Some confusion arose during a hearing in that year when a committee member read both the prepared question and its answer.

A staff member told us of a Congressman who caused some consternation when he returned to a hearing after having several cocktails at lunch. He was usually able to read reasonably well from the text prepared in advance by the Pentagon, as long as he kept his eyes on the script. On this day, however, he felt particularly confident and departed from his text. He asked a rambling question about an item in the budget and glanced only occasionally at the prepared question. A young major who served as a Pentagon back-up witness was giving testimony. He tried to recall which of the prepared questions was being referred to by the Congressman during his rambling discourse. Finally, after an extended pause, the Congressman asked, "What's the matter, Major, don't you know the answer to the question?" The major gazed thoughtfully at him for a moment and then replied, "Sir, I believe I know the answer, but I am not sure I understand the question."

Many of the questions asked of witnesses by Congressmen and Senators, other than those prepared by the committee staff or the Pentagon, are of a very general nature or refer to a relatively minor aspect of the proposal under discussion. During the Pentagon presentation of a $2 billion research and development budget for one of the military services, one Congressman stopped the testimony to indicate his displeasure with a $900,000 request for research into food service. He stated that he was familiar with the Defense Department's food service and knew "the cause of a major part of the problem." He continued: "We don't need a $900,000 research project to find out about it. The problem with the Defense Department's food service is that you don't serve grits! If you served grits, a major part of your food service problem would disappear. And you don't need $900,000 to find that out." This was the Congressman's total contribution to the discussion. The Pentagon witness was jolted by this attack on an item which represented 1/2000th of the total research and development budget request. He had expected a number of questions on crucial features of the budget proposal but was unprepared to handle questions on food service.

When committee members do ask questions that require complex answers, they often seem restless if the witness attempts to answer the question with the care it deserves. Several committee staff members mentioned that most Congressmen and Senators prefer a quick, simple answer, even if accuracy is sacrificed.

Pentagon witnesses new to the Congressional committee process are usually discouraged when they discover that committee members have not taken time to prepare for a discussion of multibillion dollar programs. More experienced Pentagon witnesses, however, have learned to take advantage of committee members' ignorance and lack of interest, and are able to skirt issues which might compromise their budget requests. A program may be behind schedule; a weapon system may not be performing as predicted; a multibillion dollar program may need more funds because of inaccurate cost estimates. But no Pentagon or industry witness is likely to mention such problems if they are not raised by committee members. When these problems reach such magnitude that they cannot be hidden, members of Congress are quick to blame the Defense Department for its lack of candor but seldom question the manner in which programs are evaluated by Congress itself.

In most cases, Pentagon officials attempt to present honest testimony but are unable to explain, in terms comprehensible to laymen, the complex reasons for program difficulties or the steps that will lead to solutions. Very often, however, the Pentagon decides that program problems are "transitory" and that forthright discussion will lead to a cutback or cancellation of funds. If a branch of the military believes the program to be essential to the service and/or to national defense, facts will be withheld from Congress as long as possible.

Pentagon witnesses are often wary of those few Senators and Congressmen who question them at length about programs experiencing difficulty. They believe that committee members use controversial programs to gain publicity and are primarily concerned with re-election, caring little about the problems of national defense. As is the case within the Pentagon itself, many officers are critical of the concept of civilian control of the military. They doubt that civilians—elected or appointed—have the ability to evaluate military activity. Their experience with Congressional committees strengthens this conviction.

The inadequacy of the committee process encourages the Pentagon practice most often scored by critics in Congress—the presentation of unrealistic cost and performance estimates for development programs. For many years Pentagon officials have tried to convince Congress that they can estimate the cost of large research and development programs to within 10% to 15% of actual figures. In fact, however, the Defense Department has never had this capability, and skyrocketing program costs have finally weakened their credibility. So far, Congress has been unwilling to admit that its own lack of capability is at least partly responsible for this Pentagon tactic.

Another aspect of the appropriation process that affects Pentagon strategy is its one-year-at-a-time approach. If, for example, the decision to proceed with the next phase of a particular program cannot be made until the middle of the next fiscal year, Pentagon officials must decide whether (1) to wait until the following year to request funds for the next phase of the program (thereby experiencing the wasteful costs of program stretch-out); or (2) to attempt to convince Congress that no risks are involved in funding the next phase of the program ahead of time. If Congress votes to provide the requested funds, the defense organization will probably spend the money whether or not it is finally needed in order to avoid Congressional criticism.

The detailed nature of annual authorization bills also affects defense spending. The Pentagon must submit very specific budget proposals each year, prepared long before programs actually get under way. Once in progress, program requirements usually change. All too often it is considered safer to spend available money for items that have been authorized rather than to seek permission to reprogram funds. The president of a major defense firm described the problem:

Planning and defending the defense budget has to occur so far in advance that when it comes time to spend the money, the services do so whether they need the product or not. Since reprogramming is difficult to accomplish and is frowned upon by the Congress, the tendency is to buy what was originally requested.

Every industry executive interviewed during our study was highly critical of the system of planning in one-year segments. Two comments are typical:

It is not until the fiscal year in which we work that we find out that we will get 20% to 25% less than we had been led to believe we would receive, from our discussions with the project manager.

* * * * *

On production contracts, Congress appropriates funds each year, and a company must be prepared to do the minimum, but be able to do more on a program in case a higher level of funds is appropriated. This is often highly inefficient. For example, on the [name] project we could make significant savings if we could plan further ahead than one year for production quantities.

The inflexibility of the one-year budgeting system has had an unusual effect on the Congressional attitude toward organizations that do not spend their entire appropriations. Such agencies are usually penalized. Specifically, the Congressional review of an organization's budget request in the following year will be much more strenuous than usual. The organization's budget will probably be reduced by the amount it failed to spend in the preceding year. As a result, Pentagon officials urge defense organizations to spend every dollar appropriated to them for the year. Prior to 1971 official notices were sent to all senior Government personnel during April or May, reminding them to use all their funds before June 30.

Firms doing business with the Government send marketing representatives to various buying offices during March, April, and May to determine which agencies will have "excess" money on June 30. Such agencies then are sent proposals for research, development, and study contracts that will help them absorb their extra funds.

We asked a Congressional staff member why Congress has this punitive attitude. We were told that "the Congress wishes to teach them a lesson, not to request any more funds than they are certain will be consumed." When we pointed out that this attitude could stem efforts to improve efficiency and reduce costs, the staff member explained that Congress is not interested in reductions below the amounts appropriated. In his opinion, Congressmen believe that when a military organization fails to spend its full appropriation, the voting public thinks that Congress has been over-generous.

An example of activities undertaken to insure that all budgeted funds are spent was described in a *Washington Post* article by Morton Mintz, on March 29, 1972:

> *Washington.*—The Navy's top admiral urged key commands last month to hurry up and spend $400 million by June 30 lest their budget for the year starting July 1 be slashed by Congress, it was disclosed yesterday on capital hill.
>
> Admiral Elmo R. Zumwalt, chief of Naval Operations, made the appeal on Feb. 9 in an unclassified message to Admiral Isaac C. Kidd, chief of Navy materiel, and sent information copies to nine other top officers.
>
> Senator William Proxmire (D-Wis.), saying he was "informed" that Zumwalt was carrying out policy for all of the armed services made "at the very highest level of government," obtained the Zumwalt directive and revealed it at a hearing of his Joint Economic Subcommittee.
>
> Proxmire also produced a memo of Feb. 18 in which the Navy Ships Systems Command, seeking to implement the Zumwalt directive, listed specific ideas for "expenditure acceleration."
>
> The senator charged that the "shocking" memos reveal that the military is doing its best to "spend, spend, spend" and, as shown by the $38 billion budget deficit, is winning the battle against those who try to economize.
>
> The Zumwalt memo exposes a desire to "get rid of money" and "play games" with the taxpayers and Congress, and can no more be justified by the Defense Department than it could by the Agriculture or Commerce Departments, Proxmire said.
>
> But Admiral Kidd said that the Zumwalt directive could save money for the taxpayers in the long run, especially because inflation will make postponed purchases cost more later. He insisted that the memo has in no way inhibited his determination to assure that funds are spent "properly and . . . correctly."
>
> Zumwalt said in the directive that President Nixon, in his January budget message, had set revised Navy "outlay targets" for Fiscal 1972 at least $400 million higher than the "targets" set in the original 1972 budget a year earlier.
>
> Zumwalt went on to say that he "fully appreciated" the difficulty of achieving such a great increase in spending in the remaining months of Fiscal 1972. But, he said, in cryptic Navy language: ". . . importance of avoiding shortfall in meeting newly established FY 72 targets to avoid resultant adverse effects on anticipated FY 1973 outlay ceilings dictate

need for top management attention. Anticipate any shortfall in FY 72
outlay target could be translated into program loss under FY 73 ceiling."

Federal agencies sometimes spend funds at the end of the year for stock-
piling. An Assistant Secretary told us that he had received a call from a
superior regarding a program for which Congress was not expected to appropriate funds in the following year. This program, to continue, would soon
require the purchase of a quantity of crucial items. Without them, the
program would have to cease operations. The senior official asked the Assistant Secretary to use excess funds to stockpile the items. Then, if Congress did
not provide the necessary appropriation, the Department could draw the items
from stockpile and keep the program alive for another year without authorization. Occasionally, the legal niceties of the authorization process are ignored.
While this is not a common practice, it is followed for those programs considered high priority by the administration, with little regard for Congressional
approval.

DEFENSE DEPARTMENT STRATEGIES

Over the years, the Defense Department has developed a number of other
strategies to deal with an unpredictable Congress. On every level of management, from a program management office to the Office of the Secretary of Defense, the common goal is to deflect controversy and to attract Federal funds.
The Pentagon is well aware of Congressional ambivalence toward defense
spending. Many members of Congress suspend their critical faculties when
listening to the prestigious members of the military who appear before them
in hearings or engage them in private lobbying attempts. On the other hand,
many members of Congress would like to trim spending whenever it seems
justifiable.

In the absence of sustained investigation and qualified analysis, these two
attitudes are difficult to reconcile. The easiest course is to cut off funds for
those programs whose financial or technical problems have surfaced in the
press or during hearings. In rebuttal, the Pentagon attempts to win the support
of Senators and Congressmen whose constituents will be affected by cutbacks
or cancellations. Industry spokesmen join the battle. But if direct tactics do
not work, the Pentagon may turn to more subtle "games." The five listed here
were each used at least twice during my four years in the Pentagon.

Game #1: Our friends on the Senate staff tell us that committee members believe we have spent too much on research and development for
Program X. They say we are not likely to obtain additional funds, even

though the R&D tasks are still incomplete. To take care of this problem, we will redefine the remaining work as Advanced Production Engineering, thereby giving Congress the idea that production is under way. This strategy will work because we asked for, and obtained, some APE funds last year, before we found that the program was not yet ready to enter production. If we *don't* ask for APE funds this year, we lose out on two counts. First, we won't obtain the funds we need to continue R&D. Second, we raise a red flag that something is wrong because they will be expecting a request for either R&D or APE funds. No request may mean an end to the entire program.

Game #2: Congressman A has requested specific information on the cost and capability of System B, but there is no law that says that we have to give it to him. System B is in hot water right now and we'd rather not have him know what is happening just before budget hearings. The committee chairman, who doesn't like troublemakers either, has told us "off the record" to ignore the Congressman's request. We have two choices. We can drag our feet and delay the submission of the data, or we can present the Congressman with so much detail that he will never figure out what is happening. His staff is small and it would take them six months to go through the masses of data we could provide.

Game #3: Although a majority of the Senate committee does not support us on this budget request, there is no real cause for alarm. The House has given us strong backing and the Senate chairman is also behind us. In fact, he has told us that he will not bring the issue to a head in his own committee because he can arrange to have the item restored by the joint Senate-House Conference Committee. We know from experience that we can depend on him.

Game #4: Congressman Z has us over a barrel. He has warned us that he will see that funds are not appropriated for our two most important programs unless we scrap our plans to close the military base in his district. It will cost us $10 million a year to keep the base open, and we don't need it at all. But it looks as though this is the price we will have to pay to get the funds we want for these two programs.

Game #5: Never give false statistics, but be selective with statistics that will support arguments for increased spending. If we want more ships, indicate that a potential enemy has more ships than the United States. Don't mention that U.S. ships are larger or have greater firepower. Or, talk about inferior troop strength in NATO—only 20 divisions compared to 100 Warsaw Pact divisions. Don't mention that a Russian troop division is about one-fifth the size of a U.S. troop division, or that an American division's firepower is greater than the firepower of five Russian divisions.

Defense Department games are not limited to dealings with Congress. When the military want to promote a program that might not be approved by the Secretary of Defense because of cost overruns or other difficulties, they reason: "Don't tell the Secretary all the problems involved in this program. We'll have everything under control in due time. No reason to upset him." This is a dangerous game, however, for there is always the possibility that a committee or staff member knows of the program's difficulties. If the Secretary is unable to counter negative reports presented during hearings, the service may lose support for a program that might otherwise have been funded.

Many Congressmen and Senators are aware that they do not hear those facts that show the Defense Department in an unfavorable light. But they are unable to elicit straight answers from Pentagon spokesmen. Senator Stuart Symington (D., Missouri), a former Secretary of the Air Force and a current member of the Senate Armed Services Committee, observed: "Getting information for this committee is like trying to dig something out of a hole." [13] Senator Stennis expressed his feelings to the Secretary of Defense during an open hearing: "Now when you send people up here before us to testify about these programs, we want *all* the facts. We don't want to have to *dig out* these facts. These people should *volunteer* these facts. All too often they just plain don't give us the facts." [14]

According to the program manager for one of the Defense Department's largest development and production programs:

> If we told the truth to the Congress, we would never get our programs approved. So we have to understate the cost and overstate the performance. . . . Our military bias is to get as much as we can get—after all, we don't know who the future enemy is or what he will have in the way of weapons. . . . We are the ones who have to fight the wars, not the people in the Congress or the average taxpayer.

And an Assistant Secretary asked, "How do you deal with an irrational Congress and obtain decisions in the best interest of the country?"

Only very recently have the shortcomings of the authorization and appropriation process received more than casual attention from the public. One reason is that both Congress and the Department of Defense are protected from criticism by the secrecy of committee proceedings. Since hearings are closed "in the interest of national security," even Congressmen and Senators who are not members of the defense committees have great difficulty obtaining information they need to conduct independent analyses of the defense budget. In the May 26, 1971, report of the House Armed Services Committee, a number of Congressmen expressed dissatisfaction with the 1972 budget and the authorization process. One of these was Congressman Michael Harrington (D., Massachusetts). Many of the Pentagon officials who had testified before the committee stated privately that they shared the Harrington opinions quoted below from the report.

> . . . I am thinking particularly of the passion for secrecy that pervades our deliberations on the Committee. Almost all of our sessions are held in secret. There seems to be a conscious effort to minimize public knowledge and discussion of defense issues, particularly those that are controversial or might expose the military to criticism. There are also very large expenditures (in excess of $1 billion) that most of the members of the Committee are not permitted to know anything about.
>
> The process has a closed circuit nature that tends to undermine effective and balanced outside review and interrogation of Defense Department requests and witnesses. Few alternative points of view are presented or, more important, listened to. There is a constant undercurrent of hurrying to go through the motions to reach the inevitable end of near unanimous approval of nearly all that is presented to us. The handful of independent and dissenting witnesses are quickly dismissed by most members as kooks or idealists who know nothing about military problems. Little effort is expended toward patient, reasoned and intensive discussion of basic national security questions and, in particular, of the key assumptions and judgments made by defense officials.
>
> I think we do ourselves, the armed forces, and our country a disservice. Instead of open discussion leading to broad, national understanding of military needs, we have held secret talks which inevitably build resentment. Instead of an exchange of views drawing the country to a consensus on defense priorities, we have acted as the military's Capitol Hill lobby incurring as we sit the distrust and dismay of so much of our citizenry who cannot, at least through our deliberations, come to a sharing of this Committee's views. . . .
>
> . . . But even the very limited explorations that I have attempted to make into the labyrinth of the Pentagon budget have not been met with responsiveness. Questions I have submitted to the Defense Department on such subjects as Soviet military research and development spending and on MIRV remained unanswered although the Committee completed action on the bill. A set of questions pertaining to the justification for the continued inclusion in the defense budget of $2.5 billion in military assistance to Southeast Asian Governments was apparently lost. Answers that I have received have often been casual and curt and sometimes calculatedly evasive or irrelevant.
>
> The climate which tolerates such a pattern of responses is traceable to the almost passive role that we of the Armed Services Committee assign ourselves. It is a role which rests, I believe, on a very fundamental mis-

conception. And even Secretary of Defense Laird has assigned a more positive function to the Congressional branch. He has stated, "Since studies within the NSC [National Security Council] and the Department of Defense focus on requirements, there is a built-in tendency to request more resources than are available. . . ." We cannot and should not expect the Department of Defense or the NSC to decide on the final allocation of resources between defense and nondefense activities. The President and ultimately the Congress must make these decisions.

We need to pay more than lip service to this reality. Congress, and the House Armed Services Committee, cannot abdicate its responsibility or permit itself to be preempted by officials who, however dedicated, have special viewpoints and interests which prevent them from objectively weighing the full range of national goals.

THE CONDUCT OF CONGRESSIONAL HEARINGS

Since relatively few people actually attend defense budget hearings, I have included here descriptions of five of the nine authorization and appropriation hearings I attended between 1969 and 1971.

#1—A Senate Hearing

During this hearing the committee was scheduled to review a request from one of the military services for several billion dollars. The money would be used for the procurement of weapon systems and equipment. All Senators assigned to the committee—16 in all—were informed of the date of the hearing by the chairman. When the hearing convened at 10:00 a.m., only the chairman and one other Senator were present. The chairman called the meeting to order and the principal Pentagon witness began to read his opening statement. While he was reading, the second Senator quietly left the room. He did not return. He had been in attendance for approximately 20 minutes. The official record subsequently released by Congress implied that he was present for the entire hearing.

At 11:30 a.m., when the second Pentagon witness was halfway through his opening statement, another committee member slowly ambled into the hearing room and took his seat at the head table with the chairman. The newcomer shuffled through some papers and finally found a list of questions prepared for him by his staff. Meanwhile, the second Pentagon witness had concluded his presentation. The chairman remarked to the witness: "I'm glad you summarized your statement. I can understand the summary quite well, and that's more than I can say about the long statement."

Next, the chairman asked the other Senator if he wished to question the witnesses. The answer was affirmative. The Senator read from his typed list of questions. After each question was answered, the Senator proceeded to the next question without further comment. He seemed unfamiliar with the questions and unsure of their meaning. Although the witnesses did not always cover all the points he had raised, the Senator never asked them to continue. He seemed to have one objective: to get through the list of prepared questions as fast as possible.

While the Senator was still reading his questions to the Pentagon witnesses, he was interrupted by the chairman, who announced that he had to leave for another appointment. The chairman thanked the witnesses for attending the meeting, handed them several lists of questions, and instructed them to submit their answers for inclusion in the official record of the hearing. Following the chairman's departure, the remaining Senator read one or two more questions. He then suggested that the witnesses simply take his list, fill in the answers, and return them for the record. He thanked the witnesses, praised them for doing a good job, and told them to keep up the good work. The meeting was then adjourned and the Pentagon officials were informed that the committee would hold no further hearings on their $4 billion procurement request.

None of the remaining 13 committee members ever appeared during the hearing. The three Senators who had attended were listed in the official report, along with the questions they had submitted to Pentagon officials. All questions and answers were printed in the record as though they had been part of the hearing proper. The hearing was classified "secret" and was not open to the public.

#2—A Senate Hearing

The purpose of this hearing was also to review the budget request of one military service for several billion dollars' worth of weapons and equipment. All 13 committee members were informed by the chairman of the date of the hearing. When the hearing began at 10:00 a.m., only the chairman and two other Senators were present.

One of the Senators interrupted the leading Pentagon witness's opening statement to ask whether his service had any night-vision equipment. The witness replied that the service was equipped with a large quantity of the equipment and invited the Senator to visit one of the displays to see it in action. Although it was not mentioned during this exchange, the Senator and his colleagues had, over the past several years, approved annual budget requests for tens of millions of dollars of night-vision equipment.

A second Senator wanted to know whether the military service was buying "enough" of a particular weapon system "to equip our boys in the field." He had heard that there might be a shortage. (The system was one for which the committee had approved sufficient funds in each of the past few years to build a sizable stockpile well beyond actual usage.)

Later in the same hearing a Pentagon witness outlined a several million dollar request to carry on advanced production engineering (APE) for a system presently undergoing research and development. None of the three Senators questioned the item, and the witnesses continued to list budget proposals. Approximately 30 minutes later, Pentagon witnesses outlined a multimillion dollar APE request for another system currently in a research and development program. At this point, one of the Senators asked for a definition of APE. The witnesses explained that it referred to tooling, production engineering, and other work required to prepare a system undergoing research and development for a subsequent production program. The Senator appeared satisfied with this answer and the witnesses continued their description of other items on the budget list. No one mentioned that in each of the past few years the Senator had voted to approve several APE budget requests, together amounting to more than $100 million. For the specific system under consideration, several million dollars for APE had been approved by this committee each year for the past three years.

The chairman adjoined the hearing shortly before noon. The Pentagon witnesses were informed that there would be no further hearings by this committee on the budget for procurement of weapons and equipment for their service.

At no time during the hearing did any of the remaining ten members of the committee enter the room.

The hearing was classified "secret" and was not open to the public.

#3—A Senate Hearing

This hearing was scheduled in order to review the total annual procurement budget for one military service. The chairman was unable to attend the meeting, and another Senate committee member was scheduled to take his place. Shortly after 10:00 a.m. the acting chairman arrived, accompanied by one other Senator. The total membership of the committee was 13. All members had been informed of the date of the hearing by the chairman.

As the two Senators sat down, a senior staff member for the committee moved his chair next to the acting chairman's place at the center of the head table. In a loud whisper he told the acting chairman that the (name of military service) procurement program was on the agenda for discussion. The acting chairman seemed surprised. The staff member then placed several sheets of paper before the Senator. These the aging Senator read with some difficulty. They included a welcoming statement addressed to the principal Pentagon witnesses and a request that they summarize their statements orally and submit their complete statements for publication in the official record.

During the summary statements the two Senators made frequent comments and asked several general questions. In addition, the senior staff member whispered almost continuously to the acting chairman and scribbled questions for him to use. From the nature of their unprompted questions, it seemed obvious that neither committee member had read the supporting material sent to them in advance by the Pentagon. This was later confirmed by one of the committee staff.

At one point during the hearing, a Pentagon witness discussed a request for $326 million for production of a particular system (here referred to as System X). Later, while another item was being discussed, the senior staff member hurriedly whispered something to the acting chairman. Apparently, he had suggested a question about System X, for the Senator immediately interrupted the witness to comment: "It seems to me that $326 *thousand* [italics added] is quite a large amount of money for System X." The two Pentagon witnesses were stunned. They did not know whether to correct the Senator's figures or simply to explain why the service needed System X. They chose the latter alternative. When the official record appeared, the Senator's figure had been changed to $326 million.

Later, while another Pentagon witness was delivering his summary statement, one of the two Senators left his place to chat in a corner with a staff member. For approximately 20 minutes their audible laughter punctuated the proceedings.

Sometime after 11:00 a.m. another committee member entered the room and took his place at the head table. A staff person approached the Senator and whispered to him at length, apparently describing the nature of the hearing to this point. The newly arrived Senator then opened his briefcase and removed about a dozen 8x12 photographs of himself, taken when he was a younger man, along with what appeared to be a travel brochure. He leafed through the brochure for several minutes while the Pentagon witness presented the details of a multibillion dollar procurement request. Then the Senator began to write messages on each of his photographs. As each was completed, it was placed separately on the large table shared by committee members and witnesses. Together, the photographs took up a large portion of the table.

After the second Pentagon witness had completed his statement, the acting chairman turned to the Senator autographing photographs and asked if he had any questions. The Senator nodded and produced two typewritten lists. He appeared unfamiliar with the lists, often stumbling over words and unsure of the meaning of the questions. Once, while listening to a witness's answer, he lost his place. When he resumed his reading, he repeated a question that had already been answered. He did not recognize his error until he had heard the answer a second time. At this point he tried to find his place. Whether he actually did no one knew, but his remaining questions had not been read before. Most of the answers provided by Pentagon witnesses were accepted without comment by the Senator.

As the Senator began to read his list of questions, the acting chairman left the table and entered a telephone booth located approximately 15 feet from the table. A moment later, the third Senator present left the room without a word to anyone.

When the Senator asking questions—now the only committee member present—was deep into his list, the acting chairman emerged noisily from the telephone booth and told the senior staff member that he wished to call a recess until the afternoon because he had to leave. It was now 11:30 a.m. and the hearing was nearing an end. The discussion between the acting chairman and the staff person grew in volume. The staff member told the chairman that the schedule would not permit a recess because the Public Works Committee hearings were scheduled for the afternoon. The acting chairman then suggested that the hearing be recessed until the following morning. (By this time the conversation was so noisy that the Senator reading questions returned to autographing photographs.) The staff member informed the acting chairman that the Joint Chiefs of Staff were scheduled to testify during the next morning's hearing. He believed it advisable, therefore, to continue the present hearing until its conclusion in about 15 or 20 minutes. The Senator decided to let the Senator with the photographs act as chairman for the remainder of the hearing. He announced his decision, walked around the table to thank the two Pentagon witnesses for their testimony, told them to "keep up the good work," and left the room.

When the noise had subsided, the new acting chairman resumed his questioning. When he had completed his list, he adjourned the meeting and thanked the witnesses.

At no time during the hearing did any of the remaining 13 committee members appear. The hearing was classified "secret" and was not open to the public.

#4—A House of Representatives Hearing

During this hearing the annual procurement budget of several billion dollars for one military service was to be reviewed. The committee consisted of ten Congressmen. The chairman had informed all his colleagues of the date of the hearing. When the meeting began at 10:00 a.m., the chairman was the only committee member present. My own minutes of the meeting are printed below.

10:05—As the principal Pentagon witness began to read his prepared statement, three Congressmen walked into the room and chatted in loud whispers with the chairman and members of the committee staff. The Pentagon witness continued to read.

10:10—One of the Congressmen left his chair to make a call from a telephone in the corner of the room.

10:20—As the second Pentagon witness began to read his prepared statement, the chairman left his place and walked over to speak with two other Congressmen.

10:25—A fifth Congressman entered the room as the second Pentagon witness was reading his statement.

10:27—A sixth Congressman entered the room and made several loud comments to another committee member. He then left the room, letting the door close with a loud slam. The Pentagon official continued to read his statement.

10:28—Another Congressman left his place to make a telephone call. After completing the call, he returned to the table and carried on a loud conversation with the committee chairman and a staff member. The second Pentagon witness thought he was being addressed and stopped reading. The chairman told him to continue. The interrupted conversation continued, at a slightly lower volume.

10:30—The conversation came to an end. Another Congressman placed a telephone call. His side of the conversation, punctuated frequently with loud laughter, could be heard throughout the room. (During this 30-minute period, the senior staff member paid close attention to the statements read by the two Pentagon witnesses.)

10:32—The Congressman who had been using the telephone most recently returned to the table. An earlier conversation between the chairman and another Congressman was resumed, again loud enough to interrupt the Pentagon witness.

11:25—The chairman left the hearing without explanation and the next senior Congressman took over as acting chairman.

11:45—The acting chairman adjourned the hearing for lunch.

The hearing was classified "secret" and was not open to the public.

#5—A House of Representatives Hearing

This hearing was scheduled to review the annual procurement budget of $4 billion for one military service. There were 41 members on the committee. Approximately half of them were present. The committee chairman announced that he would allow each member of the committee to ask questions for no more than five minutes. There were two Pentagon witnesses scheduled to testify and each read a prepared statement. During these statements, six or seven Congressmen walked in and out of the hearing room. At the end of the first statement, the chairman opened the floor to questions. Each committee member was stopped at the end of five minutes. Approximately ten Congressmen addressed questions to the first witness. At 11:45 a.m. the hearing was recessed for lunch.

The afternoon session began at 2:00 p.m. Only the chairman and two other Congressmen were present. The second Pentagon witness began to read his prepared statement.

> 2:00–2:15—Seven Congressmen entered the hearing room, one every few minutes. One Congressman spent this 15-minute period chatting with the senior committee staff person. Another Congressman walked over to talk with the chairman and then resumed his seat. He was followed by another Congressman, who talked with the chairman for a few minutes and then left the hearing. During this period the witness continued to read his statement.
> 2:18—Another Congressman entered the room and took his place at the table.
> 2:20—One Congressman left the room.
> 2:21—A Congressman who had not been present earlier entered the room.
> 2:23—Another Congressman entered the room.
> 2:24—Another Congressman arrived.
> 2:30—As the witness delivered his statement, one Congressman read his hometown newspaper. Every now and then he ripped out an article.
> 2:31—The Congressman who had left the room at 2:20 returned to his seat. Several Congressmen opened and read mail collected at noon.
> 2:32—Another Congressman entered the room.

Between 2:00 and 2:30, several committee members addressed questions to the second Pentagon witness. The Congressmen's questions indicated that none of them had read the extensive back-up material supplied by the Pentagon before the hearing. All committee members who spoke were unfamiliar with the material under discussion.

> 2:35—Another Congressman entered the room, for the first time that day.
> 2:40—Another Congressman entered the room.
> 2:45—One of the Congressmen present walked to the corner telephone and placed a call. The second Pentagon witness continued to read his statement.
> 2:47—One of the Congressmen who had earlier left the room returned.
> 2:52—A Congressman who had earlier left the room returned and again left.
> 2:53—Another Congressman entered the room for the first time that day.
> 2:58—Two Congressmen left the room. Testimony and questioning continued.
> 3:20—The chairman left the room without explanation and two other committee members followed. The Congressman who had been reading his hometown newspaper since 2:30 now laid it aside and assumed the role of chairman.
> 3:20–3:25—Several Congressmen left the room.
> 3:20–3:45—The senior committee staff member addressed several questions to the two witnesses.
> 3:55—Another Congressman left the room.
> 3:56—A Congressman who had not yet attended the day's hearing arrived and took his place.

Following the chairman's exit at 3:20 p.m., all order had disintegrated. The five-minute rule was abandoned and Congressmen spoke at random. The acting chairman did not attempt to impose any controls.

> 4:00—The chairman returned and resumed his role. Questioning of witnesses continued.
> 4:04—A Congressman left his place, spoke with the chairman and the senior staff member, and then left the room.
> 4:11—Another Congressman left the room.
> 4:15—Another Congressman left the room.
> 4:25—Another Congressman left the room. Testimony continued.
> 4:30—The chairman adjourned the hearing.

The meeting was classified "secret" and was not open to the public. Several months later the committee issued an unclassified transcript of the hearing, available to Congress and the public. The official record began with a list of committee members present at the hearing. The list included the name of any Congressman who had spent five minutes or longer in the hearing room. Anyone reading the record who had had no other access to the hearing would assume that 35 Congressmen attended an orderly meeting, listened to two senior Pentagon officials read prepared statements, and then conducted a well-disciplined question-and-answer period. In fact, a large percentage of the information printed in the record had been supplied after the hearing by the Pentagon.

COMMENTARY ON CONGRESSIONAL HEARINGS

In the above reports, several facts stand out. Few committee members attend defense budget hearings. Few, if any, prepare for the hearings. Few regard the hearings as a crucial part of the legislative process.

As Congress attempts to strengthen the weapons acquisition process, it hears more and more criticism of its own responsibility for the breakdown of the present system. In December 1971 the Senate Armed Services Committee initiated hearings on the procurement of weapon systems. An article by Jack McWethy, printed in a December 26, 1971, edition of the *Washington Post,* summarized the committee's findings.

> Congress is as much to blame for rising weapons costs as either the Pentagon or defense contractors, witnesses have told the Senate Armed Services Committee.
>
> "The budgetary process has become a ritual with no content," said Dr. William B. McLean, a weapons designer.
>
> "It occupies more than 50% of the productive time of our best technical people at the laboratory level and the full time of large numbers of technical people in Washington," continued McLean, technical director of the Naval Undersea Center, San Diego.
>
> In five days of quiet, poorly attended hearings held as Congress rushed to adjourn, witnesses leveled an unusual amount of criticism at Congress for its part in creating weapons costs overruns.
>
> Appearing several days before McLean was Gilbert W. Fitzhugh, chairman of the President's Blue Ribbon Defense Panel. In their testimony the two men said Congress—
>
> • causes costly delays in programs because the House and Senate are so slow in providing funds—often failing to appropriate defense money until the fiscal year is half over.
> • requires people responsible for developing the weapons to spend too much time on Capitol Hill and not enough time in their workshops.

- interferes too much during the research and design phase, then fails to challenge defense witnesses enough when they say a weapon is ready for production.

"One feels that life would be much more enjoyable if the amount of funding to be spent were known at the beginning of the year, whatever its amount," McLean told the committee.

Senator John C. Stennis, chairman of the Armed Services Committee, called for the hearings to investigate the way in which weapons are bought —the weapons acquisition process.

The breadth of the criticism his witnesses poured into the record left a strong impression that the rising cost of weapons cannot be blamed solely on the Pentagon, defense contractors or Congress—they're all at fault.

"It certainly is refreshing to hear your views," Stennis told two Rand Corporation weapons experts. "Most of the witnesses we get in here are asking for money."

Because the weapons acquisition process is so inefficient, witnesses explained, the end product is costing the United States far more than money.

This was a condition the Appropriations Committee already feared. In their report accompanying this year's $70.5 billion defense appropriations bill, the committee wrote: "If the geometric cost increases for weapon systems is not sharply reversed, then even significant increases in the defense budget may not insure the force levels required for our national security."

In recent years reports have been prepared for Congress by the General Accounting Office (GAO). Created to perform independent analyses for the benefit of Congress, the GAO has exposed serious management inefficiencies in a number of defense programs. The GAO is not without its own problems, however. GAO analysts often find themselves in the middle of controversy. Congressional critics who expect devastating attacks on the defense industry are disappointed with anything less. On the other hand, the GAO's exposures of mismanagement, price-fixing, and other irregularities on defense programs have alienated members of Government defense organizations and private defense firms, and Congressmen and Senators who support the military point of view.

Although it can perform a valuable service, the GAO cannot change Congressional attitudes. An Assistant Secretary who had served in the Pentagon for more than three years commented on his contacts with members of Congress: "It is frightening to discover that most Congressmen are exclusively interested in their own districts. As far as helping or supporting actions that are designed to benefit the country as a whole, Congressmen seem to have very little interest."

From time to time, the concerns which govern Congressional decisions about defense spending surface unexpectedly. For example, the Defense Department may find that it is given more money for specific programs than it has requested. In 1970 Congressman Mendel Rivers from South Carolina, chairman of the House Armed Services Committee, convinced his committee to add $1 billion to the Pentagon's budget for shipbuilding. In South Carolina the shipbuilding industry provides jobs for several thousand voters. In 1971 the same committee added $166 million to the shipbuilding budget. Chairman Rivers was probably the all-time champion at exerting influence on Pentagon decisions. By 1970 his Congressional district in South Carolina—the Charleston area—had acquired an Air Force base, an Army depot, a Navy shipyard, a Marine air station, a Marine recruit training base, two Naval hospitals, and a Naval base that includes a supply center, a weapons station, and a Polaris submarine training and operation center. Congressman Rivers' campaign slogan was: "Rivers delivers."

It is certainly reasonable for members of Congress to defend and support the interests of their constituents. What one also hopes to find, however, is some indication of a concern for the nation as a whole. We asked Defense Department officials to describe the calls and letters they received from members of Congress, in an attempt to assess the relationship between Congressional concerns and the defense budget. We learned that the Office of the Secretary of Defense and Deputy Secretary of Defense receives approximately 1,800 letters from members of Congress each month, in addition to innumerable telephone calls. The office of one Assistant Secretary received, in 1970, more than 1,000 letters and telephone calls. The majority of these contacts were related to Congressmen's and Senators' home districts: e.g., questions about complaints made by servicemen; requests for particular assignments for local servicemen; requests for information about local defense programs; reports of complaints from constituents about defense activities; requests to reverse a Defense Department decision to close a military installation; requests to enlarge a military installation; requests for additional defense contracts for particular firms or particular districts.

During periods when defense spending is being reduced, most members of Congress favor reductions only in districts other than their own. One Pentagon staff member, who had recently received many telephone calls from members of Congress objecting to defense reductions in their home districts, mentioned that the same Senators and Congressmen had demanded that defense spending be curtailed. He observed wryly that the only way to satisfy every member of Congress would be to place defense plants on wheels and pull them around from one state to another so that each Congressional district could have equal time.

Since World War II the peacetime acquisition of weapon systems has involved a large percentage of the Federal budget and the nation's work force. Not only has the United States involved itself in two extraterritorial civil wars, but military preparedness, including the continual development and production of new weapon systems, is now a major defense priority. Measured in terms of national security, tax dollars spent, or jobs dependent on the industry, the evaluation and funding of defense programs is one of the most important of Congressional responsibilities. Despite the implications of an abdication or a misuse of this authority, few members of Congress take seriously their mandate to impose rigorous controls on Defense Department activity. To monitor the weapons acquisition process responsibly, Congressional committees should be able to evaluate every major aspect of the procurement process, as well as the military and technological rationale behind the acquisition of each new system. Given the size and complexity of acquisition programs, the task is demanding and time-consuming. Success is predicated on a thorough grounding in technology, financial management, and military operations. If members of Congress take this responsibility lightly, perhaps this results from the sentiments expressed by a chairman of the Senate Armed Services Committee, the late Senator Richard Russell: "There is something about preparing for destruction that causes men to be more careless in spending money than they would be if they were building for constructive purposes." [15]

NOTES TO CHAPTER VII

1. *Congressional Directory, 92nd Congress, 1971* (Washington: Government Printing Office, 1971), pp. 302–327.
2. Ibid., pp. 302–309.
3. Ibid., pp. 310–327.
4. Ibid., pp. 302–307.
5. The House debate on the C-5A, as well as the entire Fiscal Year 1970 Military Procurement Bill, appeared in *The Congressional Record*: Wednesday, October 1, 1969, pp. H87863–H8816; Thursday, October 2, 1969, pp. H8847–H8922. In addition the *Boston Globe,* October 13, 1969, p. 21, carried an account of the exchanges later deleted from *The Congressional Record.* The hearings were also described at length in Berkeley Rice, *The C-5A Scandal* (Boston: Houghton Mifflin Company, 1971), Chapter X.
6. U.S. Senate, Armed Services Committee, Report of hearings on *Military Procurement for Fiscal Year 1970,* Part 2, May–June 1969, p. 2083.
7. *New York Review of Books,* October 23, 1969, p. 10.
8. *The Congressional Record,* October 2, 1969, in "Extension of Remarks," p. #8093.
9. Douglass Cater, for example, suggested that the ". . . Congress lacks the capacity to assimilate this outpouring of experts." See *Power in Washington: A Critical Look at Today's Struggle to Govern in the Nation's Capital* (New York: Random House, 1964), p. 133. The more serious charge was made that political leaders had abdicated their responsibilities and permitted technological elites to make decisions; see Hans J. Morgenthau, "Decision Making in the Nuclear Age," *Bulletin of the Atomic Scientists,* December 1962, pp. 7–8. Criticism of a similar nature may be found in James Burnham, *Congress and the American Tradition* (Chicago: Henry Regnery Co., 1959), pp. 190, 348. A more moderate view was given by Ralph Lapp, *The New Priesthood* (New York: Harper & Row, 1965), and by D. S. Greenberg, "Science and Congress: Machinery Is Out of Date for Handling $12 Billion in Research Programs," *Science,* October 19, 1962, pp. 417–418.
10. *Congressional Directory, 92nd Congress, 1971,* p. 262.
11. Ibid., p. 280.
12. *The Congressional Record,* March 1, 1971, pp. #2198–2204.
13. Interview with Senator Stuart Symington reported in the *Baltimore News American,* May 9, 1969.
14. Berkeley Rice, op. cit., p. 203; and the *Baltimore News American,* May 9, 1969.
15. William Proxmire, *Report from Wasteland: America's Military Industrial Complex* (New York: Praeger, 1970), p. 11.

CHAPTER VIII

Estimating the Cost of Large Development Programs

AT EACH STAGE of a major development and production program, from the generation of ideas to the delivery of a finished system, an estimate of cost is a major input in management decision making. As soon as a new system is conceived, three questions are raised:

- What will it cost?
- What will it do?
- When will it be available?

In making decisions, policy makers must weigh the potential value of the end product and its prospective date of completion against an estimate of its cost. The time/value/estimated-cost relationship is then compared with other potential uses of available funds and a decision is made to proceed or not to proceed with the project. This method of decision making has gained increasing popularity in the Department of Defense in recent years. Thus, a comprehensive understanding of costs, especially estimated future costs, is an important part of the systems development process. In evaluating complex and expensive defense systems, the view that only the defensive value of a system is significant, regardless of cost, would indeed be naive. Such a limited analysis does not lead to maximum returns for the finite resources available.

After systems are selected for development, each military service must contract for and produce those systems that are its responsibility. The services must to the best of their abilities accomplish these objectives within the budget provided in advance by the Congress and the Department of Defense. Yet the development of these systems is hardly the same as the production of fixed and known items of hardware. All along the route, from idea to systems-in-place, choices must be made that will significantly affect the ultimate costs of the acquisition process. If the services are to achieve sound financial control of these costs, it is essential that they have sound and reliable estimates of the cost implications of their choices. Reliable cost estimates must be made available to decision makers in each military service if they are to carry out their responsibilities. Unreliable estimates may be worse than no estimates at all.

The purpose of cost estimating is to produce reliable cost estimates for decision makers at all levels. Adequate cost-estimating capability depends on the availability of people and methods for making cost estimates. It also depends on the responsiveness of these people and methods to the needs of the decision makers in the services and the Office of the Secretary of Defense. Cost estimates—whether for new, advanced technology systems, or for changes in systems already in existence—are not statements of fact. Rather, they are judgments of the cost of work to be performed under certain specified conditions. Consequently, if a decision maker is to consider an estimate reliable at any stage in the acquisition process, he must have confidence in the judgment of the estimator and the likelihood that the specified conditions will occur.

Cost estimating capability is only as accurate as the information on which estimates are based. On some large, complex development programs, the degree of accuracy surrounding an estimate may be -10% to $+100\%$ or more. Decision makers must be informed about the degree of accuracy so that they will not erroneously assume that an estimate is accurate to within plus or minus 10%.

Cost estimates are required for five types of activity in the acquisition process.

1. *For planning purposes:*
   a. To prepare a cost/benefit or cost/effectiveness analysis;
   b. At major review points (e.g., at the beginning of concept formulation, full-scale development, or production);
   c. To appraise the cost impact of proposed program changes;
   d. To provide supporting data for a military service in its long-range planning.
2. *For budget preparation:*
   a. To support fund requests to the Congress;
   b. To support requests for the assignment of appropriated funds from the Office of the Secretary of Defense.
3. *For pricing a contract:*
   a. To provide a Government cost estimate independent of the contractor's estimate;
   b. To establish negotiation objectives.

4. *For pricing contract changes:*
   a. To price work added by a contract change;
   b. To price work deleted by a contract change.
5. *For progress measurement and control of ongoing programs:*
   a. To measure the planned versus actual cost of work performed to date;
   b. To develop estimates of costs needed to complete a contract.

THE DISTINCTION BETWEEN COST AND PRICE

The distinction between cost and price is not always clear in discussions of cost and price estimates. The Armed Services Procurement Regulations define "price" as contractor cost plus contractor profit, with each stated separately. When the term "cost" is used *within* the Department of Defense in reference to the acquisition process, however, it usually means the total funds required for a program. Hence, when the Office of the Secretary of Defense asks a military service for the "cost" of a particular alternative, the term "cost" normally means full cost to the Government, including contractor profit. Since contractor profit usually amounts to less than 6% of contractor costs on major development programs, the distinction between cost and price is not a particularly significant breakdown within the total resource requirements of a program.

The terms "price analysis," "price estimate," "cost analysis," and "cost estimate" overlap significantly. In practice "price analysis" and "price estimates" are terms generally used by Government procurement personnel. "Cost estimate" and "cost analysis" are terms generally used by Government comptroller personnel and higher level decision makers in the Department of Defense. In the past "price analysis" has often referred only to the process of examining and evaluating a contractor's price, without evaluation of the separate cost elements and proposed profit. The term "cost analysis" has usually meant a more comprehensive evaluation of a cost estimate, that is, an examination and evaluation of its component parts. With the improvements in cost and price analysis that have taken place within the Department of Defense in the past few years, however, the distinction between the two terms becomes less clear.

TYPES OF ESTIMATES

There are three types of cost estimates for large development or production programs, or for changes in these programs.

1. *Parametric Estimates*—Estimates derived by extrapolating costs from the actual costs of previous systems and correlating these costs with physical or performance characteristics of the systems. Examples of the characteristics correlated with costs are weight, thrust, number of circuits, speed, or range.
2. *Engineered Estimates*—Estimates derived by summarizing the estimated costs of detailed components of a system. The estimated costs of detailed components may be derived from an analysis of specific work to be performed, or by parametric estimates of detailed components.
3. *Learning Curve Estimates*—Estimates derived by extrapolating the actual cost of previous units or lots of an item produced in quantity. The learning curve estimate is also based on the assumption that some reduction in cost will take place (attributed to learning) on each subsequent lot of the item produced.

Price estimates are normally identified as one of the following two types:

1. *Standard Price Estimates*—Estimates based on an analysis of a contractor's price proposal. The analysis is conducted by one or more Government pricing specialists who seek to identify overstatements and/or understatements of contractor costs for purposes of developing Government negotiating objectives.
2. *Should-Cost Estimates*—Estimates based on analyses of a contractor's price proposal by a team of price analysts, cost analysts, industrial engineers, auditors, and technical specialists who examine the assumptions made by a contractor and the manner in which the contractor has constructed his proposed price. The development of a Should-Cost estimate is a team effort intended to produce a specific Government negotiating objective based on an estimated price for each task to be performed. In constructing the Should-Cost estimate, the Government team uses the contractor's basic input data and assumes that the contractor will establish reasonable goals for efficiency in the performance of work on the program. The development of a Should-Cost estimate normally includes:
   a. An analysis of the contractor's planned labor realization;
   b. Ratio delay studies of the contractor's operations;
   c. Analyses of make-or-buy decisions;
   d. Analyses of the rationale for, or the cost content of, the program.
   A Should-Cost analysis leads to a specific negotiation with the contractor that is designed to capture any savings identified in the quantitative analysis of the contractor's proposal.

Each type of estimate is useful under certain conditions, but each has certain weaknesses. Parametric cost estimates are particularly suitable when there is limited design information available for a particular system. For most programs the parametric approach to cost estimating is the only feasible method prior to or during the concept formulation phase. The absence of detailed information on the nature of the work to be performed precludes the application of other estimating techniques. Only after detailed contractor proposals are prepared can industrial engineering procedures be applied to the development of cost estimates. Furthermore, parametric estimating methods allow an analyst to examine, at little expense, the impact on cost of a variety of changes being considered in the performance requirements of a system. This information is particularly important during the early phases of the planning and development processes. Since parametric estimates are based on the actual cost of previous systems, they can be no better than the historical data used as input. If previous systems were not produced under price competition, or if they were not efficiently controlled, the resulting estimates for the current or proposed system would not be comparable with competitively determined costs. Unfortunately, the majority of defense system cost records have not been derived from programs competitively awarded or effectively controlled. Indeed, most of the information contained in Defense Department data banks was derived from programs conducted under cost reimbursement type contracts at a time when the Department had few effective measures of performance or control. There is another problem associated with the use of parametric estimating techniques: cost estimating relationships become obsolete very quickly under conditions of rapidly changing technology. For example, titanium, used in many new aircraft, is a light but far more expensive material than the aluminum used in previous aircraft. This tends to render obsolete previous parametric relationships of cost per pound used in estimating the cost of new aircraft.

Engineered estimates have the advantage of being tailored to specific programs and often to specific contractors. Thus, the margin of error is likely to be less than for a parametric estimate, where neither the contractor nor the detailed design is known. The engineered estimating technique has one major drawback, however. It involves many detailed analyses and runs the risk of becoming inflated through failure to identify the contributions of managers at each level of summation.

Learning curve estimates are relatively simple to calculate and to use. Like parametric estimates, however, they project past experience into the future, whether or not that experience is based on reasonable and efficient operations. As an estimating technique the learning curve applies only to quantity production programs.

The standard price estimate has two advantages. It can be prepared by a small number of personnel, and it focuses attention on a specific procurement plan and, usually, a specific contractor. As an estimating technique, it includes only minimal analysis of the efficiency of a contractor's internal operations. In contrast, a Should-Cost estimate establishes a negotiation objective that is based on a detailed analysis of a contractor's plans for performing work on a program. In most cases, the Should-Cost estimate has provided the basis for identifying potential Government savings of 25% or more of contractors' proposed costs for work to be performed. A Should-Cost analysis requires a team of 10 to 20 or more specialists and usually takes 10 or more weeks to complete, depending on the size and complexity of the contract under study.

Different types of estimates are appropriate in different situations. A parametric estimate is normally used in cost effectiveness analyses and annual budgeting activities. It is the only estimating technique applicable when little is known about the details of a program. An engineered estimate, on the other hand, is normally used in analyzing a specific program plan and often a specific contractor's proposal. It is applicable to all well-defined programs. A learning curve estimate is used on production programs where there is insufficient time to conduct a Should-Cost analysis or where the Government personnel are sure of the reasonableness of the contractor cost base to which the learning curve is to be applied.

A standard price estimate is used for small- and medium-sized programs, or for large programs when insufficient time or justification exists for conducting a more costly and time-consuming Should-Cost analysis. A Should-Cost estimate is used on large programs where the potential for cost reduction is considered significant and where the forces of price competition do not provide assurance of reasonable costs. Parts or all of the Should-Cost analysis techniques can be applied to smaller programs whenever the capability exists within the Government and the situation appears to hold a significant potential for cost reduction.

In estimating the cost of complex development and production programs, a number of factors interact to inflate or deflate the results. Our interviews with personnel throughout the Defense Department and the defense industry revealed that Government and contractor cost estimates often reflected the level of funding that officials believed would be appropriated for a particular program by the Congress and the Office of the Secretary of Defense. Because of the limited availability of funds in near-term years, some programs are planned to extend over a longer period of time than necessary. A number of officials told us that it was easier to obtain approval for a $1 billion program in increments of $200 million or less for five or more years than to obtain approval for larger dollar increments over fewer years. How much money could be obtained for a program in a particular year was believed to be dependent on many considerations: the number of other major programs in the defense budget that year, the degree of urgency that could be associated with a program, the attitude of the country and the Congress toward military activities, and pressures to reduce the defense budget.

Several contractors stated that technical uncertainty in the work to be performed was also an important factor in determining the level of a cost estimate. Allegedly, these uncertainties cause analysts to overlook required parts of programs and to underestimate costs because of difficulty in appraising technical difficulty of work to be performed.

Possibly one of the greatest single factors affecting cost estimates is the definition of the requirements of the program under consideration. A number of individuals within the Government and the defense industry told us that vague or unrealistic requirements often made it impossible to develop reasonable cost estimates. Even in those programs where the requirements had been reasonably defined, we were told that inadequate planning of work to be performed caused estimates to be lower than reasonable. One senior civilian in the Pentagon, characterized by others as an advocate for new development programs, said he disagreed with current efforts within the Pentagon to plan programs in greater detail. He explained that "planning in detail always seems to raise the estimated cost of new systems and makes them harder to sell to the Office of the Secretary of Defense and the Congress." Another senior civilian in the Pentagon told us that he was dissatisfied with the cost estimates for a defense program initiated in 1969 because they were based on the assumption that all would go well with the program, that there would be no technical difficulties or test failures.

One Pentagon official expressed his support for optimistic estimates.

> If estimates for programs are too high, everyone is the loser because the chances for the program being approved diminish rapidly. On the other hand, if the estimate is based on optimistic circumstances and is lower than the facts would justify, the chances of the program being approved will be higher because it will appear to be a smaller drain on the resources of the Department of Defense. Later, if the actual costs turn out to be much higher than the estimate, it is likely that any of several changes will have taken place to obscure responsibility for the low estimate and possibly even obscure any evidence that the estimate was low. These changes include: assignment rotations for one or more individuals involved in approving the initial estimate and any subsequent revisions to the estimate; the occurrence of unforeseen technical problems; changes in the requirements of the program; or changes in the annual funding plans for the program.

For every large Federal program, there are always supporters and opponents. Since major Federal programs compete for funds, this is unavoidable.

It means that individuals who sponsor a program have to build and maintain support for that program if it is to survive in the Federal budget process. One way to gain support is to promise substantial advantages for the expenditure of a relatively modest sum of money. On large, complex advanced technology programs, only those individuals familiar with the program and its technology in detail will really understand how much the program should cost. As one Pentagon official commented:

> Except for a very small number of people in the Pentagon and the defense industry, appraising the reasonableness of a cost estimate for a new complex program is like estimating the number of fleas on Manhattan Island. You know the number is high, but you don't have any idea how high. This is the condition in which most people find themselves—Congressmen, Senators, many senior military and civilian personnel in the Pentagon, the press, and the average citizen.

Several Government program managers commented that they had great difficulty transmitting reasonable estimates to the highest levels of the Department of Defense. They said that higher levels of management tended to reduce cost estimates as a result of their personal impressions. When this happened, the resulting estimates were usually lower than the program manager's estimates. One program manager told us that contractors would sometimes be a party to these reductions in cost estimates.

> If a contractor gives an estimate you think is unreasonably low, you can submit a higher figure to headquarters. Immediately, the contractor and headquarters get together and the contractor says, "Well now, I don't see how in the world they [the program office] can justify that." Thereafter, the headquarters often accepts the lower, more appealing, contractor estimate.[1]

One program manager said:

> Many times on the X program we were told what figures to submit in our budgets. Our budget requests were simply not accepted by higher levels until those figures were in there. A year thereafter, as it became clear that additional funds would be required for the program, other parts of the Department of Defense immediately began criticizing the program manager for not being able to estimate.[2]

In early 1971 one general officer in the Pentagon described the situation to us this way:

When estimates are put together, each level of review tries to pare the estimates down to be able to fit all the desired service programs into the budget. Then when a total budget is reduced, the estimates for individual programs are again reduced across the board to fit all desired programs into the reduced ceiling, so that no program has to be canceled.

Another senior military officer commented:

When you estimate the cost of a program which you believe the country needs, you have a tendency to be overly optimistic and to estimate the cost of doing the job with the current technical state of the art. Then, the individuals who later make the design decisions on the program include the latest accuracy, radar, electronics, etc. Everyone wants to include the best. If you try to be completely objective in making a cost estimate, you may not be listened to, or you may find you cause the cancellation of the program.

The circumstances that influence cost estimates are not new to the acquisition process. In 1962 Peck and Scherer cited findings from several case studies.

Yet not all the optimism reflected in contractor proposals is due to competitive strategy. Frequently the Government literally compels contractors to submit proposals which it knows are unrealistically optimistic. The services and their buying agencies sometimes discourage realistic cost estimates because their current budgets are inadequate to support a new program. There is a tacit assumption that "We'll work with this low figure for a while. If the program looks good, we can go back later and get an increase." Along the same line, buying agency personnel often negotiate initial cost reimbursement contract amounts which they know are unreasonably low in order to minimize the contractor's profit, which (since profit rates are fairly standard) is a function of the contract amount. Finally, military requirements have frequently placed a premium on achieving the maximum possible state of the art advance, encouraging contractors to submit very optimistic technical proposals. A weapons maker competing with other firms for a desirable new program is seldom in a favorable position to deny the service's ambitious pleas.[3]

Each cost or price estimate is based on assumptions about the degree of efficiency and the number of changes that a program will experience. In the case of parametric estimates, there is an implicit assumption that no greater efficiency or control will occur for the new program than occurred in the past, and that all the problems of the past will occur again on the new program. Engineered estimates and Should-Cost estimates, on the other hand, establish specific objectives for contractor cost performance. To compensate for in-adequacies in cost estimates, it would seem reasonable for a manager to maintain a contingency fund to cover the cost of unpredictable problems. If there is no contingency fund, or if the contingency funds are budgeted out to all parts of the program, funds will not be available when problems actually occur. A number of individuals in the Pentagon commented that they found it impossible to request funds for a program and then to withhold part of those funds for contingencies. They said that contractors inevitably learn how much has been budgeted for the program and tailor their program plans to spend the total amount available.

Several Government program managers stated that few attempts are made on higher levels of management to prevent additions to the program after the initial budget has been approved. One such official commented:

> In many cases in the past, and even today, many of the tasks, subsystems, and capabilities vital to the system were omitted because of funding limitations. Most generally these omitted items have to be incorporated at a later date, thus escalating program costs. In other cases we have gone into a program knowing full well that we only had a portion of the funds required by our own estimation thus facing an up-hill battle all the way. Many times this can be justified by the rationale that it is better to get new capabilities started than to wait forever.[4]

Another program manager made a similar comment:

> In my experience, I feel that the best possible cost estimate for the established requirement was established as a "first cut." However, in the ensuing "negotiations" with higher levels in the Department of Defense, a number of items, functions, and/or capabilities have had to be eliminated in order to reduce costs to meet available funding levels. These were substantially added back in after the Using Command's tactical situation indicated a sufficient requirement to justify reinstatement. The lesson to be learned here is obviously that insufficient money in the beginning resulted in infinitely increased cost and time schedules at a later date.[5]

Eleven out of 19 program managers interviewed confirmed that tasks, subsystems, and/or capabilities vital to the mission of their programs were omitted from early program proposals because of funding limitations imposed at the time by higher management levels within the Department of Defense. Seven of the 19 reported that the deleted systems were reinstated after program approval.[6]

Since each cost estimate is based on assumptions about the conditions under which work will be performed, those Government and industry managers responsible for performing or supervising the work need to maintain close surveillance and control of the program to insure that these conditions are enforced. This follow-up action can be particularly useful in early identification of potential problem areas. Several Government program managers commented that they are able to spot problems when they observe that a contractor's internal budgets for short-span work packages are being exceeded. When this comes to light early in a program, one of two things may happen. Corrective actions may be planned so that budgets will not be exceeded or the cost estimate may be revised to alert higher levels of management to the changes. Actually, we learned from many individuals in the Department of Defense that there is no real incentive to send up revised cost estimates to higher levels of management. This type of early warning system might cause the program to be canceled or reduced in scope. In examining the two-year history of two major defense programs, we found that major changes had been made in the work performed for each, yet in neither case had the program cost estimates been revised to reflect the changes.

There are a number of other problems that make cost estimating a difficult activity. They center around the concept of responsibility.

1. Responsibility for cost estimating within each military service is fragmented. It may be special among comptroller and procurement organizations. Other levels of the military service command structure may also have certain responsibilities. One level may be responsible for initiating an estimate, but a higher level may have the responsibility for revising the estimate. Different estimates are prepared at different stages, from concept formulation to final negotiations. But no single organization within each service is assigned the responsibility for assuring that an "appropriate" estimate has been performed—i.e., that all available techniques consistent with the state of the program definition and knowledge have been employed.

2. In many programs the responsibility for developing a cost estimate shifts from the comptroller organization to the procurement organization somewhere near the end of the concept formulation phase. It is approximately at this time that the work is being defined in detail and the Government prepares a Request-for-Proposals (RFP) that is distributed to industry. The procurement organizations at this time begin to develop negotiation price objectives. On most programs, these objectives are based on (1) informal data banks, (2) a so-called "feel" for the industry, or (3) consultation with expert engineers about the reliability of informal cost estimates received from contractors. Pricing personnel in the procurement organizations are not always aware of or interested in the cost estimates prepared by the comptroller or-

ganizations. The types of estimates are almost as numerous as the number of programs for which they are prepared. Most Government price analysts have developed their own procedures for preparing and testing negotiation price objectives. Most senior price analysts have their own records of past programs. They use these to apply their carefully guarded methods for analyzing contractor price estimates.

3. There have been very few documented instances of comptrollers' estimates matching the price of negotiated contracts, or the price of negotiated contracts matching the final cost of the program to the Government. No Government organization is responsible for making these reconciliations. Separate organizations have separate responsibilities for each of the various cost figures.

4. A fourth problem is closely related to those described above: the difference between the definition of program work used in developing a cost estimate and a price estimate. Both of these work definition structures pertain to the same overall program, but the program is subdivided differently in cost estimating and price estimating organizations to take advantage of the limited kinds of historical cost data available to each. For example, on one program a cost estimating structure was defined in terms of successively more specific subdivisions; e.g., airframe, wing, and wing box. At the same time the pricing structure was defined in terms of the functional organizations that were scheduled to perform work on the airframe; e.g., various types of engineering, manufacturing, and testing units. A comparison of the two estimates is only possible at the summary airframe level, although such a comparison may never be made.

Several industry representatives have suggested that the Government abandon the Should-Cost estimating technique and other industrial engineering methods of establishing negotiation objectives. They prefer the Government to use parametric estimates. They reason that parametric estimates and contract prices for programs will thus be sufficiently high that the need to explain cost overruns will be reduced. In the same vein, several Defense Department procurement offices suggested in 1971 that cost overrun problems could be solved by raising all cost estimates. As pointed out earlier, parametric estimates incorporate all cost growth on previous programs (resulting from inefficiency, contract changes, poor program definition, and mismanagement) into the base used for estimating the cost of new programs. This can only perpetuate cost growth experienced on successive programs. To respond realistically to the lessons of the past, the Defense Department personnel might use the parametric estimating technique to establish a private cost estimate, including contingencies for posssible cost growth from all causes. They could then allocate only a portion of the total amount available for the programs. For example, if the cost growth on past programs of a particular type had been 100%, they could use the parametric estimating technique to establish an internal budget of X and then make available X/2 to the military service for negotiating with a contractor. The drawback is that the contractor will undoubtedly discover how much has been budgeted for the program and will develop initial budgets and manning plans that will spend at least the budgeted amount. Any problems or changes which subsequently occur will have to be paid for by additional funds.

THE COST GROWTH PROBLEM

When actual costs for a program exceed the original estimate, it is often assumed that the original estimate was too low. In fact, this conclusion is not always warranted. It may be (1) that the estimate was too low, or (2) that the estimate was reasonable, but that the program was not adequately controlled to prevent inefficiency, the addition of new features, delays in design approvals, or poor workmanship on the part of the contractor or the Government. It is often extremely difficult to establish effective program controls, disapprove additions to a program, improve efficiency, or admit to failures in management and make the difficult changes that will preclude recurrence of similar problems. On the other hand, it is relatively easy to maintain that a program has experienced minor problems of inefficiency or mismanagement but that the major part of the cost growth problem can be ascribed to low estimates. If one accepts this reasoning, the solution is to increase initial cost estimates. But it is doubtful that raising the level of cost estimates will solve any part of the problem. Since contractors' internal budgets are largely determined by the amount of funds available and contractors' manning levels are based on plans to consume all the budgeted funds, higher estimates may only mean higher actual costs. Revising cost estimates upward will not stop the spiral.

A senior consultant to defense contractors gave us an example of how this happens. He told us of a discussion with an aerospace executive regarding a forthcoming space satellite program. The executive, who expected to bid on the development contract, indicated that he could probably develop a satellite for any amount from $5 to $25 million (a span of 500% from the low to the high estimate), that would achieve the minimum mission objectives specified by the customer. As soon as the company executive knew how much money the Government customer had allocated to this development program, he would know what kind of satellite to build. In his proposal he intended to emphasize the importance of cost control and his ability to deliver an effective program for the proposed cost (approximately the cost budgeted by the customer). Once the customer decided how much money he had available for the development of the satellite—say, $15 million—this contractor, like many others, would design a satellite costing at least $15 million. Neither the contractor nor the customer would ever know how much additional value (in terms of performance or new missions) might have been achieved for a $17 million satellite. Similarly, it is unlikely that they would know how much their mission requirements would be affected if they developed a $13 million satellite.

On most multihundred million dollar programs, the prices proposed by contractors usually group within a few percentage points of each other and the Government estimate for the program. On one recent multihundred million dollar development program, the proposed prices from the two competing prime contractors were within 1% of each other and within 1% of the amount allocated for the program by the military service. Occasionally, there are exceptions. One contractor may break rank and propose a substantially lower price in order to win the contract (e.g., the winning bidder on the C-5A program bid $250 million below the price of the competing firms). But most new development programs are not awarded on the basis of price competition, and since there is increasing concern about low contractor bids that are designed to obtain a buy-in position for a lucrative production contract, the low-bid approach is being discouraged.

There is additional evidence that the much maligned cost estimator may not be the cause of the cost growth problem. In the past few years each of the military services has conducted selected in-depth cost analyses of major programs and each has discovered deficiencies in contractor operations that account for 30% or more of the initial program budget. Examples of these deficiencies are:

1. Increasing contractor overhead rates. There is evidence that tighter control (e.g., fewer personnel, or faster reductions in indirect personnel as sales volume decreased) could have kept overhead rates in line with direct costs.
2. Low labor efficiency. Labor performance measured against internal company standards was found to be 50% or lower on defense programs.
3. Failure to coordinate internal schedules for the program. Required supplies were not available from vendors in the time required for efficient use of the materials.
4. Ineffective make-or-buy programs. Opportunities to purchase items at substantially lower cost than proposed by the prime contractor

were neglected in order to maintain in-house personnel levels or to build a production capability within the prime contractor plant.

In 1971 there was some evidence that the Defense Department was attempting to reduce cost growth by raising estimates—as a matter of policy. For example, on one large development program a military service buying organization devoted considerable effort to developing cost estimating relationships based on the actual cost and performance parameters of previous programs of a similar nature. Using these relationships, the buying organization prepared a cost estimate which amounted to several hundred million dollars. The estimate was then submitted to the service headquarters in the Pentagon which had recently received considerable criticism for cost growth on its development programs. To prevent recurrence of this cost growth on currently proposed programs, the headquarters organization increased the buying organization's estimate by a factor of almost 50%. This was the estimate that was then submitted to the Office of the Secretary of Defense and subsequently approved. Later, a group of investigators were sent from the Pentagon to the field office of the buying command that had prepared the initial estimate for the program. In a report on the estimating techniques employed by the field unit, the investigators explained why there were such wide differences between the two estimates.

> The Committee also noted that the estimate on the Y program in 1969 was raised by approximately X hundred million dollars when the estimate was reviewed by the Headquarters—an increase of almost 50% in the program cost estimate. Much of this difference can be attributed to an underlying philosophical difference of whether the cost estimate should be based on an ideal situation which assumes minimal engineering problems and other forms of program turbulence (i.e., funding difficulties), as well as assumptions as to whether the same contractor inefficiencies, technical problems, and funding turbulence will exist in this program as had been typical of earlier programs. There also appears to be considerable uncertainty at [name of buying command] as to what the criteria should be for a good cost estimate and the relative responsibility of the program manager to develop a high and more realistic cost estimate of his program versus a low cost estimate which will force him to manage much more aggressively but is much more likely to lead to at least some cost growth.

In this case, those officials who wanted to establish the "high and more realistic" estimate won out and the higher estimate remained in the defense budget of January 1972. Once the higher estimate was accepted, the Pentagon would expect that prospective contractors would revise their manning and work plans upward to insure that their estimates would be close to the budgeted figure. Otherwise, the contractors might be disqualified for submitting an "unrealistically low estimate" or trying to "buy-in" on the program.

Because many senior Pentagon personnel are eager to end all future cost growth, it is possible that they will adopt the relatively simple "high estimate approach" before initiating more basic control activities. As one senior appointed official in the Pentagon commented: "We have seen the problems of underestimating and the problems of overestimating, and I believe that the penalty for overestimating is less in the present environment. We had better be safe than sorry on estimates." This type of statement by a senior Pentagon official reflected a lack of knowledge of basic realities; namely, that work on a program at a contractor plant expands to consume whatever funds are budgeted, however "high" the initial estimate may be.

The focal points for government management of ongoing development and production programs are the program managers and contracting officers. These officials, their activities and responsibilities are described in the following chapter.

NOTES TO CHAPTER VIII

1. Richard J. Lorette, "The Relationship Between the Pressures on the System Program Director and the Growth of Weapon System Cost Estimates" (Boston: unpublished doctoral dissertation, Harvard Business School, 1970), p. 89.
2. Ibid., p. 83.
3. Merton J. Peck and Frederic M. Scherer, *The Weapons Acquisition Process: An Economic Analysis* (Boston: Division of Research, Harvard Business School, 1962), pp. 412–413.
4. Lorette, op. cit., p. 397.
5. Ibid.
6. Ibid., p. 446.

CHAPTER IX

Program Management

AT THE HEART of the weapons acquisition process are the individual development and production programs. The management techniques used in acquiring weapon systems have evolved over the years. On July 13, 1971, the Office of the Secretary of Defense issued Directive 5000.1 designed to improve procurement management. Directive 5000.1 refers to programs with an estimated research and development budget of more than $50 million, or an estimated production cost of more than $200 million. In 1971 more than 125 programs met these criteria.

Centralized program management was introduced into the Defense Department in the 1950s. It was a distinct departure from service tradition. Before the 1950s, task-oriented management organizations worked on several weapon systems simultaneously. In the late 1950s, however, the Department recognized the need to streamline the procurement process and introduced *ad hoc* program management offices.[1] The key person in each office is the program manager, a senior military officer. He is assisted by a deputy project manager, either military or civilian, and supervises the division chiefs within the program office.

The program manager is responsible for research, development, evaluation, procurement, deployment, and effective overall management for one weapon system program. All the activities in the program are performed by specialist staffs, or divisions, such as the following.

1. *The program control, or program management, division* directs overall systems program planning, programming, collection of cost and schedule data, performance reporting to higher levels of management, and financial management.
2. *The configuration management division* establishes and implements policies and procedures for configuration management: system equip-

ment and facility identification; specification and engineering change control; and performance reporting on all such activities.

3. *The procurement and production division* manages all procurement and production activities and supervises the planning and execution of all contracts for research studies, engineering development, tests, and production.

4. *The engineering division* manages the total system engineering function, including the integration of engineering systems and subsystems. This division is also responsible for the quality of the weapon system's technical performance.

5. *The product assurance, or test and deployment, division* plans and coordinates the test program for the weapon system.

Most division chiefs are military officers. Remaining program staff are usually civil service personnel. The staff may also include officers from defense organizations with a direct interest in the weapon system; e.g., the operational using command, the training command, and the logistics support command.

The following are descriptions of five current program management offices.

1. A $200 million development program. Staff: 64 civilians and 4 military officers. Divisions: engineering; configuration management; logistics; procurement and production; program support.

2. A $378 million development program. Staff: 28 civilians and 4 military officers. Divisions: programs; logistics; technical; procurement; configuration management.

3. A $400 million development program. Staff: 28 civilians and 4 military officers. Divisions: technical management; logistics; plans and programs; acquisition; project support.

4. A $90 million development program. Staff: 24 civilians and 4 military officers. Divisions: technical management; plans and programs; supply and maintenance; procurement and production.

5. A $200 million development program. Staff: 43 civilians and 7 military officers. Divisions: technical management; acquisition; logistics; plans and programs.

A second type of program office uses a matrix system of management. In other words, it draws its personnel from the permanent functional organizations within the Defense Department.[2] Again, the program manager is the supervisor of the development or production program. He works with personnel in the functional organizations, and other military organizations, and with contractors in private industry. He must coordinate all the work of the Government and industry personnel assigned to his program. A matrix organization may be staffed by as few as 14 people, as is, for example, the Navy's F-14 (fighter aircraft) program office. Another 92 people who work on the F-14 program are drawn from the functional organizations within the Naval Air Systems Command. They work on tasks essential to the F-14 program but are not supervised by the F-14 program manager. They may also work on other programs concurrently. Time conflicts are negotiated by the appropriate program managers.

(By way of comparison, the Air Force F-15 program management office is a self-contained unit. All 243 people in this program office work solely on the F-15 fighter aircraft. The F-15 program manager, unlike the manager of a matrix organization, directs all work connected with his program.)

Since the program manager in a matrix organization depends on specialists from many other defense organizations, his success in gaining their cooperation is crucial to the success of his program. If he is unable to maintain a healthy working relationship with specialists working on the system, the program is in jeopardy.

Figure IX-1 compares three types of program management organizations. At the present time, Air Force program offices are usually self-sufficient organizations (Type B); Navy program offices, matrix in structure (Type C); and Army program offices, a combination of features of Types B and C. No attempt has ever been made by the Defense Department to maintain a rigid distinction between Type B and Type C program management organization.

Most defense officials and contractors agree that the type of program management chosen for a development or production program should be determined by the technical complexity of the weapon system, the size of the program budget, the degree of urgency and concurrency, and the importance of the program to the defense effort. However, in 1970 the President and the Secretary of Defense were told by the Blue Ribbon Panel:

> . . . Programs were found to be organized and staffed according to prevailing procedures and preferences of the individual agencies and were generally quite rigid in structure, being within any one service relatively the same for large or small projects. They ranged from the highly structured 200-man Project Offices of the Air Force to 12-man System Project Offices in the Navy with the Army falling somewhere in between. The size generally had more to do with procedural workload than with problems. Another important factor is the way in which the services use the functional people. Regardless of size, the System Project Offices find

difficulty in keeping up with their workload. There was little to choose between them in performance. Apparently small, competent organizations can perform as well as large ones on most programs; providing the environment and the procedures allow them to concentrate on the important actions.[3]

FIGURE IX-1. FUNCTIONAL MANAGEMENT, PROGRAM MANAGEMENT, AND MATRIX ORGANIZATIONS

A. FUNCTIONAL MANAGEMENT ORGANIZATION:
   No program established.
   Includes permanent and continuing specialist staffs.

	FUNCTIONAL ACTIVITY I	FUNCTIONAL ACTIVITY II	FUNCTIONAL ACTIVITY III
PROGRAM A	——————— TASKS ——————→		
PROGRAM B	——————— TASKS ——————→		

B. PROGRAM MANAGEMENT ORGANIZATION:
   Program office established.
   Program office staff assigned for the duration of the acquisition includes specialist staffs required for program accomplishment.

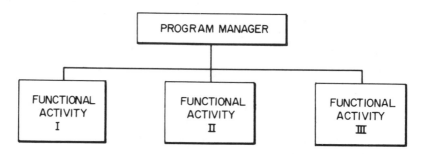

C. MATRIX ORGANIZATION:
   Interfacing of program and functional management organization.
   Management of correlated activities of functions and programs.

FUNCTIONAL ORGANIZATIONS

	I	II	III
PROGRAM A MANAGEMENT OFFICE STAFF →	PROGRAM A TASK	PROGRAM A TASK	PROGRAM A TASK
PROGRAM B MANAGEMENT OFFICE STAFF →	PROGRAM B TASK	PROGRAM B TASK	PROGRAM B TASK

THE PROGRAM MANAGER

The program manager for a major development or production program is usually an Army or Air Force colonel or a Navy captain. His assigned responsibilities are those of a top-level business executive: planning, organizing, directing, and coordinating all program activity, and evaluating performance. His immediate superior is the commander of a Government buying organization.

Program management offices were introduced into the weapons acquisition process to centralize and strengthen the management and allocation of resources for programs most critical to the nation's defense posture or most costly to the Department of Defense. As the key figure at this level of management, program managers must oversee the Department's effort to acquire, deploy, operate, and support major weapon systems of proven capability, within approved schedules and budgets. To fulfill these objectives, the program manager must:[4]

1. Establish firm and realistic system and equipment specifications;
2. Define organizational relationships and responsibilities;
3. Identify high-risk areas;
4. Explore schedule, cost, and technical performance trade-off decisions;
5. Select the best technical approaches;
6. Establish firm and realistic schedules and cost estimates;
7. Formulate realistic logistics support and operational concepts;
8. Lay the groundwork for contracting for the program.

In his negotiations with contractors, the program manager works very closely with the second principal official involved in the acquisition of a weapon system, the contracting officer. By definition[5] a contracting officer is any person, military or civilian, who is formally assigned the authority to enter into and administer contracts in the name of the United States Government. Contracting officers at different management offices perform somewhat different functions and are known by titles which describe their functions. At purchasing offices they are called "procuring contracting officers" and are normally responsible for negotiating and signing contracts. At field contract administration offices they are known as "administrative contracting officers" and are responsible for ongoing contract administration activities, such as making payments and negotiating routine contract changes. Some contracting officers are responsible for settlement of terminated contracts and are called "termination contracting officers." Most contracting officers have several responsibilities in addition to the negotiation and administration of contracts, and their career development depends upon their total performance record.

The contracting officer's responsibilities have grown as the ASPR has introduced formal management techniques, mandatory and optional contract clauses, and contract reviews into the acquisition process. Contracts now cover a number of specialized contractor activities—e.g., data management, quality control, reliability, human engineering, systems engineering, and maintainability—and the contracting officer must judge whether contract terms are being followed in all these areas. In the course of his duties, he deals with contractor representatives, other contract administrators, equipment specialists, financial managers from Government and industry, pricing specialists, small business personnel, legal counselors, industrial mobilization representatives, quality assurance personnel, and management officials from other levels of the Defense Department hierarchy. He receives instructions from the program manager that must be translated into appropriate contractual provisions, and he must have the program manager's approval for most of his administrative actions.

Many officials in Government and industry believe that the contracting officer should be the only Government agent authorized to determine procurement action.[6] But instead, contractors usually receive advice and direction from a bewildering variety of Defense Department personnel. It is often difficult for them to determine whether the contracting officer or the program manager directs contract administration.

Although the duties of the contracting officer and those of the program manager sometimes overlap, the following tasks normally fall within the province of the contracting officer:[7]

1. Administration of contracts, under the supervision of the program manager;
2. Approval of subcontract terms, conditions, and costs for compliance with prescribed make-or-buy decisions;
3. Preparation of field analyses of contract-change proposals and their impact on costs, schedules, and technical performance;
4. Evaluation of proposals for extended overtime and multishift work, for the final approval of the program manager; personal approval of spot overtime;
5. Miscellaneous duties, including quality assurance; interpretation of contract provisions; review and analysis of reports; progress surveillance; overhead negotiations; property administration; reviews and analyses of contractor systems (such as accounting, purchasing, and compliance with statutory provisions); and across-the-board support for the program managers.

The program manager exercises the following prerogatives:

1. Overall technical control, including responsibility for decisions affecting design, reliability, and trade-offs in design because of cost and schedule considerations;
2. Approval of specifications;
3. Approval of plans to subcontract;
4. Technical guidance in the selection of subcontractors;
5. Approval of contract-change proposals involving design modifications, additional costs, and changes in schedule.

Although Defense Department regulations and contracts designate the contracting officer as the final authority in all contract proceedings, the program manager is usually the only official with broad knowledge of the program and the authority to direct and control the numerous organizations involved in the program. This pragmatic reality dilutes the contracting officer's authority and often makes it difficult for him to manage contractor activities effectively.[8] Indeed, trade-off decisions involving time, cost and technical performance are often made without his knowledge by agencies outside his jurisdiction—to the detriment of the management process.

Ambiguity in job definition is only one of the conflicts that impede the management process in program offices. Program managers complain that most of the major decisions affecting the progress of their programs are made at higher levels of the Defense Department—often within the Office of the Secretary of Defense. Military officers above the program manager in the management hierarchy want to be kept informed of the progress of all programs within their jurisdiction. They also want to review all important decisions affecting their programs. As a result, program managers regularly receive instructions and requests for information from several sources:

1. Higher-level organizations within the service acquiring the weapon system;
2. The Office of the Secretary of Defense;
3. The General Accounting Office (an auditing agency which reports directly to the Congress);
4. The Defense Contract Administration Service;
5. The Defense Contract Audit Agency (an auditing agency which reports directly to the Office of the Secretary of Defense);
6. The using command (e.g., Strategic Air Command, Tactical Air Command, U.S. Army Europe);
7. The service training command;
8. The service logistics command.

The program manager's charter states that he is required to accept direction only from his military superiors within the buying organization of his service. All the organizations making demands on his time are staffed by senior officers in his service, however. If he is interested in his career, he must be responsive to their "special requests." Consequently, he does not have enough time to evaluate the many possible trade-offs within his program or the costs involved in contract-change proposals. As he forwards information from contractors to higher management levels within the Defense Department, he begins to feel like a titled errand boy, lacking sufficient status to give first priority to his own management responsibilities.

During our interviews with Army, Navy, and Air Force program managers, we heard the following comments, or variations, many times over.

> We are continually responding to requests from the Congress, OSD, and the service headquarters. All of the requests seem to be crash requests. Often the questions take the form of: "what if we do this?"

> *   *   *   *   *

> In the early parts of our program, much time was spent by the program office developing detailed, technical development plans and schedules for technical work. Each document generated further questions from higher places.

> *   *   *   *   *

> Earlier this year, we had six separate teams in the program office making studies of the program. Needless to say, this consumed my time and the time of my key people.

> *   *   *   *   *

> It seems as though we spend most of our time reacting rather than acting.

> *   *   *   *   *

> Two- and three-day requests are not uncommon during budget preparation time. In order to do an effective job on these requests we really need three to four weeks.

> *   *   *   *   *

> More than 50% of my time is spent collecting and analyzing information for higher-level personnel. Actually, we at the program office make very few decisions without higher-level concurrence.

One deputy program manager gave specific examples of the tasks that consume most of his working time:

1. Computation of the weight of the aluminum in an aircraft within 40 minutes;

2. Computation of the total cost of flight instruments and avionics gear;
3. Computation of the cost of all landing gear materials, including brakes, wheels, and tires;
4. Computation of the following statistics, within 24 hours:
   a. The average direct labor in man-hours for the first 100 aircraft;
   b. The man-hours per pound for the average empty weight for the first 100 aircraft;
   c. The cost of all other changes, identifying separately the cost of engineering, general and administrative costs; the cost of materials, sustaining engineering, and sustaining tooling—all as a percentage of the total labor cost;
   d. Airframe material costs in one dollar summary figures;
   e. A single dollar figure representing the subcontracted and vendor costs.

The chief of the program control division in one program management office made an analysis of his own activities and those of his key personnel over a six-month period. He found that more than 60% of his time, and 25 to 50% of the time of his key personnel, was spent preparing briefings and special studies. This naturally interfered with the management of the ongoing program. Discussions with other Defense Department personnel revealed similar problems in the management of functional offices. The director of a functional cost analysis office claimed that his staff had very little time to assist program offices; they were too busy with special studies commissioned by higher levels of management.

When so much time is spent dispensing information, the erosion of the program manager's function is inevitable. Does the program manager ever, in fact, exercise executive control over his program? Several program managers discussed this question.

> The program office doesn't make decisions and the contractor knows it. So, we behave in whatever way is least likely to run the risk of damaging our careers.

> * * * * *

> The authority we have is only implied. It is not explicit.

> * * * * *

> We often have to deal with dissimilar and sometimes conflicting interests among the functional offices with which we deal within the Command.

> * * * * *

> The program manager is simply spread too thin to do an effective job.

Over the period 1956–1971 a number of reports cited the problems that continued to interfere with efficient program management.

> 1956—A study of the services, weapon systems, and industrial relations revealed that:
>   • Project management conflicts with functional department management.
>   • Project management units exist at a low organizational level.
>   • Project officers lack sufficient training, rank, and continuity of assignment.
>   • Project officers lack proper approval, authority, and receive operational direction from higher authority.[9]
> 1959—Contractors quickly adapt their project administration to vertical lines; government offices are slower to effect this and have mixed requirements that prevent full organizational change.[10]
> 1961—Those concerned should provide positive and prompt support to strengthen the position of System Program Directors and Staff Officers.[11]
> 1963—The rule today is that . . . the program managers . . . have neither a substantial, well delegated, clearly defined responsibility, nor do they have authority commensurate with exercising the responsibility. . . .[12]
> 1969—The program manager is a sort of official champion of the system. In a hostile world, in which most of the senior people with whom he must deal seem bent on stopping, changing, delaying, or otherwise attacking his system, his people, or his money, he is the one dedicated support. . . . Because authority is at present so highly centralized in the Department of Defense, the program manager has little authority and is separated from those that have it by a number of intermediate staff levels which can distort and interfere but cannot help.[13]

There is one more aspect of the program manager's role which does not involve management activity but which significantly affects his performance. He must promote and defend his program before other levels of the Defense Department and before Congress. He usually feels obligated to fight continually for a bigger budget and a bigger program. This takes on particular significance at the time of annual budget hearings or whenever competing demands for funds from inside or outside the Department jeopardize the status of his program. This responsibility is interpreted individually by program managers and by higher-level procurement managers. According to a former commander of the Air Force Systems Command:

The system program manager has a continuing responsibility to determine, and to illuminate to higher levels, the full extent of growth in his program capabilities which can be realized if desired. This is a very important aspect of the program manager's job. However, it must be understood clearly that the program manager is not responsible for including this growth unless and until it has been approved. This point is so easily misunderstood that I think it should be repeated in the negative sense: The program manager is responsible that growth of the program beyond the specified performance does not occur without the approval of higher levels within the Air Force.[14]

Several program managers commented on this conflict.

The program manager's role is to sell the project whether he sees the need for it or not.

*   *   *   *   *

The program manager must be extremely optimistic in his role as program advocate.

*   *   *   *   *

As long as pressures are placed on defense personnel from the level of the program manager on up to the highest levels in the Department of Defense, we will continue to have the same deceptive behavior in dealing with the Congress as in the past.

*   *   *   *   *

Those of us in the service who are concerned with this program have to continue to sell it all the way up the line to the Office of the Secretary of Defense and the Congress, and we have to make sure that we keep the program sold to all concerned. If there is any time left over, I try to do the other jobs of program manager. My job is complicated by the fact that I often need the help of the contractor in order to sell the program effectively to higher levels, and yet I am supposed to maintain an arm's-length buyer-seller relationship with that contractor.

*   *   *   *   *

If you want to protect your program, you have to fight for it. You especially have to fight for funds. One or another program is always in trouble and someone is sure to be looking for money. They want to swap their problems for your money. It may be a provincial attitude, but I think a program manager is expected to push for his program. That means two things: first, grab for your money; second, get it into contracts and work orders as soon as possible. You have to plan and schedule your contract actions early in the fiscal year. You have to make sure you are moving your money out as planned.

*   *   *   *   *

Program managers are rewarded for making their programs bigger. No project manager was ever promoted for making his program smaller.

The problem was summed up by a general involved in acquisition management: "An advocate cannot be an impartial judge. Yet the program manager is clearly assigned both roles." The general stressed that in the annual fight for a share of the budget, the program manager must project unwavering optimism. A program must always be "going well, holding great potential, and more than worth the next increment of funds."

Procurement Personnel: Military and Civilian

The procurement of advanced weapons, equipment, and space systems requires specialized contractual negotiations and highly competent day-to-day management. Each program requires hundreds of individual decisions that affect costs, schedules, and performance. Good judgment is usually the result of years of experience and training in the fields of procurement, research and development, and business and financial management. As contracts are negotiated, awarded, and administered, program personnel must match wits with senior executives from defense contracting firms. Familiarity with private industry is therefore indispensable. Since large development programs are usually covered by cost reimbursement contracts, the experience and skill of Government managers have a direct impact on Government costs. This is particularly true for the most expensive programs, since the number of people employed is often determined as much by the amount of money available as by the complexity of the weapon system.

The capability of the program manager and his staff obviously determines the ultimate success of each weapon acquisition program. But a study of the military and civilian personnel who are assigned to program offices reveals profound deficiencies in the level of professional competence. More than 75% of the program managers interviewed complained of having too few procurement personnel, and even fewer qualified personnel. One comment was typical: "A program manager must rely on data and analyses given to him by unqualified personnel within his own organization."

In 1971 a member of a General Accounting Office team which had just completed a comprehensive study of the defense acquisition process commented: "Only 50% of the professional personnel in [name of service] procurement and production offices were qualified to do their jobs." In a separate interview a deputy program manager observed: "A program manager who has 50% of his people qualified is fortunate. Most don't."

Understaffing in program offices has always been a problem. Program managers have had particular difficulty in finding qualified professionals for financial management divisions. Table IX-1 gives the distribution of financial management staff in eight program offices, by military rank and civil service grade level.

TABLE IX-1. FINANCIAL MANAGEMENT STAFF IN EIGHT PROGRAM OFFICES

| | \multicolumn{8}{c}{Program Number} |
	1	2	3	4	5	6	7	8
Civil Service Grade								
GS-14		1						
GS-13	3		1	1	1	1	1	1
GS-12	6	6	2	1	1	1	3	4
GS-11	1	1				1	1	1
GS-9	1	1						
GS-6								1
Military Rank								
Lt. Colonel	1							1
Major	1							1
Captain	2							1
Lieutenant							1	1
Sergeant							1	1
Total	15	9	3	2	2	3	7	12

Programs 1, 2, and 8 were large, well-publicized programs that had experienced severe financial difficulty. To remedy their problems, two to five financial management specialists had recently been added to each of these offices. Each of the eight programs was running on budgets of more than $200 million, and three of the eight had budgets of more than $1 billion. Two offices with similar problems (not represented on Table IX-1) had never had more than six regularly assigned financial managers. Yet each spent approximately $500,000 for each working day.

There are at least two reasons for understaffing in program offices. The first is the low priority given by the military to the management of the acquisition process. Second is the traditional "start slow, end strong" philosophy that governs the staffing of program offices. At the beginning of any program there is a standard personnel selection process: preparation of personnel requests; validation of requirements; authorization of spaces; review of candidates; and selection, transfer, and assignment of personnel. These activities usually take weeks, sometimes months. At the same time a number of crucial program activities are taking place that require the attention of a trained staff. Plans must be prepared for contractor activity; contractor sources must be selected; contract proposals reviewed; contracts negotiated. Understaffing at this time puts the Department at a great disadvantage in negotiations with private contractors. And the decisions made at the beginning of a program determine the quality of all remaining program activities, many of which last for several years.

The problem of understaffing is compounded by the constant turnover of military personnel assigned to the program office. In its 1970 report to Congress, the General Accounting Office revealed that program management positions often go unfilled for substantial periods.[15] Of the 85 program managers in their study, only two had been assigned before the outgoing manager was released. Thirty-nine were assigned during the month in which their predecessors were released. Forty-four, or slightly more than half, were assigned from one to eighteen months after the previous program manager had been released.

In addition, no overlap between management assignments was indicated by the GAO review of the program managers' records. In our own study, we examined the records of 170 officers, who had been program managers during their military careers, to find out where they were assigned following their tour of duty in program offices. The following statistics summarize the findings:

- 57, or 34%, went into retirement, usually because their age or length of service made promotion unlikely;
- 73, or 43%, were moved to other routine assignments, some in the buying command, but most to a field operational or staff unit;
- 25, or 15%, were reassigned to other program offices, usually after the merger of two programs or deactivation of their present offices;
- 13, or 8%, left their assignments to attend senior service schools;
- 2, or 1%, died during assignment.

The records also revealed that only 16 of the 170 program managers, or 9.5%, were promoted to the rank of general officer.

In every program office we visited, the common problem among military and civilian personnel was lack of training and experience in procurement and business management. During our conversations with key staff members in more than 25 program offices, we learned that few had worked previously in any phase of the weapons acquisition management process; e.g., contract negotiation, contract administration, cost control, or financial management. Staff members expressed considerable uncertainty about the most basic requirements of their jobs. They were often unable to cope with the complex and rapidly changing demands of the programs to which they had been assigned. During the course of a program, for example, program office staff are called upon to review and analyze a multitude of contractors' reports. These reports are prepared in response to regulations and directives issued by the Pentagon or the buying command. In more than 50% of the program offices within our study, personnel did not understand the directives or the reports and were unable to judge whether or not contractors were complying with Department regulations or contract terms. We learned that some contractors assign several people the job of "keeping Government personnel happy" so that their companies can move ahead with work on their programs.

Caught in this difficult situation, program managers and other Government management personnel try to compensate for lack of training and experience by following the ASPR and other directives to the letter. By concentrating on required special studies, documentation, and coordination procedures, they leave little time for the more difficult management tasks.

Every industry manager we interviewed was unhappy about the frequent turnover of Government management personnel on program performance. The following are typical comments.

> The change of military personnel every two to three years leads to lack of responsibility on the part of both government and industry.

> *   *   *   *   *

> [Commenting on the new Defense policy of three- to four-year assignment tours for project managers]: Four years is too short a time for the assignment of a government program manager to a program. He should be there long enough to evaluate the present program and help in the source selection process for the next program. Under the present system, by the time the source selection activity takes place for the next system, all those familiar with the performance of a contractor on the last system have long been transferred.

> *   *   *   *   *

> There were three project managers on the [name] project, all of them general rank, in the space of the first three years of the project. Each had a slightly different way in which he wanted to work with us.

> *   *   *   *   *

> On this program there has been incredible mismanagement of personnel assignments. In the space of a few weeks last summer the program control director and his two principal assistants left the program. At about the same time the Director of Procurement and his principal assistant also left the program in quick succession. During the same period a new project manager was assigned.

> *   *   *   *   *

[Name of Company] would be in serious difficulty if they took their key trained men out of the project offices and periodically sent them to other places outside the field of project management. We simply could not tolerate that personnel turbulence and complete the programs on time or within the budget.

Although most supervisory positions in program management offices are filled by military officers, civilians far outnumber military personnel in the area of defense procurement. The Army, Navy, and Air Force together employ approximately 30,000 procurement personnel.[16] Of these, 12%, or 3,600, are military officers. Among the remaining 88% who are civilians, more than four-fifths are in the lower civil service grades (GS-5 to GS-12). Since most college graduates enter the civil service with grades higher than GS-8, the following analyses are limited to grades GS-9 and above. For purposes of comparison with the military, the following approximation is usually made:

Civilian	*Military*
GS-9/10	01 2nd Lieutenant/Ensign
GS-11	02 1st Lieutenant/LT (JG)
GS-12	03 Captain/Navy Lieutenant
GS-13	04 Major/Lieutenant Commander
GS-14	05 Lt. Colonel/Commander
GS-15	06 Colonel/Navy Captain
GS-16	07 Brigadier General/Rear Admiral
GS-17	08 Major General/Rear Admiral
GS-18	09 Lt. General/Vice Admiral

The Office of the Assistant Secretary of Defense (Installations and Logistics) published a report in February 1969 containing information on all Defense Department logistics personnel, including those in the field of procurement. The following statistics are taken from that report.

In 1969 no GS-18 civil service personnel were assigned by the Army, Navy, or Air Force to the procurement field. There were only four at the GS-17 level (three in the Navy, one in the Army). Total grade-level distribution, GS-9 and above, is shown in Table IX-2.

The small number of senior personnel (GS-16, -17, -18) assigned to defense procurement does not seem justified by the defense budget, since the Department spends approximately $80 million each day on procurement activities. During our review of the senior civil service positions authorized for procurement, we studied the Army Materiel Command, an organization which purchases more than $5 billion worth of weapons and equipment

TABLE IX-2. NUMBER OF CIVILIAN PERSONNEL IN PROCUREMENT: 1969

Civil Service		Military Level	
Level	Army	Navy	Air Force
GS-9/10	2,200	1,851	1,404
GS-11	2,033	1,255	1,477
GS-12	1,482	911	1,316
GS-13	717	581	706
GS-14	273	203	231
GS-15	80	77	70
GS-16	5	6	4
GS-17	1	3	0

SOURCE: Office of the Assistant Secretary of Defense (Installations and Statistics), Report of the Long Range Logistics Manpower Policy Board, February 1969.

annually. Although it employs 150,000 civilian personnel, only four positions above the GS-15 grade are authorized. This is 1% of the total number of senior civil service positions authorized for the entire Army. (The Army, Navy, and Air Force each have authorization for 400 senior civil service positions.) With so few senior positions available, civil servants with management potential are wont to look outside the procurement area for career opportunities.

During 1970 and 1971, as Assistant Secretary of the Army, I sought authorization for an increase in the number of senior civil service positions assigned to defense procurement. I learned that there is a ceiling, set by Congress, on the number of senior civil service positions authorized for the Defense Department. This ceiling, however, does not include engineers engaged in research and development (according to Public Law 313). I was advised to redefine the positions I wished to secure to include the word "engineer." Such an effort was initiated, but did not succeed. I then sought to have the authorized senior civil service positions within the Army redistributed to give greater weight to procurement, but found that each organization was intent on retaining its full authorization. Since new legislation seemed to offer the only remaining hope, my staff drafted a bill in 1970 exempting some civil service positions in procurement above the GS-15 level. The bill has won the support of the House Committee on Government Operations, as well as the Armed Services and Appropriations Committees of both the House and Senate. If it is enacted, there is a possibility that the procurement field will attract more ambitious, capable civil servants.

Not all senior civil servants in procurement are involved in high-level management. At present more than 75% of the senior civil servants in procurement are assigned to headquarters of buying organizations or staff positions within the Pentagon. Field positions are filled with lower-grade personnel. Over half of the remaining 25% are assigned routine activities involving small and medium-sized purchases. More complex procurement tasks, such as measuring progress in development programs and negotiating complex contract changes, require the kind of training and experience that few civil service personnel have.

TABLE IX-3. NUMBER OF MILITARY OFFICERS IN PROCUREMENT: 1969

Rank	Army	Navy	Air Force
W.O.	2	17	13
01	124	8	414
02	194	28	186
03	100	99	352
04	196	125	297
05	170	136	196
06	34	63	87

SOURCE: Office of the Assistant Secretary of Defense (Installations and Statistics), Report of the Long Range Logistics Manpower Policy Board, February 1969.

Table IX-3 gives statistics for military personnel in defense procurement. Although the number of high-ranking officers is higher than in the comparable civil service categories, even the senior military officers have had little formal management training, and no more than three to five years' experience in procurement activities. Such experience has usually consisted of routine purchasing.

TABLE IX-4. PERCENTAGE AGE DISTRIBUTION BY GRADE OF
DOD PROCUREMENT CIVILIANS

| | Grade | | |
Age	GS 9–12	GS 13–14	GS 15–17
Under 20	1%	0%	0%
20–29	2	1	0
30–39	15	9	2
40–49	42	42	36
50–59	32	40	53
60 and over	8	9	9

The age distribution of the civilians in program management (Table IX-4) poses a problem that will become more acute in the late 1970s. Assistant Secretary of Defense Barry Shillito pointed out that 40% of the civilian procurement force will qualify for retirement by 1975, and 60% by 1980.[17] If the Department of Defense is unable to attract and retain capable young procurement managers during the next five to ten years, problems in the procurement process may become markedly worse.

TABLE IX-5. PERCENTAGE AGE DISTRIBUTION BY RANK OF
DOD MILITARY OFFICERS (PROCUREMENT)

			Rank			
	01	02	03	04	05	06
Age						
Under 20	0%	0%	0%	0%	0%	0%
20–29	97	95	58	1	0	0
30–39	3	5	33	70	13	0
40–49	0	0	8	28	72	58
50–59	0	0	1	1	15	41
60 and over	0	0	0	1	1	1

The age distribution of military officers in procurement (Table IX-5) is comparable to civilian distribution. Military officers may retire after 20 years of service with half pay. Many who retire accept a position in private industry which provides a sizable second income. Those who do not retire until they are required to do so usually have not developed skills that are in demand in the commercial market. Consequently, it is to their financial advantage to remain in the service, despite the small likelihood of promotion.

Officers at the Grade 05 and 06 level in procurement (Lieutenant Colonel/Commander, and Colonel/Captain) usually fall into one of three categories. They are: (1) capable officers who are reasonably sure of promotion to the rank of general or admiral; or (2) capable officers who have little chance of promotion, but who are dedicated to the service of their country; or (3) officers whose performance in the service has been mediocre, who have little chance for promotion, and whose few skills are not in demand in the private sector. Officers in the first two categories can find attractive jobs in industry upon retirement. They often leave the service after 20 years despite the need for their management ability in defense procurement. This trend will continue unless they are offered meaningful incentives to remain in the service.

TABLE IX-6. EDUCATION LEVEL PERCENTAGES BY RANK OF
DOD MILITARY OFFICERS (PROCUREMENT)

			Rank			
	01	02	03	04	05	06
Education						
Less than High School	0%	1%	1%	0%	1%	0%
High School only	5	7	13	21	21	24
B.S./B.A.	80	65	72	60	42	38
Advanced Degree	15	27	15	19	37	38

Table IX-6 gives the distribution of educational level achieved by military officers in procurement. Among senior officers, 20% to 25% have high school diplomas or less education. This is true for only 5% to 7% of the junior officers. The number of senior officers in these categories has declined in recent years and will continue to decline during the 1970s, as the present junior officers are promoted.

TABLE IX-7. EDUCATION LEVEL PERCENTAGES OF
DOD PROCUREMENT CIVILIANS

Education	Percentage
Less than High School	4%
High School only	74
B.S./B.A.	20
Advanced Degree	2

Table IX-7 indicates that the education level for civil servants in procurement is far lower than for military officers. Nearly 80% of civilian personnel have had no more than a high school education. Most of the senior supervisors fall into this group. Civil service personnel recruited in the more recent past tend to be better educated than those on higher grade levels.

In general, the education level for civilians in procurement is so low that one is tempted to believe that errors may have been made in compiling statistics. Other statistics, however, indicate that civilians in other Government logistics capacities have even less education; e.g., 94% of the civil service personnel in Maintenance and 88% of those in Supply Management have high school educations or less. In fact, the average education level for civilians in defense procurement exceeds the average for the defense logistics work force as a whole.

Problems inherent in the low education attainment of civil service personnel are compounded by rigid civil service rules of tenure. According to the general counsel of the Civil Service Commission, it is a relatively easy matter to remove an incompetent worker from a job. It is only necessary to document the charge of incompetence. In the opinion of military and civilian supervisors who have actually attempted such action, however, the removal of a civil servant for cause is so lengthy and difficult a task that it is avoided in all but extreme cases. One general officer worked with a civil servant who was so incompetent that the officer was determined to have him fired. After one year of documenting instances of incompetence, the general officer was successful. In looking back, however, he admitted that he had made a mistake. Rather than spending an inordinate amount of time on the case, he felt it would have been better to assign the man in question to a position in which he could do the least harm. Conversations with other military and civilian supervisors indicate that many have adopted this attitude.

The difference between the Civil Service Commission's point of view and that of field supervisors hinges on the interpretation of the term "incompetent." It may be relatively easy to remove an individual who is flagrantly incompetent. When employees "coast"—i.e., do the least possible work within the job definition—their incompetence is more difficult to document. Supervisors in field offices and in the Pentagon usually find it easier to render such persons harmless by working around them.

Annual rating systems for civil servants are so carefully limited that it is virtually impossible to learn anything about an individual's job performance by examining his official record. Every year a civil servant's performance is rated "satisfactory," "unsatisfactory," or "outstanding." Supervisors admit that many more individuals receive "outstanding" reports than deserve them. This is usually justified as a means of promoting morale or inspiring a man to better performance in the following year. Simple objective evaluations based on actual job performance seem to have no place in the system.

The rating system for military officers is far more complex. Senior military officers prepare comprehensive evaluations each year for every officer within their jurisdiction, or more frequently if either officer changes assignment. Since most evaluations are written in superlatives, officers learn about their newly assigned men or about potential candidates for promotion by reading between the lines. The specific areas selected by supervisors for comment, together with the things left unsaid, reflect the true performance of an officer. Although ratings are often far higher than logically possible—e.g., recently 85% of the colonels in one service were rated in the "top 12%" category—the military places considerable weight on these performance reports. By the time an officer reaches the rank of lieutenant colonel or colonel, he knows that even a single report that is less than outstanding will be sufficient to destroy his chances for promotion.

For a different kind of performance rating, we asked ten presidents and vice presidents from companies with major defense and space contracts to comment on the Government personnel who managed their programs. Following are some of their opinions.

> There have been a number of useful techniques that have been introduced for management of defense procurement, but too few government personnel who know how to use them.

*   *   *   *   *

> The activities at our plant are so vast and our management systems so foreign to military personnel that a "quick trained" military officer charged with managing this system is quickly snowed, and rapidly retreats to the vu-graph level of evaluation, thereby not running the risk of revealing what he doesn't know about our operations.

*   *   *   *   *

The defense procurement process is highly complex and requires better trained experts to run it—not part-time managers.

*   *   *   *   *

Many people in Government do not have experience in dealing with industry and they often do not know how industry operates.

*   *   *   *   *

The amount of change and rotation makes the job of manning and operating a systems project office impossible. . . . There is a drought in implementation skills. The senior people in Government procurement need to have control over the selection, training, and assignment of personnel and be able to protect their men from the cannibals that would take them to be assigned somewhere else. . . . There is no significant amount of training yet for Government personnel on how to use the vast amounts of information coming into the Systems Project Offices.

*   *   *   *   *

Government personnel in the laboratories are for the most part high quality, but many of the civilians holding down jobs in the project offices are a joke.

*   *   *   *   *

One of the serious problems with the Government personnel is that they have very little understanding of industrial accounting or financial management procedures.

*   *   *   *   *

If senior personnel in the Government had the authority to terminate just the bottom 2% of the civil service each year, the civil service system would still provide great job security for the remaining 98%; but the 98% would work much more diligently to make sure they would not be in the bottom 2%. As it is now, many of them just don't care.

*   *   *   *   *

The military man who has operational experience need not be the project manager. Indeed, he should not be the project manager because it is almost impossible for him to have had sufficient training and experience in managing the acquisition process. Rather, the military men with operational experience should act in the capacity of consultants to the project manager.

*   *   *   *   *

The Government doesn't need technical specialists or operational personnel as project managers. They need business managers as project managers and technical and operational people as consultants to the project managers.

The primary reason for the frequent turnover of military personnel in program offices is the policy of rotation practiced by all branches of the Armed Services. The Report of the Blue Ribbon Panel in 1970 included a study of 174 military officers with an average service career of 24 years. The 174 officers had served in a total of 3,695 assignments, or an average of 21 per person.[18] The average officer spent eight years in operational assignments, five years in military service schools and other educational institutions, and eleven years in staff assignments.

The policy of rotation is also responsible for the failure of most military officers to gain the experience needed for their program management assignments. The services believe that rotation from one type of assignment to another at frequent intervals broadens the capabilities of their officers. Officers are then supposed to be qualified to hold any senior position. Although this concept has been useful in the past, the increasingly specialized nature of procurement management makes the concept an anachronism in the 1970s. It is obvious that a procurement officer cannot become a competent pilot without extensive training. It is often assumed by the military, however, that a pilot can become a competent procurement or program manager with little or no training. This opinion is shared by some civilian appointees in the Defense Department. As one Pentagon official frequently commented in 1970 and 1971: "What we need to do is to select more good men. If he is a good man, he ought to know how to manage."

A typical pilot spends the first five or six years after his commission on flying status, and another three years working toward a Master's degree. Nine or more years out of a possible twenty, therefore, are spent in nonprocurement activity. During the remaining eleven years, alternate three-year tours are usually spent on operational assignments. The pilot has five years remaining for on-the-job training in program management. During his tour in the program office, he must fly at least one day a month to maintain active flying status and to receive flight pay. If a meeting is scheduled with a contractor on the day his flight is scheduled, the pilot/program manager may send a delegate to the meeting in his place. One contracting executive told us that this was a common occurrence.

Dependence on rotation as an educational tool in itself does not take into account that even the most capable officers need appropriate training for management as well as operational assignments. Both the officer and the program to which he is assigned suffer when such training is lacking. As the Blue Ribbon Panel observed in 1970:

> The system of rotation not only fails to provide management and leadership needed on the job, but also has deficiencies in accomplishing its

stated purpose—the development of the officer himself. Men are not developed by being observers; they must have responsibility to assure growth. From the point of view of the position to be filled, as well as the best interests of the officer himself, his job assignments should be of sufficient duration so that he can become thoroughly involved in the work and be fully responsible for results.

Before 1970, 80% of the program managers in one service remained in their assignments for less than three years, and 60% for less than two years. During 1970, however, each service made plans to assign program managers for minimum three-year tours and to schedule transfers to coincide with natural cut-off points within their programs. Also in 1970 the Army initiated a personnel development program for procurement managers and assigned more than 50 officers to design the program. After nearly a year the senior officer on the project stated: "The improvement program itself has been hampered by the military rotation system taking officers out of their jobs in the program and moving them to another place, simply because the personnel branch noted that the time had come for a move."

In September 1970 we asked eight program managers to record the length of time their key military subordinates were assigned to their program offices. In total, there were 51 officers assigned to the eight program offices, not including the managers themselves. The officers had been assigned for periods ranging from three months to three years. The median period was nine months. In a sample of eleven officers selected from the engineering divisions of five other program offices, assignments ranged from four to 28 months. The median period was 17 months. Program managers observed that most new staff members require from six months to a year of on-the-job training before they are sufficiently qualified to make significant contributions to their programs.

Unwelcome side effects of the rotation policy have been noted since at least 1954. In that year the House Committee on Government Operations conducted hearings on the organization and administration of military research and development programs. Included in their report were the following observations.

It appears clear to the subcommittee that military personnel career requirements are basically different from those of scientists and other technical personnel, and that rotation is understandably necessary in order that military officers might familiarize themselves with a variety of military operations. The subcommittee recognizes the unique need for military rotation, but accelerated rotation programs which result in short tours of duty are both disturbing and harmful to the productivity of the research and development program.

At the commanding officer level short tours of duty might not in themselves be harmful if the officer is primarily fulfilling a military need for his having a variety of experiences. Difficulties do appear when an officer, fresh from the field and with limited technical experience, enters a research center with a view to reorganization based on limited technical qualifications.

Most scientists acknowledged that they respected a qualified line officer with an intelligent consumer point of view. Scientists realize, however, that all too often qualified officers are transferred to another assignment within a short period of time.

There was much testimony concerning an optimum period for a tour of duty for a military officer in a technical assignment. Even the Department of Defense officials admitted that a two-year tour of duty was inadequate. Although a three-year tour is apparently recommended by departmental policy, various reasons were cited for failure to adhere to this policy. Evidence of this may be found in the testimony. The testimony of our leading scientist witnesses and witnesses from the Department of Defense appeared to favor a four-year tour of duty. Such a period would permit a thorough indoctrination of an officer who might become competent enough to assume direction over certain elements of a research program.

The Department of Defense officials complained that there were not enough technical officers in uniform to permit such liberal tours of duty. The subcommittee feels that the military departments must be more willing to accept leadership and technical direction from our civilian scientists until such time as the departments are able to train a greater number of technical officers. Further, the subcommittee believes that the services could make better use of the military officers trained in technical fields; where such officers have proved especially adept or qualified in technical assignments, it would seem only reasonable that they should be rotated to closely related assignments rather than to only remotely related field assignments as the subcommittee understands to be the case in many instances.

Again in 1962 the problem of personnel instability received attention. Peck and Scherer observed in *The Weapons Acquisition Process*:

> . . . But since it usually takes one or two years for a person to obtain a thorough working knowledge of the technology and personalities involved in a complex weapons program, rotation can interfere seriously with the smooth administration of programs. The rapid turnover of U.S.

weapons project officers has been the subject of much criticism. Schlaifer, for example, found unduly short tours of duty a serious problem in the development of U.S. aircraft engines during the 1930s. More recently, the Robertson Committee concluded that the duty tours of aircraft weapons project officers should be lengthened beyond the 26 to 32 month average which prevailed during the early 1950s. Yet our case studies conducted during the late 1950s indicated that rapid turnover of project officers remained a problem.[19]

During our study we found many inexperienced military officers in management positions of great responsibility. In early 1971 one military branch appointed a general officer to head a program funded at more than $1 million a day. The officer commented that although he had never before been assigned to a position involving procurement management, he had heard of the Armed Services Procurement Regulations and was looking forward to getting acquainted with them. He added that he was "delighted to learn that the prime contractor on the program is a large firm with a fine reputation." This would "ease considerably the necessity of . . . having to exercise any significant control over the program." The fact that the primary contractors on the program were all operating under cost-reimbursement contracts did not diminish his optimism.

We visited one program office in which the chief of the financial management division was a qualified pilot. He admitted having no interest in procurement or financial management and could not understand why he had been assigned to the office. During the week in which we visited his division, we often found him chatting with fellow officers about his flying experiences. At other times he sat at his desk gazing out the window. His assistant was a major who had been assigned to the program office several months earlier. The major spent long hours in the program office, reviewing financial information and preparing reports for the program manager and headquarters. Toward the end of the week, during an informal conversation, he asked if we could contact someone in Washington about changing his assignment. His background and training—including a Master's degree—were in the field of bioastronautics. Like his supervisor, he had neither training nor experience in business administration, financial management, or procurement.

It is common for contracting officers at service buying organizations to handle assignments that far exceed their level of competence. At one field installation we met a second lieutenant who had interrupted his college education to enter the service. He was assigned responsibility for the engineering activities on a $5 million contract because of a shortage of procurement personnel, although nothing in his background qualified him for the assignment.

In Vietnam we interviewed an Army captain who was responsible for a $100 million cost-incentive contract for construction and services. He had been in the Army for less than four years. We asked him to describe his training in procurement and incentive contracting. He told us that although he had had no formal training, his current roommate had attended a short course in incentive contracting and they spent many evenings together "discussing incentive contracting and how it works."

In 1970 the General Accounting Office made a study of 25 officers holding key procurement positions.[20] Only seven met the prescribed criteria for senior positions, and only three had previously held procurement positions. One was on his first procurement assignment.

TABLE IX-8. QUALIFICATIONS OF THREE SENIOR PROCUREMENT OFFICERS: 1970

Example	Service and Rank	Procurement Experience	Procurement Training	Position Occupied
#1	Navy Captain	None	Defense Procurement Management Course (5 weeks)	Asst. Executive Director for Purchasing
#2	Army Lt. Col.	17 months	Defense Advanced Procurement Course (3 weeks)	Chief of Procurement Division
#3	Air Force	21 months	None	Chief, Weapons Systems and Major Equipment Procurement Division

Three examples were given in this report (see Table IX-8). The GAO report also noted that military officers listed as part of the procurement career program had attended an average of less than one procurement course.[21]

The problem of attracting enough qualified personnel to fill military positions within program offices becomes more pressing each year. Recently, Pentagon officials have issued numerous statements about the need to establish clearly defined military career fields in program management and procurement. This is strongly resisted, however, by most senior officers in personnel and fighting units. They fail to understand the need for a highly skilled and stable professional force to manage the weapons acquisition process, and they are also concerned that they will lose some of their most able officers to noncombat fields if they lose control of any part of the assignment and promotion process.

Most officers believe that procurement assignments will not advance—in fact, may even damage—their careers. Even if an officer has a long-term interest in procurement, he believes that success in the military depends on his returning to a combat unit and demonstrating his skill and dedication in a field activity (e.g., operating ships, aircraft, tanks, signal equipment). The attitude of senior military officers was vividly illustrated by a slogan attached to the Pentagon door of a former Air Force Chief of Staff: "Our mission is to fly and fight, and don't you forget it!" The implication was obvious: those who do not "fly and fight" are second-class members of the Air Force. Officers often refer to procurement assignments as "shore duty," i.e., assignments requiring neither skill nor hard work.

If an officer is maintaining peak mobility, he will advance in rank every two to four years (from second lieutenant/ensign to general/admiral). The Secretary of each service has nominal responsibility for military promotions. He appoints the selection board which reviews officers' records, instructs the board on promotion policy, and approves promotion lists that are forwarded to the President. In fact, however, each service's Chief of Staff directs the promotion process, although he is not specifically mentioned in the directives designating responsibility in this area. Prior to the appointment of a selection board, the military Chief of Staff makes a number of recommendations to the Secretary regarding the board's operations. In cases involving promotions to the highest ranks, the Chief of Staff may meet with the board himself to give specific instructions. In considering officers for promotion, priority is almost always given to men with command experience. Experience in fields requiring technical competence and/or management skill—e.g., program management, procurement, intelligence, communications, electronic data processing[22]—is rarely an asset. As a result, most officers look upon an assignment in one of these areas as a liability, a "dead end" in the development of their careers.

In early 1971 I interviewed a colonel who had recently returned from an assignment in Vietnam. I noted in my review of his official record that his annual performance ratings were outstanding and that he had been given important assignments throughout his career. He had attended a number of schools in the field of procurement and had been given a major procurement assignment. I suggested to him that he would be an excellent candidate for another procurement assignment, especially since the Department of Defense was having difficulty finding officers for program management positions. The colonel was obviously disturbed at this suggestion. He told me that he had consciously avoided procurement assignments in recent years because identification with that field was considered "the kiss of death" to chances for promotion to general officer.

In the spring of 1971 I met with a group of 20 officers attending the Industrial College of the Armed Forces. We talked about the need for outstanding officers in the fields of procurement and program management. During the discussion period, one officer said: "I can see the value in what you say, but the only problem is we can't get to be a general officer by doing it.

The problem is that I have to have a command to get promoted." This opinion was repeated by most of the officers I interviewed. It seems to have sound basis in fact. In May 1971 a service Secretary instructed his selection board to promote to the rank of general officer five colonels who met specific criteria in the field of procurement. When the promotion list was distributed, it contained the names of four officers who supposedly met these criteria. But not one of these officers had had any experience in the procurement of major weapon systems. The closest any one of them had come was an assignment in the determination of annual procurement requirements for their service, or a few brief assignments in the purchase of conventional products. Upon further inquiry we learned that several colonels with extensive procurement training and experience had been passed over for promotion. One or more of the following reasons was given: they had not been to Vietnam; they had not been to a senior service school; they did not have command experience in field operational units. Although senior Pentagon officials have stated that experience in procurement and program management would be major factors in promotions, there has yet to be enough concrete evidence to convince career officers of the sincerity of these pronouncements.

Management positions may lack status because there are no adequate standards by which to evaluate the effectiveness or efficiency of program management techniques and/or program managers. On August 19, 1971, Dr. John Foster, the Pentagon's senior officer for research and development, made the following statement during an address to the Armed Forces Management Association:

> Those project managers who do well will be easily identified and will be rewarded just as an outstanding ship's captain or brigade or wing commander is rewarded. Poor performance will be equally conspicuous, and the poor manager will be relieved just as he would if he did poorly while leading troops in the field.

While this is a worthy goal, few Defense Department managers believe it is attainable.

In the absence of uniform standards by which to evaluate management performance, an individual is usually judged by his conformity to traditional management procedures and his loyalty to his service. During our visits to program offices, we found that most military officers were highly motivated and worked extremely hard, despite their lack of training for the complex tasks to which they had been assigned. This motivation may come from the military tradition of doing the best job possible with the available resources. In the case of program managers, *ésprit de corps* is enhanced by each officer's belief that "his" program is "vital" to national defense. Managers' identification with their programs is so strong that there is virtually no chance that they would recommend cutbacks or cancellations because a program is no longer cost-effective. To the program manager, the acquisition of his weapon system is essential for national survival. Ordinary management concerns for reasonable cost, schedule, and performance controls seem almost unpatriotic to him in this context.

Program managers naturally want to impress their military superiors favorably in order to achieve high marks in their annual performance ratings. Since officers serve for a relatively short period in each assignment, each program manager attempts to produce spectacular results in the shortest possible time. We visited a number of military bases in Vietnam and Europe from 1969 to 1971. At each base the commanding officer gave us a briefing on program activities. Unfailingly, the briefing centered around graphs that began at a low point on the left side, signifying the time when the commander began his current assignment. From the beginning of his assignment to the present, the charts showed remarkable progress. At the time of the briefing, performance measured by the charts was at an all-time high—in every single unit. Improvement was always attributed to the current commanding officer's management ability. We looked for one commander who might begin his briefing by remarking: "When I arrived at this assignment, my predecessor was doing an outstanding job. I am pleased to say that since that time I have continued what he was doing and have maintained the same high standards." We never found him.

One colonel who had worked under three highly respected general officers over a period of five years pointed out that the present system for evaluating and rewarding performance precludes the pursuit of long-term goals. He claimed that each of the three general officers under whom he had served had "announced in staff meetings that they were not interested in long-term plans. Rather, they wanted to know what could be done tomorrow."

One general officer expressed an even more cynical point of view: "Remember, in the Government, it's the image, not the substance, that counts. If you're ineffective and your boss likes you, you're o.k. But even though you may be an effective producer, if your boss doesn't share that belief in the short run, you're in bad shape."

There are few rewards in the military for the capable performance of a long-term task. A short-term task that is done well will be attributed to the present commander and will be mentioned in his annual performance rating. Maintaining stability in program management and progressing efficiently toward long-term program goals are not seen as "rewarding" activities. They may lead to the ultimate success of a program but they do not often lead to outstanding performance ratings for the responsible officer.

A general officer in a senior procurement position discussed rewards during an interview in early 1971. "In the end analysis, the rewards to the program manager are based on whether an effective weapon system is obtained for the service or not. The question of whether or not there was a 50% overrun, or whether the acquisition was accomplished for a particular cost figure, is well down on the list of priorities."

For the past two decades many in the Defense Department have not recognized that business management skills are distinct from engineering and scientific skills. A general in one of the larger buying commands commented: "One of the causes of our current problems arises from the fact that we failed to recognize that a program manager must be a business manager and need not be an expert scientist or an expert engineer." In private industry the scientists and engineers who work on defense programs can usually count on the assistance of skilled financial and business analysts from within their own company. This support capability is rarely present in Defense Department program offices. Some Government program managers hire engineering or technical consultants from outside the Government on a part-time basis. In the area of business management, however, they are reluctant to request outside assistance because they feel this would call attention to their own lack of management capability.

In the last few years members of Congress have begun to worry about the Defense Department's failure to attract men and women capable of managing costly procurement programs. On March 19, 1970, Senator Stuart Symington testified before the Congress Joint Economic Committee:

> My able colleague (Senator Proxmire) notes that the situation with respect to the weapons acquisition process is getting worse instead of better. In this connection, does he believe that part of the problem is related to the fact that military procurement officers are not properly trained, particularly in view of the gigantic amounts of money they control, and, in addition, the fact that most of these officers are constantly being shifted from one duty station to another?

Senator Proxmire, the chairman of the committee, responded:

> There is no question in my mind that these men who have this very heavy responsibility do not have the kind of training or background which would be in many cases essential to hold down expenditures.

On December 10, 1970, the House Committee on Government Operations expressed some doubts about the effectiveness of the Defense Department's attempts to stabilize the assignment of program managers.

Secretary Packard has referred to the need for drastic reorganization of the services, but he has not spelled out any details, and there is little indication that the services share this view of the problem or are prepared to institute such changes on their own.

It is fair to ask whether the new call for expertise in program management squares with policy and practice regarding the rotation of military officers. The new goal is three-year tours of duty for program managers. It is difficult to see how three-year tours of duty for military officers will enable them to gain the degree of technical and managerial expertise that Mr. Packard emphasized so strongly. Development projects frequently are maintained for much longer periods. The concept of expertise that Admiral Rickover espouses, and Mr. Packard seems to endorse, is associated with rigorous technical training career professionalism, and longer tenure than even a three-year tour of duty.[23]

On March 9, 1971, Deputy Secretary of Defense David Packard testified before the House Armed Services Committee.

A very crucial problem area in the past has been that project officers were not doing an adequate job. This resulted from many factors, including assignment of managers who were poorly selected or who lacked proper training for the job, inflexible service rotation policies which made it impossible for a manager to stay with a program long enough to be effective, and the effects of permitting too many people to get in on what the program manager should have been doing himself. Solution of this problem requires that we select more capable project managers and staffs and leave them on the job long enough for them to be effective. We also must give project managers the special training in development and procurement they need in order to do their job properly. We are revamping and improving our Defense Weapons Systems Management Center to add this special training. The center is being relocated from Wright-Patterson Air Force Base to Fort Belvoir, effective July 1971. Finally, we must clarify the project managers' responsibility so that they are not just errand boys for already over-burdened higher staff echelons.

On December 9, 1971, Admiral H. G. Rickover discussed the problem of personnel turnover during the Senate Armed Forces Committee Hearings on the Weapon Systems Acquisition Process.

In the Defense Department there is the problem that those who are running the projects are around for only 2 to 3 years. The DOD looks for quick solutions to solve all its management problems. They designate technically inexperienced persons as "project managers." The problem is then considered solved and at once forgotten. But these managers do not have the technical skill to see to it that their project is properly conceived and carried out. Most have only the shallowest knowledge of the theory of the techniques they must deal with and little experience with the practical problems involved. Under our rotation system, they are never kept long enough on the job to acquire such skill and knowledge.

As if this did not make their task difficult enough, they are subject to constant interference from upper echelon bureaucrats pushing their personal proposals, seeking to have their "advanced" concepts put into effect. With all of these pressures upon him, the neophyte manager during his brief tour of duty will barely learn to understand these proposals, still less to weigh them and arrive at a judgment he can forcefully defend. Nevertheless, he must make decisions vitally affecting his project, decisions which may be technically unsound but will satisfy his superiors and so will take effect. This is how a project becomes irrevocably set.

Before the results of the decisions are in, the manager will have moved and a new manager, equally unqualified technically, will take his place. Naturally the new manager will feel no responsibility for prior decisions and actions; his primary ambition will be to keep the project moving in the hope that it will not fail during his own tour. Thus responsibility cannot be fixed and there is bound to be little continuity in technical direction for most of the defense developments under way today.

Although Pentagon officials, such as Deputy Secretary Packard, began to make improvements in 1970 and 1971 in the training and assignment process for military officers, it is still doubtful whether their efforts will lead to significant changes in promotion and assignment policies. The most far-reaching reform would be the establishment of a clearly defined procurement career field within the military, with senior procurement managers controlling assignments and promotions. Anything short of this will not resolve the continuing crisis in procurement management.

Among executives from private corporations working on defense programs, the need for a career field in procurement management is commonly recognized. Several references to this were made during interviews.

> The services must find a way to equate a systems acquisition job with an operational job or there's no way out of this mire.

> * * * * *

> Why does the program manager or top guy have to be a pilot? Industry doesn't run their projects with pilots. If we did, we'd be out of business in no time.

> * * * * *

> It took [name of company] ten years to establish program managers in our company in the same status as function managers. Today, they

are the same—they have the same status and cars and other accoutre-
ments. But we had to prove to our men that they could grow within the
company and make equivalent salaries, by working up through the program management chain.

*   *   *   *   *

There is a need for much more care in translating policies down
through each organizational level within the Department of Defense. The
military services need to do much more in terms of training their procurement personnel and in creating a clear procurement field. There needs
to be a separate career ladder for procurement and the career assignments need to be under the control of the people in charge of procurement.

*   *   *   *   *

There should be career progression ladders for procurement officers
and program managers, separate from the career progression ladders for
operational personnel. We see no advantage to the country in taking a
good boat commander and making him a program manager.

Although military officers supervise acquisition programs, the importance
of civil service personnel should not be underestimated. As 88% of the
procurement work force, they are at the present the only source of continuity
in program management offices. Yet, not surprisingly, it is difficult to attract
capable civil servants to careers in program management. They are reluctant
to become part of an organization in which military officers occupy most
of the senior positions. Since most supervisory jobs must be filled by military
officers of a specific rank, positions remain vacant until the appropriate
officer is found. Qualified civilian managers are usually passed over, and the
officer eventually placed in the position may have no relevant experience
or training. The GAO report of 1970 cited the case of a capable civil servant
who had entered the Defense Department procurement field as a trainee and
advanced to a position as senior negotiator. After several frustrating years
of working under military officers who knew little or nothing about program
management, he left the civil service for a job in private industry. The report
commented:

In many cases the situation inhibits the professional development of
civilians because of the lack of suitable opportunities. It also requires
civilians to work under the supervision of personnel who do not have
adequate training or experience in procurement, which encourages "tread-
mill" performance, or premature separation from Government service,
by well-qualified civilians.[24]

Many civil service jobs are routine and dull. In addition, a civil servant working in a program office does not have the same job security as his counterparts in functional offices. Although he may stay within the procurement field, he must find a new job when his program ends, often in another location, sometimes at a lower salary. There is greater security, and more opportunity for professional development and advancement, in permanent staff office positions.

The civil servants who staff program offices have usually been Government employees for the major portion of their careers, often in low-grade purchasing activities. Contractors describe them as "tired men" who have worked their way up through the civil service ranks over a period of 20 to 30 years. When a senior civil service position becomes vacant, personnel next in rank compete to fill the position and thus advance in rank. One cynical program manager commented: "It does not take these individuals long to tell you about their rights and privileges and the difficulty you would have in removing them from the system."

The GAO report discussed the demoralizing effect on civil service personnel of the present program management system.

> There is also the matter of satisfying what is sometimes referred to as a person's ego needs contrasted with his financial needs. It is generally established that today, once a person's most fundamental financial needs have been met, he develops other needs which must be satisfied. In the procurement field it is difficult for civilians to satisfy such needs, because many of the higher status positions are filled by military officers. A combination of factors (e.g., limited training compared with that provided for the military profession, limited promotion, and limited responsibility) is demoralizing to civilians and makes it difficult to encourage their professional development in the procurement field.[25]

One civil servant who had resisted the pattern of low productivity of many of his colleagues commented: "People who stay in one of these jobs for a long time may start out performing at an adequate or even an above-adequate level. But after awhile, 'the blues' set in and they become rigid in their ways and resistant to new ideas."

The problems involved in attracting and retaining qualified civilian procurement personnel are well known throughout the Defense Department. Air Force Assistant Secretary Philip Whittaker, addressing the National Contract Management Association on October 30, 1970, discussed the issue:

> . . . We are faced with a very serious problem of attracting capable young college graduates with the promise of rewarding careers in the

contracting field, training them, improving their professional standing, and then retaining them in the face of manpower reductions. As a matter of fact, one of the major concerns of many of us who work for the military departments is that these very demanding and crucially important procurement jobs are being filled with an ever-aging and thinning core of experienced personnel.

The GAO report of 1970 noted that few procurement positions were being filled by young trainees.[26] Supervisory personnel claim that this scarcity results from a lack of training programs and training spaces, low grade levels for trainees, and ineffective recruitment on college campuses. According to the report, Defense Department recruiters are working under two handicaps:

1. The Civil Service Commission requires a majority of graduate applicants to take the Federal Civil Service Entrance Examination. Most educators and students consider this unwarranted.
2. Beginning salaries for Federal employees are lower than in private industry. The Federal Employees General Pay Schedule (July 1969) and the Salary Survey of the College Placement Council (June 1969) show that Government starting salaries for business administration graduates were between $605 and $2,068 below average industry levels. (The surveys did not take into account the fringe benefits of either Government or industry positions.)

Another major problem is the lack of job security for new procurement staff. They are protected from job reductions only for the one or two years they are in training. Then they are grouped with the total job force and are the first to be separated when jobs are eliminated.

In the mid-1960s the Defense Department initiated a program to upgrade the skills of civil service personnel already in procurement management. It instituted the Civilian Career Program for Procurement Personnel. However, the program has failed to produce the corps of skilled procurement managers needed to strengthen standards and performance. In 1970 the General Accounting Office reported:

> The development of the current DOD-Wide Civilian Career Program for Procurement Personnel was a positive step toward providing qualified personnel for carrying out the procurement function. It appears, however, that an in-depth analysis of the then and future requirements of the procurement function did not precede the program formulation. Insufficient consideration was given to (1) the changes in the character of the procurement function because of new military technology, (2) the change to almost total reliance on industry for research, development,

and production and for the evolving interface role, (3) the advances in science and technology, (4) the increasing complexity of the weapons being acquired and the attendant complex decision-making problems which start early in the research and development cycle, and (5) the impact that these factors would have on the procurement positions and the broadened training and development of the personnel for these positions. . . .[27]

In the same study, the GAO found that a majority of military and civilian procurement personnel had not attended courses designated by the Defense Department as mandatory for their grade levels.

Choosing qualified individuals to attend such courses is frequently difficult. One procurement supervisor explained that "we face the problem of having so few qualified people that you send your 'dead-beats' to school where they often do not work and are not assigned grades. As such, there is no measure of performance included in their records."

In the spring of 1971 senior Pentagon officials instituted a 20-week training program, called the Defense Systems Management School, for military and civilian personnel working in program offices. Each of the military services was urged to select highly qualified individuals for the school's first session. When the first class convened, the required 60 personnel were present—15 military officers and 5 civilians from each service. A gap between military and civilian performance became increasingly obvious during the 20-week program. Most officers were interested and took full advantage of all resources. No more than two or three civil servants worked with the course material or participated in class discussion. One of the interested civilians explained that civil service personnel are often sent to training programs as a reward for loyalty and longevity of service, not on the basis of capability or potential.

Not all program personnel who seek further training are able to attend training schools. A first lieutenant who had worked in a program office for 18 months told us that he had been unable to convince his supervisor to send him to one of the short training programs, despite his lack of experience and background in program management. The workload in the organization was so heavy that it was difficult for the manager to send anyone at all to school. Several program managers said that they usually sent only those individuals whose loss would have the least harmful effect on productivity. Obviously, this means that the individual who is eager and qualified for training is often the least likely to receive it. Another problem was outlined by a civil servant enrolled in the 20-week program: "Supervisors in the field fear that if they give up a man for 20 weeks to attend a school, Government personnel specialists may conclude that the man is not needed. If the man's position is not filled during his 20-week absence, personnel specialists will ask why the position cannot be given up permanently. If the position is filled by another civil servant for the 20-week period, the man attending school is concerned that he may lose his position to his replacement."

Personnel problems within the Armed Services are certainly not limited to the field of program management. Similar problems in other military areas do not seem so difficult to remedy, however, as the following excerpt from a December 1969 article by Kenneth Turan of *The Washington Post* may suggest.

> Rear Admiral James Calvert, superintendent of the Naval Academy, announced at yesterday's annual Army-Navy Luncheon at the Touchdown Club that Coppedge, who has been athletic director since June 1968 will retire from the service in July to take the post as a civilian.
>
> The admiral said the change to a civilian director is "absolutely essential, if the Naval Academy's program is to catch and overtake those on our schedule in football and 20 other sports." Navy takes a 1–8 record, its worst in more than 20 years, into the November 29 game with Army.
>
> Admiral Calvert emphasized that "by constantly changing our athletic director every two or three years we have destroyed continuity which is necessary to an effective athletic administration," and Coppedge agreed, saying "if you had a million-and-a-half dollar business, would you want to change bosses every three years for someone who didn't have any experience?"
>
> Previously, the athletic director's post was simply another two to three year tour of duty for career Navy men. "Most directors come right from sea duty to this job," Coppedge said, "and it can take a full year to get to know the ropes. When I became director I barely knew the NCAA ground rules. How many people in the Navy do you think know about things like scheduling problems?"

MANAGEMENT OF DEFENSE PROGRAMS IN PRIVATE INDUSTRY

Most defense firms find that a task-oriented, or functional, organization is the best environment for the professional development of their employees —their most important asset. Since defense contracts usually require input from several of these functional groups, most companies superimpose upon functional organizations a matrix program office structure designed (1) to provide management direction on specific contracts, and (2) to provide a clearly defined point of contact with the customer. The person heading this program office is called a program manager.

In early 1971 we surveyed a sample of 30 program managers, 15 employed by the Defense Department and 15 in private industry. Each completed a detailed statement on his background and training. Tables IX-9 and IX-10 summarize the findings.

TABLE IX-9. 15 GOVERNMENT PROGRAM MANAGERS: 1971

Government Project Manager	Formal Education	Years of Training in Business or Industrial Practices	Number of Years' Contact with Procurement or Project Management
1	B.S. from service academy B.S. in Physics	0	1
2	B.S. Academic B.S. Mech. Eng.	0	2
3	B.S. from service academy —MBA	1	1
4	B.S.—MBA	1	1
5	B.S. Mil. Eng. M.S. Civil Eng.	0	4
6	M.S. Civil Eng. B.S. Mil. Sci.	0	4
7	B.S. from service academy M.S. Elec. Eng.	0	1
8	B.S. Mil. Sci. M.S. Elec. Eng. M.S. Ind. Eng.	1	2½
9	B.S. Bus. Adm. M.S. Log. Mgmt.	4	2
10	B.S. from service academy MBA	1	1
11	B.S. Mil. Sci. MSE Mech. Eng.	1	2½
12	B.S. Mil. Sci.	1	3
13	B.S. Mining Eng. MBA	2	1
14	B.S. Eng. M.S. Eng.	1	3
15	B.S. Physics M.S. Elec. Eng.	0	4

Fourteen of the 15 Government program managers had one year or less of formal training in the fields of procurement, contract administration, and/or industrial management. The fifteenth program manager had four years of training in these fields. Seven of the 15 Government program managers had been involved for two years or less with some segment of private industry. Most of this contact had occurred during their current assignments. Five pro-

TABLE IX-10. 15 INDUSTRY PROGRAM MANAGERS: 1971

Industry Project Manager	Formal Education	Years of Training in Business or Industrial Practices	Years in Current Business Activities	Years Since Worked in Commercial vs. Defense Projects
1	B.S. Mech. Eng.	0	14	4
2	B.S. Mech. Eng.	0	40	31
3	B.S. Elec. Eng.	0	15	15
4	B.S. Elec. Eng. B.S. Physics	0	14	11
5	B.S. Math & Eng.	0	24	24
6	B.S. Eng.	Exec. mgmt. training	16	16
7	Product Design Courses	Co. spon. mgmt. course	12	12
8	B.S. Elec. Eng.	Co. AMP course	15	15
9	B.S. Mech. Eng. Commercial Science	1	12	12
10	B.S. Elec. Eng.	0	21	21
11	B.S. Elec. Eng.	0	19	19
12	B.S. Math/Chemistry	0	19	19
13	B.S. Eng.	0	20	20
14	B.S. Elec. Eng.	0	17	17
15	B.S. Mech. Eng.	Co. spon. mgmt. course	16	16

gram managers had between two and three years' contact with industry. Three of the managers had four years' experience with industry.

All 15 industry program managers had received formal education in engineering. Only five of the 15 had any formal training in business administration. Four of these five had attended short company-sponsored courses in advanced management training; the fifth had earned an additional degree in commercial science. The experience level of industry program managers ranged from 12 to 40 years, with an average of 18 years. All had been employed in Defense Department or NASA programs for consecutive periods of four to 31 years, with little or no recent experience in commercial programs. While statistics indicated that Government program managers had more formal education than their industry counterparts, not one Government manager had worked one-third as long in program management as any industry manager.

The program manager and staff within the contracting company are generally responsible for:

1. Interpreting total contract requirements;
2. Developing a plan for fulfilling program requirements within contract budget and schedule;

3. Dividing the requirements into distinct work packages;
4. Assigning the work packages to functional groups or to outside sources ("make or buy" decisions);
5. Defining and assigning responsibility for interfaces between work packages;
6. Determining the adequacy of resources assigned to each work package, in accordance with the overall program plan;
7. Obtaining adequate funding from the Government customer to carry out the program plan;
8. Maintaining continuous program surveillance; identifying budget or schedule problems for the attention of the appropriate management levels within the company;
9. Keeping the customer and company management informed of program progress;
10. Providing liaison with the customer;
11. Realizing the full profit and sales potential of the program.

During interviews with industry personnel we learned that the critical period in program management begins with a company's decision to bid for a new development program, and continues until initial production problems have been solved. Throughout this period the program manager is the key individual in the organization. Company directives stress his importance to the company's financial health. For this reason he is always working under pressure. If he performs capably, he becomes a candidate for promotion to a higher level of company management. If he is not successful, promotion channels close quickly.

We found no definite career pattern in program management within private industry. An assignment as program manager is generally considered a broadening experience for promising company executives. Most transfers involving program managers are "lateral," i.e., into and among the company's various program and functional organizations. Although program management is considered a relatively high-risk route to general management, it is a risk for which program managers are well paid. Annual salaries for industry managers of major defense programs begin at $40,000.

As a general rule an industry program manager is evaluated in terms of customer satisfaction with the weapon system developed or produced in his program. His record in meeting schedule and cost terms is secondary, with schedule receiving the greater emphasis. Especially important is the manager's record in generating "follow-on" business. He continually attempts to expand the scope of his program by negotiating engineering change proposals or by persuading a Government agency to buy more production items. The company's need for "follow-on" business is urgent because highly qualified program personnel do not like to mark time between Government contracts. When Government funds dry up, talented employees are idle and restless. If the period between programs lasts from three to six months, personnel may move to other firms, especially if promotion or lateral transfer opportunities are available to them.

When opportunities to attract "follow-on" programs have ended, the program manager's responsibility alters considerably. This usually occurs when the program is midway into the production phase. Work then becomes relatively routine and the possibilities for contract changes or additions are virtually over. In some cases management of remaining program performance is transferred to the company's manufacturing or production department. At other times a less experienced program manager is assigned to the program.

Industry program managers told us that the organizational structure of a program office varies according to program requirements. The industry program office is usually modeled on the Government's program management organization. In general, the program manager is chosen from a management level appropriate to the size of the program. A small research or limited development program that can be performed in a narrow segment of the company is directed by a functional manager of fairly low status. He has little need for additional management staff. Larger programs, which demand inputs from broad segments of the company, require larger program offices. Program managers for major programs are accorded direct and immediate access to top management.

In many major defense firms, a small group of specialists works with the program manager to direct the work performed in the functional departments. This group includes a chief engineer and a director of program control. They remain with the program manager throughout the life of the program. Other group members come from the company's functional organizations and are phased in and out of the program as needed. These may include specialists in contracts, production, logistics, systems, technical support, data, and planning and control. The program manager of this matrix organization controls his staff's salaries, working hours, and vacations, and evaluates performance. Program support staffs range from six to 200 or more people, depending upon the size of the contract.

Not all contractors have found the matrix organization structure practical for program management. An industry program manager is expected to control costs and to present his company with a profit. Both goals demand exceptional management expertise and optimum program environment. The program manager has special problems when his staff is assigned to other profit centers as well as his own. He must depend on cooperation from the managers of his company's functional departments as he organizes his program activity. He will, for example, assign a task to the manufacturing department of the company. The manager of this department will provide the necessary manpower. The program manager will direct and coordinate the overall program activity, but the daily supervision of employees and periodic appraisals of performance are the responsibility of the functional manager. This division of authority can be a serious impediment to the success of the program.

Some major contractors have therefore elected to organize their programs as self-contained units, with each program manager comparable to the general manager of an independent company. Some firms even assign separate buildings to major programs. According to industry managers, this program organization structure provides work incentives and a sense of participation not afforded by a matrix organization. Many industry program managers believe that a group of experts working closely together on one program perform better than a collection of specialists separated by discipline or function. When the goals of a program are shared by all participants, cooperation without conflict or lost motion is optimized. In addition, top management has found that these relatively independent program management organizations are easier to monitor for contract performance.

In major development and production programs, the most difficult task is the management of engineering design and integration efforts. During the initial development period, the company's engineering departments perform a large proportion of the program work. Their tasks usually require the development of new system components and/or the integration of many components being used together for the first time.

Skilled engineers are usually dedicated to their technical specialties. If an engineer receives a comfortable salary, his principal objectives are to work on challenging technical problems and to advance the state-of-the-art. Engineers are especially sensitive to informal appraisals of their work by their peers. Since the program performance of one engineer, or an engineering task group, is usually integrated with the work of other engineering units within the company, there is considerable intragroup discussion regarding technical activity. Industry executives believe that engineers are often more sensitive to the opinions of their colleagues than to the goals of the programs to which they are assigned. As they struggle with tasks which advance the state-of-the-art, engineers working on defense programs feel particularly vulnerable. Not only must they develop new technical approaches to the development of a weapon system, but they feel that their solutions must be able to withstand the scrutiny of other engineers. It is not sufficient that the equipment they design and construct meet program performance standards. Their designs, to be assured of approval from other engineers, must be more sophisticated than previous designs, whether or not this is dictated by the program requirements.

Contractors welcome engineering achievements on defense programs that will enhance company reputation and attract new business. The technology developed on one defense contract may insure large profits from subsequent defense and commercial ventures. Contractors use various incentives to encourage engineering advances. Employee appraisal systems on which promotions and salary increases are based usually give as much weight to technological achievement as to total performance in meeting cost and schedule requirements. Appraisals of a particular department sometimes include a factor for the number of new patents developed by the department. Engineers who are responsible for new patents occasionally receive bonuses.

While engineers understandably prefer to pursue their technical objectives without constraints, limits are generally imposed by budget and schedule requirements. An engineer is expected to cooperate with his program manager, who in turn must meet the program's cost, schedule, and technical requirements. At the same time, an engineer's performance ratings and promotions are controlled by engineering supervisors who share his quest for professional excellence.

Engineers invariably spend the funds available to them. Periodically, problems arise within programs because engineers exceed their budgets. When cost, schedule, and technical performance requirements are incompatible, program managers establish priorities. In most cases, technical performance receives highest priority. Given a choice of meeting cost or schedule requirements, program managers generally prefer to meet schedules. As one contractor explained: "Missing schedule is one of the few justifications the Government has for terminating a contract for default."

In geographical areas where there is considerable movement of technical personnel between firms, program managers are especially cautious in their dealings with engineers who possess unique specialties or are unusually proficient in their fields. The exercise of overly strict cost discipline may drive such engineers to other companies in the area. Rather than run that risk, industry program managers concentrate on meeting technical and schedule needs and try to avoid conflicts over costs. This is undoubtedly one major reason for cost growth on development programs. It also explains the need for "management reserves," which amount to 3% to 8% of contract costs. Not only must funds be set aside for the unforeseeable problems which arise in all development efforts; they must cover the cost of professional curiosity and competitiveness as well.

Recent cutbacks in defense funds for weapons acquisition programs have resulted in a reduction of the defense industry's job force. For many engineers, unemployment is a totally new experience. Program managers note that it has shocked some of the remaining engineers into their first real acknowledgment of the need for cost controls.

Although program managers and procurement personnel in Government and industry program offices are dedicated to the success of their programs, "success" means something quite different to each. Among Government officials from the program office to the Pentagon, as well as in Congress and the executive branch, interpretations of defense priorities vary widely and spring from divergent values and goals. In comparison, the main industry goals are relatively simple: maintaining customer satisfaction, realizing a profit, developing the professional skills of their employees, and generating more business.

In theory, the Defense Department wants to acquire advanced weapon systems that meet performance standards and are reasonable in cost. In fact, too few Government personnel know anything about controlling cost schedules and performance. In addition, or as a result, they discourage or downgrade cost control efforts. Industry managers do not emphasize cost control if it means lessening profit or curbing the efforts of zealous engineers and other professional personnel. Unfortunately, Government officials often acquiesce to industry priorities and are persuaded that these are synonymous with national defense priorities.

A major reason for lack of balance on the program office level is the stability and expertise within industry management, as compared with the constant turnover of military program management staff, most of whom bring little more than good intentions to their assignments. Civilians in Government procurement have longevity of assignment but are often inferior in capability, training, and status; and they receive little opportunity or motivation to improve their skills.

Reform is long overdue.

NOTES TO CHAPTER IX

1. Comptroller General of the United States, Report to the Congress on *Action Required to Improve DOD Career Program for Procurement Personnel,* August 13, 1970, p. 12.
2. Ibid.
3. Report of the Blue Ribbon Panel to the President and the Secretary of Defense on the Department of Defense, July 1, 1970, p. 27.
4. Air Force Systems Command Memorandum 375-3.
5. Armed Services Procurement Regulations 1-201.3.
6. Aerospace Industries Association, Report on *The Role of the Contracting Officer,* July 1971.
7. Office of the Secretary of Defense, Report to the Secretary of Defense on *Contract Administration, Project 60,* August 26, 1963.
8. Instructions of General James Ferguson to Project Managers, Air Force Systems Command, January 24, 1970.
9. U.S. Department of Defense, Ad Hoc Study Group (Robertson Panel), *Manned Aircraft Weapon Systems, A More Vigorous Project Management,* Volume V, August 1956.
10. U.S. Department of the Navy, Aviation Division Notice 5410, "Analysis into Short and Long-Range Military Technical Effects of the Introduction of the Weapon System Concept," May 15, 1959.
11. U.S. Department of Defense, Systems Management Study Committee (Rawlings), Report to the Secretary of the Air Force, May 26, 1961.
12. Defense Industry Advisory Council, *Fundamental Issues Affecting Defense-Industry Relationships,* Washington, D.C., 1963, pp. 137–151.
13. Defense Science Board, Office of the Director of Research and Engineering, *Report of the Panel on R&D Management,* July 18, 1969.
14. National Security Industrial Association Report on *Defense Acquisition Study,* Washington, 1970.
15. Comptroller General of the United States, Report to the Congress, op. cit.
16. Office of the Assistant Secretary of Defense (Installations and Logistics), Report of the Long Range Logistics Manpower Policy Board, February 1969.
17. Address by the Honorable Barry J. Shillito, Assistant Secretary of Defense (Installations and Logistics) to the Industrial College of the Armed Forces, Washington, D.C., June 4, 1970.
18. Report of the Blue Ribbon Panel, op. cit., p. 137.
19. Merton J. Peck and Frederic M. Scherer, *The Weapons Acquisition Process: An Economic Analysis* (Boston: Division of Research, Harvard Business School, 1962), pp. 93–94.
20. Comptroller General of the United States, Report to the Congress, op. cit., p. 40.
21. Ibid., p. 16.
22. For additional information on this topic, see the Report of the Blue Ribbon Panel, p. 140.
23. U.S. House of Representatives, Committee on Government Operations, report on *Policy Changes in Weapons Systems Procurement,* December 10, 1970.
24. Comptroller General of the United States, Report to the Congress, op. cit., p. 46.
25. Ibid.
26. Ibid., p. 2.
27. Ibid., p. 14.

CHAPTER X

Government Representatives at Contractor Plants

THE DEFENSE CONTRACT ADMINISTRATION SERVICE (DCAS) was created in the early 1960s to consolidate the contract administration offices operated by individual military services. It is an organization of approximately 25,000 personnel, with headquarters at Cameron Station, Alexandria, Virginia. DCAS administers more than 80% of all defense contracts, providing the military services and contractors with uniform contract administration activities and procedures. The organization is headed by a major general or an admiral. (Leadership rotates among the three services.) This officer reports to the head of the Defense Supply Agency which falls under the jurisdiction of the Office of the Assistant Secretary of Defense (Installations and Logistics). DCAS carries out its contract administration services through 11 regional offices and approximately 100 field offices, many of which are located at defense plants. The decision to establish a resident field office at a plant is usually determined by the number and size of ongoing contracts at the plant.*

PLANT REPRESENTATIVE TASKS

Armed Services Procurement Regulation 1-406 describes 42 tasks under the heading "Contract Administration." These range from approving con-

---

* It should be noted that each of the military services retains contract administration responsibility for a small number of contractor plants, usually those that do most of their Government business with a single military service, often with a single program within that service. Since DCAS has responsibility for most plant representative offices at defense contractor locations, however, the discussion in this chapter will refer only to all field representative offices as DCAS plant representative offices.

tractor requests for payment to conducting industrial readiness field surveys and reviewing a contractor's insurance plan. The following list summarizes these tasks. Plant representatives:

1. Review and approve or disapprove contractor's request for payment under the progress payments clause;
2. Determine the allowability of costs suspended or disapproved by the Defense Contract Audit Agency;
3. Negotiate billing rates and final overhead rates with the contractor;
4. Negotiate prices and execute supplemental agreements for spare parts and other items selected through provisioning procedures;
5. Review and evaluate contractor's proposals;
6. When authorized by the purchasing office (i.e., the program management organization), negotiate and execute supplemental agreements incorporating contractor proposals resulting from change orders;
7. Review, approve or disapprove, and maintain surveillance of the contractor's procurement system;
8. Consent to the placement of subcontracts;
9. Prepare production support, surveillance, and status reports;
10. Prepare surveys of a contractor's operations before a contract is awarded to ascertain his ability to perform successfully;
11. Oversee contractor design, development, and production engineering performance;
12. Review engineering studies, designs, and proposals, and make recommendations to the program manager;
13. Review, on a continuing basis, contractor test plans and directives for compliance with contract terms; compare milestones, progress, and cost against contract requirements.

As the list above indicates, the DCAS office has major responsibility for keeping the program manager informed about the activities of the contractor and the extent to which these activities do or do not conform to the terms of a contract.

The DCAS plant representative staff can contribute to the Government's strength in negotiating contracts with the contractor. They are often more familiar with the contractor's operations and estimating methods than the Government program office staff; this knowledge can be valuable in face-to-face bargaining sessions. DCAS plant representative personnel usually negotiate small contract-changes—normally those below $350,000. In some cases, a representative of the local DCAS office will attend negotiations on larger changes held at the program office. However, geographical and organizational remoteness often keeps local DCAS plant personnel from attending negotiation sessions on major changes.

INTERNAL DCAS ORGANIZATION

The size of a DCAS plant organization can range from 30 to 240 personnel. The officer in charge of the local DCAS plant office usually holds the rank of Army or Air Force colonel or Navy captain. Although civil service personnel outnumber the military officers in the plant representative organization by as much as 20 to 1, most of the key supervisory positions are filled by military officers. As in Government program offices, the internal organization of DCAS plant offices varies from one case to the next. In most instances, however, they are divided into a number of divisions; e.g., Production, Quality Assurance (i.e., inspection and acceptance), Contract Administration, and Engineering.

The relationship between the Government program office and the DCAS plant office ranges from close cooperation to arm's-length negotiation. Difficulties occur because the program manager reports to superiors within his military service, while the senior official of the DCAS plant office reports to superiors within the DCAS regions, to the head of DCAS, and then to the head of the Defense Supply Agency. It is only at the level of the Office of the Secretary of Defense that there is a single focal point for both the program office and the DCAS plant representative.

The Government program offices and DCAS plant offices usually work closely together. But in a significant number of instances, Government program managers work directly with contractors without including representatives from the local DCAS office. On the other hand, a senior officer of one military service told us that he knew of many cases where there was a much closer relationship between the contractor and the DCAS plant representative than between the plant representative and the Government program manager. During our visits to more than 30 plant representative offices, we observed many DCAS plant representatives who thought of themselves as the contractor's "partner" rather than an independent investigator and negotiator.

The same problems identified in relation to program managers exist for DCAS plant representative offices: frequent turnover of military officers and lack of qualified personnel. There is an additional problem at plant representative offices, however—the result of the longevity of civilian officials' service at one plant. One of the primary reasons for assigning Government personnel to a contractor's plant is to strengthen cost control and quality of work being performed.[1] When personnel have been assigned to the same DCAS plant office for a number of years, these goals may be neglected. At any defense plant, programs come and go; military personnel come and go; Government program offices come and go. But the civilian personnel in the DCAS plant offices and the senior executives in the plant remain on the scene. Senior personnel from DCAS plant offices are often invited by contractors to use the facilities of the company's executive dining room. Years pass and the same individuals work together on many programs. DCAS people begin to identify with the long-term stability and growth of their plant.

Proximity may quite naturally result in close friendship. But close friendship among the parties at a negotiating table may easily mean that some negotiators will not present strong arguments for their side of the case. One officer in charge of a DCAS region told us that the civilians in his region had held assignments at the same contractor plants for an average of more than 10 years. One Government auditor had been assigned to the same plant for 25 years, and other Government personnel approached this longevity. The officer stated that this situation is common in plant representative offices throughout the United States.

The senior officer at one plant representative office resisted attempts by a team of Government auditors and industrial engineers to make an in-depth analysis of the contractor's price proposal for a major program. He justified his resistance on the grounds that "they've been our contractor for 30 years and we don't want to jeopardize that relationship." In a similar case, individuals in the plant representative office refused to make any cost information available to a team of Government auditors unless they received a specific release from the contractor. This action was justified with the same reasoning cited in the first example.

A vice president of a defense contracting firm commented on the role of Government plant representatives:

> I think the plant representative can play a valuable role. The plant representative can represent the contractor's views. Our plant representative has served as a buffer between us and the program office and often made our case better than we did. We find that it is highly incumbent on the contractor personnel to develop a good working relationship with the civil servants at the plant representative office.

It is not easy to identify inefficiency, poor quality, or inadequate controls. Negotiating meaningful agreements in order to have these deficiencies corrected is an even more difficult task, and often an unpleasant one. If they have any doubts about whether or not there are problems in a large contractor's internal operations, DCAS representatives find it easier to look the other way and to postpone a comprehensive investigation until the situation becomes more serious. Seeking out instances of poor quality or inadequate controls may endanger close friendships.

A management consultant to the defense and aerospace industry who has conducted contract negotiation classes for more than 14,000 industry personnel provides the following advice in his manual on contract negotiation:

> This [mention of the friendship problem] is not intended to infer that a buyer, whether a Government buyer or one employed in private industry, is making under-the-table deals or that there is anything ethically wrong in the relationship. It is just that, in many cases, familiarity may not breed contempt, but may breed friendship which prevents the buyer from doing the most effective job at the negotiation table. The seller, of course, should attempt to analyze the buyer's basic attitudes and conduct himself accordingly. Many firms maintain a dossier on the buyers with which they do business.

Since the number of Government employees and the promotion opportunities at a plant representative office are determined by the amount and type of the defense business at the plant, it is understandable that Government representatives assigned to a plant for a number of years would want the contractor to obtain new business. There is another reason for the DCAS plant representatives' eagerness to maintain or increase the level of defense business at a contractor plant. Declining business frequently means that there will be increases in the contractor's indirect cost rate, unless someone at the plant undertakes the difficult task of reducing indirect costs along with direct costs. As discussed later in this report, indirect costs in the defense and aerospace industry frequently account for 50% or more of a contractor's costs. These costs consist largely (approximately 70%) of personnel costs. Thus, reducing them means removing personnel from a contractor's payroll—a painful task under any circumstances. If a contractor does not maintain effective control of indirect costs in a period of declining sales, then the indirect cost rate, as a percentage of direct costs, increases. When this occurs, program cost growth begins. Cost growth means that the contractor, the DCAS plant representative, and the Government program office may be criticized by higher levels within the Department of Defense, and possibly by the Congress and the press.

Recently, senior DCAS officials have taken steps to reduce the length of time served by Government personnel at one contractor plant. The new policy would limit the assignment of a DCAS resident to a period of no more than three years. In the spring of 1971, as attempts were being made to implement this policy, one senior DCAS officer stated that he had received many telephone calls from Congressional offices, objecting to the new policy on the grounds that it posed an inconvenience for the Congressmen's constituents. The fact that the earlier policy was likely to mean higher costs for the bulk of the Congressmen's constituents was seldom discussed.

One industry manager for a major defense program offered some suggestions for improved performance at plant representative offices.

> What the military services need is a larger number of better trained, more knowledgeable, and courageous plant representatives. I know from my own experiences and from observing other contractors on this program that the courage and capability of the Program Manager and the senior officer at the plant representative office are major influences on the contractors. In the interest of minimizing their problems, the Program Manager and the individuals at the plant representative office sometimes become proponents of the contractors. Even in those cases where they do not, they often give up too soon in trying to bring about effective change in a contractor plant. Sometimes the Program Manager or other Government personnel conduct a management survey of one of our plants, but they don't do anything about taking the next step, because they aren't sure what to do.

In March 1971 the Air Force Association issued a report on the weapons acquisition process in which a number of similar observations were made.

> . . . Some of the shortcomings identified were: undermanning of the plant representative offices; inexperienced personnel; too low military grades to be effective; and personnel becoming "contractor oriented" due to long tours of duty at the same plant. Some experts in Air Force financial management have indicated that a potential source of savings is the area of determining standard hours for work packages and the allocation and control of overhead. The responsibility for monitoring and evaluating the reasonableness of plant overhead might be assigned to the local plant representative office, if the personnel assigned were adequately trained in contractor methods of accounting for and controlling overhead.[2]

In fact, plant representatives have for years been assigned the responsibility for monitoring and evaluating the reasonableness of plant overhead. The Air Force Association was unaware of this, it would seem.

In many cases, the Government program manager receives monthly progress reports from the plant representative. For each contract, these reports identify the latest negotiated target cost, budgeted dollars by months, and the ceiling price. In addition, the reports contain a statement of the costs charged to each contract during the past month and a brief progress report for each contract.

The officer in charge of one DCAS region said that his personnel monitor the rate at which contractors spend money, but they have few qualifications to undertake any analysis of a contractor's efficiency or the reasonableness of his costs.

Responsibility for contractor overhead costs is perceived differently from one DCAS office to the next. In one case, a visitor from the Pentagon pointed out to a plant representative that the contractor's overhead rate had increased 40% in a period of four years. The representative responded that he had no responsibility for contractor overhead costs. His job was simply to see that the contractor produced a good quality product on schedule. In another case, at a Government-owned plant operated by a contractor, a Government auditor had determined that the contractor's overhead costs were excessive and that $82.5 million should be removed from the contractor's current proposal for a large production contract. The Government plant representative subsequently sent a letter to the Government program manager commenting on the auditor's report, part of which is excerpted here.

> The price analyst considers this (the level of overhead costs) a contractor management function and to say that indirect people are excess because the ratio of indirect to direct is unfavorable when compared to other periods of time, is not reasonable. The contractor is entitled to his costs, and if we think they are too high, we should seek a cheaper facility, but since we have engaged him, then he is entitled to his costs.

If one were to adopt this logic one could only conclude that the Government should pay whatever the contractor requested because the size, complexity, and importance of the program made it almost impossible for another contractor to complete the program.

Government plant representatives have tasks other than management duties. They are required to act as hosts to visiting dignitaries from higher levels in the military services, from DCAS, the Office of the Secretary of Defense, the General Accounting Office, Congressional committees, or any other part of the Government. Local plant representatives are expected to work with the contractor to plan itineraries for these visitors, and then to accompany the visitors when they arrive at the plant. While protocol may require this hospitality, there is an even stronger reason for plant representative personnel to accompany the visitors at all times. Both contractor and Government personnel at all levels agree that visiting Government officials often provide informal "guidance" to contractors without the knowledge of the Government program manager or the DCAS plant resident personnel. This guidance may or may not be in line with management decisions made by the Government program office or the plant representative. In order to protect their own interests and preserve order in the conduct of the program, plant representative personnel make every effort to accompany Government visitors wherever they go.

How frequently do Government personnel visit the plant? A plant representative who was later promoted to the rank of general officer, and who held the senior procurement policy position in his service, discussed his experience as the senior Government representative at a large aerospace plant in southern California. He said that when he was assigned to the job, he was amazed to discover the frequency and number of Government personnel visiting the plant. At the end of two years, he found that the average was more than 300 visitors per month during the winter and more than 150 visitors per month during the summer. This plant may have had more visitors than usual because of the large and controversial nature of its program, but comments from other plant representatives indicate that most large contractor plants receive visits from Government personnel at a rate of 50 or more a month. In the summer of 1971 a senior executive of one defense firm told us that he had "a total of three Congressional and GAO investigating teams resident in his plant continually for the past three months."

The lack of enthusiasm one finds at many plant representative offices may, in part, result from a sense of despair. The job assigned is impossible to perform with the capability available. The 42 tasks assigned by ASPR 1-406 represent an undertaking of immense proportions. Recruiting efforts to obtain better qualified personnel are not always successful. In fact, DCAS often has difficulty recruiting and retaining qualified college graduates. Most graduates are interested in a reasonable opportunity for advancement and continued employment. At the present time, DCAS does not offer civil servants any assurance of promotion opportunities and continued employment. Once new employees emerge from the DCAS training program of one or two years, they are no longer protected from a civil service reduction-in-force. When such a reduction occurs, individuals with lowest seniority are the first to be released. Seniority rights presented major problems for the Department of Defense in the required reductions in civilian personnel which took place in 1970 and 1971. Senior civilian and military personnel could find no effective recourse to terminating hundreds of college graduates, while hundreds of less desirable, low-output personnel with more seniority remained on the payroll. For example, more than half of the 200 recent college graduates brought into the Chicago DCAS office in 1968 were given termination notices in 1970 because of reductions-in-force directed from higher levels. This pattern was repeated at DCAS offices throughout the United States. As a result, DCAS recruiting personnel have found it difficult to recruit high-quality college graduates for their training programs.

The responsibility for improving the overall situation rests, not on the individuals assigned to the plant representative offices, but on higher-level Government officials who have structured the present system and have the authority to change it.

In many respects, the management duties of Government plant representatives, as well as program managers and contracting officers, depend on the contracts which define the work to be accomplished by contractors. These types of contracts are described in the following chapter.

NOTES TO CHAPTER X

1. Report of the Blue Ribbon Panel to the President and the Secretary of Defense on the Department of Defense, July 1, 1970, p. 191.
2. Air Force Association, *Study of the Weapons Acquisition Process*, March 1971.

CHAPTER XI

Types of Contracts

A CONTRACT is an agreement between a buyer (in this case, the Government) and a seller (the contractor) stating the functions each will perform in a particular transaction.* Such agreements vary in size: a one-page purchase order may be an adequate contract for a standard commercial item. In the case of complex, specialized equipment, a contract may include a thousand or more pages. There are two general types of contracts in Government procurement—cost-reimbursement and fixed-price. Under a cost-reimbursement contract, the contractor promises that he will try to meet the performance requirements or goals of the contract within the negotiated schedule and estimated cost. In return, he is entitled to reimbursement of his costs, and a profit (normally referred to as "fee"). Under a fixed-price contract, the contractor *guarantees* performance of the terms of the contract. In exchange for the guarantee, the Government is obligated to pay a specified price.

In 1970 the Department of Defense wrote more than ten million contracts (5,000 per working hour). A small portion of these contracts represents a major part of all defense contract awards. In 1970, 4,605 contracts, each for $1 million or more, constituted 67.4% of total defense prime contract awards. (These 4,605 contracts represented less than 0.1% of the total defense contracts awarded in that year.)[1]

---

* Federal Procurement Regulation 1-1.208 states: "Contract means establishment of a binding legal relation basically obligating the seller to furnish personal property or non-personal services (including construction) and the buyer to pay therefor. It includes all types of commitments which obligate the Government to an expenditure of funds and which, except as otherwise authorized, are in writing. In addition to a two-signature document, it includes all transactions resulting from acceptance of offers by awards or notices of awards; agreements and job orders or task letters issued thereunder; letter contracts; letters of intent; and orders; such as purchase orders, under which the contract becomes effective by written acceptance or performance. It also includes contract modifications."

In writing contracts the Government fits the terms to a wide range of defense procurements. If a cost-reimbursement procurement offers a contractor certain benefits beyond the immediate contract (e.g., commercial applications), the contractor may be willing to perform the work without profit and may even be willing to share the costs. In other situations the Government may provide an incentive fee to encourage the contractor to exert special effort on some aspects of the work. Fixed-price contracts may be written with labor or material escalation clauses or incentive features covering schedule, cost, or technical performance.

"Time-and-material" and "labor-hour" contracts combine features of fixed-price and cost-reimbursement contracts, and are used mainly for engineering design, repair, or overhaul jobs. Payment is based upon direct labor hours paid at fixed hourly rates and the actual cost of materials, both subject to a specified ceiling.

Three other contractual arrangements should be mentioned: letter contracts, basic agreements, and basic ordering agreements. Letter contracts are simply preliminary agreements for beginning work before a definitive contract is negotiated. Basic agreements are also preliminary agreements, but unlike letter contracts, they are not enforcible. They merely define the general provisions applicable to a future contract award. Basic ordering agreements resemble basic agreements, but include a description of the supplies or services to be furnished. These agreements are intended as time-saving devices in dealing with contractors on a recurring basis.

The Government, like any other buyer, wants its suppliers to assume a fair risk in procurement situations. Therefore, it prefers to use fixed-price contracts whenever possible. However, the Government officially recognizes the unusual risks of filling certain of its needs, and therefore authorizes several types of contracts with varying degrees of risk. The contract type is chosen by the procuring contract officer on the basis of the item or service to be purchased.

The underlying assumption of defense contracting is that a contractor will seek to maximize his profits. The Armed Services Procurement Regulation states:

> Profit, generally, is the basic motive of business enterprise. Both the Government and its defense contractors should be concerned with harnessing this motive to work for the truly effective and economical contract performance required in the interest of national defense. To this end, the parties should seek to negotiate and use the contract type best calculated to stimulate outstanding performance. The objective should be to insure that outstandingly effective and economical performance is met by high profits, mediocre performance by mediocre profits, and poor performance by low profits or losses. The proper application of these ob-

jectives on a contract by contract basis should normally result in a range of profit rates.[2]

FIXED-PRICE CONTRACTS

The Armed Services Procurement Regulation provides for four basic types of the fixed-price contracts:

1. Firm fixed-price
2. Fixed-price with escalation
3. Fixed-price incentive
4. Fixed-price redeterminable

Although all four limit the price for the completed job, each allocates risk to the contractor differently.

The *firm fixed-price contract* is the simplest of the four types. In this case, the contractor theoretically accepts all risks in exchange for the stated price. The Government is required to make no price adjustment for the original work after the contract is awarded, regardless of the contractor's actual cost experience in meeting it. Exceptions occur in cases of Government-approved contract changes made in response to changes in military requirements, technology, and funding. Changes may also be made in cases involving the "Truth in Pricing" Law (87-653). This provides that the Government is entitled to a reduction in price if it finds that the contractor did not disclose information available to him at the time of the negotiation which rendered his estimates inaccurate. In implementing this law, the Armed Services Procurement Regulation states:

> Cost or pricing data . . . is satisfied when all facts reasonably available to the contractor up to the time of agreement on price and which might reasonably be expected to affect the price negotiations are accurately disclosed to the contracting officer or his representative. The definition of cost or pricing data embraces more than historical accounting data; it also includes, where applicable, such factors as vendor quotations, nonrecurring costs, changes in production methods and production or procurement volume, unit cost trends such as those associated with labor efficiency, and make-or-buy decisions or any other management decisions which could reasonably be expected to have a significant bearing on costs under the proposed contract. In short, cost or pricing data consists of all facts which can reasonably be expected to contribute to sound estimates of future costs as well to the validity of costs already incurred. Cost or pricing data, being factual, is that type of information

which can be verified. Because the contractor's certificate pertains to "cost or pricing data," it does not make representations as to the accuracy of the contractor's judgment on the estimated portion of future costs or projections. It does, however, apply to the data upon which the contractor's judgment is based. This distinction between fact and judgment should be clearly understood.[3]

Firm fixed-price contracts closely resemble commercial contracts. The *Defense Procurement Handbook* uses the following terms to describe them:

> At a specified price, the contractor assumes all financial risks of performance. His profit depends entirely on his ability to control his costs. The Government bears no risk of loss under the contract. A firm fixed-price contract thus gives the contractor the maximum incentive (i) to avoid waste and (ii) to use production and subcontracting methods that will save labor and materials.
>
> The firm fixed-price contract has another great advantage for the Government: it is relatively easy and inexpensive to administer. It also benefits the contractor. The Government does not monitor his costs, so he does not have to conform his accounting methods to DOD audit procedures. His administrative costs are therefore lowered too.[4]

Realistically, two important conditions should exist before a firm fixed-price contract is negotiated: (1) reasonably definite design or performance specifications must be available; and (2) the contracting parties must be able to establish at the outset prices that are judged to be fair and reasonable.[5] In formally advertised procurements, the existence of definite specifications and adequate competition satisfies these conditions.

Even when price competition is not present, a firm fixed-price contract may be appropriate if one of the following conditions exists: (1) historical price comparisons can be made; (2) available cost or pricing data permit realistic estimates of probable performance costs; or (3) contract performance uncertainties can be so clearly identified that their impact on price can be evaluated. When none of these conditions exists, the use of a fixed-price contract with an incentive feature, or a cost-reimbursement type of contract, is normally considered more appropriate.

Fixed-price contracts with escalation provide for the upward or downward revision of the contract price when specific conditions occur. Escalation clauses in Government procurement fall into two broad classes: price escalation, and labor and/or material escalation.[6] Price escalation permits price adjustments based on changes in the price of certain materials (e.g., steel, aluminum, brass, bronze). Adjustments may be based on changes in (1) published or established prices of specific materials used in the project, or (2) the actual prices of the purchased materials. (Established prices can be defined as those set by the contractor for similar materials sold in the open market.) Labor or material escalation provides for similar adjustments in price on the basis of changes in wage rates and/or material costs for a particular procurement. In return for an escalation clause, a contractor must agree to eliminate from his estimate contingency allowances for increased labor and/or materials costs. It is important to note that escalation clauses protect the contractor only against *changes* in labor rates or material prices; they are not operative when the contractor makes incorrect estimates for required labor or materials.

The Armed Services Procurement Regulation discourages the use of escalation clauses because of the difficulty of administering them.[7] As a result, the clauses are normally used only for programs extending over two or more years.

Fixed-price incentive contracts are intended to encourage contractors to improve their cost and/or equipment and schedule performance. Simply stated, they seek to provide contractors with a profit incentive to reduce costs, improve the performance of the item to be produced, or meet or exceed a specified schedule. The most common fixed-price incentive contracts are those containing incentives on cost only. However, in many large development contracts, the incentive feature pertains to technical performance and schedules as well. These are called "multiple-incentive" contracts.

The two basic types of incentive contracts are fixed-price incentive (FPI) and cost-plus-incentive-fee (CPIF). The fixed-price incentive contract includes a ceiling price that limits the cost liability of the Government. The cost-plus-incentive-fee contract does not have a ceiling price. Since it is to the Government's advantage to have the contractor assume cost risk, the fixed-price incentive contract is preferred to the cost-plus-incentive-fee contract whenever costs and performance are reasonably certain.

Under a contract with cost incentives, the contractor's profit is determined by the amount that his costs underrun or overrun the target cost. The Government and the contractor share cost overruns or underruns according to a formula negotiated before the award of the contract. If the cost-sharing formula is 80/20, the Government retains $.80 and the contractor keeps $.20 of every dollar by which the contractor underruns target cost. In the case of an overrun, the Government pays $.80 of every dollar expended over target cost and the contractor pays $.20. Contract profit or fee is thus a function of the contractor's control of costs. Incentive patterns for technical performance may be arranged to reflect such product characteristics as range, speed, maneuverability, reliability, maintainability, and interchangeability. In terms of delivery or schedule, contractor rewards or penalties may be related to such measures as test completion dates or prototype acceptance dates.[8]

Before a fixed-price incentive contract is awarded, the Government and the contractor negotiate the following elements:

1. Target cost;
2. Target profit—the negotiated profit for work performed at target cost;
3. Ceiling price—the total dollar amount for which the Government will be liable;
4. Sharing formula—the arrangement for Government and contractor cost sharing below ceiling price.

After the work specified by a fixed-price incentive contract is completed, the contractor and the Government negotiate the final costs of the contract and share the overruns or underruns according to the cost-sharing formula being used. To illustrate: assume that the cost-sharing formula is 80/20; the target cost is $100; the target profit is $10; and the ceiling price is $120. In this case, the contractor would have to reduce costs to $90 ($10 below target cost) to earn a total profit of $12 (the target profit of $10 plus 20 percent of the $10 underrun). Since there is no ceiling on profit, it can increase indefinitely as the amount of underrun increases. At the same time, there is no guaranteed minimum profit. If the contractor spends more than $120 (ceiling price), he will incur a loss on the contract.

Fixed-price redeterminable contracts provide for (1) prospective redetermination at a specified time or times during performance; or (2) retroactive price redetermination after contract completion.[9] The prospective form of redetermination establishes, in effect, a *series* of firm fixed prices under one binding agreement. It is designed for use when firm and reasonable prices can be negotiated only for a portion of the contract period at the time of a contract award. A firm fixed price is negotiated for deliveries to be made during a specified initial period; thereafter, and at specified intervals, the price is subject to prospective redetermination.

Prospective redetermination at stated intervals is limited to situations in which:

1. A firm fixed-price contract is not suitable;
2. The contractor's accounting system is adequate for price redetermination purposes;
3. The prospective pricing period will conform with the operation of the contractor's accounting system;
4. There is reasonable assurance that timely redetermination will take place.

In the case of a retroactive redetermination contract, a ceiling price is established at the time of contract award. (The Armed Services Procurement Regulation specifies that the ceiling price should place a reasonable amount of risk on the contractor.)[10] Subsequent negotiations adjust the final price within the ceiling. Retroactive redetermination contracts are limited to research or development procurements with an estimated cost of $100,000 or less. Written approval for the use of this type of contract must be obtained from a management level higher than the defense procurement organization, and a review team must determine that the contractor's accounting system is adequate.

COST-REIMBURSEMENT CONTRACTS

The Armed Services Procurement Regulation provides for four basic types of cost-reimbursement contract:

1. Cost-plus-fixed-fee
2. Cost-reimbursement-without-fee
3. Cost-sharing
4. Cost-plus-incentive-fee

The Government contracting officer normally uses a cost-reimbursement contract when the magnitude of the uncertainties in the work to be performed precludes the use of an acceptable fixed-price arrangement. Under cost-reimbursement contracts, the Government is obligated to reimburse the contractor for all costs that are allowable and allocable to the contract. Allowable costs are defined by section 15 of the Armed Services Procurement Regulation. The usual unallowable costs are interest and advertising expense. A cost-reimbursement contract includes, however, a cost limitation beyond which the contractor will not be reimbursed—and beyond which he need not continue to work (if the Government does not provide additional funds). The limitation may be increased during the course of the contract but this may be done only by the contracting officer, in writing.

Because the Government bears the major portion of the financial risk, Congress has limited the amount of profit or fee that can be negotiated for work performed under cost-reimbursement contracts.[11] The fee limitation is described below.

1. Experimental, research, or development contracts: the fee can be no more than 15% of the estimated cost.

2. Supply or service contracts: the fee can be no more than 10% of the estimated cost.

The Armed Services Procurement Regulation now extends these statutory fee limits to cost-plus-incentive-fee contracts.[12] In such cases, however, the limits apply to the relationship of maximum fee to target cost as established at the time of contract execution.

A cost-reimbursement contract may be used only after a formal determination is made that any other contract type will be more costly or that it is impractical to secure supplies or services of the kind or quality required in any other way. It is ordinarily used in the following situations:[13]

1. When research and development work is procured;
2. When the scope and nature of the work required cannot be definitely described or its cost accurately estimated;
3. When there is doubt that the project can be completed successfully;
4. When production specifications are incomplete.

A type of cost-reimbursement contract that is prohibited by law is the cost-plus-a-percentage-of-cost arrangement. Under this type of contract, the contractor receives payment for the actual cost of performance, plus a specified percentage of such costs as a fee. Its undesirable feature is the automatic increase in fee as costs increase. Such contracts are generally considered wasteful and costly since the contract provides no incentive to promote efficient and economical contractor performance.[14]

The following clause is included in all cost-reimbursement contracts. It effectively reduces a contractor's financial risk to close to zero:

> It is estimated that the total cost to the Government for the performance of this contract, exclusive of any fee, will not exceed the estimated cost set forth in the schedule, and the contractor agrees to use his best efforts to perform the work specified in the schedule and all obligations under this contract within such estimated costs. If, at any time, the contractor has reason to believe that the costs which he expects to incur in the performance of this contract in the next succeeding sixty (60) days, when added to all costs previously incurred, will exceed seventy-five percent (75%) of the estimated cost then set forth in the schedule, or if, at any time, the contractor has reason to believe that the total cost to the Government for the performance of this contract, exclusive of any fee, will be greater or substantially less than the then estimated cost thereof, the contractor shall notify the contracting officer in writing to that effect, giving his revised estimate of such total cost for the performance of this contract.

> . . . the Government shall not be obligated to reimburse the contrac-
> tor for costs incurred in excess of the estimated cost set forth in the
> schedule, and the contractor shall not be obligated to continue perform-
> ance under the contract (including actions under the termination clause)
> or otherwise to incur costs in excess of the estimated cost set forth in the
> schedule, unless and until the contracting officer shall have notified the
> contractor in writing that such estimated cost has been increased and
> shall have specified in such notice a revised estimated cost which shall
> thereupon constitute the estimated cost of performance of this contract.
> No notice, communication or representation in any other form or from
> any person other than the contracting officer shall affect the estimated
> cost of this contract. In the absence of the specified notice, the Govern-
> ment shall not be obligated to reimburse the contractor for any costs in
> excess of the estimated cost set forth in the schedule, whether those ex-
> cess costs were incurred during the course of the contract or as a result
> of termination.[15]

Cost-reimbursement contracts place a heavy administrative burden on both Government and contractor. The contractor must have, or establish, an accounting system that is acceptable to the Department of Defense. Because title to all property purchased by the contractor and charged to the contract passes to the Government, both contractor and Government must compile comprehensive property records. This is a substantial administrative under-taking.

Cost-plus-fixed-fee contracts are the most prevalent type of cost-reimburse-ment contract. Under this type of contract, the contractor has a right to be reimbursed for all costs determined to be allowable, reasonable, and allocable. He is also paid a fixed-dollar profit or fee for his services, with the dollar amount of the fee established before work begins. Cost-plus-fixed-fee con-tracts provide the contractor very little incentive to manage his costs effec-tively. He may even find it advisable to increase his direct costs. By so doing, he may be able to charge more of his overhead or indirect costs to the contract. He may also be able to justify high estimates on future con-tracts.

Cost-plus-fixed-fee contracts can be written in one of two forms: com-pletion or term. The completion contract describes the scope of work and a definite goal or target, and normally requires delivery of a specific weapon system. The term contract describes the scope of work in general terms and obligates the contractor to maintain a specified level of effort for a stated period of time to the research and development program. Because the completion contract requires that the contractor assume more obligations than the term contract, the former is generally preferred by the Government.[16]

Cost-reimbursement-without-fee contracts (cost contract) are identical to the cost-plus-fixed-fee contracts, except that no profit or fee is paid to the contractor. They are used principally for (1) research and development work performed by educational or other nonprofit institutions, and (2) work on facilities, usually in connection with work on another contract.

Cost-sharing contracts are designed for research or development procurements when the contractor is to be reimbursed in accordance with a predetermined sharing agreement. Over and above the contractor's costs, no fee is paid. Unless a project involves work sponsored jointly with an educational institution or a cost-sharing arrangement with a foreign government, cost-sharing contracts are seldom used. Exceptions may be made if, for example, the contracting officer can find evidence that there is a high probability that the contractor will receive substantial commercial benefits, and if written approval is obtained from the head of the Government procuring activity. The use of this contract solely because a contractor is willing to share costs is contrary to Defense Department policy: it is likely to limit competition.

Cost-plus-incentive-fee contracts are part of the cost-reimbursement group. As in the case of fixed-price incentive contracts, the Government and contractor negotiate a target cost, a target profit, a sharing formula, a maximum profit, and, in some cases, a minimum profit. The sharing formula is used to determine how much profit will be paid to the contractor. When cost is the only incentive, the sharing formula is based on the relationship between the negotiated target cost and the final total allowable costs.

Unlike a fixed-price incentive contract, the cost-plus-incentive-fee contract has no ceiling price and the contractor is reimbursed for all allowable costs. If the actual costs exceed the target cost, the actual profit paid is less than the target profit. If the actual costs are less than the target cost, the actual profit paid is greater than the target profit. In no case can the actual profit be higher than the maximum profit stipulated in the contract. Incentive patterns for schedule and technical performance may be arranged in a similar fashion.

The cost-plus-incentive-fee contract is intended for use primarily for development and test activities when a cost-reimbursement type of contract is found necessary, and when a target and a profit adjustment formula can be negotiated to provide the contractor with a positive incentive for effective management.[17]

The *cost-plus-award-fee contract* is a variety of cost-plus-incentive-fee contract. The contract contains a base fee (generally 3% or less) and provision for the fee to be adjusted upward on the basis of the contractor's performance, evaluated after-the-fact in accordance with criteria set forth in the contract. The cost-plus-award-fee differs basically from other types of incentive arrangements, however: there is no mathematical formula established at the outset for the determination of profit. Instead, the amount of the award fee is based on recommendations of a Government Award Fee Evaluation Board and cannot be disputed by the contractor (i.e., the contract has no "disputes" clause). The total fee on these contracts may range from 2% to 13% of costs, depending upon the nature of the work to be performed and the performance record of the contractor on previous programs.

TIME-AND-MATERIALS CONTRACTS

A time-and-materials contract provides for payment to the contractor for supplies or services on the basis of incurred direct labor hours (at fixed hourly rates) and materials (at cost). The rate to be paid for each hour of direct labor is negotiated by the Government and the contractor and set forth in the contract; it includes direct and indirect labor, overhead, and profit. The cost of materials may include other items (such as handling costs) insofar as they are excluded from the direct labor rate.

Since the contractor is paid for work actually performed, a time-and-materials contract does not provide the contractor with a positive profit incentive to control material costs or to manage his labor force effectively. Consequently, the Government and contractor negotiate a ceiling price. This type of contract is intended for use when it is not possible to estimate the extent or duration of the work or to anticipate costs with any reasonable degree of confidence at the time the contract is signed. Such conditions are often encountered in procuring (1) engineering design services related to production of supplies; (2) engineering design and manufacture of special tooling and special machine tools; (3) repair, maintenance, or overhaul work; and (4) work performed in emergency situations. Since a time-and-materials contract does not encourage effective management control by the contractor, its use is discouraged by the Department of Defense.

LABOR-HOUR CONTRACTS

A labor-hour contract is simply a variation of a time-and-materials contract, differing only to the extent that no materials are supplied by the contractor. Both contracts bear a resemblance to the illegal cost-plus-a-percentage-of-cost contract. Because the amount of profit is determined by the amount of time or material expended, the greater the labor and materials, the higher the profits. Nonetheless, these types of contracts are suitable for small procurements when specific scientific, engineering, or other professional services cannot be found within the Government.

LETTER CONTRACTS

A letter contract is a preliminary contractual document. It authorizes the contractor to start work on a procurement immediately. He may prepare drawings, order materials, and begin production procedures that would otherwise be delayed pending negotiation of a definitive contract. Letter contracts are used to save time in the procurement process—time required for a contractor to prepare a price proposal, time required for the Govenment to audit the proposal, and time required to negotiate and agree on a firm contract. A letter contract contains no definite overall pricing arrangements. The Government is committed, however, to reimburse the contractor for costs incurred during the life of the letter contract, up to a specified amount. If a letter contract is not converted into a definitive contract in the shortest possible time, it takes on the characteristics of the cost-plus-a-percentage-of-cost contract.

A letter contract is intended for use only when *both* of the following conditions exist: (1) in the interests of national defense a binding agreement is necessary so that work can begin immediately; and (2) a definitive contract cannot be negotiated soon enough to satisfy the needs of the project.[18]

To Government officials the letter contract is the least desirable type of contract. In a sole-source situation, however, its use may strengthen the Government's bargaining position. This is especially true when the time pressures are working against the Government. If the Government and the contractor fail to agree on price or other contract terms, the "disputes" clause of the letter contract allows the Government to make a unilateral price determination. The contractor then has the option of appealing the decision to the Armed Services Board of Contract Appeals, or to the civil courts.

The lack of definition of the work to be performed under a letter contract tends to encourage contractors to expand the work. This, in turn, encourages the growth of program cost estimates. In addition, while the contractor is working under the letter contract, he is accumulating actual costs. The longer a contractor is allowed to work under the letter contract, the less the uncertainty about the total cost of the work. When total cost information is already available, it becomes particularly difficult for the Government contracting officer or program manager to negotiate a fixed price that is tight enough to provide an incentive for the contractor to control his costs.[19]

In recent years, Defense Department letter contracts have frequently extended over periods of many months and even years. On the A7D Navy air-craft program, a letter contract was in effect for more than two years. On the Air Force F-111 aircraft program, a $571 million letter contract was in effect for more than 18 months. Later in the F-111 program, a production letter contract for a program of nearly $2 billion was in effect for two years.

During 1970 and 1971 the Department of Defense took action to reduce the number of letter contracts outstanding. In 1968 letter contracts outstand-ing accounted for $4.7 billion. By the end of 1970 that total had been reduced to $1.2 billion, and the value of Defense Department letter contracts over six months old had been reduced from $2.4 billion in 1968 to less than $1 bil-lion.[20]

ANALYSIS OF CONTRACT TYPES

The Defense Department's attitude toward fixed-price contracting has gone through many changes over the past two decades. In 1952 fixed-price con-tracts represented 82% of defense prime contract awards. By 1961 this had dropped to 58%. Defense Secretary Robert McNamara raised the percentage to 79% in 1966; by 1970 fixed-price percentage had dropped to 74%.[21]

Although the percentage of fixed-price contracts is partly a function of the type of work to be performed, it is heavily influenced by Pentagon policy. The McNamara administration used fixed-price contracts to shift the burden of cost control from the Department of Defense to the contractor. After 1969 the Laird-Packard influence led to a decline in fixed-price contracting and an increase in the use of cost-reimbursement contracts for research and de-velopment work. The Laird-Packard administration believed that large re-search and development programs are impeded by rigid fixed-price contracts because they reduce the government's ability to observe what is happening during the life of the contract.

In theory, the Defense Department selects a contract type that will provide a reasonable distribution of risk between Government and industry. Defense policy calls for the percentage of negotiated profits on a contract to vary with the type of contract. Fixed-price contracts provide the greatest risk to con-tractors and award the highest profit rate. Cost-plus-fixed-fee contracts have the least risk for contractors and award the lowest profits. In 1970 the average negotiated profit rates for defense prime contracts were the following:[22]

Firm fixed-price contracts	11.1%
Fixed-price incentive contracts	9.6
Cost-plus-incentive-fee contracts	7.7
Cost-plus-fixed-fee contracts	5.9

Although fixed-price contracts are still preferred over other types, defense policy stipulates that they should be used only when "reasonably definite design or performance specifications are available and fair prices can be initially established."[23] They present contractors with a number of advantages and disadvantages. They involve a higher profit potential, minimum Government control, and minimum Government auditing. On the other hand, the contractor may have to assume all financial and technical risk and the risk of greater liability for work being performed. A senior industry executive told us that fixed-price contracts ran into difficulties because of increasing Government involvement in defense programs during the 1960s. In his view, "when the Defense Department began to emphasize fixed-price contracts, they took with them many of the techniques and controls that were only appropriate for cost-reimbursement contracts." Many defense procurement officials agree with this observation. They explain that increased Government controls were necessary because fixed-price contracts were being written for programs in which the element of uncertainty was too high. The standard fixed-price contract was inappropriate in these instances. Numerous contract changes effectively converted fixed-price contracts into cost-reimbursement contracts. On the F-111 development program, for example, contract changes occurred at an average rate of one per hour.

In addition to contract changes, other methods have been used by the Government and contractors to transform fixed-price contracts into de facto cost-reimbursement contracts. A well-known textbook on the negotiation and management of defense contracts offers the following advice:

> . . . in the face of the growing practice by Federal agencies to award fixed-price research contracts, what should be the negotiation position of the contractor? Take the contract! Negotiate a statement of work or specification so broad that delivery of the contract end item (usually a feasibility report or at most a prototype) would be acceptable whatever may be the result of the research. Who can challenge the effectiveness of a study, system, model, or report? The report could be nothing more than a paragraph indicating that the research reached a dead end not meriting the expenditure of additional funds.[24]

A common method for diluting the effect of a fixed-price contract involves incremental definition of the work to be performed. On one large defense program, a contractor negotiated a letter contract for more than $90 million. As time passed, the contractor performed work and was paid by the Government. Later, the work already accomplished was defined and a fixed-price contract was negotiated. Obviously, the contract provided little or no incentive to the contractor to control his costs; it was merely used as an instrument for the transfer of funds. This method of defining and negotiating work does avoid discomforting cost overruns and technical performance shortfalls—simply because the contract is negotiated after the fact. In 1967, four-and-a-half years after the award of the F-111 development contract, less than 50% of the development program was included in the fixed-price incentive contract. The contract was being defined incrementally.

Until 1960 cost-reimbursement contracts were virtually standard for research and development programs.[25] During the decade of the 1960s fixed-price contracts were negotiated for many research and development programs, including the F-111, C-5A, AH-56A Cheyenne helicopter, and Short Range Attack Missile (SRAM). Although defense officials believed that fixed-price contracts would automatically mean better control and less cost growth, the Department's own unwillingness to enforce the contracts undermined their effectiveness. Contract changes and broad statements of work, along with contractors' failure to perform (e.g., the C-5A aircraft, Cheyenne helicopter, F-111 aircraft, and the MKII Avionics) became commonplace. Clearly, fixed-price contracts by themselves do not solve the problems of cost growth and schedule slippage.

As noted earlier, the Defense Department returned to cost-reimbursement contracts for research and development work in the 1970s.[26] Under a cost-reimbursement contract, contractors must agree to accept a variety of Government controls and reviews administered by a program manager and his staff, defense auditors, and contract administration personnel. Theoretically at least, the Government has the right to terminate a fixed-price contract for default if the contractor fails to perform acording to its terms, i.e., the Government may stop payment on the contract and may charge the contractor with the cost of procuring the specified items from another source. Cost-reimbursement type contracts, on the other hand, contain no default clause, and the contractor does not incur such a risk. A review of defense practice reveals that contracts for major systems or subsystems are rarely canceled for default, however, even when Government personnel believe that the contractor has failed to perform according to the terms of the contract. Contracts are usually so complex that a contractor can successfully argue that formal or informal direction from a Government official was responsible for his failure to perform. Cancellation of a contract for default is also an unwelcome alternative for the Government because it causes a delay in the completion of a program. Another source must be solicited and developed before the weapon system can be acquired by the Government. So when a contractor fails to perform, the Government often amends the contract and allows an increase in price. Or it may cancel the contract "for the convenience of the Government" (i.e., at no cost to the contractor), writing a new contract with the same contractor for a narrower statement of work. Outright cancellation of a program or a change in contractors is rarely considered by Pentagon personnel. This means that once a significant investment has been made with a contractor on a major program, most realistic options have largely disappeared for the Government.

During the 1960s a major defense electronics program operating under a fixed-price incentive contract experienced growth of nearly 100%. Several industry executives told us that it was widespread knowledge that the contractor had intentionally underbid because of expected follow-on production. Once in 1969 an Assistant Secretary in the Pentagon directed the military buying agency to make whatever contract changes were necessary to cover the contractor's costs on the program.

In some cases, a contractor who fails to perform may be required to accept some loss along with the contract change. For example, contract changes forced contractors to absorb losses on the C-5A program, the F-111 program, the Short Range Attack Missile (SRAM) program, and the AH-56A Cheyenne helicopter program.

Government personnel cite several disadvantages that accompany cost-reimbursement contracts. Contractor profit becomes a function of the costs estimated at the outset of a program. Thus, it is not affected by the quality of the contractor's work. After a cost-reimbursement contract has been awarded, there is little or no incentive (in some cases even a negative incentive) to simplify design, improve deliveries, or control costs. Other cost-reimbursement contract deficiencies are described below:

1. Neither the Government nor the contractor is penalized for failure to achieve adequate preplanning and program definition with respect to trade-off decisions for technical performance, schedules, and costs. (Performance failure in these areas can lead to costly redevelopment efforts.) While false starts and dead ends are inevitable in research and development work, the cost-reimbursement contract provides almost no incentive to reduce their occurrence.
2. The penalty for incurring unnecessary costs, or costs of questionable value, is not determined in absolute dollars, but in the percentage that the profit bears to the total cost. This is a questionable penalty, at best. In fact, as cited earlier in this report, it may be to a contractor's advantage to extend work on a program (at additional cost only to the Government) in order to keep his personnel employed.
3. The contract provides little incentive for contractors to assign their best people to the program: highly qualified personnel may be more profitably assigned to work where performance determines profits.
4. There is no reward for efficiency and no penalty for its absence, even

in those overhead and administrative areas which do not impinge on the technical effort. It is particularly difficult—perhaps impossible—for Government personnel to monitor overhead and administration, since efficiency in these areas depends on thousands of small decisions made by contractor personnel.

5. Since cost-reimbursement contracts contain inadequate self-policing controls, the Government believes it necessary to impose external administrative controls in areas such as wages and salaries, bonus and pension plans, insurance, material utilization, disposal of scrap, overtime, extra shifts, and purchasing. Such controls are difficult to implement. Frequently, the contractor assigns additional control personnel in an attempt to monitor Government control personnel, and vice versa.

6. The contractor is not penalized for overestimating his technical performance and delivery capabilities or for underestimating costs.

7. Since profit is determined by estimated costs at the time of contract negotiation rather than by performance, a cost-reimbursement contract appeals more to the inefficient than to the efficient contractor.

COMMENTARY ON INCENTIVE CONTRACTS

During the 1960s incentive contracts were used to provide contractors with incentives lacking in cost-reimbursement contracts. They were structured so that a contractor's fee might fall above or below a target amount, depending upon his performance in the area of cost, schedule, and/or technical achievement. Incentive contracts were intended to communicate the Government's objectives and to motivate the contractor's management to achieve them.[27] Many Defense Department officials believed incentive contracts to be an effective means for controlling procurement costs. By increasing the total profit as actual costs are reduced below the target, the contracts were supposed to encourage contractors to achieve cost underruns. Many officials believed that the contracts placed greater financial risk on the contractor, since the Government would no longer absorb cost overruns.[28]

In the past few years there has been increasing evidence that incentive contracts do not accomplish the Government's management objectives. Several Government contracting officers told us that contractors were much more interested in the level of contract ceiling prices than they were in target costs. Indeed, defense industry groups are trying to convince the Defense Department to revise its budgeting system so that contract budget levels will be established at the ceiling price, rather than the lower target price.

In May 1968 the Logistics Management Institute studied six separate reports on the effectiveness of incentive contracting. They summarized their findings—all unfavorable to incentive contracting:

1. Extra-contractual considerations dominate over profit or fee. A contractor rarely seeks to maximize profit during the short run of a single contract. He is more interested in taking actions that will expand company operations, lead to increased future business, enhance company image and reputation, benefit his nondefense business, or relieve such immediate problems as loss of skilled personnel and a narrow base for fixed costs.
2. No significant correlation can be found to exist between cost sharing ratios and overruns or underruns.
3. Incentives have not been significantly effective as protection against cost growth on programs.
4. Contractors establish upper limits on profit on Government contracts. Those limits pertain to individual contracts and to overall business with the Government. A large profit or fee on a contract arouses suspicions of cost padding and profiteering, making future negotiations more difficult and possibly damaging company reputation. Sometimes an investigation results and exaggerates the consequences. A high profit on overall Government business results in renegotiation, and some of the profit increments gained may be taken away. Contractors go to great lengths to avoid investigation and to avoid refunds resulting from renegotiation.
5. Incentives are costly to negotiate and administer. The process of making a contract change is much more complex when an incentive arrangement is involved.
6. Contractors will not sacrifice performance attainment for profit. Performance is of such importance to company image and future business acquisition that all performance incentives provide little, if any, additional motivation to the contractor.
7. It is often difficult to pass incentive motivation to the people who carry out the contract effort on a day-to-day basis, because it is difficult to relate individual activity with specific contracts. Many workers' time cannot be associated with individual contracts in such a way that they usually know what contract they are working on and what the incentive arrangement is.[29]

In a more recent study of 94 Air Force contracts, the RAND Corporation concluded that contract cost growth was not influenced by type of contract.[30] In March 1971 the Army Procurement Research Office arrived at similar conclusions after an analysis of 200 Army incentive contracts. The Army study revealed that (1) there was no difference in the cost overrun experience for incentive contracts and cost-reimbursement contracts and (2) incentive contracts tended to have higher targets and higher administrative costs than cost-reimbursement contracts.[31]

The RAND Corporation report by Irving Fisher on incentive contracts concluded that "incentive contracts probably are not saving the Government much money through increased efficiency and better cost control. Consequently, the merits of incentive contracts will have to be judged on other grounds."

Several executives from one major defense firm readily agreed that they were much more concerned about exceeding a contract ceiling and covering their costs than they were about trying to figure out how to earn maximum profit on the contract. The senior executive of this group commented:

> There is always something we can spend money on to make the product better. A cost underrun simply is not considered a realistic possibility for us. Furthermore, when we enter into a major development program, we simply don't have the definition of the program that would enable us to come up with an estimate in which we have any reasonable confidence. As such, our primary concern is avoiding a loss. Most of us feel that our stockholders are much more concerned about a loss on any significant contract than they are about how low our profits are as a percentage of sales.

One factor that contributes to incentive contracts' lack of effectiveness is the low share that contractors have to carry in the event of a cost overrun. Most incentive contracts are written so that contractors must pay no more than 20 cents, and usually less, of each dollar increase in costs above the target cost. Since the contractor's share of cost overruns is tax deductible, and since large defense contractors are in the 50%-or-higher tax bracket, the actual cost of each dollar overrun to a contractor is 10 cents, and often less. To state this another way: if the contractor spends an additional dollar on direct or overhead costs (thus enhancing his commercial business or future defense business) and charges the cost to the incentive contract, the dollar investment will cost the contractor no more than 10 cents. Thus, in many cases, it is to the contractor's advantage to spend as much on a contract as the market will bear.[32]

Executives from defense contractor firms and defense management consulting firms told us that when contractors incur costs above the negotiated target cost, the Government will provide additional support in four areas:

1. Discretionary independent research and development activities, which improve a firm's technical capabilities and enable it to prepare for future commercial and Government business;

2. Investment in facilities and equipment;
3. Additional engineering and scientific personnel who will then be available to prepare proposals for new projects;
4. Overhead expense that would otherwise be absorbed by fixed-price defense contracts or by commercial work.

Many Government personnel told us that many of the problems associated with incentive contracting result from the Government's limited capability for negotiating and administering these complex contracts. The rapid turnover of military procurement personnel and the limited procurement training of many Government civilian and military personnel contribute to the problem.

Many Government personnel assigned to field procurement organizations believe that incentive contracts reduce their responsibility for measuring and controlling performance. More than half of these procurement personnel told us that they were much less concerned about cost overruns on incentive contracts because contractors would have to pay for part of any overrun. Most of these individuals seemed aware of the loopholes cited in the studies above.

There were also indications of the Government's diminished concern about cost growth on incentive contracts in the case of the C-5A program. In January 1967 the Air Force C-5A program office requested permission from the Pentagon to discontinue the requirement for Lockheed to report cost information to the Government. To support this request, the program office argued that the fixed-price incentive contract provided Lockheed with sufficient incentive to control costs, and that the program office had no need for the cost information. While such permission was not granted, interviews with Government personnel assigned to the C-5A program office revealed that the cost performance information received from Lockheed was neither understood nor used. The personnel in the program office did not have the training in industrial management that would have enabled them to understand the information.

Many factors undermine the effectiveness of incentive contracting. Not the least of these is the fear expressed by some industry executives that earning profits higher than negotiated target profits would embarrass their Government contracting officers, causing them to negotiate lower costs on subsequent contracts.

TOTAL PACKAGE PROCUREMENT

During the early 1960s the Defense Department heard from a number of Government and industry officials that the method of defense contracting itself caused contractors to underestimate the cost of development programs. It was argued that contractors intentionally underestimated the cost of development programs in order to win the contract and place themselves in a "sole source" position for the follow-on production contracts. Robert Charles, then Assistant Secretary of the Air Force, was particularly concerned over this weakness in the defense procurement process. To attack this problem, he designed a new method of contracting: contractors would be asked at the beginning of a program to bid on a total program package, consisting of the development, production, and spare-part support work. Charles argued that this would bring the maximum amount of competition into defense procurement because contractors would no longer be able to make low bids on a development program and subsequently make up their losses by bidding high on the follow-on production and support contracts. In effect, Charles conceived of a multi-year contract for all phases of a program to replace the numerous contract negotiations of the past.

The purpose of the new total-package contract, generally of a fixed-price incentive type, was to end the need for Government control of contractors' activities. Charles recognized the limited day-to-day management capabilities of the Department of Defense. He thought that the total package procurement concept offered Government the opportunity to shift the major risk and major program management responsibility to contractors. Many defense managers looked to this new contracting concept as the great hope for defense procurement, substantially relieving the Government of day-to-day decision making for weapon systems development and production.

Lieutenant General Terhune, Vice Commander of the Air Force Systems Command, summarized the Government's view of total package procurement in 1968:

> As you know, total package procurement contracting envisions that development, production, and support requirements for a system are procured under one contract. Price and performance commitments are obtained during the contract definition phase.
> To date, all total package contracts have been fixed-price incentive.
> Our major objectives in total package procurement are to:
> Inhibit "buy-in,"
> Permit the Government to use competition effectively,
> Encourage industry to design for economic production,
> Motivate the contractor to obtain supplies and services from the most efficient source, whether in-house or by subcontract,
> Obtain long-term commitments leading to program stability and continuity,
> Enforce design discipline,
> Encourage efficiency,

> Better control changes,
> Motivate the contractor to control cost,
> Foster program discipline on the part of the contractor and the Government. . . .[33]

During the 1960s total package procurement contracts were written for a number of major defense programs, including the multibillion dollar C-5A transport aircraft program. At the time of the preparation of the C-5A contract, a number of individuals in the Pentagon urged Secretary Charles to try the contract first on a smaller program less susceptible to change. They had reservations about using the new contracting method on the C-5A because of the likelihood of contract changes, or failure of the contractor to perform. The Government would be operating with reduced visibility of contractor operations because of the fixed-price type of contract. The C-5A total package contract might extend for eight years and involve more than $2 billion.

It is generally recognized that for any contract to be enforceable, each side must have some viable recourse in the event that the other side fails to perform. At the time of the signing of the total package procurement contract for the C-5A with the Lockheed Aircraft Corporation, it was not at all clear that the Government had such recourse. Once the Government made a sizable investment in the C-5A development program, it seemed unlikely that it would withdraw from Lockheed in the event of poor performance and take the program to another contractor. When these reservations were expressed to senior Air Force officials, they elicited little concern because no one believed that the Lockheed Aircraft Corporation, the largest defense contractor in the United States, would fail to perform according to the terms of the initial contract. When pressed for an answer on the course of action available to the Government in the event of Lockheed's failure to perform, one senior Air Force official commented in 1965: "We will get the sheriff and go to Atlanta" (where the C-5A program was located).

Reservations about the use of the total package contract on the C-5A were voiced even without knowledge of the repricing clause in the contract. This clause permitted Lockheed to make up its losses on the initial contract, if orders were placed for subsequent purchases of the C-5A aircraft.[34] The existence of this clause was unknown to most of the Pentagon officials involved in the procurement decisions for the C-5A.

Viewing the C-5A total package contract from the perspective of several years, it appears that the critics were correct. The C-5A program did encounter serious cost problems, as did several other total package programs. The "urgent" need for the C-5A program prevented the Government from canceling the contract and seeking another producer. In the end, the Air Force chose to convert the C-5A contract to a cost-reimbursement contract and to require Lockheed to sustain a substantial, but not total, loss on the program. A similar decision was made when difficulties occurred on the Lockheed contract for the development of the Army's AH-56A Cheyenne Helicopter.

A number of senior executives in defense firms expressed dissatisfaction with the Defense Department's decision to release defense firms from their contractual commitments. One executive, referring to a program with cost problems similar to those on the C-5A, summarized a widespread feeling:

> I don't see how you can run a system of contracting unless you hold a contractor responsible for how he performs. On the [name] program, the prime contractor is asking to be bailed out. He is not asking for a loan. The contractor underbid the [name] program and everyone knew it. If you don't hold us accountable for performance and for what we promise, you can expect these situations to occur time and time again.

In an address to a George Washington University Research and Development Conference on November 7, 1968, Secretary Charles commented on the impact of a possible failure of the total package concept:

> If industry fails to respond, if we finally learn that this industry is unable or unwilling to accept the risks of competition, then I suspect we will be in for several rounds of increasing Government controls that will leave the industry's management without much risk, to be sure, and without much managerial freedom to boot. I think we will all be much better off if industry can prove that the pendulum has not swung too far.

By 1972 it appeared that Secretary Charles had lost his argument for the new contracting method. Total package procurement was abolished by the Deputy Secretary of Defense and most senior officials of the Pentagon had come to the conclusion that the task of program control on major defense contracts could not be delegated by the Government to the performing contractors. There did not appear to be any contractual mechanism that could do the job.

As the Department of Defense reverted to the policy of the 1950s (writing separate contracts for development, production, and support, and using cost-reimbursement contracts for development work), many defense officials expressed concern that the problems of cost growth, schedule slippage, and technical performance shortfalls that characterized the defense programs of the 1950s and early 1960s would occur again in the 1970s. Although Deputy Secretary of Defense David Packard directed that a number of changes be made to improve the capability of defense procurement managers, many Pentagon officials doubted that his directives would be implemented at the numerous defense field procurement organizations. At the same time, there were increasing numbers of defense officials who began to question a fundamental premise of defense contracting; namely, that different profit levels on an individual contract could be used to motivate contractors to perform more efficiently and effectively. Nonetheless, the official position on incentive contracts remained unchanged.

NOTES TO CHAPTER XI

1. Office of the Assistant Secretary of Defense (Comptroller), Directorate of Information Operations, *Military Prime Contract Awards, Fiscal Year 1970.*
2. Armed Services Procurement Regulation 3-402.
3. Armed Services Procurement Regulation 3-807(e) and NASA Procurement Regulation 3.807-3(i).
4. Office of the Secretary of Defense, *Defense Procurement Handbook,* 1968, p. V-7.
5. Armed Services Procurement Regulation 3-404.2.
6. Armed Services Procurement Regulation 3-404.3.
7. Armed Services Procurement Regulation 3-404.3(b).
8. For a detailed treatment of incentive contracts and discussions of structuring and negotiation techniques, see *DOD Incentive Contracting Guide,* prepared by the Office of the Assistant Secretary of Defense (Installations and Logistics), 1969.
9. Armed Services Procurement Regulation 3-404.5-7.
10. Ibid.
11. 10 U.S. Code 2306(d).
12. Armed Services Procurement Regulation 3-405.4(c).
13. *Defense Procurement Handbook,* p. V-23.
14. Ibid.
15. Armed Services Procurement Regulation 7-203.3 and 7-402.2; NASA Procurement Regulation 7.203-3 and 7.402-2.
16. *Defense Procurement Handbook,* p. V-26.
17. Armed Services Procurement Regulation 3-405.4.
18. *Defense Procurement Handbook,* p. V-26.
19. Richard J. Lorette, "The Relationship Between the Pressures on the System Program Director and the Growth of Weapon System Cost Estimates" (Boston: unpublished doctoral dissertation, Harvard Business School, 1967), p. 216.
20. Office of the Assistant Secretary of Defense (Comptroller), Directorate of Information Operations, *Letter Contracts and Change Orders, Fiscal Year 1970.*
21. *Military Prime Contract Awards,* op. cit.
22. Office of the Assistant Secretary of Defense (Comptroller), Directorate of Information Operations, *Profit Rates on Negotiated Prime Contracts, Fiscal Year 1970.*
23. Armed Services Procurement Regulation 3-404.2.
24. Francis Pace, *Negotiation and Management of Defense Contracts* (New York: Wiley-Interscience, 1970), pp. 200–201.
25. Statement by Assistant Secretary of Defense Perkins McGuire cited in the U.S. House of Representatives Armed Services Committee Hearings Pursuant to Section 4, Public Law 86-89, 86th Cong., 1st Sess., 1960, p. 163.
26. U.S. Department of Defense Directive 5000.1, July 1971.
27. U.S. Department of Defense and NASA, *Incentive Contracting Guide* (Washington: Government Printing Office, 1969).
28. Irving N. Fisher, *Controlling Defense Procurement Costs: An Evaluation of Incentive Contracting Experience* (Santa Barbara: RAND Corporation Report, November 1968).
29. Logistics Management Institute, *An Examination of the Foundations of Incentive Contracts,* LMI Task 66-67, May 1968.

30. *A Preliminary Analysis of Contractual Outcomes for 94 AFSC Contracts* (Santa Barbara: RAND Corporation Report, WN 7117, December 1970).
31. Army Procurement Office, *An Analysis of 200 Army Incentive Contracts,* Fort Lee, Virginia, March 1971.
32. Bruce Backe, "Low Fees May Undermine Incentive Goals," *Aviation Week and Space Technology,* January 11, 1965, pp. 69–72.
33. Lieutenant General Charles H. Terhune, Jr., USAF, "Defense Contracting—The Problem of Distribution of Risk," an address at the 1968 Western Briefing Conference on Government Contracts, San Francisco.
34. The repricing clause on the C-5A contract is discussed at length in Berkeley Rice, *The C-5A Scandal* (Boston: Houghton Mifflin Company, 1971).

CHAPTER XII

Methods of Government Procurement

THE DEFENSE PROCUREMENT ACT passed by Congress in 1947 provides for two methods of procurement—formal advertising and negotiation.

FORMAL ADVERTISING

Formal advertising—calling for sealed bids from contractors—is the traditional method of Government contracting. Under current defense regulations, formal advertising must be used except when it is impracticable or when the program is covered by one of 17 exceptions (described later in this chapter).

Formal advertising is divided into four procedures.[1]

1. The preparation of invitations for contractor bids (IFB's).
2. The publication and distribution of the IFB's. (To ensure that an adequate number of bidders will apply to the procuring agency, the Government contracting officer must publish a notice of the invitation in *Commerce Business Daily,*[2] requesting that qualified sources interested in bidding respond with statement to that effect.)
3. The opening, recording, and evaluating of bids received.
4. The awarding of a fixed-price contract to the contractor whose bid offers the best price and other advantages to the Government.

Formal advertising has two main goals. One is to gain for the Government the benefits of full and free competition; the other is to give all qualified sources equal competitive opportunity. The procedures of formal advertising are often described as rigid or mechanical: they are established by law and regulation and, in general, cannot be varied.

Effective use of formal advertising depends on competition; there must be at least two qualified sources willing to bid on the basis of an IFB. For formal advertising to be practical, specifications must be sufficiently precise to allow bids to be evaluated on a common basis. If the technical requirements of the desired item or service are not adequately defined, bidders cannot outline their proposals in sufficient detail. Major defense research and development programs do not lend themselves to formal advertising because they cannot be described with sufficiently detailed specifications at the time a contractor is to be selected.

"Two-step" formal advertising is a special case of formal advertising; it is used for procurements when specifications for the item to be procured are not adequate to permit full competition. In the first step, interested bidders are required to submit technical proposals in response to an invitation for bids. These proposals do not include prices; they are evaluated simply on a technical basis. During this first stage, prospective contractors are free to meet with Government personnel to discuss and adjust the details of the proposals they have submitted. The second stage requires all bidders whose technical proposals are considered acceptable to submit firm prices based on these proposals. Except that each of these contractors bids on his own technical proposal, the normal rules and procedures for formal advertising are followed. One of the advantages of two-step formal advertising is that it places the burden on contractors for developing creative approaches to military problems. By using this method of procurement the Government seeks to derive the benefits of the knowledge, expertise, and inventiveness of interested contractors.

NEGOTIATED PROCUREMENTS

Negotiation is the method for selecting a contractor without formal advertising and formal price competition. The rules and regulations for employing the negotiation method specify that the selection of a contractor will be made to the best advantage of the Government, price and other factors considered.[3] Theoretically, factors other than the lowest bid can play the major role in the selection process. In practice, however, there is a regulation requiring the Government to justify the choice of someone other than the low bidder. This gives the low bidder more of an advantage than the regulations would lead the casual observer to believe. (This point is discussed at greater length in Chapters XIII and XIV.)

In procurement by negotiation, the Department of Defense seeks to interest a large number of qualified bidders. Negotiation supplants formal advertising as a procurement method when one, or both, of the following conditions exist:

(1) the Government and the bidders need to be able to discuss the procurement, either before or after contractor proposals are submitted, in order to be certain that there is an adequate understanding of specifications; (2) there is some condition (e.g., highly specialized technology or a highly classified procurement) that makes it necessary to restrict the number of bidders.

Under current Government procedures for negotiation, the IFB is replaced by the "request for proposal" (RFP). In the RFP, the Government asks interested contractors to submit proposals outlining (1) technical and (2) management approaches for a specific program, and (3) cost estimates for the work. When the proposals are received, the Government program manager and his staff, the contracting officer, and other Government personnel with relevant specialties evaluate the proposals. They then conduct negotiations with those firms whose offers are considered technically acceptable and whose estimated costs fall within a reasonable range. The negotiations involve analysis, investigation, exploration, and bargaining with respect to costs, profit, performance requirements, delivery schedules, and provisions for future changes. Rarely, if ever, does the Government accept contractor proposals without any discussion. In negotiation, unlike formal advertising, the contracting officer may use a fixed-price, incentive, or cost-reimbursement contract. Only fixed-price contracts are used in formally advertised procurements.

The procedures for negotiated procurements are similar in many ways to formal advertising procedures. Whenever possible, negotiated procurements are competitive. But unlike formal advertising, the competition in negotiated procurements may or may not involve price. For example, contractors may compete to provide the most comprehensive and credible technical plan for the work to be performed, or the lowest cost estimate within a range believed to be acceptable to the Government—intending to negotiate the price to a higher level at a later date.

Proposals made under negotiating procedures are not opened and read in public, as they are in formal advertising. As in formal advertising, however, the terms of each proposal are recorded, and each proposal is evaluated against the requirements of the RFP. As in formal advertising, the award is to be made to the best advantage of the Government, price and other factors considered.

It is simply not practical for many Government procurements to be conducted through formal advertising. Contracts for research and development programs, for example, normally are awarded through negotiation because the Government wants to evaluate contractors' technical capabilities, technical approaches, and management ability, as well as costs. Procurement by negotiation allows the Department of Defense to select the contractor who seems best prepared to meet all the requirements of the program, and to meet them on the terms most satisfactory to the Government. Furthermore, negotiation enables the Government to be relatively flexible. For example, vital skills, or a wartime production base, consisting of one, two, or more contractors in essential fields (e.g., aircraft or ammunition), may be developed and maintained through educational orders. These orders are designed to familiarize the manufacturer with defense systems.

Nonetheless, by law, negotiation is intended to be the exception rather than the rule in defense procurement. A procurement may be accomplished through negotiation only if the procurement falls into one of the following 17 categories:

1. A national emergency (declared at the outset of the Korean War and remaining in effect as of early 1972);
2. Public exigency;
3. Purchases not in excess of $2,500;
4. Personal or professional services;
5. Services of educational institutions;
6. Purchases outside the United States;
7. Medicines or medical supplies;
8. Supplies purchased for authorized resale;
9. Perishable or nonperishable subsistence supplies;
10. Supplies or services for which it is impractical to secure competition by formal advertising;
11. Experimental, developmental, or research work;
12. Classified purchases;
13. Technical equipment requiring standardization and interchangeability of parts;
14. Technical or specialized supplies requiring substantial initial investment or extended period of preparation for manufacture;
15. Negotiation after advertising;
16. Purchases in the interest of national defense or industrial mobilization;
17. Procurement otherwise authorized by law, e.g., architectural or engineering services for preparing specifications for public works, utilities, naval vessels, or aircraft construction.[4]

A more complete description of the 17 exceptions is contained in Section III of the Armed Services Procurement Regulation.

Permission to conduct a procurement through negotiation is usually obtained by the contracting officer by submitting written determinations that justify the exception. These must then be signed by the contracting officer, the head of the procuring activity, or the Secretary of a military department.

Prior to World War II virtually all defense procurement was accomplished by formal advertising; during the 1960s and early 1970s by far the largest part of defense procurement has been accomplished through negotiation. In every year since the beginning of the Korean War, more than 80% of all military procurement dollars have been awarded through negotiation. Almost two-thirds of the negotiated contracts have been approved under three of the 17 negotiation exceptions:[5]

- Exception 14: Technical or specialized supplies requiring substantial initial investment or extended period of preparation for manufacture.
- Exception 11: Experimental, developmental, or research work.
- Exception 10: Supplies or services for which it is impractical to secure competition by formal advertising.

Senior officials in the Office of the Secretary of Defense believe that rapid changes in world events and available technology will continue to make negotiation the primary method of defense procurement. At the present time, the negotiation method is used for aircraft, engines, complex electronic systems, missiles, and other weapon systems for which the military services know little more than the desired performance characteristics. Proposals from contractors are as much suggestions of how work can be performed as they are price quotations.

During the 1950s and 1960s, Congress frequently criticized the Department of Defense for extensive use of negotiated procurements rather than formal advertising. Defense Department personnel normally attributed this criticism to political expediency or the failure of Congress to understand the nature of the procurement process. By 1969, however, members of Congress had begun to realize the need for negotiated procurement. In 1969 the House of Representatives' Government Operations Committee, in considering the establishment of a Commission on Government Procurement, made the following observations:

> The procurement laws call for advertised bidding as the preferred method, but only ten to twelve percent of the procurement dollars are spent in this manner. To justify negotiated bidding, which is the exception in the laws but the rule in practice, determinations and findings have to be made in a wide variety of procurement categories excepted from advertised bidding and frequently these determinations are routine and relatively meaningless but consume large amounts of time and paperwork.
>
> Whereas competitive advertised bidding is long established and continues to be beneficial and should be vigorously pursued, the Government's interests are not protected by attempting to purchase through advertised bidding when the conditions or circumstances for such bidding are inappropriate. It would seem that in view of the large and continuing

volume of Government procurement which has to be negotiated rather than advertised, new statutory rules can be written to clarify and strengthen competitive negotiations, and to closely regulate sole-source negotiations and contracts.[6]

Regardless of whether formal advertising or negotiation is employed, the stated objective of the procurement process is to encourage efficient and optimal performance. In the pursuit of this objective, a variety of procurement plans and innovations have been attempted. Before 1952 the "fly before you buy" concept was practiced; i.e., the Government tested various prototypes before choosing a contractor for further development and procurement. Build-up for the Korean conflict and rapid development of technology convinced the Department that lead-time from development to operational use had to be reduced. As a result, development and production programs in the late 1950s and early 1960s were often "concurrent"—overlapping. Concurrency between development and production programs created such uncertainties that contractors refused to consider contracts with firm fixed prices. Consequently, cost-reimbursement and incentive contracts were used to reduce the risks for contractors.

Commercial procurement and Government procurement involve two different approaches. For most commercial procurements, the buyer places an order with a seller using a fixed-price contract arrived at through competitive bids or through negotiation with one or more suppliers. The seller usually makes the investment needed for the development of the item to be procured. For Government procurement of major weapon systems, a contractor may find it impossible to develop the necessary technical knowledge, experience, and capital investment on his own. The requisite technical knowledge is usually difficult to learn without specific experience in the development of the same or similar systems. Thus, in order to insure adequate competition, the Government frequently contracts with a number of firms during the conceptual phase of a program. Later, when the system is ready for full-scale development, the program is usually shifted to competitive negotiated procurement.

The Department of Defense has devised elaborate formal procedures for evaluating and selecting contractors for major programs. These procedures will be described in Chapter XIII.

COMPETITION IN DEFENSE PROCUREMENT

One of the problems posed by negotiated procurement is the absence of free market forces that would reduce the contractor's price. While competitive forces in negotiation may, in some cases, drive down estimated costs to an unrealistic level, vagueness in the description of the work to be performed frequently provides an opportunity for later contract changes that will increase the cost.

In 1971 less than 12% of defense procurements were awarded through formally advertised competitive procurement; the remaining 88% were awarded through negotiated procurement. No more than 25% of the negotiated procurements were conducted in situations where more than one contractor was a contender for the award. Thus, no more than 37% of defense procurement was awarded through competition of any form.[7]

In early 1971 GAO reported that a higher percentage of defense contracts could be awarded competitively. In preparing its report, the GAO studied 54 contracts, valued at $33 million, that had been awarded noncompetitively. After detailed study, the GAO concluded that 36 (67%) of these contracts should have been awarded on a competitive basis because other suppliers were available who could have delivered the requested items at lower prices within similar time limits. These 36 contracts had a total value of $31.5 million. If one uses the estimates from the RAND Corporation and the Office of the Secretary of Defense (Installations and Logistics) that a contract price can usually be reduced by 25% when genuine price competition exists, the savings from the limited GAO sample of 54 contracts would have amounted to nearly $8 million.[8]

In a comparison of the sole-source negotiated vs. competitive procurement costs of components in six weapon systems, we observed that competition in specific contract awards effected savings of from 17% to 49%, with an average of slightly less than 25%.

On November 21, 1969, the Battelle Memorial Institute's Columbus (Ohio) Laboratories issued an unclassified study of procurement alternatives for the MBT-70 tank. In this report the Battelle researchers identified 20 items that were procured in both a sole-source negotiated and a competitive environment. The median savings for the 20 competitive procurements was 30% and the average savings was 32%. It should be pointed out that, unlike the RAND study or the study conducted in association with our research, the Battelle study was limited largely to subsystems or components. However, it is not clear that this makes any differences in the results. In summary, it seems reasonable to assume that a 25% reduction in a contract price can be achieved in many, if not most, cases when competition is introduced.

Four factors make competitive procurements less desirable than single-source procurement.

First, competition requires more time and effort than single-source procurement. Additional care must be taken in developing work statements and

RFP's to insure that each interested bidder submits a proposal on the same basis. Competition requires the difficult and time-consuming task of evaluating proposals and selecting the best contractor from among two or more firms, each of whom has a variety of strengths and weaknesses. The planning and accomplishment of these tasks often adds months to procurement time.

Second, competition increases the likelihood of protests and disputes from one or more contractors. Losing contractors often contend that the Government gave special information to the winning contractor or that the winning contractor exerted political influence. Many losing contractors are unable to admit to the deficiencies that caused them to lose the source selection. Consequently, contracting officers must take particular care to document and justify each decision made in a competitive procurement. This documentation may be used in a hearing requested by a losing contractor, or by the losing contractor's Congressman or Senator.

Third, competition frequently disrupts long-established relationships between Government and industry personnel who have worked together on the procurement of a particular item. Once Government personnel (or personnel in any buying organization, commercial or Government) develop a comfortable relationship with the personnel in one supplier organization, they naturally wish to continue the relationship and prefer not to take the time to build a new relationship with a different supplier—unless it is necessary to buy the item at a lower cost. Without the forces of a free marketplace, this necessity rarely exists.

Fourth, with competition the Government buying organization must evaluate the production quality and capability of competing contractors. The selection of a new, lower-cost producer may introduce problems of quality and reliability that the buying command will probably have to explain to higher level personnel in the Government.

As a result of these factors, senior officials in the Department of Defense are often confronted with active resistance in their continuing efforts to develop and maintain a high degree of competition in the defense procurement process.

The focus of any competition is the source selection process discussed in the following chapter.

NOTES TO CHAPTER XII

1. Office of the Secretary of Defense, *Procurement Training Handbook,* 1970, Chapter VIII.
2. *Commerce Business Daily* is published by the Government Printing Office. It lists all un-classified, pending, and accomplished procurement transactions in excess of $10,000. It is available to the public on a subscription basis.
3. Office of the Secretary of Defense, *Procurement Training Handbook,* 1970, Chapter VIII.
4. Armed Services Procurement Regulation, Section 2, Part 5.
5. Office of Statistical Services, Office of the Assistant Secretary of Defense (Comptroller).
6. U.S. House of Representatives, Government Operations Committee, Commission on Gov-ernment Procurement, Report 91-468, 91st Cong., 1st Sess., August 12, 1969.
7. Office of the Assistant Secretary of Defense (Installations and Logistics), *DOD Logistics Performance Measurement and Evaluation Report,* March 31, 1971.
8. Comptroller General of the United States, *More Competition in Emergency Defense Pro-curement Found Possible,* Report B-171156, March 25, 1971.

CHAPTER XIII

The Source Selection Process

THE DEPARTMENT OF DEFENSE defines *source selection* as "the process wherein the requirements, facts, recommendations, and Government policy relevant to an award decision in a competitive* procurement of a system are examined and the decision is made." [1] To select a contractor for a development or production program, the Defense Department makes a formal evaluation of the proposals submitted by interested contractors. The primary objective of the source selection process is "to assure impartial, equitable, and comprehensive evaluation, resulting in the selection of that contractor whose proposal offers optimum satisfaction of the Government's cost, schedule, and performance objectives for the system." [2]

The procurement of any system for which development costs are expected to exceed $25 million, or for which production costs will exceed $100 million, must involve the use of formal source selection procedures. The exception to this occurs when the contractor selected for the procurement of a system is the same contractor who developed or produced the item under earlier contracts. Even if a program does not meet the $25/$100 million criterion, the Department of Defense can choose to apply formal source selection procedures. Situations under which such a decision would be made include those in which:

1. The contract is for a systems-oriented development program;
2. The item has potential for substantial follow-on production;
3. The program involves complex management interrelationships among associate or other prime contractors;

---

* The term "competitive" as it is used in the definition may or may not include price competition. Competition may be based on design excellence, responsiveness to Government requests, or overall quality of contractor proposals, rather than price.

4. The program is believed to have sensitive economic or political implications.

FORMAL SOURCE SELECTION GROUPS

When the Office of the Secretary of Defense assigns responsibility for the development, production, installation, and operation of a system, it designates one individual to be the *Source Selection Authority* (see Figure XIII-1). In a few rare cases, this individual is the Secretary of Defense (e.g., the F-111 program). In most cases, however, the Secretary of Defense delegates this authority to the Secretary of the military service acquiring the system. This authority

FIGURE XIII-1. FORMAL SOURCE SELECTION GROUPS

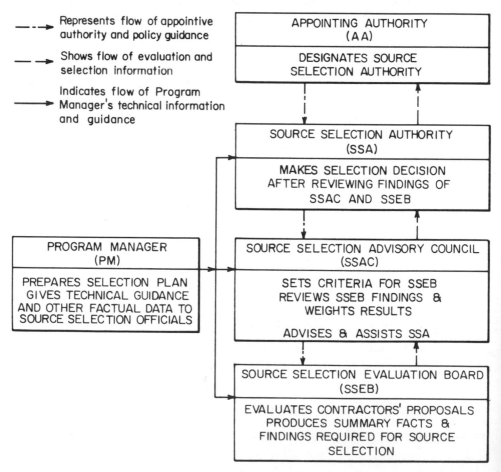

is then usually delegated by the service Secretary to an official at a lower management level. In no case is the Source Selection Authority someone below the level of buying command chief.

The Source Selection Authority has four responsibilities.

1. He appoints the Source Selection Advisory Council.
2. He reviews and approves the schedule for proposal evaluation, source selection, and contract negotiation.
3. He provides guidance to the Source Selection Advisory Council and the Source Selection Evaluation Board.
4. He decides which contractor will win the contract award.

The *Source Selection Advisory Council,* appointed by the Source Selection Authority, consists of senior military and civilian personnel from the functional organizations involved in procuring the weapon system; e.g., the using command, the logistics command, and research and development agencies. Other Government agencies also have representatives on the Source Selection Advisory Council (e.g., the Atomic Energy Commission, NASA) when they are concerned with the development or operation of the particular defense system.

The Advisory Council normally consists of fewer than a dozen officials who act as advisors and staff to the Source Selection Authority. The specific responsibilities of the Advisory Council include:

1. Establishing the criteria by which contractor proposals are to be evaluated;
2. Establishing the weights to be given to each of these criteria;
3. Appointing the Source Selection Evaluation Board;
4. Reviewing and approving the evaluation plan prepared by the Source Selection Evaluation Board;
5. Reviewing the Evaluation Board's findings and applying the criteria to the Board's results;
6. Preparing a summary of the Board's analysis and findings;
7. Briefing the Source Selection Authority on the results of the evaluation.

The *Source Selection Evaluation Board* is usually a joint military-civilian group representing the functional and technical areas involved in the development, production, installation, and operation of the weapon system. The Board evaluates and scores the proposals submitted by competing contractors. Proposals are evaluated according to criteria established in the Request for Proposal (RFP) and by the Source Selection Advisory Council.

Figure XIII-2 exemplifies the manner in which the Source Selection Advi-

FIGURE XIII-2. SAMPLE PROPOSAL EVALUATION WEIGHTS

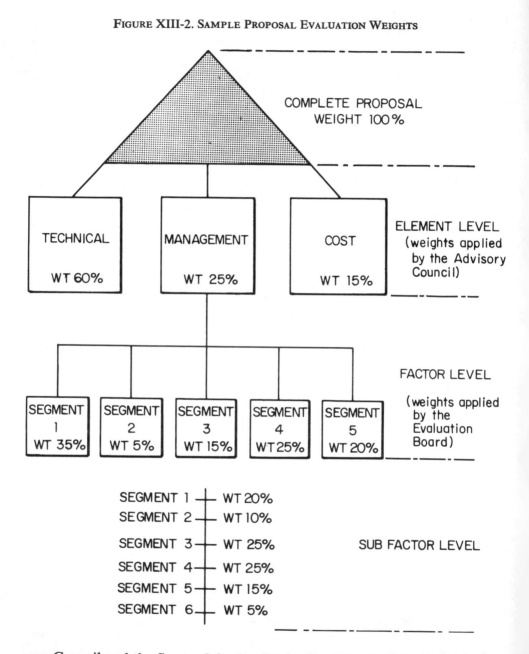

sory Council and the Source Selection Evaluation Board apply weights to the various sections of contractor proposals, for purposes of evaluation. (The numbers in the figure are simply illustrative.)

For a small, relatively simple procurement program, the Source Selection Evaluation Board may consist of 10 to 20 members. The membership may be

300 or more for a large, complex procurement program. The Board often structures its evaluation procedures according to the RFP. In conducting an evaluation, the Evaluation Board establishes working groups. These groups also consist of representatives from organizations having an interest in the system. They are organized into teams which evaluate specific aspects of contractors' proposals. Some teams evaluate costs; others, technical approaches; still others, management techniques.

The Source Selection Evaluation Board, aided by its working groups, evaluates proposals but does not recommend specific contractors. The Board cannot make recommendations because it does not know the weights to be applied by the Advisory Council to the various sections of each proposal. After the Evaluation Board completes its work, the Advisory Council applies weights to the proposals and reviews the work done by the Evaluation Board, adding its judgments to those of the Board. The actual source selection is made by the Source Selection Authority, based on the analyses and recommendations of the Advisory Council. In other words, the decision maker is at least two levels removed from the actual work of evaluation.

Government program management officials work closely with the groups conducting the source selection process. For example, a program management office prepares a selection plan for the use of the Source Selection Authority and the Source Selection Advisory Council. The plan includes recommendations for proposal evaluation criteria, proposal evaluation techniques, the functional areas to be represented on the Advisory Council, the composition of the Evaluation Board, and the scheduling of all evaluation activity that occurs between the receipt of contractor proposals and the signing of a contract. The Department of Defense usually tries to complete the source selection process within 18 weeks.

The program management office usually prepares the list of contractors who will be requested to submit proposals. In screening potential contractors for this list, the program office receives help from technical personnel familiar with the weapon system to be acquired. They study company brochures, performance records, and the other available information in order to identify contractors with the capability to develop and/or produce the weapon system. If a contractor seems to have this capability and is not on the Government's list of disbarred, ineligible, or suspended contractors, it is placed on the approved list. In addition, a synopsis of the planned procurement is published in the *Commerce Business Daily,* and contractors who want to be considered for the list can submit "letters of interest" to the procuring organization. These contractors are screened along with those recommended by the program management office. The final list is approved by the Source Selection Advisory Council, and the official RFP is issued to all contractors on the approved list.

It is Defense Department policy to list only those contractors that are considered "responsible"; that is, capable of fulfilling the terms of the proposed procurement contract. In other words, the Government contracting officer must predict companies' future performance.[3] A "responsible" contractor is one having adequate financial resources, or the ability to obtain such resources during the performance of the contract. The company must also be able to demonstrate its ability to comply with the required delivery or technical performance schedule, to be given a place on the approved list.

In deciding whether a potential contractor is "responsible," the Defense Department considers the company's business commitments, both commercial and governmental. Specifically, the prospective contractor must have the right kind of experience and operational controls, and employees with the necessary technical skills. Lastly, the company should have a satisfactory record of performance if it has previously been a Government contractor.

The Request for Proposals

A formal Request for Proposal (RFP) may consist of 1,000 or more pages (if the program is one of the top 50 in size). It states performance and design requirements for the weapon system and lists specific information that the contractor must provide regarding schedules, costs, logistics, quality control, testing, management, past experience, and personnel. Under the direction of the program manager, a variety of personnel participate in the preparation of an RFP. These include individuals from Government organizations, as well as defense companies who hope to be selected for the contract.

Contractors try to influence the Government program office to include weapon system requirements in the RFP that will give their companies a particular advantage when proposals are being evaluated. Walter B. Wentz, an individual experienced in defense marketing, summarized the role of contractors in the preparation of the RFP:

> The successful firm must forecast requirements with accuracy and must also assist the customer in defining requirements. The seller can virtually exclude competition by convincing the customer that the firm's unique approach to the design and fabrication of a particular system is precisely what the customer needs to fulfill the mission.[4]

On major defense programs the RFP can be a very sizable document. Listed below are the number of pages included in the RFP's for four development and production programs that were active in 1972:

Program	Request for Proposals (Number of Pages)
A	1,287
B	2,460
C	1,156
D	2,000

RFP's are subject to frequent changes. Statistics are available for two of the above programs. On Program B, the Department of Defense made 1,800 formal changes in the RFP during the four-month proposal-preparation period and the subsequent seven-month evaluation period. For a comparable period of time, there were 1,200 formal changes in Program A's RFP.

Industry executives criticize the organization of the RFP's. Several told us that most RFP's seem to be prepared by compiling suggestions from several different organizations, each of which has prepared its requirements for the weapon system independently. As a result, RFP's specify some performance standards for the weapon system in too much detail and leave gaps in other sections. RFP's also fail to indicate the relative importance of the various weapon system requirements. This is important for a company to know when attempting to prepare a balanced contract proposal.

CONTRACTOR PROPOSALS

In response to the RFP, contractors submit proposals that normally contain three major sections: (1) technical; (2) management; and (3) cost. The amount of detail in each section is usually left to the discretion of the contractor. Information must be presented in sufficient depth to enable Government personnel to evaluate the company's capabilities. A proposal will include detailed systems definitions, work plans, engineering analyses, organization and management plans, facilities, cost estimates, logistics plans, and systems integration plans, to name but a few topics.

A typical contractor proposal will be divided as follows:

Proposal Section	No. of Pages	% of Total
1. Total System Integration	1,080	5%
2. Technical	15,395	67
3. Operational	1,005	4
4. Logistics	410	2
5. Management/Production	845	4
6. Contracting/Procurement	650	3
7. Cost	3,605	15
Total	22,990	100%

For some programs, the Department of Defense sets limits on the length of contract proposals. By so doing, the Department hopes to force contractors to concentrate on the most important issues. It also hopes to receive proposals that can be evaluated by the limited number of Government personnel available. For the four programs listed above, page limits were not specified. Proposals were therefore very long.

Program	Average Number of Pages in Contractors' Proposals
A	38,000
B	23,000
C	27,000
D	38,000

In December 1969 the Aerospace Industries Association (AIA) issued a report based on an analysis of defense contractor proposals. They concluded that the information requested by the Government was excessive in each of the seven categories listed above. They were particularly critical of the "cost" category. The cost-data requirements for a fixed-price program could be satisfied, they stated, in 500 pages. Two hundred pages were sufficient for a cost-reimbursement contract. They also reported that much of the required cost data was of no possible use in the source selection process. For the C-5A program, for example, one contractor prepared a proposal that included 39 volumes of cost information, as required by the RFP. When the Air Force distributed the volumes to the officials charged with evaluating them, it found that no recipient was designated for four of the 39 volumes. These four volumes were never considered in the evaluation process. On smaller programs, the AIA reported, "contractors have been required to submit reams of supporting cost material which they are satisfied are either never looked at or are considered only in the case of the two or three final contenders for the contract award." [5]

The five competitors on the C-5A program submitted proposals that totaled 240,000 pages. With all the required copies, the proposals weighed 35 tons. [6]

Some progress is being made in limiting the size of RFP's and contractor proposals. In 1971, for example, the RFP for one major program was reduced in complexity, and the average size of the contractors' proposals was slightly less than 10,000 pages. But with the usual absence of page limits, contractors include any information that they feel will enhance their competitive positions. In the technical section of their proposals, companies describe how they plan to meet performance specifications set forth in the RFP. The more complex and detailed the performance specifications, the longer the proposal. In the management section of their proposals, companies seek to convince the Government that they have the necessary manpower and appropriate management techniques to manage and control the program successfully. This section also includes a description of the contractor's cost reduction plans; a make-or-buy analysis for items that might be subcontracted; configuration management plans; subcontractor management plans; program organization plans; and reports on past management performance. In the absence of general standards for measuring management effectiveness, the contractor is encouraged to include enough information to satisfy the management analysts assigned to the Source Selection Evaluation Board.

In the cost section, contractors are required to present cost estimates for the acquisition program, a description of the methods used to develop these estimates, and techniques used to measure and control actual costs as they are incurred. Here, again, contractors include extensive descriptive material on proposed cost planning and control techniques in the hopes of obtaining a favorable rating. They may include such management techniques as performance budgeting, equivalent unit costing, performance measurement, and milestone costing.

Government teams evaluating the cost section of contractor proposals use information received from the Defense Contract Audit Agency (DCAA) and the Defense Contract Administration Service (DCAS), as well as the information contained in the proposals. The cost evaluation teams compare contractors' cost proposals in order to identify unusual variations from one contractor to another. If variations are found, teams may request clarification from DCAA, DCAS, or the contractor.

THE EVALUATION PROCESS

While cost groups are evaluating the cost sections of contractors' proposals, other working groups on the Source Selection Evaluation Board are studying other parts of the proposals. These groups use the evaluation criteria approved by the Source Selection Advisory Council. The normal evaluation report includes a numerical score, combined with a written explanation of the evaluation results. An example of the scoring method used by one military service is shown below:

	10	High probability of exceeding
Above normal	9	—requirements without excessive
	8	risk or cost.

Normal	7 6 5 }—Meets minimum solicitation re- quirements.	
Below normal	4 3 2 }—Does not meet solicitation re- quirements but has correction potential.	
Unacceptable	1—Does not meet minimum require- ments or involves unacceptable risk and drastic reorientation to correct.	

Another military service uses the following scoring mechanism:

Technical Section of the Proposal	Management Section of the Proposal	Numerical Scores
Outstanding	Outstanding	10
Excellent	Well above average	8–9
Good	Above average	6–7
Adequate	Average	5
Fair	Below average	3–4
Deficient, poor	Well below average	1–2
Seriously deficient, inadequate	Unsatisfactory	0

Source Selection Evaluation Boards use numerical scores to summarize the evaluations made by working groups. On a major program, evaluation teams may include several hundred people, and the number of individual items to be appraised may also reach that number.

When a procurement program is formally advertised, the contracting officer has a relatively easy task of selecting a winning contractor: he selects the company which submits the lowest bid. When contracts are to be negotiated for a major acquisition program, however, the Source Selection Authority must evaluate differences among contractors with respect to costs, schedules, quality, past performance, technical approaches, and technical capabilities.

The Source Selection Advisory Council receives the Source Selection Evaluation Board's report and prepares its own analysis for the Source Selection Authority. This analysis summarizes the highlights of each contractor's proposal and applies weights to the items scored in the evaluation report. The report to the Source Selection Authority includes appraisals of proposed schedules, costs, technical performance, management, and any other considerations that may affect the procurement. This procedure—the application of weights by the Advisory Council—was established to separate the functions of evaluation and selection, thereby providing checks and balances in the source selection process.

Although the Government team that will negotiate the procurement contract is not normally considered part of the source selection process, the team actually plays a vital subsidiary role. In some cases, the Source Selection Authority decides that contracts should be negotiated (but not signed) with each of the bidders before a winner is selected. This technique has been used because the Government's negotiating position is weakened as soon as a winner is announced. During contract competition, each company works feverishly to satisfy Government requirements. When the winning contractor is chosen, the Government provides few incentives to insure that reasonable negotiations will continue.

One of the principal criticisms of the formal source selection process is its use of scarce Government resources for extended periods of time. The following illustrations, from the records of the Army, Navy, and Air Force, provide an indication of the considerable effort involved.

Program A—118 Government personnel applied 26,400 manhours in a six-week period to evaluate proposals from three prospective contractors (an average of 225 hours per man).

Program B—140 Government personnel applied 40,000 manhours in a 13-week period to evaluate proposals from three prospective contractors (an average of 285 hours per man).

Program C—292 Government personnel applied 99,000 manhours in a 13-week period to evaluate proposals from four prospective contractors (an average of 338 hours per man).

Program D—350 Government personnel applied 182,000 manhours in a 26-week period to evaluate proposals from four prospective contractors (an average of 520 hours per man).

Program E—22 Government personnel applied 5,600 manhours in a six-and-a-half week period to evaluate seven prospective contractors (an average of 250 hours per man). This program was a small one, involving routine vehicles.

Program F—300 Government personnel applied 110,000 manhours in a 12-week period to evaluate three prospective contractors (an average of 365 hours per man).

Program G—400 Government personnel required five months (no manhours available) to evaluate three prospective contractors.

In 1970 the President's Blue Ribbon Panel criticized the source selection process, citing the following problems:

1. The process is too time-consuming and complex.
2. The scores of competing contractors tend to be very close.
3. The large number of items evaluated in each proposal levels out the overall ratings.
4. The numerical scores obscure more important issues.
5. The process wastes time and scarce resources.

The Panel recommended that source selection procedures be simplified. It also recommended that RFP's call for a greatly reduced volume of information, and that the military services should experiment with the use of outside experts on source selection boards to produce a broader perspective in making contract decisions.[7]

The following illustration shows the total source selection process in operation. The numbers have been disguised.

Source Selection for the Development of System XYZ

The Source Selection Advisory Council met four times: first, to approve the source selection plan prepared by the program office and to provide guidance to the Evaluation Board in the scoring of the proposals; second, to review the progress of the Evaluation Board shortly after the evaluation process had begun; third, at the completion of the work of the Evaluation Board, to review and analyze the Board's findings; and, fourth, to present a summary and analysis to the Source Selection Authority.

The Source Selection Evaluation Board consisted of 112 professional personnel who worked on the evaluation of proposals from four contractors for a period of eight weeks. The Evaluation Board identified 165 separate areas for scoring. Only three numbers were used in the scoring: 9 = good, 5 = adequate, and 0 = inadequate.

The Advisory Council decided to assign the following weights to the sections of the proposals: technical = 60%, management = 25%, and cost = 15%. At the completion of the evaluation, the total weighted scores for the four prospective contractors were as follows:

Contractor A	480
Contractor B	460
Contractor C	400
Contractor D	275

The scores of the two leading contractors differed by less than 5%.

Management Section. The management sections of the proposals were evaluated in terms of management techniques and management competence. The management scores (included in the total scores shown above) are listed below:

Contractor A	145
Contractor B	151
Contractor C	122
Contractor D	135

Management evaluation scores for the two leading contractors differed by less than 4%.

Cost Section. The Evaluation Board examined contractors' cost estimates in terms of "most probable cost"; that is, the team made its own cost estimates, using the financial information supplied by contractors wherever possible. The Board also used cost information from previous programs similar to the present program. Once the independent estimate had been made by the evaluation team, each contractor's proposed cost was rated as "unrealistic" or "realistic," according to how much it differed from the most-probable-cost. A factor of more, or less, than 25% was used. The most-probable-costs for the four contractors are shown below.

	Most-Probable-Cost
Contractor A	$374–414 million
Contractor B	$405–459 million
Contractor C	$360–405 million
Contractor D	$420–475 million

These were the total estimated budgets for a full-scale development program for the weapon system in question. Each of the above contractors was given a full score of 82 in the cost area, since each contractor's cost estimate was within 25% of the most-probable-cost established by the evaluation team. The proposed costs submitted by the first three contractors were within 5% of each other. The fourth contractor was within 10% of the costs submitted by the first three.

The contractors were even closer in calculating production costs for the development program. Each had been asked to bid on 320 items. The bids submitted are shown below.

Contractor A	$1.53 billion
Contractor B	$1.68 billion
Contractor C	$1.56 billion
Contractor D	$1.73 billion

Contractors A and B differed in their estimates by less than 10%; contractors A and C by less than 2%.

The Weighting of Evaluation Scores

The following table shows how technical, systems engineering, and management sections of a contractor's proposal are weighted in the source selection process. In this example the total technical evaluation was weighted by a factor of 0.5; the systems engineering evaluation, by a factor of 0.3; and the management evaluation, by a factor of 0.2. The cost proposal was evaluated by a separate group, and the resulting report was provided separately to the Source Selection Authority.

The percentage figures appearing on the left side of the page, in the following table, represent the weights applied to each major subdivision within the three overall areas of evaluation. The percentage figures appearing on the right side of the page represent the weights within each subdivision.

Source Selection Problem Areas

Although the source selection process provides a formal means for selecting a contractor, it is not at all clear that the process provides for selection of the contractor that will provide the best product for the cost. Estimates of time, cost, and technical performance are seldom matched by actual performance. This inconsistency adds to the difficulty of evaluating proposals. Moreover, evaluation criteria, particularly for the management sections of contractors' proposals, are not sufficiently sophisticated to mark distinctions between contractors.

The most important lesson that contractors have learned from their experience with the source selection process is the importance of reaching the customer before submitting a formal proposal. Contractors know that members of an Evaluation Board have relatively wide latitude in grading the 100 or more technical concepts and approaches contained in a contractor proposal. Therefore, the bidders try to influence the judgments made by evaluation team members even before the formal source selection process begins. The judgments made by Board members naturally reflect their own level of comprehension and their own estimates of the feasibility of the approach being described. If a Board member does not understand a particular contractor's approach to a technical problem, he may downgrade the proposal. This can have a damaging effect on the contractor's score, since evaluations based on a

I. TECHNICAL APPROACH, TOTAL = 0.5

30% A. *System Design Concept*

1. Analysis and understanding of mission requirements. — 20%
2. System analysis and trade-offs. — 20
3. System synthesis and integration. — 20
4. Configuration rationale, general arrangement and aerodynamic qualities. — 20
5. Growth potential. — 20

100%

15% B. *Design Characteristics*

1. Airframe—general arrangement and weight. — 30%
2. Propulsion installation and fuel system. — 10
3. Structures and materials. — 10
4. Stability and control. — 10
5. Crew station. — 10
6. Armament. — 5
7. Fire control system. — 15
8. Navigation system. — 5
9. Ancillary system. — 5

100%

15% C. *Performance Capability*

1. Energy maneuverability. — 15%
2. Turn capability. — 15
3. Acceleration. — 15
4. Range. — 15
5. Loiter. — 10
6. Maximum Mach number. — 10
7. Rate of climb. — 5
8. Combat ceiling. — 5
9. Cruise speed. — 5
10. Take-off distance. — 3
11. Landing distance. — 2

100%

30% D. *Operational Effectiveness*

1. Missile engagement capability. — 15%
2. Gun engagement capability. — 15
3. Stability and control. — 10
4. Cockpit visibility. — 10
5. Armament flexibility. — 10
6. Electronic counter-measures. — 5
7. Survivability. — 10
8. Mission flexibility. — 10
9. Mission reliability. — 10
10. Availability. — 5

100%

10%   E. *Logistics*

1. Integrated logistics system plan.   10%
2. Maintenance approach.   20
3. Support equipment approach.   20
4. Spares and supply approach.   10
5. Personnel and training plans.   10
6. Technical data and manuals plan.   10
7. Contractor support services plan.   10
8. Test and demonstration plan.   10

100%   100%

II. SYSTEMS ENGINEERING APPROACH, TOTAL = 0.3

40%   A. *Systems Analysis*

1. Fundamental approach.   10%
2. Methodology, models.   10
3. Definition of critical parameters and trade-off areas.   10
4. Completeness of proposed analysis.   10
5. Demonstrated competence.   20
6. Resources and organization.   20
7. Related experience and past performance.   20

                                                                         100%
40%   B. *Approach to System Requirements*

1. Fundamental approach.   10%
2. Compatibility with DOD regulations.   10
3. Adequacy of existing methods and procedures.   20
4. Proposed verifications, tests and demonstrations.   20
5. Proposed demonstration of guarantees and incentives.   10
6. Personnel and organization.   10
7. Related experience and past performance.   20

                                                                         100%
20%   C. *Approach to System Integration*

1. Fundamental approach to system synthesis.   10%
2. Identification of critical interface and integration problems.   20
3. Integration methods and procedures.   20
4. Compatibility with DOD and subcontractor procedures.   20
5. Organizational set-up and personnel.   10
6. Related experience and past performance.   20

100%   100%

III. MANAGEMENT, TOTAL = 0.2

40%   A. *Organizational and Personnel*

1. Contractor organization.   10%
2. Program organization.   40
3. Personnel qualification and experience.   40
4. Organizational interface relationships.   10

                                                                         100%

35%   B. *Management System*
1. Planning of major activities.   25%
2. Management control systems for cost/schedule/technical performance.   20
3. Change control.   15
4. Engineering plan.   10
5. Configuration management plan.   5
6. Data management plan.   5
7. Procurement and production plan.   5
8. Facilities plan.   5
9. Test and evaluation plan.   10
                                                                   ———————
                                                                        100%
25%   C. *Contractor Competence and Probability*
                              of Successful Performance
1. Meeting of performance requirements.   25%
2. Quality of design, test, and manufacturing.   25
3. Schedule control.   20
4. Cost control.   20
5. Correction of deficiencies.   10
                                                                   ———————
———————   100%
100%

reviewer's limited knowledge are not likely to be challenged. Such evaluations
will be buried in the complexities of the source selection process. It is therefore
in the contractors' best interest to be sure that evaluation team members are
well-informed regarding their technical proposals. A contractor also initiates
extensive contracts with Government personnel to find out which parts of a
proposal are considered more important than other parts, in terms of the
weights assigned by the Evaluation Board and the Advisory Council.

The close relationship that sometimes exists between a Government program manager and a contractor can influence the source selection process. It
is not unusual for a program manager to encourage a contractor to submit
a low bid, and then to accept the bid, even though both parties realize that
the budget is far too low to cover program costs. In these cases, the program
manager is naturally inclined to accept contract changes proposed by the contractor that increase the program budget. While it is difficult to document instances of this practice, many individuals in Government and industry admit
that it exists.

A lack of experience or demonstrated capability can be a major stumbling
block for a contractor desiring to enter the defense field. Most Government
buying agencies emphasize experience, especially when evaluating the management section of a contractor's proposal. On the other hand, experienced
contractors face hazards also. "Double counting" of experience factors, at different levels of the evaluation process, is common. The Source Selection Eval-

uation Board may downgrade a firm because of poor performance on a previous contract. The Source Selection Advisory Council, upon reviewing the Evaluation Board's findings, may further downgrade the firm because of its own familiarity with the same performance difficulties. A favorable rating of contractor performance may also be magnified. In both cases, the three-level source selection hierarchy makes differences among contractors seem greater than they actually are.

Since contractors need to "sell" their technical and management capabilities to government officials, many of them maintain as many personnel as possible on their payrolls. In the absence of other measures of contractors' capabilities, the size and experience level of a contractor's work force is often used by Government evaluation teams as a measure of competence. The chief of a DCAS region criticized this aspect of the source selection process: "We lead contractors down the path of building large technical and engineering staffs, to satisfy the corresponding large staffs in customer organizations, and to create the impression of a massive capability."

INDUSTRY VIEWS OF THE SOURCE SELECTION PROCESS

Interviews with defense industry executives revealed widespread dissatisfaction with current source selection procedures. Excerpts from ten of these interviews are printed here.

> Executive #1—What contracting officer is questioned when he makes
> an award to a big company? The company is blamed in this case if
> something goes wrong. But if the contracting officer selects a small
> company and something goes wrong, the contracting officer may be
> criticized for not selecting the larger, better-known firm.
>
> The safest thing for Government personnel to do when operating
> in a cost-type environment is to give the contract to the contractor
> who is the largest and best-known.
>
> From my discussions with Government personnel, it appears to
> me that they are continually asking themselves the question: "What
> is the safest thing to do and the best way to avoid criticism?"
> Executive #2—In the source selection process the Government has
> gone too far in the development of source selection systems and
> procedures and not far enough in terms of training their own per-
> sonnel to make the judgments required by the systems.
> Executive #3—In some cases, companies will underbid with the idea
> of getting their foot in the door and then raising their price through
> contract changes. But in order for a buying agency to select other

than the lowest bidder and punish a contractor playing that game, the contracting officer has to be very knowledgeable and strong. By selecting a contractor other than the lowest bidder, he can be sure that he will have to devote a considerable amount of time to defending his decision.

Executive #4—The major problem in doing business with the Government is waste. Five teams from different contractor plants spend millions of dollars proposing the [name] missile, and yet there is only one winner. DOD should restrict competition severely and, at most have only two or three competitors for a major program.

Executive #5—The Armed Services Procurement Regulations say that the basis of source selection should be "price and other factors." If a contracting officer does not select the lowest bidder, however, he has to write up a comprehensive justification and defend it, and face a protest—which often means a lot of extra work and possible delays in a program.

Executive #6—The best way to select a contractor for a major program is to base the selection on related experiences of personnel, derived from a specific list of names of contractor personnel who will, in fact, be assigned to a program.

Executive #7—The only effective way to evaluate a contractor in the source selection process is to see how he did on the last job. Even here, the evaluation may come down to an appraisal of the abilities of the specific individuals assigned to a program.

Executive #8—The defense procurement system would be improved if the Government told contractors outright how much money they had and what it was generally that they wanted. They might then be able to select a contractor with the most reasonable proposal for a fixed amount of money. As it is, the schedule, and performance, is fixed, and you find out how much money is available, and then the game becomes one of trying to convince the Government that you can do something nobody can do. At the present time, the contractors find out how much money is available for a program, but it's all done under the table.

When a company does a good job or a poor job on a program, many of the individuals in the Government who know about this are transferred to other locations by the time the next program comes along. As a result, much of the source selection process is based on promises and "brochuremanship," rather than proven performance.

The GAO and the Congress looking over the shoulder of the project manager and his superiors cause them to do what is the apparently safe thing—the action which is least susceptible to criticism in the short run.

For example, it is apparently the safest course of action to make
an award to the lowest cost estimate; it is apparently the safest
course of action to select the proposal with the greatest proposed
range and payload; it is apparently the safest course of action to
accept the shortest schedule; it is apparently the safest course of
action to agree to performance specifications larger than the minimum needed, so as to allow a margin for slippage or error; it is
apparently the safest course of action to make a decision that will
not be able to be measured for three or more years. At such time,
the individuals who made or approved the decisions will likely have
been transferred. There will also be a different Congress at that time.

Executive #9—The Government sets up the source selection process on
the basis that the Government will not provide information to the
contractors on the amount of funds available for the program. Then
the project manager or his representative tells the contractors under-
the-table, "Here is how much money we have—$9.7 million. So
don't come in over $10 million or we'll have to drop you."

Executive #10—Source selection boards are very concerned that they
may be embarrassed by their decision, so they take the apparently
safest course of action, or possibly better stated, the course of action
least likely to be criticized. This also means that source selection
boards are cautious about risking a decision to go with new ideas.

One might ask why contractors participate in a particular source selection
when they are dissatisfied with the manner in which it is being conducted. One
senior industry executive provided the following answer:

> I would like to ask whether anybody really believes that a contractor
> can make the decision *not* to bid on a major procurement for which he
> is one of a very small number of highly qualified and competent sources,
> without at the same time making the decision that he no longer wishes
> to remain active in the defense contracting business. The fact is that we
> are not and we would not be making decisions with regard to individual
> proposals; we would be making decisions with regard to our status and
> relationship—our continuing participation in the field.

Criticism of the source selection process comes from Government as well as
industry. A former Pentagon official told us: "Our present source selection
procedure provides no assurance that it will result in the development of the
best product, but it does select a contractor in an environment relatively free
from special-interest groups." Another Pentagon official told us: "The source
selection procedures that we now use in the DOD are no better than throwing
a dart at a dart board."

For one major defense program, the Source Selection Evaluation Board recommended the contractor with the lowest bid. The members of the Advisory Council then prepared an analysis that provided strong evidence that the contractor could not perform the job for the quoted price and that unless the price were adjusted through contract changes, the contractor would incur serious losses. The Source Selection Authority elected to accept the lowest bidder. He decided that he "could not go to the Congress and tell them that I refused to accept the low bid of one of the largest defense contractors, who claimed that he could do the job and was willing to place his reputation on the line with a fixed-price contract." The lowest bidder received the contract, and four years later the program was in serious financial difficulty. In order to complete the program, the Defense Department was forced to arrange additional funding.

Another problem was cited by Government personnel as affecting the source selection process. Senior industry representatives complain directly to an Assistant Secretary or to other senior Government officials whenever they are dissatisfied with the way they are treated by Government personnel during the source selection process. Senior Pentagon officials may tell contractors to work out problems with lower-level Government personnel on their own, or they may inject themselves into the controversy. Since many senior Government personnel are former associates of these contractors they do not often take the former course of action.

It should be clearly stated that no more than a few Pentagon officials allow unprincipled favoritism to play a role in the source selection process. While some Pentagon officials are appointed to their positions with an inadequate knowledge of the negotiating tactics of Government and industry, they usually acquire such knowledge within a year. Officials who fail to resist pressures from contractors for special assistance are regarded unfavorably by most of their peers. The judgment is that they are unaware of what is happening, or are too weak to withstand industry pressure.

Some Pentagon officials are trying to improve present source selection procedures. One alternative approach involves prototype evaluations rather than paper-proposal evaluations wherever feasible. The high cost of defense systems is expected to limit the use of prototype competition, but the concept of prototype competition is not new to the Department of Defense. Most of the aircraft competitions prior to World War II were based on evaluation of flying prototypes. Approximately 50 sample-aircraft competitions were held by the Army between 1934 and 1940. Most of the aircraft used extensively during World War II were chosen through prototype competition, including the B-17, -24, -25, -26, and -29; the A-20 and -24; and the P-38, -39, -40, and -47.[8] In 1939 prototype competition was abandoned because it was considered too time-consuming for emergency procurement. Since then, proposal and paper-design competition have been the primary methods of selecting sources for the development of aircraft and other major defense systems.

SOURCE SELECTION PROTESTS

Contractors often find it difficult to learn why they did not win a particular contract. Although Government debriefing conferences are held for losing contractors, Defense Department personnel are circumspect in their explanations. They do not want to encourage losing contractors to appeal contract decisions to higher levels within the Department.

A losing contractor has the right to file a protest to the contracting officer or to higher authorities in the Defense Department. Contractors can appeal either before or after the actual contract award. If the protest is made to the contracting officer and he rules against the protest, the losing contractor may then appeal the decision to higher levels of the Defense Department, or directly to the General Accounting Office. Upon receipt of a protest at the GAO, the Defense Department is asked to submit a report to the protestor, who then replies. If any significant new issues are raised, the GAO may refer the protestor's brief to the Department of Defense for comment. After the GAO has solicited and evaluated the relevant facts, it renders a decision that is binding on the Department of Defense.

A dissatisfied contractor has no real alternative to the protest procedure. He may choose to solicit the assistance of his Congressman, but this is usually neither timely nor effective. The most effective means to avoid protest situations is for a contractor to maintain frequent and informal discussions with the procuring agency and to make known his questions or issues during the source selection process so that the RFP or the selection procedures can be modified, if appropriate, prior to the closing of the proposal deadline. While the dissatisfied contractor is free to attempt to use the courts and injunction proceedings to stop a contract award and to overturn a source selection decision, there is little evidence available to indicate that this course of action is worth the time and effort required.

THE INFLUENCE OF CONGRESS ON THE SOURCE SELECTION PROCESS

When a contractor loses a competition for a major program, the allegation is often made that the winning contractor "had an inside track" or "had Congressional influence." These kinds of comments leave individuals in Government, industry, and the public-at-large suspicious that source selection decisions are, in fact, the result of "deals" involving industry, the military, and Congress. The "deal" theory has, in the eyes of some, been given credence by the practice of having Senators and Congressmen announce contract awards to firms in their districts. (In the past, the Defense Department routinely gave certain Congressmen and Senators a few hours' advance notice of contract awards being made in their districts or states. Thus, the Congressman or Senator could be the first to make public announcement of the contract award. As of 1971, that practice appears to have stopped, although many Congressmen and Senators still use the occasion of a contract award to derive as much publicity and credit as possible.)

The widespread suspicion about Congressional involvement in the source selection process prompted me to seek to identify the specific role played by Congress. On the basis of my interviews and personal experiences with Government and industry personnel involved in defense procurement, I found that the members of Congress rarely, if ever, cause an award to be made to a particular contractor. From a review of source selection decisions made during the course of a four-year period, it would appear that only one of several hundred decisions was made on the basis of Congressional influence. In the one case, the alleged influence—if it occurred at all—was exercised at a level above the military chain of command, and above the service Assistant Secretary level.

It is nonetheless clear that a number of Congressmen and Senators frequently make their wishes known to decision makers in the Department of Defense and attempt to influence decisions that will increase defense employment in their districts and states.

As discussed in Chapter VII, Congressmen and Senators sometimes seek to influence defense spending in their areas by calls to military and civilian decision makers in behalf of contractors seeking to win contract awards. Our interviews and personal experiences indicate that such inquiries have little, if any, identifiable effect on decisions. In most cases, the individual contacted by a Congressman or Senator simply fails to mention the inquiry to individuals further down the line in the source selection process.

Pentagon decision makers often receive telephone calls pertaining to major defense programs from Senators and Congressmen representing virtually all the leading contenders for contract awards. In most cases, Congressmen and Senators make the inquiry out of an expressed sense of duty to "look after those good people down in. . . ." Even if a senior military or civilian official in the Pentagon is inclined to accede to the requests of a Congressman or Senator, he is likely to have a justifiable fear that news of such direction from his office would soon find its way to the losing contractors, whose Congressmen and Senators would delight in sponsoring an investigation by the GAO to expose such an action.

When a contractor performing work on a defense contract produces unacceptable results, or simply fails to live up to the terms of the contract, officials of the Department of Defense may contemplate action to cancel the contract for default and to charge the contractor the cost of procuring the contract items from another source. News of this impending action, and its implication for local employment, usually arouses Congressional interest and causes telephone calls to be made from the Congress to the Pentagon to seek to have the Department of Defense undertake methods other than contract cancellation to correct the problem. In one case in which an FBI report had supported allegations of fraudulent actions on the part of a contractor, a senior Senator from the contractor's state asked an Assistant Secretary to meet with him in his office. When the Assistant Secretary arrived, there were two Senators and eight Congressmen present. After hearing the evidence to support the allegations of fraudulent actions, most of the individuals present at the meeting commented that it appeared that the Department of Defense had done the correct thing, and the Congressional delegation requested that the responsible individuals be punished but that the contract remain in the Congressional district. In this case, the Congressmen and Senators were successful in their request.

When a contract award is announced, it is not unusual for senior military and civilian personnel in the Pentagon to receive inquiries from Congressmen or Senators who want specific and detailed information as to why a contractor in their own district or state was not selected. These inquiries usually end as soon as the information is made available to the Congressman and he is able to assure the contractor that he is "looking out for his best interests."

Probably the most wasteful form of Congressional influence is that of seeking to have the Department of Defense issue more contracts for an item than are actually needed. In one case, the Department of Defense was faced with reducing requirements for an item used extensively in Vietnam. Senior officials in the Defense Department made the decision to reduce the number of contractor sources to two (in order to retain competition), and to cease buying from higher-cost producers. Two influential members of Congress learned that a firm in their state would no longer be used as a source for the item. After several unsuccessful telephone calls to the Pentagon, the Congressmen were able to influence Congress to include a stipulation in the defense procurement legislation that required the Department of Defense to maintain three producers of the item in question. This decision was made by the Congressmen after they had received several briefings by Department of Defense personnel to acquaint them with the fact that maintaining three producers would require a premium payment of several million dollars.

In a similar case, several Congressmen and Senators called senior military and civilian officials in the Department of Defense to seek to have additional sources of supply retained for an item that already existed in stockpile in substantial numbers, was not urgently required, and could be purchased at a savings of several million dollars per year from fewer suppliers. While the Department of Defense was successful in this case in holding to its decision to have fewer producers, the Congressmen and Senators continued their criticism for several months. One Congressman objecting to the decision pointed out twice during a 20-minute meeting that he "was a supporter of the military-industrial complex" and he thought it was appropriate for the Defense Department to do whatever it could to support him.

Source Selection in Commercial Business

It is difficult to find a parallel to the defense source selection process in the commercial world. Most commercial contract awards are based on price competition resulting in a fixed-price contract. In those cases where a competitive negotiated procurement takes place, the process appears much less formal than the Defense Department process. In addition, a commercial RFP calls for much less detail, and the prospective contractor's previous performance plays a greater role than it does in defense source selection.

In March 1970 the Logistics Management Institute in Bethesda, Maryland, issued a report comparing commercial practices with defense procurement practices. The report cited four major differences:

1. The use of past experience in dealing with a supplier generally is given heavy weight in award of a contract. Past experience, in this sense, covers ease of managing the relationship as well as technical performance of the product or quality of the work. Some companies are put on favored commercial lists; others are barred from future awards.

2. It is considered essential in the commercial world that the purchasing staffs be knowledgeable about the products and processes of key suppliers or have such knowledge readily at hand. Satisfying this condition is an easy matter in many cases where the purchasing firm has similar operations to those of its suppliers and, therefore, has the required expertise. In other cases, as with merchandising companies, the needed technical know-how is not automatically available and the development of purchasing specialists includes a thorough schooling in

the business of the suppliers who must be dealt with. In general much greater emphasis is placed on technical and market knowledge in commercial purchasing than in defense procurement.

3. The processes, management structure, financial condition, and reputation of a potential new supplier of a key item are carefully examined before that supplier is approved as a candidate for a share of the business. The reviews conducted relate the operations and practices of the prospective supplier to those of others in the same industry. Recommendations for improvement are made, and often are a condition for qualification as a supplier. The reviews and advice are not routinely continued once the firm becomes a supplier, but there is no hesitation on the part of the purchaser to move in with a review team if quality or timely delivery is in jeopardy or if such service is called for by the supplier (this situation evidently is not rare). Chronic demand for assistance from the supplier, however, can lead to discontinuance of the relationship.

4. Commercial purchasers recognize the potential peril to them if key suppliers develop serious problems. They protect against such problems by maintaining two or more sources of supply which are unlikely to be affected by the same calamity (e.g., strike, flood, financial failure). They monitor the financial condition and market success of suppliers carefully.

If multiple sources of supply are not needed to achieve sound price agreements, if a sole-source supplier is in sound financial condition, and if additional sources are not a means for avoiding possible problems (e.g., if a strike that would affect one supplier would affect all his competitors), then the commercial purchasing organization does not have any reluctance about a sole-source arrangement. There is aversion, however, to relationships which account for the bulk of the supplier's business in the given product line. It is believed that motivation for efficiency and innovation is likely to be lacking in such cases.[9]

In an article appearing in the April 1972 *Newsletter of the National Contract Management Association,* H. W. Neffner, Vice President of the Boeing Company, discussed several differences between source selection in the commercial world (e.g., 747 aircraft subcontracts) and source selection on defense programs. He noted that in commercial source selection for the 747 program, no more than seven people were assigned to the evaluation boards for each major subcontract. The proposals for each prospective source were contained in a single document covering the extent of investment in facilities; capability to provide engineering personnel and engineering test facilities; the degree of design responsibility accepted and the terms of acceptance; and the maximum profit deemed necessary for the financing and program risk assumed. He stated:

> In major Government programs, the review and approval sequence goes through a number of echelons quite frequently up to the Secretary of a Military Service and often all the way to the Secretary of Defense. Final decisions in such cases may take 1 to 5 months and there have been cases where the review and approval cycle has taken, in our own experience, 8 months or longer. This, of course, has also required some supplementary proposal action, redefinition and inevitably the updating of a proposal. On the 747 major contract review there were 3 levels of management approval ending up at the top corporate management. This process required an average of one week for each source selected. . . .
>
> . . . the quality of the management that followed the source selection decision making contributed much more to the satisfactory performance of these major subcontracts than the quality of the actual final decisions which represented the selection. Since this is not a novel viewpoint in commercial source selection, but is rather a generally accepted fact of life, it tends to explain and justify the considerable disparity between the commercial practice which relies so very little on the accumulation of large amounts of data from each prospective source prior to the decision and the reliance instead on the largely subjective evaluations of a smaller number of evaluators and participants in the decision-making process, each of whom was expected to make significant personal contributions to the decision.

As noted earlier, the GAO, the Congress, and possibly even the courts may need to study a Defense Department contract award decision. This is one crucial reason for the lengthy documentation involved in the source selection process for each major military weapon acquisition program, although it does not justify the inadequacies and redundancies of the process.

Notes to Chapter XIII

1. U.S. Department of Defense Directive 4105.62, 1965.
2. Ibid.
3. Armed Services Procurement Regulation 1-900.
4. Walter B. Wentz, "Aerospace Discovers Marketing," *Journal of Marketing*, April 1967, p. 27.
5. Aerospace Industries Association, *Study of U.S. Air Force Requests for Proposals*, Washington, D.C., December 1969.
6. Aerospace Industries Association, *Study on Source Selection and Contract Definition for Three Air Force Programs*, Washington, D.C., 1969.
7. Report of the Blue Ribbon Panel to the President and the Secretary of Defense on the Department of Defense, July 1, 1970, Appendix E.
8. Wesley Frank Craven and James Lee Cate, *The Army Air Force in World War II* (Chicago: University of Chicago Press, Volume I, 1958), p. 109.
9. Logistics Management Institute, Report on the *DOD Contractor Relationship—Preliminary Review*, Task 69–21, March 1970, pp. 15–16.

"It's not the type of ball game we would choose to play, but it's the only ball game in town."

Defense Industry Executive

CHAPTER XIV

Defense Marketing

DEFENSE MARKETING takes two forms: (1) the marketing of ideas and programs by Government personnel to higher levels in the Department of Defense and the Congress; (2) the marketing of a company's capabilities by industry personnel seeking to win a Government contract award.

Internal marketing activities (within the Defense Department) have been discussed at length in Chapters V and VI. Further discussion in the present chapter will be limited to a brief summary of major marketing activities and problems. This summary will serve as an introduction to the marketing activities of defense and aerospace contractors.

GOVERNMENT INTERNAL MARKETING

In preparation for the annual appropriation process, each military service justifies its programs to the Office of the Secretary of Defense and to the Congress. The senior officials engaged in this process are the Secretaries of the Army, Navy, and Air Force, who find themselves acting as chief marketing representatives for their services.

During the decade of the 1960s the sum of the budget requests of the military services has always exceeded the total amount that the President and the Bureau of the Budget have considered reasonable for defense. As a result, the military services inevitably find themselves competing with each other for funds. In preparation for the annual budget process, the senior military and civilian personnel in each service conduct extensive marketing strategy sessions. The purpose of these sessions is to determine the most effective manner of "selling" their programs to the Office of the Secretary of Defense. The marketing process begins when the Secretary of Defense requests each military service to determine what it can accomplish with a specified amount of money. Traditionally, this amount is less than enough to carry out all the programs desired by each service. The services then seek to convince the Secretary that the low budget would result in cancellation of several essential programs. As one Assistant Secretary commented:

> If we presented the Office of the Secretary of Defense with a balanced, practical program at a low budget level, they would accept it, and the senior military officers in our service would feel as though we let them down. So we play the game that the other services play and we present an unbalanced response that makes it appear that a catastrophe will occur if we have to live with the reduced budget level. Sometimes the analysts in the Office of the Secretary of Defense spot this strategy and sometimes they don't. There are too few of them to know as much as we know about our programs. It's a bit like the game played by the mayor of a city who tells the city council that he must have approval of the budget level he requests or he will be required to delete free milk for the school children.

As part of their marketing strategy, the services underestimate the cost of the programs they request, in the hopes of obtaining approval to begin the programs. Additional funds for the programs are obtained later through requests for supplementary funds, reprogramming from other, less desirable programs, or by requesting additional funds for the programs in a subsequent year.

The reprogramming of funds after the original amounts have been approved by the Congress is a common practice. As part of their marketing strategy, officials include items in a budget request that are really unnecessary or of low priority but which are likely to be approved by the Office of the Secretary of Defense and the Congress, and thus to provide a "safe haven" for funds. Once the budget is approved the funds may be reprogrammed to programs that were underbudgeted. While the program to which funds are reprogrammed may not be essential to national defense, it may be the favorite of a military chief-of-staff, e.g., it may strengthen the service in relation to the other services. In the words of one senior defense official, "The underestimating and reprogramming games are played because the services know that if they tell the Office of the Secretary of Defense what some of these desired programs will cost they will never be approved."

The military services employ similar strategies when they appear before Congressional committees at annual budget hearings and seek funds to carry out their plans and programs. Unlike the Office of the Secretary of Defense, however, the Congress has little capability to evaluate the reasonableness of alternative military service budget levels or to challenge service cost estimates. To make the best possible sales presentation to Congress, the services frequently do not present all the relevant facts about a particular program. Defense officials do not consider this practice to be dishonest, but rather a part of necessary marketing activity—especially if they believe that the requested programs are urgently needed, and are not likely to be approved by Congress if all aspects of the program are reported. Defense witnesses to Congressional committees are instructed by their superiors to answer all questions asked, but not to volunteer any information. Briefings and answers are carefully prepared ahead of time so that Congress will hear only what is likely to enhance favored programs' chances for funding.

In following the strategy described above, if one is requesting additional ships, one selects those statistics and arguments that will support the request for more ships. Pentagon officials may compare the complement of U.S. ships with a larger number of ships operated by a potential enemy, without mentioning the much larger size or greater firepower of U.S. ships. In another case, officials may compare the more than 100 Warsaw Pact troop divisions in Europe with the 20 or fewer NATO divisions, without pointing out that a Russian troop division is approximately one-fifth the size of a U.S. troop division, or that the firepower of a U.S. troop division exceeds the firepower of five Russian troop divisions.

In brief then, this is the marketing game for winning Congressional approval for annual defense budgets. A similar marketing activity takes place after programs are approved and under way. Service representatives present only the most favorable information about ongoing programs to the Office of the Secretary of Defense or the Congress in order to maintain previously approved funding levels. Military or civilian officials who do not support the strategies described above are considered disloyal team members.

Orr Kelly, staff writer for the *Washington Evening Star,* reported an instance of marketing difficulties on April 10, 1970, in an article entitled, "Cost Coverup on Navy Plane Riles Pentagon":

> Top defense officials are furious with the Navy for covering up a sharp increase in the cost of its F-14 fighter planes.
>
> The cost increase—apparently at least suspected by the Navy as long ago as the fall of 1969—did not come to light until last week when a letter to the Navy from Grumman Aircraft, maker of the plane, was made public. When reporters questioned Pentagon press spokesman Jerry W. Friedheim about the delay in revealing the apparent cost increase, he replied: "If it's any consolation to you, Mr. Packard shares your frustration."

Deputy Defense Secretary David Packard generally is in charge of the day-to-day running of the Pentagon and of management of such programs as the F-14.

Other officials said both he and Defense Secretary Melvin R. Laird— who has had to contend with complaints from his former colleagues on Capitol Hill about the coverup of the F-14's cost problem—are furious with the Navy.

Although Laird and Packard both have emphasized on a number of occasions that the F-14 contract was signed just before they assumed office and was written in a form they do not approve, they apparently were not kept fully informed of the growing cost problems that may mean an addition of at least $1 million to the cost of each of the 710 planes the Navy hopes to buy.

Internal defense marketing takes other forms, too. The president of a large defense company reported that several senior officers from one service had contacted him and strongly urged him not to submit a proposal to produce an item currently under development by another contractor. They explained that such a proposal would "muddy the water" and "run the risk of having the current large development program canceled." The large development program was already in serious technical difficulty and had experienced substantial cost overruns.

INDUSTRY MARKETING TO THE GOVERNMENT

Defense contractors' marketing activities begin long before the Government issuance of a Request for Proposal (RFP). The first step in defense marketing is market research. Companies try to determine which programs are being considered by each military service, which Government offices are likely to obtain funds for procurement, and which contractors have a reasonable chance of winning a contract because of their defense business experience. An interested contractor cannot afford to postpone his marketing efforts until the issuance of an RFP. By that time, most interested contractors have aggressive marketing efforts well under way.

There are three ways for defense and aerospace contractors to gain market research information:

1. Direct contact with technical and management representatives of Government agencies and other contractor organizations;
2. Government publications;
3. Commercial magazines, trade publications, and marketing intelligence firms.

The variety of marketing activities carried on before submission of a proposal for a particular program are called "pre-selling" activities. These are usually grouped into four broad categories.

1. Gathering information, as described above; planning marketing strategy; forecasting defense areas and customers with business potential; and identifying specific customer requirements.
2. Developing informal relationships with a large variety of Government technical specialists and management personnel.
3. Seeking to influence the priorities and bid-evaluation procedures of a military service so that they favor a particular contractor.
4. Anticipating future military needs, designing systems that meet these needs, and offering them to the interested military service.

The efforts of this pre-selling activity frequently result in the submission of unsolicited proposals to a military service.

Most large defense and aerospace firms have small offices in Washington, D.C., and in other locations near military buying agencies throughout the United States. Contractor representatives assigned to these offices are supposed to develop and maintain working relationships with Government personnel. They are selected on the basis of their personal qualities, the ability to meet and converse with people, rather than their technical skills. Technical skills are provided by specialists from the contractor's plant who are periodically scheduled to meet influential Pentagon buying officials. One defense contractor in our study maintains field representatives at the following locations:

- Washington, D.C. (near the Pentagon, the Congress, and the headquarters of the three military service buying commands).
- Lexington, Massachusetts (near the Air Force Electronics Systems Division).
- Colts Neck, New Jersey (near the Army's Electronics Command).
- Rome, New York (near the Air Force Air Development Center).
- Dayton, Ohio (near the Air Force Aeronautical Systems Division).
- Fort Walton Beach, Florida (near Pensacola Naval Air Station).
- Huntsville, Alabama (near Redstone Arsenal).
- Houston, Texas (near the Manned Space Center).
- Hawthorn, California (near Edwards Air Force Test Base).
- Colorado Springs, Colorado (near NORAD headquarters).

The representatives at these field offices are expected to keep track of the current status of Government programs, funding availability, technical and management approaches preferred by Government personnel, and activities of competitors.

Contractors told us that they maintained contact with a large number of Government agencies during the course of a major program. One contractor working on an Air Force development program cited 23 separate Government organizations with an active interest in the program. These were:

Organization	Function
Headquarters, U.S. Air Force Headquarters, Air Force Systems Command	Direction and guidance
Aeronautical Systems Division of Air Force Systems Command	Total program management responsibility
Air Force Plant Representative Office Defense Contract Administration Service Regional Office	Administration of government/industry contracts and plant surveillance
Air Force Flight Test Center Air Force Missile Development Center Arnold Engineering Center Armament Development and Test Center Air Force Special Weapons Center	Flight test programs and engineering services
Air Force Logistics Command Air Training Center Aerospace Medical Division	Assistance in total systems integration
Air Force Flight Dynamics Laboratory Air Force Avionics Laboratory Air Force Weapons Laboratory Air Force Material Laboratory	Support and assistance in the integration of advance technology
National Aeronautics and Space Administration President's Scientific Advisory Board Aeronautical Systems Division Advisory Group RAND Corporation	Special studies and analyses of particular or unique phases of the program
Strategic Air Command	The using command

Government personnel at the Pentagon and at military buying offices in the field are frequently visited by contractor representatives, both local and out-of-town, who seek to assist them in developing and clarifying system requirements and technical approaches, and to describe ("sell") their company's capabilities. In addition, industry personnel provide suggestions for new guns, aircraft systems, radar, guidance systems, tanks, helicopters, rockets, boosters, trucks, armored personnel carriers, and a variety of other weapon systems. In preparing for these sales presentations, industry personnel collect statistics on the capabilities of potential enemies to strengthen their case for a new weapon system. Not only technical personnel from defense firms visit Government offices in Washington, D.C., and elsewhere. General managers and staff management specialists also visit and try to influence Government officials with respect to management techniques, cost estimates, and the need for particular weapon systems.

When a Government procurement organization gets ready to issue an RFP, industry representatives use their contacts to gain a detailed understanding of the system to be acquired and the complex requirements described (often ambiguously) in the RFP. During their visits, industry personnel assist in the preparation of technical management sections to be included in the RFP. After receiving a variety of suggestions from industry personnel, Government officials combine their own ideas with the most useful (or most persuasively marketed) ideas presented by industry representatives and prepare the final RFP.

Marketing, as described above, plays such an important role in defining Government requirements for major development programs that most industry managers believe it is a prerequisite for winning a contract. A contractor who waits until an RFP is issued or a notice of a planned procurement appears in the *Commerce Business Daily* rarely, if ever, wins a major procurement contract. By the time the notice appears in the *Commerce Business Daily* several individual contractors will have spent thousands of manhours constructing dummy RFP's of their own, in an attempt to anticipate the content of the Government's document. For one large procurement, a contractor prepared a thousand-page draft RFP as a guide for internal proposal preparation activities. This was done several months before the official RFP was issued. The actual RFP did bear a close resemblance to the contractor's dummy.

Contractors devote a major part of their pre-selling activity to acquainting military customers with the technical approaches they plan to propose. Contractors believe that technical procedures that are not understood, or that are considered high-risk, by Government evaluators will not receive a high rating in the source selection evaluation.

Professor E. B. Roberts of the Massachusetts Institute of Technology has conducted numerous studies of the activities of contractors who are selected for contract awards. He has this advice to offer to defense contractors:

> If you have not been in on the pre-RFP phase of the procurement, begin by saying, "We should probably no-bid this RFP, unless this is an exceptional situation in which overall strategy reasons cause us to bid." But, in general, you should expect to lose the award unless you have already been in close contact with the technical people in the customer's organization. You ought to feel that you have established a good relationship with the technical group issuing the RFP. Don't ask the first question that so many companies ask. In a number of our studies we found that companies first ask, "Do we have technical competence in this area?" That is a relevant question to ask, but it is not the correct first question.

You should first inquire, "Have we demonstrated whatever technical competence we have to the particular organization that has issued this RFP?" [1]

In a survey of defense contractors, Roberts asked: "Was contact established with the customer's technical personnel (i.e., those responsible for this procurement) following receipt of the RFP but prior to proposal submission?" Roberts pointed out that although these contacts were usually illegal according to the Armed Services Procurement Regulation, they often occurred. He found that 50% of the contract winners and 30% of the losers had been in contact with Government technical personnel during this period. Roberts also asked contractors: "Was the technical approach of your proposal in any way designed to satisfy known technical preferences of the customer?" Sixty-eight percent of the winners knew and responded to technical preferences of the customer; only 33% of the losers did so.

Several industry personnel told us that they made it a practice of talking to as many Government personnel as possible when they were seeking to win a procurement or were already engaged in a major defense program. They believed that these contacts were important because so many individuals in the Department of Defense have the power to block actions, or to delay actions, but very few can make the decision to go ahead with a course of action that is not fully coordinated with all interested organizations.

Other industry representatives told us that they found it useful to have extensive contacts with Government personnel in order to learn the names of those individuals who would be assigned to Source Selection Evaluation Boards and Source Selection Advisory Councils. "Aerospace contractors have an intelligence network as good as the CIA," said one Government program manager; "their network is able to discover what is happening within the Government as well as within the competing firms."

Industry personnel in our study indicated that they usually knew approximately how much the Government was planning to spend on a particular procurement. On industry executive commented: "Very often in defense procurements, soon after a Request for Proposal is issued, there is a leak from the Government—intended or unintended—that the Government only has X amount of funds available for the procurement. Sometimes this is not even in the form of a leak, but the program manager will tell contractors directly the amount of funds set aside for this procurement."

A management consulting firm that claims to have trained more than 15,000 contractor personnel has published a handbook on negotiation. It contains the following advice on how to obtain procurement information from the Government:

In many cases, the only recourse is to go in and ask. The regulations state that the buyer is not supposed to tell the seller whether or not he is in the zone of consideration or the number or identity of other bidders. Some buyers are more skillful at withholding this type of information than others. The ability of the buyer to keep the seller in doubt as to his position is one of the buyer's principal bargaining strengths. Many buyers, however, do not realize this, or do not seem to care, and will provide the seller with information with regard to his competitive position. In other cases, the technical personnel involved in the procurement will provide the seller with information as to his competitive standing. In extreme cases, they may even provide information as to the Government's objective in the procurement or the amount of money available. If this information can be secured, of course, it provides a valuable bargaining tool to the seller. Even if, when the buyer is approached, he follows the regulations and refuses to give the seller any information regarding his position, his attitude or the manner in which he greets the seller may provide the seller with some indication as to where he stands.

One senior Pentagon official, previously employed in the defense industry, told us that while he was with industry he would regularly see secret documents sent by Government personnel to the Deputy Secretary of Defense and not intended to be seen by industry personnel. These documents pertained to particular programs of interest to the contractor and provided valuable information on available funding, technical thresholds for program review, and features of the program considered critical by the Department of Defense. In our meetings with two defense contractor firms, copies of numbered Secret Development Concept Papers marked "not for distribution to industry" were produced as examples of the results of marketing research.

Extensive market intelligence and pre-selling activities for one major program frequently require the efforts of hundreds of personnel from a contractor's organization. These individuals travel extensively to the various military organizations involved in the planned procurement. A senior industry executive told us that during one month in 1971, 245 technical personnel from his plant spent 65% of their time attending meetings or traveling in connection with customer relations, market research, or pre-selling activities. Senior personnel from another defense company told us that the planning, pre-selling, and proposal activity for one major defense program had cost the firm $25 million; they did not win the contract. During the proposal preparation phase of the C-5A program, Boeing, Lockheed, and Douglas, the three contenders, claimed to have a total of nearly 6,000 personnel working full-time on the engineering, production, and cost problems involved in the program.

A contractor's proposal preparation activities are not always paid for by the contractor. Indeed, a large contractor with a number of current defense contracts may be able to charge most of his marketing expenses as an indirect cost to be absorbed by his other defense contracts. On the other hand, a contractor with little or no defense business is required to bear the entire cost of the marketing and proposal preparation activity without Government support. An exception to this rule occurs when the Government agrees to pay for a part of the contractors' costs of bidding on a program by agreeing to contract with the leading contenders for a specified amount of proposal preparation effort. This practice has been followed on a few of the largest defense programs during recent years. On all small and medium-sized programs, and many large programs, however, the marketing and proposal costs must either be absorbed by other defense contracts within the contractor plant, or be deducted from a contractor's profits.

In deciding whether or not to bid on a defense procurement, contractors seek to determine the answers to several questions. First, has sufficient market research been accomplished to determine the nature of the requirement and the actual objectives of the Government personnel responsible for the procurement? Second, has there been sufficient pre-selling activity to insure that Government personnel understand and accept the company's capabilities? Third, has it been determined that an actual competition will take place and that the evaluation personnel are not already committed to another contractor? Fourth, is the company willing and able to prepare a superior proposal?

Some companies consider a number of additional factors in determining whether or not they will bid on a particular program. The president of one defense company stated that his firm preferred to bid on programs that involved substantial advances in technology. Explaining his rationale, he said, "If we build something that is well within the state of the art, we don't sell many of them. The things we sell lots of are those that are advanced right up to the state of the art, or 20% beyond—and, of course, these are often the programs that get into trouble during the development phase."

Once a contractor has decided to compete for a particular contract award, the management of the firm seeks to develop a winning strategy. One strategy is to try to submit the lowest bid and to obtain ratings of at least "satisfactory" on all other aspects of the proposal. Another strategy is to submit a superior technical proposal, with a price within a competitive range. Throughout the source selection process, market intelligence information continues to be crucial. Even after a contractor has submitted a proposal to the Government, changes in the proposal can be made and accepted if the changes are believed by the Government to be in its best interest.

A former Pentagon official, who had been responsible for reviewing major procurement actions, reported the following account of a major defense program valued at several hundred million dollars. Contractor A had submitted a superior technical proposal and a price estimate that was 42% higher than the estimate submitted by the next leading competitor, Contractor B. Contractor A learned that his bid was high and submitted an amendment to his proposal. He lowered his price to a level 31% above Contractor B's estimate. On the day the source selection decision was to be made, Contractor A called the Source Selection Authority and indicated that further refinements had been made in his price estimate. His new estimate was now only 5% above Contractor B's. Later that day, the Source Selection Authority made the decision in favor of Contractor A. Three years later, Contractor A revealed that there would be a substantial increase in the cost of the program, thereby raising the total cost to a figure far above the original price quoted by Contractor B. The Pentagon decided that because of the "urgent" nature of the program, the additional funds would be made available. After making a three-year investment in the equipment, designs, tooling, and experience of the winning contractor, the Department did not feel it had the option of changing contractors. The winning contractor's pricing strategy had resulted in a contract award, and in continued support for several years beyond the original deadline. As a senior industry executive commented, "It's not the type of ball game we would choose to play, but it's the only ball game in town."

The history of one completed program provides insight into the benefits of winning an initial development contract, regardless of the high cost of winning. In 1951 a major defense contractor won the development contract for the design and fabrication of two prototypes of an advanced weapon system. In 1968, 17 years later, the program was still active and the weapon system was still under production. By 1968 the contractor who had won the development competition in 1951 had received 82 contracts directly related to the program. These included 27 production contracts, 21 modification contracts, 14 contracts for spare parts and ground equipment, 10 contracts for training, four contracts for testing, four for engineering, and two for miscellaneous items. This single program had provided a major portion of a business career for hundreds of people in the contractor's organization.

When defense spending is reduced, defense contractors worry about losing financial support for their technical personnel. All industry executives in our study admitted that the 1970–1971 phase-down in Federal defense spending had caused them to make a number of personnel reductions, but they all believed that other contractors would be more seriously affected by the phase-down than they were.

As defense firms have grown larger, there has been much more emphasis on survival and growth than on the traditional business goal of profit maximization. In 1958 Arch Patton, director of McKinsey & Co., Inc., studied 642 defense corporations. In an article in the *Harvard Business Review,* he noted that executive compensation was increasing by a function of sales volume, in the airframe industry and in U.S. industry at large.[2] This observation is supported by our own studies. A group of senior executives from a leading defense firm told us that at industry association meetings and cocktail parties, defense industry managers are congratulated for winning new contracts and commiserated with for losing a competition or having a program come to an end. Profit, on the other hand, is rarely the reason for praise or sympathy. Profit, they thought, would take care of itself. Sales volumes was the focus of attention.

Pressure within the defense industry for maintaining and building sales volume is not a new phenomenon. The following comments from *The Weapons Acquisition Process* apply as well today as they did in 1962:

> . . . Thus, contractors may be maximizing profits when they support and advocate programs with little military value; when they perform operations in-house which could be done more efficiently by other firms; when they choose technical approaches which, although not best from the Government's point of view, enhance their own competitive position; when they design into their weapons capabilities and features far exceeding what is really needed; etc. Yet profit maximization narrowly defined does not explain all such activities. Contractors may have other objectives which lead to behavior inconsistent with the Government's objectives. For example, marginal or worthless programs may be "sold" vigorously to preserve stability of employment. In some cases of this sort, the secondary role of the profit maximization objective is shown by company offers to accept very low profit rates. Similarly, firms may maintain unnecessarily large staffs primarily to avoid the extremely unpleasant task of laying off personnel.
>
> Most of these examples suggest unfavorable program outcomes in terms of costs higher than they need be. The evidence in our case studies indicates that problems like those mentioned here are not uncommon features of U.S. weapons programs. These problems are translated into program cost overruns when contractors submit initial estimates which reflect what the program would cost if conducted efficiently, but when the actual conduct of the program fails to achieve the predicted levels of efficiency.[3]

One defense executive commented on the reasons for continuing optimism in bidding for defense projects.

> If a job may cost $2 million to accomplish and the Government can only justify $1 million, we know we must submit a bid within that range if we hope to obtain that contract.

We wish to win the bid, regardless of price, for a number of reasons. First, we may see the contract as a key job with a great future potential. Second, we may desire to maintain a technical competence in the specific area of the contract. Third, we may decide it is better to cover some of our overhead rather than none at all. Therefore, we may decide to bid on a contract with an estimate at half the price we believe is valid. This does not mean that we have to lie to the Government. But we do have to make certain assumptions in developing our final bid.

We may have to assume:

1. First-try 100% design success;
2. Fully efficient utilization of personnel;
3. No delays;
4. No required changes by either the Government or the contractor;
5. No allowance for failure or error.

An Assistant Secretary in the Defense Department who had recently held a position in industry expressed a similar point of view. "The name of the game is 'damn the costs and win the competition anyway.' In order to win a contract, a contractor proposal has to state: the technology is in hand!" The same official told us that in his view the management sections of contractor proposals are worth very little. In his experience, they "simply appeared to be a playback of the last three speeches given by senior officials of the military department responsible for the procurement."

In 1970 the National Security Industrial Association—an association of defense contractors—completed a study of problems in the acquisition process. In this study, the Association provided a rationale for the practice of underbidding in defense marketing:

> For its part, industry feels it must employ the competitive tactics called for by the environment of the defense marketplace. A contractor who does a thorough and realistic job of analyzing and pricing the technical risks inherent in his proposed approach to systems development knows that he is likely to find himself the loser to a more optimistic competitor. In brief, in the environment of a buyer's market, optimism seems essential to survival. This inevitably is a more compelling motivation to the seller than risk minimization through objective realism in his proposals, the probable end result of which is losing business.[4]

At the time of the 1970–1971 phase-down in defense spending, many senior Government and industry officials suggested that the tendency toward excessive optimism in contractor bidding would increase. One Pentagon Assistant Secretary commented: "In a tight competitive environment, with a decreasing defense budget, the services as well as contractors tend to be even more optimistic about promising what they can do for the limited funds."

During the course of our interviews with defense industry personnel, the president of one defense firm claimed that representatives of five Governmental agencies (Army, Navy, Air Force, Federal Aviation Agency, and NASA) had told him on separate occasions that he had lost various contracts because his bid was too honest. On one of these contracts, he had informed the Government program manager that the program would require 18 months and $1.6 million to complete. The program manager replied that if a contractor wanted to win the job, he would have to bid $700,000 and claim that the job could be accomplished in seven months. The company president decided not to bid on the contract. The winning contractor bid $700,000 and seven months. The actual costs of the project exceeded $1.6 million; it was completed in two years.

Eugene B. Fubini, former Director of Defense Research and Engineering, expressed his concern over these matters at a press conference on the occasion of his resignation from the Department of Defense in mid-1965. He stated that in their desire to obtain research contracts, "contractors do not always face up to their responsibilities" in deciding upon the feasibility of technical proposals. He also attacked the tendency of these companies, once contracts are obtained, to "goldplate" specifications and performance, overcomplicating and raising the price for the work being accomplished.[5]

When David Packard was Deputy Secretary of Defense, he frequently warned contractors about the excessive optimism of their proposals. Speaking in August 1970 at the annual meeting of the Armed Forces Management Association, Secretary Packard commented:

> The Defense Department has been led down the garden path for years on sophisticated systems that you promised would do all kinds of things for some optimistic cost. Too frequently we have been wrong in listening to you, and more frequently you have been unable to deliver on either of these promises—what it would do or what it would cost.[6]

Several months earlier, Secretary Packard had addressed an industry group:

> . . . A related question is costing. I know you have been wrestling with this problem for some time, and I have only one thing to say on this subject now. You have to eliminate this business of buying in. Neither the Department of Defense nor the Congress will continue to tolerate large cost overruns which relate to unrealistic pricing at the time of award, or to inadequate management of the job during the contract.[7]

It seems clear from our interviews with industry personnel that there are numerous pressures on contractors to submit optimistic proposals. When defense business is declining, contractors are faced with the problem of holding their organizations together and meeting their payrolls. In such circumstances, if they believe that greater optimism in various aspects of a proposal will assist in obtaining a contract, they will seek this advantage. They will also prepare attractive or optimistic proposals in order to obtain contracts that will provide them with the opportunity to improve their technical capabilities and facilities, and/or associate the company's name with the leaders in new technology.

Our interviews revealed that for many firms, only 25% or fewer of the proposals submitted to the Department of Defense were successful. Representatives from several firms indicated that their success rate was 15% or less. They all stated that intensive marketing activity was necessary simply to survive in the defense business. We also found that the level of a contractor's activity in preparing unsolicited proposals was a function of the firm's unused capacity. As unused capacity grows, contractors direct the efforts of idle personnel to proposal preparation. The availability of extra personnel was cited as a "strength" by a winning contractor in his proposal for a development program. His proposal contained the following statement:

> In addition, because of cutbacks in the space program, the space division can make available large numbers of personnel (several thousand) skilled in all aspects of aircraft weapon system management, engineering, manufacturing, and logistics support on a schedule which phases ideally with the [name] program.

In discussing defense marketing with industry executives, we found that the motivation for these efforts was often preservation rather than expansion. And the military services encourage these activities out of similar motives: they seek more highly sophisticated weapons and equipment in order to maintain or increase their own effectiveness.

Defense industry managers told us that proposals to the Government should include evidence to support six claims:

1. The contractor has an intense interest in the program and will assure that it receives top-level attention by assigning a program manager from a high level of the company's organization.
2. The contractor understands the need for the system, the work that must be done, and the problems that are likely to be encountered.
3. The contractor has a reasonable plan for designing and producing the system and for solving the anticipated problems.
4. The contractor is qualified by previous experience and current capabilities to accomplish the job.
5. The contractor has the required manpower, facilities, and management

systems to carry out the project and to identify problems in time to take corrective action.

6. The price proposed by the contractor is reasonable and within the funds available for the project. (The advantages of a low bid were discussed earlier.)

In preparing proposals for major systems, most defense contractors employ technical and management consultants to supplement their own capabilities. Thus, contractor proposals sometimes reflect the viewpoints of consultants who may not continue to be associated with the program if the contractor wins the contract award. In this regard, several industry executives explained that many proposals simply told Government personnel what they wanted to hear. These same executives believe that many of the Government personnel reviewing the management section of their proposals do not understand the management techniques required by higher levels of the Government.

The preparation of a proposal for a major defense system requires the efforts of the best technical and management personnel available to a contractor organization. In 1963 Congressman George P. Miller commented on this state of affairs in a Congressional report on science and technology:

> The best qualified scientists and engineers are engaged in writing proposals and, when the proposals are successfully sold to the Government, the scientists are put on a new proposal. Then second-rate scientists are given the job of performing work while the more highly regarded people scout for new business.[8]

The Blue Ribbon Panel summarized a number of problems in the field of defense marketing:

> One serious weakness of industry is the tendency toward over-responsiveness to every expressed or implied desire of Department of Defense personnel. Over-responsiveness should not be substituted for the exercise of responsibility. As a management team member, it is the responsibility of industry to point out to the Department the true nature of acquisitions and developments as seen by industry. For example, the following are areas in which industry has demonstrated an over-responsiveness on specific developments:
> (1) Unquestioned acceptance of inefficient and unnecessary management control system requirements and related data items.
> (2) Failure to point out the potential risks associated with the inherent technical uncertainties in the development of a specific weapon system.

(3) Overoptimistic cost estimates and, in some cases, unwarranted buy-ins.

(4) Unquestioned acceptance and, in some cases, promotion of overly sophisticated design solutions to satisfy the stated requirements.[9]

Department of Defense officials and defense industry executives agree that the problems cited above do exist. They point out, however, that the present source selection process makes it highly unlikely that any firm wishing to continue to receive contracts will cease to respond to every preference of Government personnel involved in the process.

COMMERCIAL VERSUS DEFENSE MARKETING

Some of the differences between commercial and defense marketing stem from the large size and scope of defense projects. Others result from the defense source selection process, the need to justify funds on an annual basis, the difficulty of convincing Congress to approve programs with inherent uncertainties, and the need to provide formal justification for any Government decision involving the award of millions of dollars to a particular business firm.

Pre-selling. Defense marketing usually involves substantially more pre-selling activity than is required for most commercial industrial marketing. While pre-selling activities are not unknown in commercial marketing, they are usually far more limited in terms of the number of personnel and number of organizations involved.

Past performance. Commercial procurement decisions are more frequently influenced by the reputation and past performance of a contractor than are defense procurement decisions. Although the Department of Defense attempts to evaluate past performance and to weight this factor in the source selection process, judgments in this area have been very difficult to defend before the General Accounting Office and the Congress.

Justification of a procurement decision. The need for extensive documentation and justification of a procurement decision is another attribute of defense marketing and source selection that differentiates it from commercial marketing and source selection. Normally, few if any outside organizations challenge the decision of a commercial contracting officer or purchasing agent. By contrast, in defense procurement decisions are frequently challenged by losing competitors, the GAO, or the Congress.

Demonstrated performance versus predicted performance. In commercial marketing the emphasis is more often on the demonstrated capabilities of a product or service, whereas in defense marketing the emphasis is on predicted performance. This is because commercial firms normally sell a specific product, whereas defense firms usually sell a capability to design and produce a product never produced before.

Channels of distribution. Channels of distribution are frequently important marketing considerations for commercial firms. In contrast, defense firms normally market and deliver direct to the Government buyer. Further distribution of the product is the responsibility of the Government, not the contractor.

Advertising. Advertising frequently plays a major role in commercial industrial marketing. In defense marketing advertising plays a much less significant role. It is largely devoted to institutional advertising designed to strengthen the company's image.

Selective disclosure of information. The practice of disclosing only selected information to a customer is part of commercial and defense marketing. In commercial activities, buyers and sellers recognize that a seller will select information that presents the best view of the product and withhold or delay publication of information neutral or harmful to the product. These activities are frequently rationalized as prudent marketing strategy. In defense marketing, these activities may be viewed by the defense firms as wise marketing strategy, but to Government personnel and the Congress, withholding information necessary for a fair decision on the use of public funds is not acceptable. Defense firms that engage in this practice may be severely criticized by the Government for unethical behavior, and run the risk of a Congressional investigation and public disclosure of their activities.

Compensation of salesmen. In commercial marketing, the compensation of salesmen is frequently based on a commission, and bonuses or prizes are paid as a reward for meeting specific sales quotas. While bonuses are customary and allowable in the defense industry, sales personnel are rarely compensated by commission. Furthermore, in the defense industry, the distinction between a line manager and a salesman is less clear than in commercial marketing.

Many of the differences between commercial and defense marketing may be explained by the fact that source selection decisions in commercial contracting are considered private matters, involving reciprocity and a variety of other special considerations. Marketing and source selection in the defense business are considered public matters, subject to the scrutiny of the Congress and the GAO. Reciprocity is not a consideration. Decisions must be justified as the result of fair and equal treatment of all interested contractors.

NOTES TO CHAPTER XIV

1. E. B. Roberts, "How the U.S. Buys Research," *Science and Technology,* September 1964, pp. 70–77; and "Strategy for Winning R&D Contracts," Massachusetts Institute of Technology Working Paper, July 1965.
2. Arch Patton, "Annual Report on Executive Compensation," *Harvard Business Review,* September–October 1958, pp. 128–132.
3. Merton J. Peck and Frederic M. Scherer, *The Weapons Acquisition Process: An Economic Analysis* (Boston: Division of Research, Harvard Business School, 1962), p. 458.
4. National Security Industrial Association, *Defense Acquisition Study, Final Report,* Washington, D.C., July 1, 1970, p. 4.
5. Eugene B. Fubini, Director of Defense Research and Engineering, quoted in *The New York Times,* July 4, 1965, p. 16.
6. David Packard, Deputy Secretary of Defense, address to the annual meeting of the Armed Forces Management Association, Los Angeles, August 1970.
7. ———, Address to the Aerospace Industries Association, Williamsburg, Virginia, May 22, 1969.
8. U.S. House of Representatives, Report of the Committee on Science and Astronautics, Panel on Science and Technology, 1963, p. 88.
9. Report of the Blue Ribbon Panel to the President and the Secretary of Defense on the Department of Defense, July 1, 1970, p. 85.

CHAPTER XV

Profits in the Defense Industry

THE TERM "PROFIT" in general business usage refers to the proceeds derived from business sales after all related expenses have been deducted. In the defense business, profit has the same meaning for contractors involved in fixed-price contracting. A different situation exists for defense contractors working under cost-reimbursement contracts: the contractor receives a predetermined amount of profit regardless of his actual costs. Hence, an increase in costs does not mean a corresponding decrease in profits. Indeed, if the increased costs result from contract changes, they may even mean an increase in profits. In addition to this unusual profit feature, the manner in which the Defense Department negotiates profits for all contract types differs from commercial practice. In commercial business, profits associated with various types of work are usually determined by the amount of competition, the demand for a product, and often the investment required to produce the product. By contrast, a defense contractor's profits are negotiated primarily as a function of the estimated cost of a program. The higher the estimated costs of a program, the higher the profit that is likely to be negotiated.

Defense profit policies apply only to negotiated contracts. They do not apply when price competition exists, since in these cases the Defense Department merely selects contractors with the lowest total price if all other factors are equal. When price competition exists, the Defense Department relies upon the forces of competition to produce the lowest total price and is not concerned with the level of contractor profit. When price competition does not exist, however, the price is not subject to competitive pressures but is determined through mutual agreement by the parties to the contract. In 1971 negotiated contracts of this type amounted to $29.5 billion (89% of all defense procurement dollars).

The method of determining defense contract profit percentages (to be applied to the estimate of total cost) is described in the Armed Services Procurement Regulation (ASPR) Section 3-808. This section of ASPR sets forth a set of "weighted guidelines" that are intended for use by Government contracting officers in establishing profit objectives in negotiations with contractors. Once the profit percentage is developed through negotiation, it is applied to the various elements of the estimated contract costs. These amounts are then summed to arrive at a total dollar profit for the contract.

Armed Services Procurement Regulation 3-808(a) states defense profit policy in the following terms:

> It is the policy of the Department of Defense to utilize profit to stimulate efficient contract performance. Profit generally is the basic motive of business enterprise. The Government and defense contractors should be concerned with harnessing this motive to work for more effective and economical contract performance. Negotiation of very low profits, the use of historical averages, or the automatic application of a predetermined percentage to the total estimated cost of a product, does not provide the motivation to accomplish such performance.

In spite of the flexibility of the official policy, the profit negotiated on most defense cost-reimbursement contracts appears to correspond to a historical average in the vicinity of 7%. This figure is well below the statutory limit of 15% imposed by the Congress on the total cost-reimbursement research and development work undertaken by a defense firm in any one year. For all Federal agencies, the statutory limitations on cost-reimbursement profits are shown below:

- 15% for research and development work.
- 10% for all others, including supply and construction work.
- 6% for architectural and engineering work.[1]

The profit percentage that the Government negotiates with a contractor rarely represents the final contractor profit. Two factors, either separately or jointly, can cause the final profit to be lower than the negotiated profit. First, the contractor may enter into a contract that will provide for reduced profits to the extent that actual costs exceed planned costs (incentive contracts). Profits under these contracts may also be reduced for late deliveries or for inferior technical performance. Second, for purposes of profit calculation, the Department of Defense does not recognize certain types of contractor costs, such as interest, advertising, and entertainment. These costs must be deducted from the negotiated profit before the final profit is calculated. In recent years these unallowable costs have ranged from 1% to 2% of sales.

Profit rates on negotiated defense contracts vary by type of contract. The purpose of this is to make the profit a function of the risk assumed by the contractor; the higher the risk, the higher the negotiated profit rate. Table XV-1 shows the average profit rate for negotiated defense contracts during the period 1964–1970.

TABLE XV-1. AVERAGE PROFIT RATES FOR NEGOTIATED
DEFENSE CONTRACTS: 1964–1970

Type of Contract	Negotiated Profit Rate
Firm fixed-price	11.1%
Fixed-price incentive	9.9
Cost-plus-incentive-fee	7.5
Cost-plus-fixed-fee	6.5

SOURCE: *100 Companies Receiving the Largest Dollar Volume of Prime Contract Awards, Fiscal Year 1970*, Office of the Assistant Secretary of Defense (Comptroller), Directorate of Information Operations.

The use of the Defense Weighted Guidelines has had the effect of increasing the negotiated profit rate for defense contractors. Table XV-2 presents the lower profit rates that existed before Defense Weighted Guidelines were introduced in 1964.

TABLE XV-2. AVERAGE PROFIT RATES FOR NEGOTIATED
DEFENSE CONTRACTS: BEFORE 1964

Type of Contract	Negotiated Profit Rate
Firm fixed price	9.0%
Fixed-price incentive	8.9
Cost-plus-incentive-fee	6.0
Cost-plus-fixed-fee	6.2

SOURCE: *100 Companies Receiving the Largest Dollar Volume of Prime Contract Awards, Fiscal Year 1970*, Office of the Assistant Secretary of Defense (Comptroller), Directorate of Information Operations.

Despite the apparent increase in profit figures caused by the introduction of the Weighted Guidelines, we heard many criticisms about them from executives of small and medium-sized defense firms. Four representative comments from these interviews are included below:

> Executive #1—The people who are using the weighted guidelines do not appear to understand how they are used. They are often bound by specific profit percentages that were historical rates. The idea of the weighted guidelines is a vast improvement over the independent guess of the contracting officer. Now all we have to do is get the guidelines used.

Executive #2—The weighted guidelines have no basis in reality. In some cases we can justify 15% profit with the weighted guidelines, but we are never able to negotiate profit that high. All the contracting officers are afraid to take the plunge.

Executive #3—Only lip service is given to the weighted guidelines in negotiating $100,000 contracts. At this level, it's the historical rate that is important.

Executive #4—It may well be that the weighted guidelines are being used with the few large contractors who influence the averages, but I can assure you that the weighted guidelines are not being used with the small and medium-sized contractors. The trouble with the defense statistics is that they always show profit results as averages for all defense contracts. They seem to overlook the fact that there is no such thing as a monolithic defense industry. A more accurate description would be to print the statistics for the largest 20 or 30 contractors, and then print the statistics that apply to all the rest. The small guys simply don't have the negotiating strength that the large contractors have.

The fact that only 30 out of several thousand defense prime contractors were awarded 50% of the defense procurement dollars in 1970 [2] provides some support for the statement made by the fourth executive cited above. This point will be considered in a later section of this chapter.

MEASURES OF PROFITABILITY

There are a number of ways to measure profitability. The Defense Department usually refers to profits as a percentage of sales. Return on sales is easy to calculate and to understand. It is difficult, however, to find individuals in the business world who would make investments or evaluate companies on this measure of profit. An illustration can summarize a major weakness in measuring profitability in these terms. If a contractor uses Government-owned equipment in a Government-owned plant, and receives frequent progress payments, he may have a relatively small investment in his defense operations. Thus, on a $1 million contract for which he receives a profit of $100,000 and invests $200,000, profit would represent a 10% return on sales and a 50% return on investment. Another example that low profit as a percentage of sales can be misleading is found in a case decided by the Tax Court involving Air Force contracts (North American Aviation Inc. *v.* Renegotiation Board, 1962). In that case, the contract provided for 8%

profit on sales. The Tax Court found, however, that the contracts returned 612% and 802% profit on the contractor's investment in two succeeding years.[3]

Profitability can also be measured in terms of percentage return on equity capital invested (ECI). ECI includes the dollars assigned to capital shares, retained earnings, and other capital reserves. This base (ECI) reflects capital supplied by stockholders as well as earnings retained in the company for future growth. The rate of return on ECI is calculated by dividing profits by equity capital. This measure of profitability is significant to the owners of the business, since it represents the return on the owner's capital.

A third measure of profitability is percentage return on total capital invested (TCI). TCI in this case means the capital provided for the business by creditors as well as the owners. The rate of return on TCI, therefore, reflects profit earned on the capital available to produce that profit, regardless of the source that provided it.

On March 17, 1971, the GAO submitted a comprehensive report to the Congress.[4] The following paragraphs are excerpts from that report.

Profit data for various categories of large DOD contractors
We were interested in seeing whether profit rates varied for contractors of various sizes and types. For this purpose the 74 largest DOD contractors were divided into the following three categories.
   1. *High-volume defense contractors*—Contractors having:
      (a) At least 10% of total company business in defense sales.
      (b) Over $200 million in average annual defense sales.
   2. *Medium-volume defense contractors*—Contractors having:
      (a) At least 10% of total company business in defense sales.
      (b) Average annual defense sales of less than $200 million.
   3. *Commercially oriented defense contractors*—Contractors having:
      (a) Less than 10% of total company business in defense sales.
      (b) Substantial defense business.
The data shown in schedules 5 through 10 represent the same data shown in schedule 1 but segregated into the three categories of contractors. Some of the more significant points follow.

Sales
The major part of defense work is concentrated in 32 high-volume defense contractors, as shown in the breakdown of sales data for 74 large DOD contractors for the four-year period 1966 through 1969 [see Table XV-3]. The 13 commercially oriented contractors account for about the same amount of commercial sales as do the 61 defense-oriented contractors.

TABLE XV-3. ANNUAL AVERAGE SALES FOR 74 LARGE
DEPARTMENT OF DEFENSE CONTRACTORS: 1966–1969
(in billions of dollars)

| Sales Category | Defense-oriented Contractors | | | 13 Commercially Oriented Contractors |
	32 High Volume	29 Medium Volume	All 61	
DOD	$19.0	$2.6	$21.6	$ 2.0
Other defense agencies	2.8	0.1	2.9	0.4
Commercial	27.5	6.5	34.0	32.9
Total	$49.3	$9.2	$58.5	$35.3

SOURCE: Comptroller General of the United States, *Defense Industry Profit Study.*
General Accounting Office Report Number B-159896, Washington, D.C., March 17, 1971.

Profit on sales

Profit as a percentage of sales is lowest on DOD sales; slightly higher on other defense agency sales, except for the medium-volume contractors, and significantly higher on commercial sales. The operations of the large commercially oriented defense contractors, as a group, appear to be more profitable than those of the defense-oriented contractors, as shown [in Table XV-4].

TABLE XV-4. PROFIT/SALES AVERAGES FOR 74 LARGE
DEPARTMENT OF DEFENSE CONTRACTORS: 1966–1969

| Sales Category | Defense-oriented Contractors | | | 13 Commercially Oriented Contractors |
	32 High Volume	29 Medium Volume	All 61	
DOD	3.8%	6.1%	4.1%	6.5%
Other defense agencies	4.4	3.7	4.4	8.1
Commercial	8.2	8.6	8.3	11.6
Overall	6.3	7.8	6.5	11.2

SOURCE: See Table XV-3.

Return on TCI

The commercially oriented contractors had an average 15.2% rate of return on TCI compared with an average 12.3% rate of return for the defense-oriented contractors. It is interesting to note that the average rate of return on DOD work was almost the same for commercially oriented and defense-oriented contractors (11.1% and 11.2% respectively). Thus, as shown [in Table XV-5], a major part of the overall difference in rates of return is attributable to commercial work on which the defense-oriented contractors averaged 12.6% return on TCI and the commercially oriented companies averaged 15.4%. In addition, the commercially oriented companies had a much greater proportion of their sales from their more profitable commercial customers.

TABLE XV-5. RETURN ON TCI FOR 74 LARGE DEPARTMENT
OF DEFENSE CONTRACTORS: 1965–1969

	Defense-oriented Contractors			13 Commercially Oriented Contractors
Sales Category	32 High Volume	29 Medium Volume	All 61	
DOD	11.0%	12.2%	11.2%	11.1%
Other defense agencies	16.3	6.4	15.3	14.1
Commercial	12.6	12.3	12.6	15.4
Overall	12.3	12.2	12.3	15.2

SOURCE: See Table XV-3.

Return on ECI

As shown [in Table XV-6] the three classes of contractors compare very closely on return on ECI, the averages for the four-year period being 22.7% for 32 high-volume defense contractors, 21.4% for 29 medium-volume defense contractors, 23.1% for the commercially oriented contractors.

The defense-oriented contractors were able to approach the commercially oriented contractors in return on ECI because a smaller part of TCI of the defense contractors was ECI. In other words, the defense contractors in our study relied on borrowed capital for a greater proportion of their capital needs.

TABLE XV-6. RETURN ON ECI FOR 74 LARGE DEPARTMENT
OF DEFENSE CONTRACTORS: 1965–1969

	Defense-oriented Contractors			13 Commercially Oriented Contractors
Sales Category	32 High Volume	29 Medium Volume	All 61	
DOD	21.4%	21.9%	21.5%	18.4%
Other defense agencies	31.6	10.3	29.6	21.8
Commercial	22.8	21.4	22.5	23.3
Overall	22.7	21.4	22.5	23.1

SOURCE: See Table XV-3.

Turnover rates of TCI and ECI

The average annual capital turnover rates, determined by dividing sales by capital, were higher for the defense-oriented contractors than for the commercially oriented contractors. Also the rates were higher for the high-volume defense contractors than for the medium-volume contractors. As mentioned before, this reflects the effect of Government-furnished capital in the form of progress payments, cost reimbursements, facilities, and equipment. A summary of the turnover rates for the various categories of contractors is given in Table XV-7.

TABLE XV-7. TURNOVER RATES OF TCI AND ECI FOR 74 LARGE
DEPARTMENT OF DEFENSE CONTRACTORS: 1965–1969

Sales Category	Defense-oriented Contractors			13 Commercially Oriented Contractors
	32 High Volume	29 Medium Volume	All 61	
Turnover of TCI:				
DOD	2.5	1.8	2.4	1.6
Other defense agencies	3.4	1.3	3.2	1.7
Commercial	1.4	1.3	1.4	1.3
Overall	1.7	1.4	1.7	1.3
Turnover of ECI:				
DOD	5.6	3.6	5.3	2.8
Other defense agencies	7.1	2.8	6.7	2.7
Commercial	2.8	2.5	2.7	2.0
Overall	3.6	2.7	3.4	2.1

SOURCE: See Table XV-3.

The GAO study included nine ammunition contractors with profits on TCI and equity that were 2.5 times greater than those earned by the total GAO sample of 74 companies. The defense sales of the ammunition firms represented only 3% of the total sales of the GAO sample.

The GAO also conducted a separate analysis of the profits of 12 major defense contractors whose contract awards for aircraft, missile, or space work averaged more than 80% of their total annual defense contract awards for the periods 1966 through 1969. Contract awards to these 12 companies accounted for more than 55% of the total Defense Department contract awards for aircraft, missile, or space work during the years covered by the study. The total annual average defense sales of the 12 companies together amounted to more than $9 billion per year for all products.

The average profit return on sales to the Defense Department for these 12 contractors was the same (4.3%) as the average profit for the major defense contractors in the main part of the GAO study cited above. The return on TCI for the 12 large aerospace firms, however, was 12.9%, or 33% higher than the 9.6% earned by the 53 other large defense contractors. (The 53 contractors do not include the nine ammunition producers.) Furthermore, the return on equity for the aerospace firms was 28%, or 65% higher than that earned by the 53 other defense firms. This difference is explained by the higher debt-to-equity ratios of the aerospace firms as well as their higher capital turnover (i.e., sales/capital) ratios.

The separate analysis of the 12 major aerospace firms provides a significant input to the analysis of defense profits for the total 74 defense firms in the GAO sample. Rather than a uniform sample of 74 firms with defense profits on TCI and ECI slightly below those earned on commercial work, it can now be seen that 53 defense contractors (72% of the sample) earned almost 60% of the sample sales volume and made profits on TCI and ECI significantly below that earned on commercial work, while 12 large aerospace firms and nine ammunition contractors earned defense profits on TCI and ECI significantly above those earned on commercial work.

Certainly a wide range of realized profits is not by itself an indication of a weakness in defense profit and financing policies. It may simply be due to differences in contractors' performance or the varying degrees of risk associated with different types of defense products and different contractual arrangements. But in the case of the GAO study cited above, the wide range of profits is caused by a wide range of capital turnover ratios, not a wide distribution of profit on sales. In turn, the wide range of capital turnover ratios (resulting from the provision of Government-owned facilities, equipment, and unusually favorable contract financing terms) has enabled the largest defense contractors to maintain a substantially lower sales-to-capital ratio than other defense contractors and commercial firms.

To illustrate the impact of turnover on profit opportunities, Table XV-8, prepared from information collected by the Logistics Management Institute, compares the profit performance of a sample of 35 defense contractors and 208 commercial companies selected from six SIC codes of the FTC-SEC list of durable goods firms. In the table the firms in the defense and commercial

TABLE XV-8. COMPARATIVE PROFIT PERFORMANCE OF SELECTED DEFENSE AND COMMERCIAL DURABLE GOODS FIRMS: 1965–1967

Quarter	35 Defense Firms			208 Commercial Durable Goods Firms		
	Profit/ Sales	Sales/ Capital	Profit/ Capital	Profit/ Sales	Sales/ Capital	Profit/ Capital
Top	6.1%	5.2	31.4%	20.7%	1.8	37.1%
Third	5.3	4.1	21.8	10.5	2.4	24.8
Second	5.6	2.6	14.5	9.6	2.0	19.0
Bottom	2.7	2.2	6.1	5.5	1.9	10.4
Average	4.9	3.2	15.5	11.6	2.0	22.9

SOURCE: Industry Advisory Council, Report to the Secretary of Defense by the Subcommittee to consider *Defense Industry Contract Financing*, June 11, 1971.

categories were divided into four equal groups of contractors, in terms of profitability as measured by return on capital.

As shown in Table XV-8, the capital turnover for the 35 defense firms ranged from a low of 2.2 to a high of 5.2 while the profit return on capital ranged from a low of 6.1% to a high of 31.4%. The profits in terms of return on sales maintain the relatively narrow range of 2.7% to 6.1%. In this case, capital turnover is the most important factor affecting the profit opportunity presented to the defense contractor and, to a much lesser extent, the negotiated return on sales.

For the commercial firms, a similar analysis results in a very different finding. In this case, capital turnover bears no relationship to profitability. Rather, return on capital is largely determined by return on sales throughout this range. In addition, it is interesting to note that the capital turnover of the 35 defense firms was 50% higher than the 208 commercial durable goods firms.

The GAO study of defense profits also includes an analysis of 146 defense contracts. These 146 contracts showed an average 6.9% return on sales, 26% return on TCI, and 56% return on ECI. In comparison with the GAO measures of profitability for the defense industry, the information on the 146 contracts presents a markedly different picture. The 6.9% return on sales is generally in line with the profit figures from the sample of 74 defense contractors. But the 26% return on capital is 130% higher than the 11.1% return on capital for the 74 defense contractors. In addition, the 56% return on equity is 160% higher than the 21.5% return on equity for the 74 defense contractors. It seems clear from these data that the 146 contracts are not typical of the defense contracts that produced the lower profit figures for the sample of 74 defense contractors. The 146 contracts are the largest contracts drawn from 37 defense contractor plants. Thirty-four of these plants are listed among the largest defense contractors in the country. These data support the contention that it is misleading to average the profit data for all defense contractors. The defense industry may well consist of a few large contractors who are able to manage capital turnover effectively and thereby obtain a relatively high return on TCI and equity, while the majority of defense contractors earn profits substantially below the commercial average. Averaging all these data together presents an erroneous image of a defense industry with profit earnings on TCI and equity only slightly below the commercial durable goods averages.

Additional evidence to support the above analysis is provided by a separate profit study conducted by the Office of the Secretary of Defense. This revealed that one of the five largest defense contractors had a return on TCI of more than 50%, and another of the five largest had a return on TCI of more than

70%.[5] The return on equity for the second contractor, for the year of the defense-sponsored study, was in excess of 100%. These figures represent an unusually high level of profitability for most business firms.

The GAO profit study revealed a less attractive profit picture for sub-contractors than for prime contractors. The study included profit and invest-ment data from ten companies that perform about 80% of their defense work under subcontracts and only 20% under prime contracts. Generally speak-ing, defense sales for these companies were for raw or semifinished materials rather than completed end products. Defense work accounted for approxi-mately 9% of their total sales; commercial work accounted for 91%. Their sales to other defense agencies were relatively insignificant. The ten subcon-tractors earned a higher profit on sales on defense business (7.1%) than was earned by the 74 large defense contractors (4.3%). The subcontractors, however, had a lower rate of return on total capital and equity capital than the major defense contractors. This was because the majority of these sub-contractors provided raw materials to prime contractors and were not reim-bursed until delivery of their products. Thus, their progess payments were relatively small and they used few Government-owned facilities. The relatively small amount of Government capital they had, however, resulted in a higher rate of return on their investment for defense work as compared with their commercial work. Their capital turnover rates were lower than those of the 74 large defense contractors but were higher for defense work than for com-mercial work, as shown in Table XV-9.

TABLE XV-9. CAPITAL TURNOVER RATES FOR 10 MAJOR DEFENSE SUBCONTRACTORS
AND 74 LARGE DEFENSE CONTRACTORS: 1966–1969

Average	*10 Major Defense Subcontractors*	*74 Large Defense Contractors*
Profit as % of sales:		
DOD	7.1%	4.3%
Commercial	7.5	9.9
Profit as % of TCI:		
DOD	9.4%	11.2%
Commercial	7.8	14.0
Profit as % of ECI:		
DOD	15.4%	21.1%
Commercial	12.2	22.9
Turnover of TCI (Sales/TCI):		
DOD	1.1%	2.3%
Commercial	0.9	1.3
Turnover of ECI (Sales/ECI):		
DOD	2.2%	4.9%
Commercial	1.6	2.3

SOURCE: Comptroller General of the United States, *Defense Industry Profit Study*. General Accounting Office Report Number B-159896, Washington, D.C., March 17, 1971, p. 31.

It is significant that the capital turnover for the ten major defense sub-contractors is less than half the turnover for the 74 large defense subcon-tractors. Here again, it appears that the smaller the contractor, the greater the likelihood that return on TCI and equity is much more closely a function of return on sales. The large defense contractors have a greater opportunity to create high capital turnover ratios by negotiating with the Government to supply much of the required capital (in the form of Government-owned facilities, equipment, and more frequent progress payments).

COST REDUCTION INVESTMENTS

Most commercial business firms are rewarded with higher profits for making cost reduction investments. Under the current defense profit policy, a cost-reducing investment is not rewarded, and in some cases such an investment may even be penalized. During negotiation of a contract price, the target profit increases or decreases with the contractor's cost estimate. Even after negotiation, there may not be an incentive for a contractor to reduce costs on those contracts where cost reductions will result in a higher profit on the current contract, because such an action will affect future profits. Since future contract prices are heavily dependent upon the projection of present actual costs, the profits for future periods can be lowered by meaningful cost reductions on current work. When costs are reduced be-cause of an increase in labor-saving equipment, the penalty on profitability can be twofold. The cost base for determining profit is reduced, and the capital is increased.

Table XV-10 presents an illustration of the reverse incentive for cost re-duction described above.

TABLE XV-10. COST REDUCTION INVESTMENT

	Before	*After*
	(in millions of dollars)	
Allowable Costs	$100	$90
Profit on Costs	10%	10%
Dollar Profit	$ 10	$ 9
Capital Employed	$ 30	$38
Profit on Capital	33%	24%

SOURCE: Industry Advisory Council, Report to the Secretary of Defense by the Subcommittee to consider *Defense Industry Contract Financing*, June 11, 1971, p. 45.

Under the defense cost-based profit policy, the investment of $8 million in cost-reducing equipment to save $10 million in costs hurts the contractor in two ways:

1. If the allowable cost base is reduced for any reason and the profit percentage remains the same, the contractor's negotiated profit dollars are reduced.
2. If the cost base is reduced because of an increase in labor-saving equipment, the base for determining profit return on capital is increased, thus reducing return on TCI.

Few would maintain that defense contractors are motivated solely by profit, or that their actions are completely determined by the incentives built into defense profit policy. In order to win future awards, a contractor must maintain facilities and technical capabilities that are competitive with the rest of the industry. It is true, however, that the current defense profit policy acts as a constraint on capital investment rather than a stimulus. At best, it fails to reward contractors adequately for cost reductions; at worst, it provides incentives to keep costs high and capital investment at the lowest possible level, thereby increasing capital turnover and maximizing return on capital. This profit policy, then, rewards those contractors who maintain high labor-intensive operations while introducing only the minimum labor-saving capital additions required to obtain government business.

DEFENSE CONTRACTOR INVESTMENTS

The Logistics Management Institute collected financial data from a sample of 65 defense contractors for the year 1967 to examine defense contractor investments. The data shown in Table XV-11 reveal a pronounced inverse relationship between percent of Government business and investment in facilities.

TABLE XV-11. FACILITIES CAPITAL INVESTMENT: 65 DEFENSE CONTRACTORS

% Government Sales	Number of Contractors	Facilities Capital Investment for Each Dollar of Cost
25–50%	25	$.185
50–75%	24	.146
75–100%	10	.083

SOURCE: Industry Advisory Council, Report to the Secretary of Defense by the Subcommittee to consider *Defense Industry Contract Financing*, June 11, 1971, p. 45.

A Logistics Management Institute sample of 233 commercial durable goods firms selected from the *Standard and Poor's* "Financial Summary" revealed an average facilities capital investment of $.32 for each dollar of cost in 1967. This facilities capital investment ranges from 75% to 300% higher than the capital investment for the 65 defense firms in the sample shown above.

The 233 commercial firms in the *Standard and Poor's* sample all meet the following three criteria:

1. Financial data for the company were listed in *Standard and Poor's* "Financial Summary" for the year 1966. (There were approximately 900 companies having data included in this service.)
2. The company submitted regular financial reports to the Securities and Exchange Commission.
3. The SIC industry group code used by the Securities and Exchange Commission placed the company in industry groups 34 through 39, which includes all durable goods manufacturers other than primary metals and extractive industries.[6]

The very nature of the defense business causes some volatility in earnings as spending increases in times of conflict and decreases in times of peace. Nonetheless, these swings are magnified by a profit policy that is solely or largely dependent on level of sales. Defense spending fluctuates with the level of national defense needs. But since defense contractor profits are based on level of costs, total profits realized by contractors are solely a function of volume of business. Although a contractor's assets may remain relatively constant, his profits can range from high (in periods of high sales) to low (in periods of low sales). Contractors' earnings would become more stable to the degree that profits could be based on capital employed, while assets and asset distribution remain relatively constant.

A Proposal for an Improved Profit Policy

By 1972 senior officials of the Defense Department began testing a revision to the cost-based profit policy. The new policy recognizes contractor capital employed, as well as costs, in determining negotiated profit objectives. Sources of capital (i.e., debt or equity) are not considered. Capital employed is segregated into four classes in determining the profit objective. These four classes are: operating capital, land, buildings, and equipment. The profit paid by the Defense Department on contractor capital employed would equal the average profit on capital earned by a sample of commercial durable goods firms, adjusted upward to reflect the unallowable costs on defense contracts, thus making defense contractor profit opportunities more nearly comparable with commercial profit opportunities. The proposed profit policy would determine a negotiated profit objective through considerations of both cost and capital. In 1973 the thinking in the Department of Defense was that, as a starting point, half of the profit objective would be determined by the cost level and half by capital employed. The portion of the profit objective determined by level of costs is intended to provide an incentive for a contractor to compete for sales volume in order to fill costly excess capacity. The capital portion of the profit objective is intended to reduce inequities in profit-on-capital opportunities, to provide an incentive for cost-reducing investments, and to dampen the swings in defense contractor earnings caused by wide fluctuations in sales level.

The proposed change in defense profit policy has received widely mixed reactions within the Defense Department and among industry executives. Predictably, large defense firms with a high capital turnover are not enthusiastic about the new proposal. The president of one of these firms commented: "Now the Defense Department wants to take away from us the opportunity to manage capital turnover. Today, that's the only thing we have left in the defense business to make any profit." Equally predictable, the small and medium-sized defense firms with low capital turnover support the new proposal. Senior officers of the Western Electrical Manufacturers Association (WEMA), one of the few defense industry associations composed mainly of small and medium-sized firms, reported to the Deputy Secretary of Defense during an industry association meeting on April 8, 1971, that many of its members would welcome such a change in defense profit policy. Within the Defense Department, the division of views on the proposed new profit policy was more difficult to identify with particular interest groups. Some defense officials argued that the proposed policy was so complex that it would not be understood or correctly implemented by Government contracting officers. They argued that the profit policy in the field must be extremely simple if it is to be effective. In their view the limited effectiveness of the weighted guidelines was due in large part to the failure of contracting officers to take the time and effort to understand the policy. Other defense officials believed that the proposed profit policy would have a harmful effect on the defense profits of the largest defense contractors, and that such a change at this time would depress further an already depressed industry.

Pentagon officials who support the proposed change argue that the new policy would begin to correct a long-standing inequity that favors a few large firms able to develop and maintain high capital turnover ratios, while thousands of smaller defense contractors experience much lower profits.

In addition to the criticisms described above, five major arguments have been advanced by firms with high capital turnover ratios against the proposed profit policy. A summary of their arguments, and the rebuttals advanced by the supporters of the new policy, are listed below:

1. *The new profit policy fails to recognize "human capital."*

ARGUMENT: People are the most valuable asset of many defense contractors. By failing to recognize "human capital" in its new profit policy, the Department of Defense is penalizing those contractors who, although they may have little capital, have a high investment in human resources.

REBUTTAL: The proposed profit-on-capital policy is based on average profit on capital from a sample of commercial durable goods firms. While these commercial firms did not capitalize the human skills of their employees, nonetheless, skills are directly reflected in the average profit return of 20.2% on capital. All business firms have human assets that are not capitalized; hence, return on capital is implicitly a reward for human as well as capital resources. Defense contractors will be reimbursed for their highly skilled technical and management talent through labor and salary costs (direct labor and overhead are allowable costs) and profit, half of which is to be based on cost and half on capital. This profit is a reward for both human and capital resources. The new profit-on-capital policy will not be applied to consulting or engineering services, or level-of-effort contracts.

2. *The new profit policy is "retroactive."*

ARGUMENT: Contractor capital investment is a product of the current profit policy. The adoption of a profit policy that recognizes capital without giving contractors an opportunity to alter their investment policy is, in effect, "retroactive" and, hence, unfair.

REBUTTAL: The new profit-on-capital policy will affect only new contracts, and thus will gradually phase-in over a four-year period as existing contracts are replaced. Only by implementing a new profit policy will the Defense Department reduce the present inequities in profit on capital opportunity, raise the profits on low-profit contracts, and provide incentives for cost-reducing capital investment.

3. *The use of a profit-on-capital objective means excessive Government regulation.*

ARGUMENT: A profit-on-capital objective amounts to a guaranteed and a limited return on capital and makes the defense industry a utility.

REBUTTAL: The above argument reveals a misunderstanding of the new profit policy. In cases where there is no competitive free market to determine the price of defense procurements, the Department will negotiate the contract price with the contractor (and, in this sense, perhaps there would be some Government regulation). The contracting officer currently uses the 100% cost-based weighted guidelines to determine his profit objective for negotiations. Under the new profit policy, instead of considering only costs, the contracting officer would weigh both cost and capital inputs equally to determine profit objectives for negotiations with contractors.

4. *Capital cannot be accurately and simply allocated to a contract.*

ARGUMENT: Defense contractors' records do not readily lend themselves to the allocation of capital to defense contracts. Any such allocations will be artificial and create administrative complexities.

REBUTTAL: Over the past few years the Defense Department, NASA, and the GAO have allocated capital to contracts. The problems they have experienced are minimal. Fixed assets may be allocated in the same manner as indirect costs are presently allocated.

5. *Negotiated defense procurement includes a range of business that is too diverse to justify the application of a single profit-on-capital standard.*

ARGUMENT: It is impossible to justify a single profit-on-capital standard that would apply to research and development as well as production, or to the electronics industry and the aerospace industry. There should be a different policy to reflect the varying levels of capital investment required in each industry.

REBUTTAL: It would be administratively complex, if not impossible, for the Defense Department to develop and defend a different profit-on-capital standard for each industry or type of procurement. Such a policy would also be subject to attack as unfair to individual industries and would amount to excessive Government regulation. The profit-on-capital policy will, however, vary with contract type, as does the present policy, to reflect the different levels of risk associated with the four basic types of contracts.

EUROPEAN DEFENSE CONTRACTING AND PROFIT NEGOTIATION

In European defense contracting the contract document is substantially smaller and less complex than U.S. defense contracts. For example, in contrast to a U.S. development contract with hundreds of pages, a French contract for a major aircraft system may include no more than 50 pages. Of these, 30 to 35 pages are required for a work statement specifying performance in terms of range, speed, weight, flight ceiling, etc.

In Britain defense contracting practices are similar to those in the United States. Here, contracts are more detailed than in Germany or France. In addition, Britain has been more active in adopting incentive contracting and other management control activities common to U.S. defense contracting. Our interviews revealed, however, that British government and industry personnel are becoming increasingly skeptical of the value of the incentive contracting mechanism.

In Britain, France, and Germany we found that government personnel believe they were often at a disadvantage in negotiating with industry. Many individuals expressed their concern over the lack of quality cost information to strengthen the government's position during contract negotiations. British contractors commented on the long duration of time that often existed between beginning work on a program and completing negotiations with the government. In some cases, negotiations continue until after a program is completed before a contract is signed.

The British government is currently employing a number of the same cost analysis techniques included in the U.S. Should-Cost methodology. British technical audit review teams examine a contractor's past performance on similar programs and plans for performing work on current programs. The technical audit team includes both accounting and engineering personnel who examine contractors' technical plans for performance and who challenge the basis for the plans and their costs whenever the initial evidence is not convincing. Based on the technical audit team review, a report is prepared and is used in negotiations with the contractor by the government purchasing office.

With respect to profit negotiations, practices in France and Germany appear to parallel those in the United States. Profit is negotiated as a function of anticipated costs for a program. In Britain, however, the situation is quite different. The computation of contractor profits includes consideration of the total capital employed by a firm. This practice is accomplished by an annual negotiation with each contractor based on an estimate of the capital to be employed during the forthcoming year. The negotiation results in the development of a ratio consisting of the cost of production divided by the capital employed, based on the firm's business as a whole. The ratio is then used to calculate percentage of profit on cost for individual contracts. For example, if profits are to be paid at 20% on capital employed and the annual cost of the company divided by capital employed is two-to-one, then the overall profit percentage to be applied to the cost of the specific contract would be 10%. The total capital employed is comprised of the cost of fixed assets (buildings and equipment), net current assets (current assets less current liabilities), and progress payments.

Defense contractors are reviewed for excess profits in Britain as are the contractors in the United States. The criteria for determining that profits are excess are much clearer in Britain, however. In Britain the simple determination of excess profits is made when a contractor's return on capital employed exceeds 27%. Nonetheless, some concerns were expressed by representatives of the British Defense Ministry about the current profit determination system. They believed that the computation of capital turnover (sales/capital employed) for an entire company tended to be too gross a measure of capital employed on a particular government program. This argument is advanced because government progress payments reduce a contractor's capital requirements for its government work, in comparison with its commercial work. Hence, a contractor could have a low capital turnover for its commercial work, and yet receive the benefit of this low turnover in profit calculations for its government work where the capital requirements would be much lower because of government progress payments. Because of these problems, the British profit policy is being re-evaluated to eliminate inequities. It is clear, however, that the British believe that the use of a capital-employed calculation in computing contractor profits avoids the very significant inequities that would exist if they were to employ a cost-based profit system comparable to that employed in the United States.

NOTES TO CHAPTER XV

1. The Armed Services Procurement Act, 10. U.S.C. 2306(d).
2. Office of the Assistant Secretary of Defense (Comptroller), Directorate of Information Operations, *100 Companies Receiving the Largest Dollar Volume of Prime Contract Awards, Fiscal Year 1970.*
3. U.S. Congress, Joint Economic Committee, Report of the Subcommittee on Economy in Government, *The Economics of Military Procurement,* May 1969.
4. Comptroller General of the United States, *Defense Industry Profit Study,* Report B-159896, March 17, 1971.
5. Interview with representatives of the Office of the Assistant Secretary of Defense (Installations and Logistics).
6. Industry Advisory Council, Report to the Secretary of Defense by the Subcommittee to consider *Defense Industry Contract Financing,* June 11, 1971, Appendix I.

CHAPTER **XVI**

Indirect Costs in the Defense Industry

A CONTRACTOR'S PROGRAM COSTS consist of direct and indirect costs. Direct costs are those that benefit a particular program directly. Indirect costs are for activities that provide common benefits to more than one program. The cost of operating the accounting department and the personnel department and the depreciation of a building are examples of indirect costs. Indirect costs also include the cost of bid and proposal activities, independent research and development, and other technical efforts. They represent a large share of the cost of the weapons acquisition process. Between 40% and 70% of the costs incurred on a defense contract are likely to be indirect costs. Unlike direct costs, very few standards have been established for comparing overhead costs among contractors or for appraising the reasonableness of a particular contractor's indirect costs. As much as 70% of the indirect costs in the defense business is for indirect labor and labor-related costs. The remaining 30% is for items such as plant and equipment, supplies, travel, and purchased services. Because of the size of indirect costs in defense procurement and the manner in which they are negotiated between Government and industry, this element of total procurement costs is singled out for separate discussion.

THE USE OF RATES IN INDIRECT COST NEGOTIATIONS

In contract negotiations, Government procurement personnel seek to negotiate indirect costs that are equivalent to indirect costs in a price competitive environment. A number of problems arise in accomplishing this goal. Unlike direct costs, indirect costs are not often negotiated as an absolute amount. Rather, they are negotiated (usually once a year) as a rate—a percentage of direct costs. For example, a negotiated indirect cost rate may be 100%,

150%, or 250% of direct costs, depending on the nature of the contractor's work and the manner in which he chooses to divide his cost accounts between direct and indirect.

In practice, indirect costs vary from one contractor to another. Two contractors in the same type of work may have indirect cost rates that vary by as much as 30 or more percentage points, depending on the manner in which they choose to define direct and indirect costs. As a practical matter, most defense contractors have found it to their advantage to define their cost accounts in the way that maximizes direct cost charges to defense contracts. Low indirect rates do not necessarily result in lower quoted prices for a product, but they appeal to Government contracting officers. With a low indirect cost rate, a contractor seems to be applying more direct labor and material to performance of a contract than a competitor with a higher indirect rate. As one industry director of pricing commented: "Time after time, I have found that the Government contracting officer is much more interested in the indirect rate than he is in the amount of indirect costs or what is or is not included in the indirect cost accounts. I have been told: 'get your indirect rate down to 105%, and I don't care what you do with those costs.'" Comments such as these were heard many times during our interviews with contractor personnel. It appears from our discussions with both Government and industry representatives that the heavy workloads placed on Government contracting personnel, coupled with their limited knowledge of contractor operations, lead them to emphasize the indirect *rate*, rather than the absolute amount of indirect costs.

Many contractor personnel find that the emphasis on indirect rates encourages contractors to play games with their cost accounts. As one defense executive commented: "We budget and control indirect costs as packages in our plant, not as rates. If the contracting officer wants a lower rate, we'll give him one, but it will be by re-defining our cost accounts from indirect to direct categories." This practice of shifting costs from direct to indirect and back again is common throughout the defense industry. Public accounting standards are generally limited to presenting an accurate picture of a company's operating results in a particular year, and as such have little influence on internal allocations of costs among various projects. Consequently, the shifting of costs from direct to indirect or vice versa can easily be construed as falling within generally accepted accounting principles. In fact, accounting principles have little to say about this practice. Contractors make changes in their accounting systems, within the law, to maintain the most advantageous position in bidding on a negotiated Government procurement.

Bid and proposal expenses, independent research and development expenses, and expenses for other technical effort are all legitimate charges to indirect cost accounts. They provide the contractor with flexibility in the manner in which he identifies his costs. One of the major factors motivating contractors to maintain fluidity in these accounts is the need to retain competent scientific and technical personnel during periods of undercapacity. By assigning personnel to one or another of these accounts, a contractor is able to retain the technical capability partially or totally at Government expense. In addition, he hopes that their work will lead to future Government or commercial business, or at least to a higher cost base for application of negotiated Government profit rates. Government and contractor representatives also told us that there is no clear distinction between much of the work charged to bid and proposal accounts, independent research and development accounts, and other technical accounts.

The practice of negotiating and applying indirect costs to defense contracts through the use of a rate means that defense procurement is conducted largely on the assumption that indirect costs are 100% variable with direct expenses. For example, assume that a contractor has negotiated direct costs on a contract at $10 million. Assume also that his indirect cost rate is 100%. Therefore, the total cost will be negotiated for $20 million, with possible minor adjustments of the indirect rate. After the contractor begins work on the contract, additional work is identified and a contract change is negotiated between the Government and the contractor. Assume that the additional direct cost required by the added work is negotiated at $1 million. Thereafter, the total cost of the added work will be $2 million. In effect, the Government is assuming that an incremental direct cost causes a parallel increase in indirect costs.

Some Government personnel challenge the validity of the example described above by pointing out that the Government auditor will visit the contractor plant at the end of the year to ascertain whether or not the indirect costs have in fact risen in direct proportion to the direct costs. If they have not, the contracting officer will reduce the contractor's price accordingly. The point is, however, that the contractor is aware of this practice. Any effective company comptroller or project manager will take action to make sure that the indirect cost does not fall below the negotiated rate. This objective can be accomplished most easily by hiring additional personnel, or by providing salary increases, chargeable to the Government on the current contract. A manager from one defense contractor firm reported that he had received a call from his comptroller indicating that a recent increase in sales had caused the actual indirect cost rate to fall below the negotiated level. The comptroller was concerned about this rate reduction, lest the Government contracting officer reduce its contract prices. In order to prevent this from happening, the manager and the comptroller agreed to hire additional personnel to perform tasks chargeable to indirect cost accounts, personnel who would possibly contribute to the long-term growth of the company in defense or commercial sales.

Obviously, motives for increasing costs do not apply to a commercial firm where price competition is a major factor. But they do apply for companies in the defense business, where the majority of the procurement dollars are negotiated in a sole-source environment. In short, the larger the proportion of a firm's sales that are negotiated with the Government, the greater the opportunity for the practices described above.

The current Defense Department policy of negotiating and controlling contractor indirect costs as a percentage of direct costs often results in unnecessary costs. In a price-competitive environment, business managers find that they must make continuous effort to control and reduce costs, or they will soon find themselves priced out of their market. Their internal organizations have a natural tendency to grow in size and cost unless continuous efforts are made to reduce costs. In the defense procurement environment, pressures to reduce costs do not exist.

Indirect cost rates are usually supposed to be negotiated between Government and industry once a year. The workload placed on Government negotiators is so great, however, that negotiations with a particular contractor may be delayed by a year or more. Most contractors commented that they could usually calculate in advance the indirect cost rate that they would be able to negotiate with the Government. These negotiations usually were based on an extrapolation of the trend of actual costs over recent years. If the trend line was increasing, the contractor was usually able to make a change in his cost accounting procedures every year or so to achieve an increasing total cost base.

Government representatives at one Defense Contract Administration Service regional office who were responsible for negotiating indirect cost rates with contractors told us that they usually emphasized indirect rate trend lines because the rate was reasonably easy to measure, and because the actual content of indirect costs varied from one contractor to another. They said they simply did not have the data, the time, or the capability to make any comprehensive analysis of the reasonableness of the absolute amount of contractor indirect costs at contractor plants within their region.

So far we have assumed that a contractor has a single indirect cost rate. In fact, however, the situation is usually more complex. A medium-sized defense contractor may have as many as 10 to 12 indirect cost rates applying to various types of direct costs within his contractor plant. Each of these rates is negotiated plant-wide each year with the local Government representatives, with a normal delay of one or two years. The indirect cost rates apply to various types of direct costs, e.g., engineering, manufacturing, testing, material.

CONTROL OF INDIRECT COSTS

Several factors tend to reduce the effectiveness of Government attempts to promote control of indirect costs. First, the Government program manager and contracting officer often believe that responsibility for indirect cost rates rests with the Government plant representative. But the Government plant representative has little incentive to enforce control and reduction of indirect costs. He is not likely to receive any thanks from the program manager or his superiors for such activity because the contractor may become less cooperative as a result. Furthermore, if he takes firm action in negotiating with the contractor, he runs the risk of making his job at the plant more difficult. He may even be reprimanded by his superiors if the contractor issues a formal or informal complaint. These factors usually convince Government plant representatives to accept whatever the contractor offers after superficial discussion and negotiation. One senior military officer assigned to a Government plant representative office commented: "I believe it is up to the contractor to control his overhead. We can only monitor it." He also stated that an incentive contract reduced his responsibility for taking any actions to control or reduce contractor costs. Attempts by Government personnel to control indirect costs are undermined by the policy of negotiating indirect costs as a percentage of direct costs. When direct labor or material costs increase as a result of contract changes or overruns, contractors are encouraged to increase indirect cost charges.

For their part, contractors seldom spend less than the amount negotiated with the Government, for fear that their contract price will be reduced. They build their indirect costs to consume at least the amount allowed by the negotiated rate. Any subsequent cutback in direct costs then creates an increase or overrun in the indirect cost area. Thereafter, when the number of indirect labor personnel are reduced, the lower-paid employees are released first. This causes the average indirect labor rate to increase. Senior representatives of six management consulting and public accounting firms told us that, with proper incentives, indirect costs in the defense industry could be reduced by 25% to 35%.

When the level of defense spending began to decline in 1969, indirect cost rates began to increase. Commenting on this situation, the *Wall Street Journal* published a feature article on February 6, 1969. Excerpts from this article are printed below.

> What does a company do with employees it has no work for? It may retrain them for different jobs or transfer them to another office, factory or production line. It may take on business it wouldn't ordinarily handle

just to give the employees something to do. It may even invent tasks to keep the workers busy or lend them to another company, until business picks up enough for them to resume their old jobs. Indeed, say executives, about the only thing a savvy company won't do with temporarily unneeded employees these days is lay them off. . . .

. . . The Makework Strategy. The change is measured most dramatically by the willingness of many companies to dig up minor assignments if they can't think of any other way to keep valued employees on the payroll. Most companies hate to admit this practice publicly for fear of arousing shareholders' wrath, but there's no doubt it is growing.

In an article printed on March 22, 1970, the *Los Angeles Times* made the following comments:

Overhead can become a fearsome albatross. Executives of one major Southern California aerospace firm freely admit that the firm has passed up development of many promising commercial products invented in its plants. Addition of some of the overhead cost would price the product out of the market, they explained. The solution sometimes was to license the product to a small firm which had only ordinary "overhead." In short, the big firm was too inefficient from an overall cost standpoint to compete in a commercial market.

CHAPTER XVII

Preparing a Negotiation Objective

As the Government prepares to negotiate a contract, it seeks to develop a price objective for the negotiations. First, a contractor's proposal is analyzed. Audits and technical evaluations are made to check the historical costs on which the proposal has been based. The price analysis of a contractor proposal also includes a review of cost histories of similar programs. Use of historical cost information as a basis for appraising contractor cost proposals assumes that the factors affecting past performance will occur again. Such an assumption may not help the Government to obtain the lowest reasonable cost for a contract.

Historical cost estimating ratios used in a Government price analysis are based on relationships such as:

1. Cost per pound of airframe.
2. Cost per pound of specific thrust.
3. Learning or cost improvement curves.
4. Actual experience on the same or similar work.
5. Historical direct or indirect labor rates.

Having established a price objective, Government negotiators negotiate from this baseline, usually downward, until an agreement is reached with the contractor. This traditional method of price analysis involves little or no attempt to determine what the program should cost under reasonably efficient conditions. Price analysis based on historical cost experience is frequently referred to as the "will-cost" pricing method. With this method of pricing in a noncompetitive environment, the Government is considered to be at a distinct disadvantage, since the primary basis of the negotiation is the contractor's price proposal and past cost experience. It is particularly difficult for Government negotiators to detect overly liberal estimates of the number of manhours and machine hours required to perform complex, specialized engineering, production, and assembly operations.

Several industry executives told us that they were not concerned about the role played by Government auditors in price negotiations because they were able to support a wide range of price proposals by shifting costs between direct and indirect cost accounts. Addressing this drawback in present Government pricing techniques, the Army Audit Agency published a report in October 1969. It included the following comments:

> In several instances, the reasonableness of prices was not readily determinable by reference to the contract administration files and records of negotiation. Examination of contract files disclosed that (i) contractors had not been requested to submit required certificates showing accurate, complete, and current data, (ii) contractor proposals did not provide sufficient details to permit meaningful analysis or comparison with Government estimates, (iii) Government estimates were either not prepared or lacked sufficient depth, (iv) Government price analyses were either not performed or were too restrictive, and (v) technical and professional assistance was either not requested or not given consideration in reaching procurement pricing decisions.[1]

In 1962 Peck and Scherer had commented on similar problems:

> Our case study interviews revealed a general consensus that the average productivity of engineers in the weapons industry, and especially on the staffs of aircraft, guided missile, and warship prime contractors, was extremely low. We have found two independent studies of the problem which confirmed this common view. . . .
>
> One questionnaire survey elicited 148 responses from scientists and engineers, 80% of whom worked on Government projects. The study concluded that improved utilization of scientific and engineering manpower would give increased output yields of up to 100 times, the most likely potential increase being estimated at 10 times. Reasons for the low indicated productivity included the use of engineers on routine jobs, assignments of little or no value, unnecessary duplication of effort, high turnover (the average survey respondent changed jobs every 3.3 years), and effort spent on unassigned projects. The authors cited as underlying causes of these problems the difficulty of keeping informed on technical advances, Government duplication of projects, design competitions, duplication by prime contractors of subcontractor's work, the mass engineering philosophy inspired by operation under cost reimbursement contracts, and inadequate management.[2]

Peck and Scherer drew the following conclusion from their analysis of Government pricing techniques:

> If the Government is unable to determine how much a product it buys should cost, there may be little pressure on the producer to reach the highest level of efficiency, and his costs may tend toward the Government's upper limit. If this happens, then past cost experience—often the most convenient standard for gauging efficiency—will be a misleading indicator in the next time period. If this process of setting present standards from loose past standards is perpetuated, accumulating inefficiency will result.[3]

In the latter half of the 1960s many defense officials were concerned about the inadequacy of traditional Government pricing techniques for procurements in which price competition did not exist. They believed that if contract prices were to reflect economical and efficient performance practices, and realistic costs, Government contract negotiators would need to undertake more comprehensive analysis in preparing their negotiation objectives. Indeed, Armed Services Procurement Regulation 3-807.2(c) indicates that Government cost analysis should be aimed at forming an opinion of "realistic price," defined as "one that is influenced strongly by the prospect of what it *should cost* [italics added] to perform if the contractor operates with reasonable economy and efficiency." Traditional price analysis techniques were not accomplishing this objective for procurements conducted without price competition —procurements that constitute the bulk of defense procurement spending.

Since there are no price competitive forces at work in sole source procurements, contractors are liberal in their estimates, especially in pricing more than one year in advance. As noted earlier, contractors may also build in substantial contingency factors and attempt to increase overhead rates to support an increase in capability. Accepting contractors' cost histories as a baseline for projections is an implicit acceptance of uneconomical or inefficient practices of the past.

THE SHOULD-COST ANALYSIS

Faced with this limitation, several officials within the Department of Defense, under the direction of the Assistant Secretary of Defense (Comptroller), Robert N. Anthony, sponsored the development of a new pricing technique, called the Should-Cost analysis. This technique begins with an in-depth analysis of a contractor's management, cost estimating, and production practices to identify and measure the effects of poor performance. From a baseline developed by eliminating costs resulting from inefficiencies, projections are made for the current procurement. The objective is to foster improved industrial practices by setting realistic contract prices.

The Should-Cost technique had its beginnings in the civilian economy. For many years a large, nationwide consumer goods chain has used this method with its suppliers of appliances, hard goods, and other items. The company has been able to obtain consistently low prices from supplying companies. Suppliers have been encouraged to develop more efficient ways to manufacture their products, in order to retain the sizable orders of the retail chain. The buying power of the chain is so large that it can insist on the use of Should-Cost techniques with its suppliers.

Should-Cost contract pricing depends on the coordinated efforts of a team of Government specialists in engineering, pricing, auditing, procurement, and management. A team is also involved in the more traditional method of Government price analysis, but many of the team members do their work without leaving their offices. They rely on historical data and a contractor's proposal and make no further investigation. Under the Should-Cost approach, the team spends several weeks at a contractor's plant, reviewing in detail the company's engineering and manufacturing operations, accounting procedures, cost estimating systems, purchasing procedures, make-or-buy decisions, and other elements of cost and management control. Standard industrial engineering techniques are used to identify uneconomical or inefficient practices in the contractor's operation, and to formulate the Government's negotiation position. A negotiation objective that is based on Should-Cost procedures must be supported by facts rather than the subjective judgments of the analysts.

The Should-Cost study for a multimillion dollar defense production contract is comprehensive in scope and normally includes analyses of the following aspects of a contractor's operations:[4]

1. Factory labor
   (Usually separated into individual sections; e.g., fabrication, assembly, inspection, processing, and testing)
2. Quality control labor
3. Material handling labor
4. Tool fabrication labor
5. Production engineering labor
6. Model shop or experimental fabrication labor
7. Engineering labor
   (Usually separated into subdivisions; e.g., system design, product design, drafting, research and development laboratories, field support, and engineering design)

8. Factory overhead
9. Material overhead
10. Engineering overhead
11. Direct materials
12. Subcontracts
13. Pooled materials
14. Other direct costs
15. Interdivision cost transfers
16. Tooling material
17. Tooling and equipment maintenance
18. Outside processing expense
19. Field support labor
20. Packaging
21. Overtime premium
22. General and administrative tasks
23. Independent research and development
24. Bidding and proposal work
25. Profit or fee, including incentive arrangements

A more useful technique developed by industrial engineers for improving productivity is the sampling of work habits. "Ratio delay" is one of the most direct and uncomplicated forms of work sampling. Observations of a particular work area or department are made at random times. The observer records the number of people in the area who are working and the number who are not. Whereas other work sampling techniques call for the observer to record the kinds of tasks workers are engaged in, ratio delay simply classifies the laborers as "working" or "not working." When the number of observations is sufficiently large, the results of the study are usually statistically valid. Thus, in a short period of time, a Government Should-Cost team may establish the level of activity for groups of workers in the contractor's plant. The technique is considered conservative in its estimate of worker inactivity, since any worker involved in any task is considered working, regardless of the relevance of the task to the job at hand.

A Should-Cost study also utilizes time studies, technical estimates, historical trends, improvement curves, machine utilization studies, equivalent unit costing, and regression analysis and correlation. Bids are obtained from other companies to ascertain the reasonableness of a contractor's make-or-buy decisions. A description of each of these techniques is contained in the Army Materiel Command Should-Cost Guide (AMCP-715-7).

In late 1967 senior officials in the Department of Defense were concerned over the high price of the TF-30 jet engine (for the F-111 aircraft) produced by Pratt and Whitney. Under the leadership of a senior Navy procurement official, Gordon Rule, a Defense Department team began the first Government Should-Cost study. It resulted in a significant reduction in the price of the engines and demonstrated the usefulness of the technique, both for lowering costs on the current contract and for identifying long range improvements in contractor operations.[5]

It was not until 1970, however, that subsequent Should-Cost studies were conducted. In that year the Army adopted the Should-Cost techniques and began to apply them to major procurements for missiles, aircraft, and a variety of other weapons and equipment. By 1971 the Air Force also began limited use of the Should-Cost technique. By the end of 1971 the Department of Defense had conducted more than 20 Should-Cost studies. These led to significant price reductions. A summary of the results of six of these studies is shown in Table XVII-1.

TABLE XVII-1. RESULTS OF SIX SHOULD-COST STUDIES
(in millions of dollars)

Program	Contractor Proposed Price	Should-Cost Price	Contractor Proposed Price as a Percentage of Should-Cost Price
1	$93.9	$77.1	121%
2	95.8	64.0	149
3	13.9	9.0	155
4	1,439.0	764.0	188
5	24.8	18.9	138
6	40.2	30.4	132
Totals	$1,707.6	$963.4	

The differences between the contractors' proposed prices and the Should-Cost prices may seem surprisingly large. One might suppose that the Government teams employed unrealistic standards in deriving their price objectives. It is interesting to note, however, that the six Should-Cost studies listed above were all conducted by different Government teams. In addition, the primary data used in constructing the Should-Cost price objective were derived from data developed by the contractors for their internal use, not from artificial standards developed by Government personnel. In order to understand the nature of Should-Cost findings, it is useful to review examples of inefficient or unacceptable costs from reports of the six studies listed above.

1. *Idle workers.* During the conduct of the Should-Cost study, ratio delay studies showed that 38% of the assembly and subassembly workers were idle. The statistics highlighted an imbalance between the work force and the work tasks. The incidence of idleness was widespread throughout the assembly and subassembly areas. Sampling was

conducted on a comprehensive basis throughout these areas.

2. *One-Tenth hour upward rounding.* For this method of price estimating, labor is estimated at a minimum of 1/10th of an hour for each operation. Thus, if a unit of work requires 1/100th of an hour to perform, the contractor would estimate the cost at 1/10th of an hour. The elimination of this method of upward rounding in preference for a 100-hour upward rounding technique resulted in savings of more than $1 million for one program.

3. *Inadequate make-or-buy analyses.* It was discovered that printed circuit boards made by one contractor could be purchased from another source for one-half the current price. This resulted in savings of $84,-000 to the Government on one contract. A common component of another system was being manufactured by the prime contractor when the same component could be purchased at nearly one-half the current price. This resulted in savings of $463,000 on one contract. Another component required for the same system was being manufactured by the prime contractor when it could be purchased at a price reduction of approximately 40%. This resulted in savings of $240,526 on one contract.

4. *Accepting high quotes from subcontractors.* One contractor made it a practice to accept the high quote among subcontractors bidding on its sole-source program.

5. *Switching of items from one account to another.* In the preparation of a contractor proposal, it was discovered that there was considerable switching of cost items from direct to indirect cost categories and vice versa, in order to justify the highest prices for the sole source proposal. This practice occurred most frequently for costs related to bid and proposal activities, business development activities, independent research and development activities, and other technical activities.

6. *Costs included for additional work.* The contractor price estimate for direct engineering labor included provisions for design work beyond the task statement, and for contract changes not known to the buying agency.

One military buying agency commented on Should-Cost activities at one contractor plant: "Several examples were found where departments had been operating at an unacceptably low efficiency for an extended period of time, with no extraordinary management attention being devoted to this condition." Members of another Should-Cost team not involved in the studies cited above commented: "The data which are available on factory labor performance against company developed standards present an extremely poor situation. The ratio of standard hours to actual hours ranges from 1:6 all the way to 1:20."

One military buying agency produced a list of eight summary findings that represented the results of its Should-Cost activities:

1. Direct labor   —Overstated in most cases
2. Manufacturing,   —Overstated and often misapplied
   engineering
3. Material use variances—Higher than past experience
4. Overhead   —Extensive inactivity in indirect labor accounts
5. Equipment   —Higher than current experience for equip-
   maintenance and   ment of similar age
   modification
6. General and   —Subsidizing other programs
   administrative
7. Purchasing   —Often noncompetitive
8. Make-or-buy analyses—No apparent cost considerations

An industry executive told us that it is common practice at his plant and other defense plants to conduct make-or-buy analyses without cost considerations. He said that his firm made these decisions simply on the basis of their own available capacity and the degree of difficulty involved in making the item in question. He also said:

> The Government review of contractor make-or-buy programs is a sham. It takes very little imagination on the part of the contractor to provide a justification that will support whatever decisions he wants to make. The sophistication on the Government side simply isn't there.

Most Should-Cost studies indicate that many make-or-buy decisions are not made in the best interest of the Government. In 1964 Scherer pointed out that contractors reduced their subcontracting as their sales declined, regardless of cost considerations.[6]

THE GAO REVIEW OF SHOULD-COST STUDIES

As a result of the substantial differences between contractors' proposed prices and Should-Cost prices, the Joint Economic Committee of the Congress in 1969 requested the GAO to undertake an independent examination of the Should-Cost technique and to "study the feasibility of incorporating into its audit and review of contractor performance the Should-Cost method of estimating contractor costs on the basis of industrial engineering and financial management principles."[7] Subsequently, the GAO selected four defense contractors for study with Should-Cost techniques. On February 26, 1971, the GAO issued a report to the Congress on its findings.

> On the basis of four trial reviews applying should-cost techniques, the General Accounting Office has concluded that such reviews can be extremely beneficial and that it should make should-cost type reviews in the future.
>
> GAO found a number of areas at each of four contractor plants where increased management attention could result in lower costs to the Government. For example,
> * Improvements were needed in production planning and control;
> * There was a need for increased competition in the procurement of material from subcontractors, and
> * Higher quality engineering talent was utilized than was required by the nature of the work being performed.
>
> GAO brought the specific findings to the attention of appropriate contractor and agency officials and made suggestions for improvements.
>
> Although should-cost review techniques primarily are intended to find out how contractors' operations can be improved, they also lead to disclosures of areas where Government contracting or administration practices affect contract costs adversely. GAO noted instances of excessive packaging requirements, failure to consolidate purchasing, and excessive testing requirements.
>
> The total savings which could accrue to the Government as a result of the GAO reviews and the resulting improvements in contractor and Government management practices cannot be determined readily because the effects on costs of certain of the suggestions could not be measured readily. In those instances where they could be determined, the savings amounted to almost $6 million.[8]

The $6 million in savings reported appeared in categories very similar to those identified in the Department of Defense studies:[9]

GAO Observation	*Potential Cost Savings*
a. Savings attainable through a contractor's implementation of an effective production control system	$3,100,000
b. Increased use of competition by a prime contractor in awarding subcontracts	150,000
c. Reduction in labor cost by elimination of costs related to engineering organizations and skills which are no longer required to support items being produced	99,000
d. Reduction in annual contractor procurement costs through use of economic order quantity techniques	297,000

GAO Observation	Potential Cost Savings
e. Reduction in the level of packaging requirements for spare parts produced for use in overhaul activities within the continental United States	600,000
f. Change from extensive contractor acceptance test procedures to more realistic testing for the purpose of product verification	1,100,000
g. Consolidation of Government and contractor operated motor pools located at the same location, and utilization of regularly scheduled service rather than chauffeured service to and from airports	209,000
h. Elimination of prime contractor profit on subcontracted effort where about 90% of the total effort is subcontracted to one vendor and the prime contractor has minimal responsibility	77,000
i. Reduction in indirect labor force due to a more efficient use of personnel	75,000
Total	$5,707,000

The GAO analysis also pointed out the need for increased price competition in the procurement of material, even in those cases where contractors' procurement systems had been approved by representatives of the Department of Defense. The review of the procurement practices of one contractor indicated:

> A lack of effective price competition in the awarding of subcontracts. In the past, the Department of Defense has established that changes from noncompetitive to competitive procurements result in savings averaging 25%. On this basis we estimated that effective price competition would have reduced material procurement costs by about $560,000 for four prior production contracts.
>
> At the conclusion of our review, contractor officials agreed with us on the need for increased competition, and informed us that they would take action to obtain improved price competition on the material purchases for follow-on contracts. This action could reduce the costs on the next contract by about $150,000.[10]

The following comments from the GAO report explain the deficiencies noted in companies' production planning and control systems.

> A production planning and control system is supposed to achieve efficient performance by coordinating and guiding the physical activities of manufacturing a product. We found that one (out of four) contractor's production control system was in need of improvement because

- the manufacturing schedule did not include provisions for all parts which were to be manufactured,
- manufacturing start and finish dates had not been established for parts included on the schedule,
- utilization of production equipment was not scheduled to make the most efficient use of available machines,
- economic lot sizes had not been established for the manufacture of all parts, and
- reported machine setup time exceeded the allowable by over 100%.

This condition had been recognized by the cognizant Government plant representatives as early as March 1967, but no action was taken to request the contractor to establish a completely integrated production control system or to monitor the contractor's efforts in this area. When we brought our observations to the attention of contractor officials, they agreed that their production control system should be improved and advised us that a group had been formed in October 1969 to implement an improved program.

On the basis of current levels of production, an investment of about $580,000 to design and implement an effective production control system could result in estimated annual savings of about $3.1 million. These savings will result from the elimination of about 139 indirect labor positions in the material production control department and the reduction of about 10% of the direct manufacturing labor force.[11]

QUALITY VARIATIONS IN SHOULD-COST STUDIES

Once a Should-Cost study is conducted, its future effectiveness depends on a qualified and aggressive Government negotiator. Although the Department of Defense has not successfully negotiated all the savings indicated by the Should-Cost analyses conducted to date, there have been significant price reductions.

Not all the Should-Cost studies are of high quality, however. A number of Pentagon officials commented that one of the military services was reluctant to conduct Should-Cost studies. It was simply "going through the motions" to comply with Department directives. It is clear that the Should-Cost technique shows that many past management practices have been ineffective. For this reason many officials are not enthusiastic supporters. One management consultant working for a company experiencing a Should-Cost study by the "reluctant" military service told us that "they (i.e., the military service) found less than half the fat in the contractor's estimates. Based on the capabilities and the attitude of the individuals assigned to the team, both we and the contractor were surprised that they found as much as they did."

A representative of another management consulting firm made a similar comment about the Should-Cost studies conducted by the same military service.

> The [name of the service] is not conducting a Should-Cost study of that program. Rather, they are simply conducting a fact-finding exercise. There is little or no attempt to turn the findings into a price objective and to negotiate the price with the contractor. The chief of the team thinks he is an expert, but it is clear to us that he is very naive about what actually occurs within a contractor organization.

On the whole, however, most of the Should-Cost studies conducted by the Department of Defense have been of high quality. Some industry executives reluctantly admitted that studies of their companies were of much higher quality than they had expected, and had even revealed some problems in their own organizations that surprised them. Representative comments from these executives are listed below:

> Executive #1—The Should-Cost study performed on our plant was well done. It was well organized with high quality personnel.
> Executive #2—The Should-Cost figures came as a shock to us. We did not agree with all the recommendations but we did adopt 11 of their recommendations which resulted in savings of approximately $1.3 million in 1970.
> Executive #3—It was a painful exercise, but I believe it has been some help in improving our operations.

Problems in Conducting Should-Cost Studies

Should-Cost teams run into several kinds of problems. The following were typical.

1. *Criticism from company executives*

One contractor undergoing a Should-Cost study characterized the six-week plant review by the Should-Cost team as a poor substitute for the long-standing experience of plant managers. Disparaging comments were made to team members and to defense officials well above the level of the team chief. With the strong support of a senior Pentagon official, however, the team completed its assignment. After many discussions between the Should-Cost team chief and the company managers, the industry personnel agreed that their proposed labor efficiency of 39.4% against their own work standards was probably too low for the proposal under review. Plant executives then suggested a new labor efficiency rate of 49% against their own standards—after the labor efficiency level was brought to the attention of the company president by the Should-Cost team chief. In a private discussion, the president commented that he had "no idea that the proposed labor efficiency was so low."

2. Reprisals

A senior military officer assigned to a Should-Cost team had an unblemished record in his annual fitness reports, including two "outstanding" evaluations from his current supervisor. The supervisor did not support the Should-Cost activities imposed by a higher management level, however, and directed the officer to prepare a minority report opposing the recommendations of the majority of the team. The officer indicated that the facts uncovered at the defense plant would not support a dissenting report and that he believed the majority report to be reasonable. Subsequently, the officer received a performance rating from his superior that was far below "outstanding" but slightly above a rating of "unsatisfactory" (that would enable him to appeal the rating). The low fitness report for an officer at his senior grade level was likely to preclude any further chance of promotion within the military service.

3. Discounting of Should-Cost information

A senior executive from a firm undergoing a Should-Cost study admitted to Pentagon officials that Should-Cost techniques were useful in managing a firm. He hastened to point out, however, that the Should-Cost effort "should be divorced completely from the pricing of any particular contract, and similarly should not be used for post-award audit of any contract or program." He disapproved of the Should-Cost techniques because they "created an adversary relationship between the contractor and the government and could result in a severe deterioration of the climate for effective future negotiations." The executive must have been referring to the strains placed on companies whose inefficient operations have been revealed by Should-Cost studies—shaking up their usual attempts to justify high cost estimates.

To the extent that Should-Cost studies reveal inefficiencies in a company's operations, industry managers will try to convince their superiors that the studies are not valid. They feel that the findings are an indictment of their past performance. One particularly cooperative company president admitted that the Should-Cost study revealed opportunities for improvement that he had been unaware of, but he was deeply concerned about the effect that public announcement of the findings would have on the public and on stockholders. In his opinion, the image of the company and its stock performance might be damaged.

4. *Difficulty in maintaining qualified Should-Cost teams*

One Pentagon sponsor of the Should-Cost program discussed two dangers threatening the effectiveness of future Should-Cost studies. The first was the assignment of teams with marginally qualified personnel. He stated that the Defense Department did not have enough qualified analysts to conduct more than a few Should-Cost studies at a time. If the quality of Should-Cost studies should deteriorate, the whole program would be criticized by Government and industry personnel eager to discredit the procedure. A second danger was the result of the price reductions effected by early Should-Cost studies. The Pentagon official pointed out that future studies might be judged, not on the quality of the analysis undertaken, but on the size of the reductions achieved. "If the quality of the Should-Cost program is to be maintained at a high level," he said, "we should give equal recognition and rewards to a Should-Cost team that identifies zero savings, or the need for a higher price, as we do for one that identifies significant savings, as long as the quality of the analysis remains high."

On the same topic, several Pentagon officials commented that the outstanding results from the initial Should-Cost studies raised the possibility that future teams would simply select a low cost figure and then seek to develop a rationale to justify the figure. Through 1973, however, there has been no evidence that Should-Cost teams have adopted such practices. Directors of Should-Cost programs in two of the military services have established training programs to acquaint prospective team members with problem areas, and insure quality performance through a study of earlier Should-Cost studies.

SUMMARY OBSERVATIONS FROM SHOULD-COST EXPERIENCES

Source selection and contract negotiations flounder because contractors' estimates are not adequate guides for determining what a program should cost or will cost. They are heavily influenced by marketing factors. In a price competitive environment with the possibility of sole-source follow-on work, unreasonably low estimates are common. In the sole-source noncompetitive environment that constitutes a high percentage of defense procurements, inefficiency and padding of costs seem equally common. There are very few incentives in a sole-source environment for industry management to make the difficult decisions that can result in lower costs.

We asked one Should-Cost team chief to describe team reactions to their findings. He responded:

> I believe most of the team members were surprised that by their efforts they could uncover areas in [name of company] where there were opportunities for greater efficiency. There is no question that it was a revelation for team members to see how contract costs could be substantially influenced by various treatment of overhead accounts. I believe all members of the team were enthusiastic about the effort—at least they all worked hard and for long hours. As for myself, it was a tremendous learning opportunity which should have occurred ten years earlier.

The same team chief was asked to describe the reaction of Government buying agency personnel to Should-Cost analyses. He commented:

> Over the period of the on-site study, it was evident that the personnel at the Government contracting officer level had a greater kinship with the contractor than they did with those who were challenging contractor estimates. From time to time one could hear identical comments advanced by the contractor and the routine Government contracting personnel on the same controversial point. I spent considerable effort trying to break up this feeling of "togetherness," including arranging for the contracting officer to be replaced. The senior officers above the contracting officer, however, did not share this togetherness attitude with the contractor. They were surprised at the total dollar estimated saving developed by the Should-Cost team, but they supported our efforts.

A senior executive of a company investigated by a Should-Cost team commented:

> The Should-Cost technique is an extremely useful tool for studying and improving the efficiency of any manufacturing business, and is sometimes used by contractors for that purpose. Government contractors should be encouraged to establish, in-house, the capability and procedures for the use of the technique on a continuing basis. The Government could encourage this continuing self-examination and improvement by reviewing contractors' capabilities and procedures for the internal application of the Should-Cost technique, and the contractors' utilization of the technique. The Government should then withhold any Should-

Cost studies of a contractor by the Government upon a finding that the contractor's capabilities in this field were adequate.

In its report on application of Should-Cost concepts, the GAO supported the Defense Department decision to continue Should-Cost studies. The GAO also concluded that the "traditional Government pre-award reviews of contractor proposals, and the day-to-day functional audits and reviews of contractor management, have not been fully effective." [12]

It seems clear from Should-Cost studies that senior managers at many defense firms are not aware of the number of extra employees working in their organizations. Many of these companies do not adhere to work standards that would be acceptable in commercial industry. Many do not set up management control systems as strict as those in commercial industry. One defense company executive who had recently been transferred from the commercial division of his company told us that he "was amazed at the looseness of the defense operation compared to my previous experience in commercial divisions." He said that he was assigned to head the defense division because top management wanted someone in the organization who had not become satisfied with the inefficiency of the defense division's operations.

A senior procurement official from one of the military services compiled a series of "lessons learned" from the Should-Cost activities of his service. One of these lessons is summarized below:

> When you are engaged in a study and negotiation even comparable to the [name of contractor] exercise, you should expect resistance and criticism from your efforts.
>
> Obviously, if your assignment is in reality an adversary proceeding, you should expect resistance and criticism from your opposite number— the contractor—but when it comes from people in Government, who should be supporting your efforts, you will naturally be chagrined.
>
> This "home front" resistance can be much more brutal than that from a contractor. We were even criticized by some of our own people for getting [name of contractor] to amend the letter contract to permit us to make a contracting officer's unilateral decision.
>
> If, however, you have obtained proper terms of reference and assurance of top level support, you need not panic at the opposition to your efforts. Actually, some of these attempts to interfere with and thwart your efforts could be highly amusing if they did not come from grown men who are getting paid by the Government, and thus should think first about the Government's best interests.

Another conclusion can be drawn from the Defense Department's experiences with Should-Cost studies. The successful conduct of a Should-Cost study, by itself, provides no assurance that the Government will achieve cost savings. To achieve any savings, four steps must be followed:

1. Locate the unnecessary costs.
2. Collect clear evidence of the unnecessary costs for use in negotiations with the contractor.
3. Negotiate the savings that have been identified into the contract to reduce the contract price.
4. Maintain control over the ongoing program so that contract changes and other types of cost growth do not erode the savings achieved.

If any one of these four steps is ignored, Should-Cost studies will be fruitless. The experience of the Defense Department suggests that savings of several hundred million dollars per year could be achieved if the Should-Cost technique were used for all large procurements. But without careful control of the quality of the studies, and attention to the four steps outlined above, any potential savings could fail to materialize.

NOTES TO CHAPTER XVII

1. U.S. Army Audit Agency, Headquarters, *Summary Analysis of Audit Findings, Fiscal Year 1969,* October 1969.
2. Merton J. Peck and Frederic M. Scherer, *The Weapons Acquisition Process: An Economic Analysis* (Boston: Division of Research, Harvard Business School, 1962), pp. 515–516.
3. Ibid., p. 510.
4. For a complete description of the Should-Cost technique, see Army Materiel Command pamphlet 715-7, October 20, 1970.
5. For further information on the Pratt and Whitney case, see Hearings before a subcommittee of the Committee on Government Operations, U.S. House of Representatives, 91st Cong., 1st Sess., on *H.R. 474—Government Procurement and Contracting,* Part 5.
6. Frederic M. Scherer, *The Weapons Acquisition Process: Economic Incentives* (Boston: Division of Research, Harvard Business School, 1964), p. 61.
7. U.S. Congress, Joint Economic Committee, Report by the Subcommittee on Economy in Government, *The Economics of Military Procurement,* May 1969.
8. General Accounting Office, Report to the Congress, *Application of "Should-Cost" Concepts in Reviews of Contractors' Operations,* February 26, 1971, pp. 1–2.
9. Ibid., p. 33.
10. Ibid., p. 9.
11. Ibid.
12. Ibid., p. 13.

CHAPTER **XVIII**

Negotiating Contracts

NEGOTIATION is usually defined as a process of discussion, persuasion, and logical argument leading to mutually acceptable contract terms, including price. In the Government procurement process, negotiation between Government and industry does not only take place before a contract is signed. In fact, the process of negotiation continues throughout the entire life of many contracts. For a major development program, negotiation determines the initial statement of work, price, and other contractual terms. Once the contract is signed, negotiations continue for a large variety of ongoing program activities. For example:

1. Negotiating contract changes; the price of work to be added and the price of work to be deleted by a change; the effects on schedules and technical performance resulting from the change;
2. Negotiating the interpretation of the contract terms;
3. Negotiating the Government acceptance of designs;
4. Negotiating the Government acceptance of prototypes and initial production units;
5. Negotiating the price and acceptability of various reports and other documentation required by the Government;
6. Negotiating the work statements and prices for tasks required for the project that were not foreseen at the time of the initial contract negotiations.

Negotiating for a development program is a difficult task for both Government and industry. If the program calls for the development of a new aircraft, missile, satellite, or electronic system, both the Government and the contractor must develop work statements and estimated prices for projects that may have little in common with previous projects.

In most negotiations for development program contracts, Government personnel have very limited capability to appraise the reasonableness of a contractor's estimates. Price negotiations frequently concentrate on profit rates, overhead rates, progress curve slopes, and labor wage rates. The situation in the early 1970s is much the same as it was in 1964 when Scherer described it in the second volume of *The Weapons Acquisition Process*.[1] One improvement in the negotiation process is the increased use of the Should-Cost technique described in the preceding chapter.

The negotiation of an initial contract for a major development program may consume a period of several weeks or even months. Because of the urgent nature of most large development programs, Government contracting personnel are frequently under pressure from their superiors to complete negotiations so that the contractor can begin work. This pressure frequently leads to the signing of letter contracts, as was the case for the F-111, C-5A, AH-56, Cheyenne Helicopter, Minuteman missile, and many other programs.

The negotiation process for a major program is not confined to the contracting officers representing Government and industry. Although the negotiation may begin at that level, contractors frequently contact more important Government officials—perhaps even the Secretary of a military service or the Deputy Secretary of Defense—in an attempt to have them intervene with the Government contracting officer, to persuade him to be more "lenient." In some cases, senior defense officials will inject themselves into the negotiation process, thereby discouraging the Government contracting officer from doing whatever he can to obtain the best terms for the Government. Gordon W. Rule, chief negotiator for the Navy, commented on this practice:

> Anyone familiar with Government contracting knows that many Government contractors—and the larger they are, the more they do it—rarely confine their negotiating activities to the negotiator. They constantly and continuously attempt to run left end on the negotiator and maneuver to get what they think they are entitled to get, from any source they can. One of the largest Government contractors I know will barely talk with the negotiator cognizant of that company's contracts and will always try to negotiate at the very highest levels in the activity. Many more try this technique until they learn how unwise it is, but the point I wish to make is that when the highest levels permit themselves to be used during a negotiation, they are themselves guilty of interference in the negotiations.
>
> I do not think that industry should be criticized as much for engaging in these practices as should those who make it possible. If those in authority who are not directly connected with a negotiation—and thus never know what the facts are, or what is going on—would only make it clear that they cannot be approached during a negotiation, the negotiator

would know that he had strong top-side backing and his effectiveness would be immeasurably and immediately enhanced.

Interference by those not connected with the negotiations weakens the negotiator's position in the eyes of the contractor with whom he is dealing, which is just exactly what many of the contractors are seeking to do.[2]

VARIATIONS IN COMPETENCE AND VIEWPOINTS OF NEGOTIATORS

The competence of Government negotiators varies from one case to the next. Some negotiators have a reputation for competence and fairness in their dealings with industry and are able to present a strong case for the Government. Others are known to be only marginally competent, either too rigid or too timid in their presentation of the government's case.

Industry negotiators, taken as a group, range from strong and competent to weak and unprepared. Rarely, if ever, however, are negotiators for large defense contractors less than competent. If a negotiator employed by a major defense contractor becomes ineffective, he is either fired or placed in a harmless position. The absence of civil service tenure regulations provides a freedom in personnel selection and transfer that is not available to the Government.

Senior individuals in Government and industry have somewhat different views of the atmosphere and strategy of a negotiation. Government officials define a negotiation as a meeting between two parties seeking to arrive at a fair, mutually acceptable settlement through objective presentation of facts, without the use of deception. One senior defense policy maker even expressed his concern to us that defense negotiators might be too aggressive in dealing with industry. The senior industry executives we met, on the other hand, never worried that their subordinates might be too aggressive in dealing with the Government. Several did express their belief, however, that they usually "outgunned" the Government at each negotiation. Several ridiculed the idea that a negotiation is a process for arriving at a fair, mutually agreeable settlement. Rather, they described negotiation as "obtaining as much as you can from the Government," or a "big game in which we try to outwit the opponent without letting him know that he is being outwitted."

The differing views on the negotiation process are best described in excerpts from two negotiation manuals. The first is from a manual prepared by a firm that trains Government negotiating personnel. The second is from a negotiation manual prepared by a firm that has been called the leading organization for training defense industry negotiating personnel.

GOVERNMENT

. . . It is important that negotiations be conducted in an atmosphere of cordiality, friendliness, and mutual trust. Each party must respect the other's interests, and each must be willing to evaluate open-mindedly the positions and arguments expressed by the other. And, as we have stressed before, both parties must be strongly motivated to reach agreement on the procurement in question.

One of the best ways to make the atmosphere propitious for subsequent bargaining is to open the proceedings on an informal note; by telling a joke, by expressing the Government's gratitude to the contractor's representatives for journeying to the place of negotiation, by general conversation on matters of mutual interest, and so forth. In addition, once personal introductions and necessary housekeeping matters have been disposed of, it may be advisable for the negotiator to make a few introductory remarks, restating the principles and objectives of the negotiation. For example, he might point out that while each side will be striving to obtain for itself the most favorable arrangement possible, it is not in the interest of either party to enter into an agreement that is obviously unfair or prejudicial to the interests of the other. He might assure the contractor's representatives that he will make every effort to be completely objective in assessing any and all proposals they offer. He might also make it clear that he expects them to be just as scrupulous in reviewing his suggestions, since only on that basis will it be possible to work out a mutually acceptable agreement. . . .

INDUSTRY

. . . An individual who confuses private "ethics" and business morality does not make an effective negotiator. Negotiators must learn to be impersonal and objective in their negotiation and subordinate their own personal sense of "ethics" to the prime purpose of securing the best deal they can for their principals. A negotiator must understand the principles of the game in which he is engaged and must appreciate the fact that complete "honesty" is neither desirable nor practicable. . . .

Henry Taylor, the British statesman, once stated with respect to international negotiation that "falsehood ceases to be falsehood when it is understood on all sides that the truth is not expected to be spoken." In negotiation, it is necessary to tell the truth as one sees it, but not necessarily the whole truth. Many years ago a business executive in briefing his associates prior to their testifying before a Government committee told them to "parry every question with answers which, while perfectly truthful, are evasive of bottom facts."

Few of the Government personnel we met had been told they were about to participate in a negotiation session where the "truth is not expected to be spoken." Certainly this view contradicts that expressed by senior Government policy makers.

In addition to the capabilities of Government and industry negotiators, a number of other factors affect their relative bargaining positions in a particular negotiating session. The Government negotiation position is strengthened by such factors as:

1. The availability of an alternate contractor;
2. A competing program that produces a similar weapon system for the same military service;
3. The availability of credible cost analyses for the program;
4. Strong support for the Government negotiator from higher level Government personnel;
5. A threat of cancellation of the program by higher-level Government personnel.

On the other hand, a contractor's negotiation position is strengthened by such factors as:

1. Designation of the program as "urgent";
2. The inability of another contractor to perform work on the program;
3. The limited amount of time available to the Government to arrive at a contract agreement;
4. The availability of extensive supporting data for cost and schedule projections;
5. Contacts at higher levels in the Government with officials who will remind the Government negotiator that the negotiation should be "fair" and not prejudicial to the contractor.

Administrative pressures on Government negotiators may also help to strengthen a contractor's bargaining position. These pressures include: (1) a heavy workload; (2) the need to obligate Government funds before the end of a fiscal year; and (3) the awareness that performance will be judged by rapidity in concluding negotiations, and the ability to negotiate a reasonable profit percentage of sales, regardless of the level of costs. Several defense procurement officials told us that one of the points on which Government negotiators are judged is their ability to complete their negotiations on schedule.

Many Government personnel told us about the importance of negotiating a contract with the two or three finalists before the winning contractor is selected. Repeatedly, the comment was made by Government officials that there is a sharp change in the attitude of industry personnel from the day before the winner is selected to the day after a company is chosen. One Government program manager made a typical comment:

. . . once contractors find themselves in a sole-source position they become extremely difficult to deal with price-wise and every other-wise, for that matter. The attitude, generally speaking, under a sole-source situation, appears to be one whereby the contractor believes he has a license to make everything he can under any sole-source arrangement with the Government.[3]

One Pentagon Assistant Secretary made a similar comment about the problems of negotiating with contractors in a sole-source environment:

We are over the barrel again with [name of contractor] because we have invested a large amount of research and development funds into developing their capability and they know we need the program. We are in the same fix with another contractor on the [name] program. We have been shouting to the Congress about the need and urgency of both of these programs, and as a result, we now find ourselves in a weak negotiating position with the contractors who know that a delay would endanger our relationship with the Congress.

An industry executive told us that his firm had never had an overrun on a major program. He went on to point out, however, that he had also been successful in negotiating research and development contracts on a year-to-year basis, so that work that did not get done in one year was included in the negotiated work statement for the following year. When we pointed out that the situation he described sounded like an illegal cost-plus-a-percentage-of-cost contract, he commented:

There are ways of getting around that problem. We simply write the contract each year as a cost-reimbursement, or fixed-price type of contract, depending on the current mood of the defense policy makers. No one ever figures out that the same work in two consecutive years may be used as the basis for calculating fee. Actually, we don't intend it that way either, but when we come to the end of the year and we have not accomplished all the work, we're not about to take a loss on the contract.

NEGOTIATION TACTICS

A number of tactics are used periodically by representatives of both Government and industry in the conduct of a negotiation. The ones most frequently mentioned are listed below:

1. Place the other party on the defensive by pointing out an extreme implication of the position he has advanced.
2. Make several small concessions, and then point out that the other party is being unreasonable by not making the same number of concessions in its position.
3. Indicate that the position advanced by the other party would never be accepted by your superiors.
4. Have one team member take an extreme position on an issue, while by contrast, the actual position as expressed by the chief negotiator is far more moderate and conciliatory.
5. Appeal to patriotism and the country's urgent need for the program, which is suffering because of the intransigence of the other party.
6. Set forth an issue on which the negotiator intends to compromise, then use it as proof of willingness to concede a point.
7. Walk out of a session to let industry executives know that you are simply unable to arrive at a position. Indicate that you believe that your position is reasonable, and that you want to talk with your superiors about appealing to a higher authority.
8. Recess when tempers are heated so that members of both sides can engage in congenial conversation. A coffee break may provide such an opportunity.

In addition to the tactics cited above, we identified several tactics periodically used by Government contracting officers in their negotiations with contractors.

1. Threaten to keep work from the contractor.
2. Threaten to have high-ranking officers consult with the firm's top management.
3. Threaten to audit the contractor's operations during performance of the contract.
4. Threaten to notify the GAO.
5. Threaten to notify the Renegotiation Board.

The tactics described above seem mild when compared to one described in a negotiation manual by an organization that claims to have trained more than 14,000 representatives of leading firms.

> Outright lies are used more often in negotiation than the average negotiator would care to admit. Obviously, neither side expects the other to tell the whole truth. If this were not so, then each would be expected to make known to the other all the information at its disposal including its minimum and maximum positions. Such a procedure would make negotiation impossible. Distinguishing between proper negotiation "puffing"

and outright lies is very difficult, if not impossible, since any such determination would undoubtedly reflect the personal sense of "ethics" of the person making it. Even in the case of very "ethical" persons, their judgment as to whether or not a misstatement is a lie or a permissible negotiation technique is affected by whether they tell it or their opponent does. It is sad but true that often it is "whose ox is getting gored" that determines the rightness or wrongness of an action rather than any inherent philosophical criteria.

Most large contractors (and many small contractors) have learned another tactic of the negotiating game. They include items in their proposals that the Government negotiator can cite as disallowable, thus providing the Government negotiator with examples to include in his reports—to show his superiors that he is earning his salary and saving the Government sizable amounts of money. When high-level Government personnel visit field buying agencies, procurement personnel often present a summary of their activities by showing a chart containing: (1) the amount proposed by contractors in the form of costs or fees; (2) the amount negotiated with contractors, and (3) the difference between the two (which can be attributed to the good work of the Government negotiators). For these reasons, contractors frequently include profit figures in their proposals that are several percentage points higher than they believe can be negotiated. Dean Francis Pace of the University of California at Los Angeles (UCLA) cites several reasons for this practice.

> Generally, profit should be quoted optimistically by 2–5 percentage points for at least 4 reasons.
> - The contractor may be pleasantly surprised by the outright acceptance of a profit higher than expected.
> - If the Government insists on tight targets or risky contract incentives, the contractor should have room to negotiate package deals with favorable profit tradeoffs.
> - Regardless of the negotiation outcome, the Contracting Officer will have difficulty justifying the award of a higher profit than that proposed by the contractor; whereas his file will look good if he negotiates a lower profit.
> - Even at median assigned weights, it is easy to derive a profit objective of 10–15% by means of the weighted guidelines method of profit determination.[4]

Two additional negotiation tactics, less well known but highly effective, have been employed on recent defense programs. The first is called the "guaranteed-performance"; the second, the "disclaimer-clause."

In the guaranteed performance tactic, the contractor accepts a performance penalty clause in return for the Government's acceptance of his proposed price. It is important to the success of the tactic, however, that the penalties associated with performance failure be far less severe than the gain accruing to the contractor in receiving a higher price. The use of the performance penalty clause can effectively change a rigid fixed-price contract into a cost-reimbursement contract, with a limited penalty for the contractor if he fails to perform. Theoretically, if a contractor fails to meet the performance requirements of a fixed-price contract, the Government has the right to charge him for the cost of procuring the item from another source. With a performance penalty clause in the contract, however, the Government cannot cancel the contract for default.

A performance guarantee clause was included in the development contract for the F-111 aircraft. The contract was nominally a fixed-price incentive contract, but the Government had few options available to force the contractor to meet stipulated performance requirements. The F-111 development contract listed ten specifications, including speed, ferry range, combat ceiling, weight, and acceleration. The 207 early models of the F-111 delivered by April 1970 met only eight of the specifications. Deficiencies ranged from 3% (required landing distance) to 85% (dash distance close to the target top speed). Under the guaranteed performance clause, however, the maximum penalty that could be assessed the contractor—even if all planes failed all ten specifications—was $1,750,000. This was considerably less than the cost of one F-111 aircraft.[5]

The disclaimer-clause tactic is used when a contractor is bidding on a follow-on development or production contract. The contractor proposes that a clause be included in the new contract that frees him from responsibility for any failures resulting from poor design, poor workmanship, or incorrect decisions made on earlier contracts. Through the use of this clause, a contractor who has negotiated a production contract for a weapon system that he designed under an earlier contract can claim additional funds from the Government if it is discovered that he failed to perform effectively on the earlier contract. In 1970 one contractor submitted a claim for $6 million on a fixed-price production contract because of "failure to have adequate facilities and equipment to perform the work on the part of the Government." The same contractor, on an earlier completed contract, was responsible for developing the facilities and equipment to perform the production work. This contractor made it a practice to insist that such a clause be included in all follow-on contracts with the Government. This effectively freed him from any responsibility for design deficiencies that were discovered during a production contract, and it obligated the Government to provide him with additional funds for facilities and equipment in order to receive the weapon system.

CONTRACTOR SIZE AS A FACTOR IN NEGOTIATIONS

Discussions with Government and industry personnel reveal that small contractors have a much weaker negotiating position than large contractors. With small contractors, Government negotiators usually feel more secure, and they are less fearful that the contractor will complain to higher levels in the Government. In addition, the Government often has an alternative source for the product or service being purchased and can turn to the alternate source with a relatively small penalty in terms of dollars or time.

In contrast, several Government representatives said that they were careful not to antagonize large contractors during negotiations because "their capability is needed for the defense of the country." Fear of antagonizing the contractor is also fostered by the disparity in grade level, pay, and status among Government and industry negotiators. In a typical negotiation for a development program, the industry team is made up of industry vice presidents. The Government team of military and civilian personnel may be headed by a GS-13 (civil service grade equivalent to a major) or GS-14 (civil service grade equivalent to lieutenant colonel). These people are responsible for negotiating contracts of several tens of millions of dollars with industry. For example, the industry negotiators for one major aircraft development program were an executive vice president and second vice president. The Government team was headed by a GS-13 civilian. At a later date, the GS-13 was replaced by a brigadier general. While the general was a conscientious commander of his organization, he had very little training or experience in negotiating contracts.

The situation described above is not uncommon in defense procurement. Gordon Rule, the senior negotiator for the Navy, reported to the Joint Economic Committee of the Congress in mid-1969 that "it is common to see one $12,000-a-year Government purchaser negotiating with teams of industry officials who average $40,000 a year each—and the $40,000 ultimately comes from the taxpayer." Several Government and industry officials told us that the problem of unequal power could not be explained simply in terms of salary levels, however. It was, they said, much more a function of: (1) support for Government negotiators from higher level Government personnel; (2) the training and supervision they receive; and (3) the availability of technical experts from other parts of the Government.

Commenting on the discrepancy in the negotiating capabilities between Government and industry, the Blue Ribbon Panel wrote:

> There is a particular urgency in the matter of upgrading personnel involved in contract negotiation and in the system of promotions and reward for the negotiators. That the overwhelming proportion of defense procurement actions take the form of negotiated contracts is a fact of life and should be recognized as such. Department of Defense personnel who negotiate this great number and dollar value of contracts are involved with negotiators from industry who are key personnel with lifetimes of experience, and paid by industry much higher than the pay received by the defense contract negotiators. The defense negotiator is at a disadvantage, to say the least. Skills of Government negotiators obtained through experience are often wasted by the existing system of rewards which appears to promote the most capable negotiators to supervisory positions, thereby removing them from direct negotiating activities. Contract negotiation is a special skill, different from and often more difficult to develop or acquire than are administrative or supervisory skills. A system of rewards for negotiators, which is commensurate with their skills and does not necessarily require their removal from active negotiations, should be developed.[6]

While there is general recognition of this problem, there have been few changes to correct these deficiencies. New courses have been instituted to train negotiators, but the civil service tenure regulations make it extremely difficult for the Department of Defense to rid itself of marginal producers.

NOTES TO CHAPTER XVIII

1. Frederic M. Scherer, *The Weapons Acquisition Process: Economic Incentives* (Boston: Division of Research, Harvard Business School, 1964), p. 205.
2. Gordon W. Rule, Address to the U.S. Army Logistics Management Center, Fort Lee, Virginia, February 3, 1964.
3. Richard J. Lorette, "The Relationship Between the Pressures on the System Program Director and the Growth of Weapon System Cost Estimates" (Boston: unpublished doctoral dissertation, Harvard Business School, 1967), p. 417.
4. Francis Pace, *Negotiation and Management of Defense Contracts* (New York: Wiley-Interscience, 1970), p. 567.
5. "Senators Find Secret Clause in F-111 Order May Assure Profits Despite Soaring Costs," *Wall Street Journal*, April 23, 1970, p. 5.
6. Report of the Blue Ribbon Panel to the President and the Secretary of Defense on the Department of Defense, July 1, 1970, p. 95.

CHAPTER XIX

Contract Changes

THE PREPARATION of a contract for the development or production of a major weapon system requires thousands of Government manhours. The statement of work is developed, contract sources are identified and solicited, proposals are analyzed, and the contract is finally negotiated. One might expect that the resulting agreement would require little if any change during the period of performance. Such is not the case, however. The negotiation and control of contract changes are two of the primary responsibilities for Government and industry personnel involved in the management of large defense programs. It is not uncommon for a program to experience contract changes at a rate exceeding one per hour, or more than 2,000 per year. Each of these changes may affect the contract schedule and cost, and the technical performance of the weapon system. Changes may involve the addition of new work, the deletion of work, or the modification of work currently specified in the contract.

This chapter will deal with the types of changes, the significance of contract changes, the causes of contract changes, and methods of dealing with contract change problems.

Because any contract is a bilateral agreement between a defense company and the Government, changes must be agreed to by the two contractual parties. The formal legal document that reflects the altered contractual requirements is called a "Supplemental Agreement." The Supplemental Agreement is negotiated much as the original contract was. In fact, if the contract changes are far-reaching, and if there has been no turnover among the Government and industry negotiators, these same individuals may negotiate the Supplemental Agreement.

AUTHOR'S NOTE: The research of Professor James S. Reece at the Harvard Business School provided the major input to this chapter.

The second document that plays an important role in the change procedure is the Contract Change Notice (CCN), or—its more recent name—the Change Order. Unlike the Supplemental Agreement, the Change Order is not a bilateral agreement. Rather, it represents a unilateral action by the Government authorizing the contractor to perform according to a new or altered requirement, and expressing the Government's intention to negotiate a Supplemental Agreement with the contractor to incorporate the new requirement into the contract.

Since 1863 [1] defense contracts have contained a change clause that authorizes a Government contracting officer to direct a change unilaterally (without the consent of the contractor). The clause normally takes the form described below:

> The contracting officer may at any time, by a written order, and without notice to the sureties, make changes, within the general scope of this contract, in any one or more of the following: (i) drawings, designs, or specifications, where the supplies to be furnished are to be specially manufactured for the Government in accordance therewith; (ii) method of shipment or packing; and (iii) place of delivery. If any such change causes an increase or decrease in the cost of, or the time required for, the performance of any part of the work under this contract, whether changed or not changed by any such order, an equitable adjustment shall be made in the contract price or delivery schedule, or both, and the contract shall be modified in writing accordingly. . . . Failure to agree to any adjustment shall be a dispute concerning a question of fact within the meaning of the clause of this contract entitled "Disputes." However, nothing in this clause shall excuse the contractor from proceeding with the contract as changed. [2]

Thus, the contractor cannot refuse to accept the change. And he must proceed with the work even in the absence of an agreement about the effect of the change on contract costs, schedules, and technical requirements.

In practice, there is not a one-to-one relationship between Change Orders and Supplemental Agreements. The Government usually accumulates several Change Orders before it negotiates a single Supplemental Agreement. Each Change Order may be negotiated as a separate item in a Supplemental Agreement that incorporates as many as 50 Change Orders. Change Orders are accumulated because the time required for negotiation of a single one often does not warrant the time and expense of an exclusive negotiating session.

The directions given to a contractor in a Change Order may be the result of a strictly unilateral Government decision (e.g., deliver 100 aircraft this year instead of 150). Or the Change Order may authorize the contractor to perform new or changed tasks in accordance with a written proposal submitted by the company. The proposed changes may have been suggested by the contractor, a subcontractor, or one of several Government agencies (e.g., the buying agency, using agency, logistics agency, training agency). The contractor is often the first to recognize the need for engineering changes in a weapon system. The Government is in charge of changes in military requirements and relates them to the system being produced.

Contract change proposals from contractors take several forms. For a crucial amendment to a contract (such as the addition of a new version of an aircraft), the proposal is similar to one prepared for a new program. In other cases, a proposal may suggest that certain contractual performance requirements be relaxed or that deficiencies in contract specifications be corrected. The most common change proposals alter the hardware being produced under the contract. These proposals are called Engineering Change Proposals (ECP's) and are the type referred to in most discussions of contract changes.

A single Change Order often authorizes a contractor to perform the work described in several Engineering Change Proposals. There are several reasons for this practice. First, it is more economical. Second, a single change in work may require several related Engineering Change Proposals (e.g., when a prime contractor and several of his subcontractors are affected by the same change, or when different engineering designs are affected by the same change). On the other hand, a single Engineering Change Proposal may result in the issuance of several Change Orders. For example, one contractor may have several contracts (e.g., research and development, production, support) for the same program, and one Engineering Change Proposal may affect all of them. A Change Order would then be issued for each contract (and ultimately, each Change Order would be incorporated into a separate Supplemental Agreement).

When an idea for a change is generated within a Government or industry organization, the idea is documented in a change proposal and submitted to the Government Program office for analysis. If the Government approves the change, a Change Order is issued to the contractor, authorizing him (and/or his subcontractors) to perform the work described in the Engineering Change Proposal. Finally, the Government and the contractor negotiate a Supplemental Agreement incorporating the Change Order into the basic contract.

During the decade of the 1960s the term "constructive change" appeared with increasing frequency in books and articles on Government contracting. To effect a constructive change, the contractor performs work as a result of one or both of the following conditions: (1) a nonwritten technical directive from the contracting officer or another Government official, and/or (2) the impossibility of fulfilling a Government-approved specification.

The change clause in defense contracts expressly provides equitable adjustments only where the changes are made "by written order" of the contracting officer or his authorized representative. Nonetheless, courts and appeals boards have held that a "constructive" Change Order (with the same authority as a written order) is in effect when the contractor is required by the words or conduct of authorized Government representatives to perform different or additional work under the contract.[3] Instructions affecting the change may be written or oral; and specific terms such as "order," "direct," or "require" need not be used if the contractor's work is, in fact, changed. A change may result from the failure of Government personnel to act, as well as from a positive course of action. Constructive Change Orders may occur when:

- A Government or contracting officer unjustifiably rejects work, thereby requiring the contractor to perform rework or additional work not required by the contract.
- Government inspectors or other authorized personnel require excessive tests or a higher standard of performance than called for by the specification.
- The contractor's costs are increased by a change in the time, place, or manner of inspection, or in quality control requirements.
- The contract does not specify how the work is to be accomplished and the Government's representative insists that it be accomplished in a certain way, although the work could be performed satisfactorily by a less expensive method.
- The contractor incurs additional costs because he is forced by action of a Government official to alter the sequence in which the work is performed.
- The contracting officer directs performance not legally required by the contract as a result of his interpretation of the contract.
- The contractor is entitled to a time extension because of an excusable delay, and the contracting officer acts in such a way as to require the contractor to adhere to the original contract performance schedule despite notice of the contractor's claim to an extension of time. This is called "acceleration" of performance. It may also occur where the contracting officer recognizes an excusable delay, but for a shorter period than is justified, so that the time extension granted is insufficient and the contractor is forced to speed up the work.
- The Government's specifications contain inconsistencies or other errors, the correction of which is, in fact, required for performance of the contract work contemplated by the parties. In such a case the contractor has been entitled to an equitable adjustment under the changes clause to compensate him for extra work caused by the defects in the specifications, even though the increase in cost was not caused by an express Change Order.[4]

As a result of the use of constructive changes, Government program officers and contractors often authorize changes outside the provisions of the change clause of the contract, confident that the contractor will not lose money by such action. In the early 1960s many improperly authorized or implemented changes were interpreted as "constructive" by the courts and boards of appeal. Today, Government procurement officials often make adjustments without appealing to courts or appeal boards on the grounds that they would be directed to do so if the situation were allowed to go to the courts.

TYPES OF CHANGES

Changes in weapon system contracts may be classified as configuration changes, task changes, or program changes.

Configuration changes alter the configuration of a system being built for delivery to the Government. They may change or delete an existing part, or add a new one. For example, a change that alters the structure of any part or component of a production aircraft is a configuration change. Configuration changes are authorized in Engineering Change Proposals and are frequently referred to as engineering changes.

Although configuration changes often lead to changes in tasks performed in the defense plant (e.g., lengthening the wing span of an aircraft changes many manufacturing tasks), the term "task change" does not usually refer to changes in hardware. Task changes, for example, may restructure test programs or feasibility studies. Although task changes are not like engineering changes, in practice proposed task changes are usually supported by Engineering Change Proposals. For this reason, they are also frequently referred to as engineering changes.

Program changes involve major—and usually very costly—revisions to quantities, technical performance specifications, delivery schedules, or rate of funding for a program.* For example, the F-111 aircraft program experienced a number of program changes. Initial Government plans (in 1962) called for the building of approximately 1,700 aircraft in two versions. By 1970 Government plans called for 547 aircraft in one version. During the intervening eight years, a number of program changes led to this transformation of program definition.

---

* It should be noted that the variables are usually interrelated. For example, a change in quantity will usually involve alterations in the schedule and/or rate of funding. Similarly, added technical capabilities may cause the schedule to be extended and/or the funding rate to be increased.

The Significance of Contract Changes

Table XIX-1 presents the number and value of the Change Orders awarded during the five-year period, 1966–1970.

Table XIX-1. Number and Cost of Change Orders Awarded by the Department of Defense: 1966–1970

Year	Number	Billions of Dollars
1966	15,927	$1.574
1967	12,165	1.725
1968	12,563	2.651
1969	10,663	1.855
1970	8,965	1.600

Source: Office of the Assistant Secretary of Defense (Comptroller), Directorate of Information Operations, *Change Orders and Letter Contracts, 1966–1970.*

The total value of the contract changes awarded over the five-year period was more than $7 billion—a large sum even in the field of defense procurement. Yet these figures understate the full significance of the changes. Since a formal Change Order may include several engineering changes, the negotiation and control problems involved in these changes may be even more burdensome than the figures suggest. In 1969, for example, the Defense Department buying agency with the fewest Change Orders (the Army Materiel Command) approved more than 19,000 engineering changes. This represents an approval rate of more than eight per hour. If we make the conservative assumption that the number of engineering changes for the Navy and Air Force was also limited to 19,000 each, the Department of Defense would have been involved in the approval of approximately 60,000 engineering changes for the year, averaging in the vicinity of $150,000 each.[5]

Another way to evaluate the significance of contract changes is to examine program cost growth resulting from changes. A Logistics Management Institute study of 139 weapon system contracts, with original prices totaling $15.3 billion, identified cost growth of $7.6 billion, or almost 50%.[6] This growth occurred over a period of three to five years and the contracts studied were for aircraft, missiles, tanks, ships, and electronics systems. The cost growth on individual contracts ranged from −21% (i.e., final costs were 79% of the estimated costs of the basic program) to 184% (i.e., final costs were 284% of the original program's cost estimate).

To avoid confusion, the terms "cost growth" and "overrun" should be explained at this point. They are not synonymous, although it is common to hear all increases in weapon system program costs referred to as "overruns." A cost overrun is defined as that sum of money spent on a program in excess of contract price. If a contract price or a planned total cost for a program is changed upward by a significant amount, there may be no cost overrun recorded although, in fact, there is substantial cost growth. Cost growth is the increase in program expenditures above the price of the *original* program plan. It results from (1) changed program requirements; (2) technical difficulties; and/or (3) inefficiency.*

In March 1971, seven years after the Logistics Management Institute study cited above, the GAO issued a report of cost changes in 52 weapon systems. Despite the intervening span of eight years, the findings of the GAO study and the LMI study are very similar. The GAO found that there had been a net increase of $23.9 billion in the total cost of the 52 weapon system programs. Quantity changes had a net impact of adding $2.4 billion, while other changes (e.g., engineering, schedule, and economic) accounted for more than $21

TABLE XIX-2. ANALYSIS OF COST CHANGES FOR 52 DEFENSE
WEAPONS PROGRAMS AS OF JUNE 30, 1970

Type of Cost Change	Total Dollars (Billions)	
Quantity Change:		
Increase	$12.6	
Decrease	10.2	
Net		$ 2.4
Other Changes:		
Engineering Changes	$ 4.1	
Support Changes	1.3	
Schedule Changes	2.6	
Economic Changes	4.0	
Estimate Changes	6.1	
Sundry Changes	1.1	
Unidentified Changes	2.3	
Total		21.5
Total		$23.9

SOURCE: Comptroller General of the United States, Report to the Congress on the *Acquisition of Major Weapon Systems*, March 18, 1971, p. 61.

billion. The specific figures from the GAO study are shown in Table XIX-2. The definitions used by the GAO for the "Other Changes" are listed below:

---

* "Inefficiency" as used here may be the result of poor cost control (the usual meaning of inefficiency), or a poor cost estimate of the original program. Unfortunately, there is no effective way to isolate these two different causes of the cost variance.

Engineering Changes—an alteration in the established physical or func-
    tional characteristics of a system.
Support Changes—a change in spare parts, ancillary equipment, war-
    ranty provisions, and Government-furnished equip-
    ment.
Schedule Changes—adjustments in the delivery schedule, completion
    date, or some intermediate milestone of development
    or production.
Economic Changes—changes reflecting the influence of one or more fac-
    tors in the economy.
Estimate Changes—corrections in an initial estimate.
Sundry Changes—miscellaneous.
Unidentified Changes—unexplained by the Department of Defense.

It is obvious that there is considerable overlap in the definition of the various
types of changes. Indeed, many changes could be placed in any one of several
categories listed above.

The F-111 program provides an illustration of the extent of the role of contract changes in program management. General Dynamics, the prime contractor for the F-111 program, originally agreed to build 1,726 aircraft for $5.5
billion, or $3.2 million per aircraft. By mid-1970 the Air Force planned to
spend $7.5 billion for only 547 aircraft, or $13.8 million per aircraft. In testimony before the Senate Permanent Investigation Committee, on March 25,
1970, Air Force representatives told Senator McClellan that General Dynamics Corporation was still approximately $400 million below the contract ceil-
ing beyond which profits disappear. The senior Air Force witness indicated
that the major share of the cost growth would be accounted for in Change
Orders financed by the Government. During the height of the F-111 program
(1967 and 1968), General Dynamics Corporation experienced an average of
750 contract changes per year. Although the 1,500 changes that were approved during that two-year period amounted to a cost increase of $1.5 bil-
lion, it is important to note that more than 90% of the contract changes
brought increases of less than $200,000 each. The major share of the $1.5
billion increase was concentrated in a few changes.

Not all contract changes have a direct impact on costs. An examination of
2,271 Air Force contract changes revealed that 33%, or 774, required no contract price adjustment. However, 66%, or 1,497, did require contract price
adjustments, and more than 90% were upward adjustments. The net impact
of the 1,497 changes was an increase in contract prices of $241 million. A
separate study of Army contract changes was conducted by the Army Materiel Command. It included an examination of contract changes for 21 programs at six commodity commands (aviation systems, electronics, tank and

automotive, munitions, missiles, and mobility equipment). The study team concluded that 74% of the contract changes in the survey required an upward adjustment in contract price.

Government procurement and controller personnel told us that the primary problem they face in managing the contract change process is inadequate analysis of the incremental value of changes and the added resources required to accomplish the work affected by the changes. Several officers commented that there were often "very few if any objective criteria for measuring the value of a proposed contract change. If a change is needed, we are told that it is needed now, and that any delay in approving the change will cost additional funds or will delay the program schedule. In the face of this pressure, no one wants to take the responsibility for incurring additional costs or experiencing a schedule slippage."

Before proceeding with a discussion of the causes of changes, it may be useful to examine a partial list of actual changes for two specific programs. (The full list provided by program management staff included several esoteric technical changes that are not self-explanatory.)

Partial List of Contract Changes from Two Major Aircraft Programs
- Changes in the airframe, caused by limitations in the Government-furnished electrical system.
- Changes in the avionics, caused by changes in the Government-furnished auto-pilot.
- Extension of the delivery schedule.
- Change of delivery rate, from four per month to seven per month.
- Increase in the crew from four to six men.
- Addition of corrosion protection.
- Addition of alternate mission equipment.
- Redefinition of the flight test program to include eight instead of five aircraft.
- Change in the instrumentation to incorporate new flight instruments.
- Addition of flight instruments utilizing tape.
- Modification in crew compartments.
- Addition of audible fire warning.
- Deletion of forward cargo door.
- Change in the approved weight, from 85,000 lbs. to 97,000 lbs.
- Change in the requirements of the configuration management system.
- Change in the requirements for reliability assurance.
- Increase of fatigue testing.
- Change in the requirements for cost performance reporting.
- Increase in the scope of the fatigue test program.
- Change in the value engineering requirement in the contract.
- Addition of an interior corrosion preventative.

- Reduction in the system maintainability requirement.
- Reduction in the altitude required for maximum speed.
- Addition of penetration aids.
- Increase in the training requirements for military personnel.
- Increase in data to support the added requirements of aircraft.
- Addition of spare parts.
- Reduction in the manufacturing support required.
- Change of cooling requirements.
- Addition of gun cameras.
- Addition of a multichannel recorder.
- Addition of camouflage paint.

CAUSES OF CONTRACT CHANGES

A contract change is generated when Government or industry personnel are able to convince the appropriate Government decision makers that the need for change warrants the projected cost. There are several aspects to the changes made on defense programs. Changes in funding are made as a military service prepares its annual budget for presentation to the Congress. Budget strategy involves periodic reductions in the requested funding for approved programs in order to provide leeway for the introduction of new programs. Often these budget changes cause major problems for contractors. The following comments represent industry managers' reactions to funding changes:

> INDUSTRY EXECUTIVE #1—We have just learned that we have to re-plan our program to accommodate a seven-month gap in Government funding. This is going to cause a significant increase in the cost of the program. Next year, I imagine, we will have a GAO team in our plant trying to figure out the cause of the cost increase.

Interviews with Government personnel revealed that funding was reduced to release funds for other programs.

> INDUSTRY EXECUTIVE #2—The planned "buy" of our program changes from month to month. It is just impossible to plan for any efficient kind of production with this amount of funding turbulence.
>
> INDUSTRY EXECUTIVE #3—On this program there has been uncertainty in the annual quantities to be bought by the Government each year for the past six years. We have to be ready to produce at a variety of different production levels.

Ten Government program managers cited funding instability—i.e., changes in amount of funds available for their programs—as one of their most serious problems.

There are a number of reasons for continued "improvement" changes and additions during the course of a weapon system's development and production. One of these is the long duration of most programs. A former Navy officer who had been responsible for program management activities described the situation: "The genesis of improvement changes is that the Government often does not really know what it wants the contractor to do. The Government wants a weapon system to meet the enemy threat that will prevail five to seven years or more from now. This implies tremendous uncertainty in writing the contract today." [7] Changes occur, in other words, because the Government decides, or the contractor convinces the Government, that the system should include a new feature. One form of improvement change is the "optional accessory" change. These are changes involving system capabilities that were considered desirable at the time the initial program was planned. If they had been included in the original program plan, however, the related costs might have prevented the program from receiving approval from senior decision makers in the Government. So the features were deleted at the time of initial program approval, and were then re-introduced during the development or production program when the likelihood of approval was greater.*

Another situation leading to improvement changes is known in the defense business as "goldplating." This means that changes are added for which the incremental benefits do not seem to justify the incremental costs. Whether a change is classified as a "worthwhile improvement" or "unnecessary goldplating" depends to a great extent on who is making the cost/benefit evaluation. The possibility of goldplating underlines the fact that fallible individuals, not impersonal Government and industry "experts," originate and justify ideas for changes.

Within Government and industry, there are always different groups who have opposing views on any given change, or even on the topic of changes in general. For example, let us consider engineers—both in Government and industry. New weapon systems (e.g., aircraft) consist of subsystems (e.g., airframe, propulsion, avionics), which again consist of smaller subsystems. At

---

* Professor James S. Reece of the Harvard Business School faculty labeled these changes "optional accessory" changes. He noted the similarity of the situation to one in which a customer decides to purchase a new car because it sells for only $2,500. Before the purchase is completed, he has often purchased a series of extra-cost options that increase the cost of the car to $3,000.

the lowest level, there are work packages of manageable size that are assigned to individual engineers. This process of subdivision takes place both in defense plants, where most of the actual engineering design is accomplished, and in the smaller governmental units (e.g., systems engineering divisions or laboratories), where the Government monitors the contractors' engineering work. Thus, at some level in the subdivision of the program, there are counterpart engineering departments in the Government and industry program organizations—i.e., engineers in each of the two organizations responsible for the design and performance of the same piece of hardware. These engineers are all likely to be civilians with similar academic training. Consequently, they are able to communicate with each other easily. Both groups want their piece of hardware to achieve "engineering excellence"—in terms of engineering design concepts and performance. Both groups experience the satisfaction of a job well done when this excellence is achieved, and both receive financial and other rewards from their respective organizations when they achieve this excellence. Evaluations by peers and superiors in either group are not affected by the cost of attaining this engineering excellence, as long as funds are ultimately made available for the job. Neither are rewards for practicing economies likely to be forthcoming in either group. This, then, is the environment in which improvement changes are made. A number of these changes are bound to be labeled as "goldplating" by cost-conscious observers.

In conducting interviews on engineering changes, Professor Reece heard the following comments:[8]

- Industry program manager: "Engineering is essentially a level-of-effort activity—they keep inventing things whether there is a need or not."
- Industry industrial engineer: "On one program I was on, the contractor and Government tried to cut down on changes, allowing only 'safety of flight' changes. So the engineers—both ours and theirs—just called all the changes 'safety of flight,' whether they really were or not."
- Management consultant specializing in Government contracting: "There is good rapport between Government and contractor technical people. They talk together, and informally create a change; then paperwork formalizes it."
- Air Force colonel in the procurement field: "Our System Project Office engineers always want the 'latest and greatest.' "
- Industry program manager: "The input for change decisions comes from below the Government project manager, from people who have a vested interest in some particular aspect of the system."
- Contractor program manager: "Over-designing and studying a problem to death are tendencies of our engineers which we must always be on the watch for."

A second group that initiate improvement changes in weapon systems are the users—i.e., the military groups that will eventually operate the system.* The users naturally demand reliable weapon systems. The systems must also be superior in capability to any potential enemy's weapons. Because of the time involved in acquiring each weapon system, there are bound to be advances made in weapons technology during the course of the program. The users believe that unless improvement changes are made, their new weapon system may be obsolete by the time it is finally available to them. They argue that any technical advances known to U.S. engineers are also available to a potential enemy. This is a powerful incentive to add improved features to any system under development or in production.

The concerns of the user command are indeed understandable. The problem is that there is often no effective control force within the using command to restrict improvement changes in terms of real need. This is because users and buyers of weapon systems are from different organizations within the same military service. And it is the buyer, not the user, who is responsible for the cost of the systems. For example, in the Air Force the Aeronautical Systems Division of the Air Force Systems Command is responsible for procuring all aircraft for the Air Force, yet the Air Force Systems Command does not use these aircraft. The users are the Tactical Air Command, the Strategic Air Command, and the Air Training Command, all headed by officers who have no responsibility for the cost of developing or producing the systems. The users ask for improvements solely in terms of perceived military "urgency."

Although the separation of Government buyer from Government user may in theory establish a healthy balance, the pressures for introducing improvement changes appear to outmatch the countervailing forces to use available money wisely. As described earlier, the engineering staff in the buying office, working in conjunction with the contractor's engineers, may be inventing improvement changes. Program managers are usually military officers who have been rotated among various organizations within their service. Today's program manager for an aircraft program may have been a pilot in the using command six months ago. He is likely to have had very little training in business management.[9] His user orientation, together with his lack of business management training, renders him largely incapable of understanding the need to limit improvement changes. Since his rank is lower than senior officers in the using command who are arguing for improvement changes, he is unlikely to quibble. These senior officers will be preparing his annual performance report

---

* For example, the two primary users of the F-111 aircraft are the Air Force Tactical Air Command and the Air Force Strategic Air Command.

when he is transferred back to a using command after his present assignment.

Officials charged with the responsibility for managing development and production programs—ranging from Pentagon policy makers to Government and industry program managers to the schedule and cost controllers in industry plants—speak disparagingly of contract changes and the problems that result from them. Although they do not believe that contract changes can be eliminated entirely, most of them think that the number of changes on most programs is unnecessarily high. But they find that management considerations are seldom heeded. The following are typical comments.

- Government program manager: "It is human nature and particularly the human nature of technical people to try to improve a product to the maximum degree that either time or dollars will permit. Therefore, delayed program decisions, continued study, and/or development, only to preserve a future option, result in continued cost-generating changes which invariably increase the weight, complexity, and cost of the ultimate system."
- Industry senior vice president: "There is a strong tendency for both the contractor and the military services to keep inventing on a contract—and not simply to perform against the initial specifications."
- Director of contracting and pricing for a major aerospace firm: "We need to take much firmer steps to freeze designs once the initial design is completed. Under the present situation, people in Government and industry keep trying to improve upon the first design so that we have a second and a third and even more designs before we go into production."

Design problems are another reason for contract changes. The main goal of a development program is to resolve engineering problems, a process that by its very nature generates change. It is during the course of a development program that contractors begin to do the work they outlined in response to the Government RFP. As a contractor transforms his paper designs into actual hardware, it often becomes apparent that certain approaches will not work. When this happens, the contractor must submit an Engineering Change Proposal describing an alternative approach, since the Government has already approved the initial approach as part of the original contract.

The following comments touch on this problem:

- Senior military procurement officer: "The most serious deficiencies in our weapons acquisition process are in the engineering area. We find that inadequate technical appraisals are made and inadequate technical data packages are prepared during development programs."
- U.S. Army Audit Agency report: "In some cases, the need to negotiate

changes to existing contracts resulted from (i) errors or omissions in specifications used for the initial contract and (ii) inadequate reviews of specifications prior to negotiations. Further, extensive and sometimes costly delays were noted in negotiating the price for modifications which already had been incorporated by the contractor after consent by the Government." [10]

- Senior Government manager at a production directorate: "Design engineers usually don't develop designs that can be effectively produced at the end of a development program. We find that we have to go out to the contractor and have him redesign the item for production, during the phase of the program called Advanced Production Engineering. If the initial design has been poorly done, we can spend tens of millions of dollars during Advanced Production Engineering to accomplish jobs that should have been done during the development program."

- Pentagon procurement official: "When aircraft weight, ceiling, or cost objectives can't be met, contractors are issued change notices because the military services want the product even if it doesn't meet all the specifications. If the weight is high or the flight ceiling is low, the military service will still accept the aircraft because they would rather have a plane that almost meets the specifications than no new plane at all. Making contract changes to accept the plane is the only alternative to not having the planes. The contractors know this situation well."

Several Government representatives told us that a contractor proposes more and more changes as he finds himself in difficulty with the program. The following account was related by a senior Government engineer who had worked on several development programs.

Whenever a contractor begins to have difficulties, he begins to shave other contract areas to find ways to cover his costs. In other words, minor problem areas on the program which might otherwise have been uncontested, had things gone well, are now actively sought out and written up as Engineering Change Proposals to improve the contractor's position. The contractor begins to go over the contract with a fine-toothed comb, hoping to discover marginal areas which he can use to his advantage. If loopholes or errors are discovered, the contractor can then submit change proposals to his advantage. The contractor has sufficient manpower and time to develop the paperwork necessary to support his proposal. The Government often does not have the time or qualified personnel to effectively challenge a proposed change.

A number of related comments were made by Government and industry personnel:

- Senior Government program manager: "In my view, many unessential changes have been proposed by contractors on my program."
- Vice president of a leading defense firm: "There is a tendency in the Department of Defense to believe that they are writing better contracts because they are tougher. The honesty they tried to create has back-fired and integrity has gone out the window. . . . One industry weapon used to retaliate is the Engineering Change Proposal. You can ECP the program to death." [11]
- Vice president of a defense firm: "When I was with [name of company], it was a frequently repeated statement that we would bid to lose money on the initial contract and then make money on the contract changes."
- Senior vice president of a leading defense firm: "Contract changes represent one of our major problems. Changing requirements, changing specifications, etc. We certainly contribute to this problem ourselves, but so does the government."

EVALUATING CONTRACT CHANGE PROPOSALS

A contractor's proposal or a Government directive for a contract change carries with it a substantial requirement for analysis by both Government and industry. A reasonable approach to managing changes should include at least the following four steps:

1. Notification of both parties to the contract as soon as a potential change situation is recognized;
2. Development of a thorough mutual understanding of change problems before solutions are proposed;
3. Evaluation of alternative courses of action;
4. Evaluation of the impact on schedule, cost, and technical performance for each change *before* its approval.

In reality, this process rarely occurs in the orderly manner described above. The Government office is pressured by the using command and the contractor to approve the change first and make the analysis later, if at all. This analysis is a time-consuming procedure. In order to arrive at a reasonable decision on a change and the cost to be paid for the change, an analyst seeks to learn the cost, schedule, and technical performance impact of work added, work deleted, and work altered. The analysis may require hundreds, or thousands, of manhours. The time required to make a decision and to implement a change may range from one or two weeks to 300 or more days. This includes the preparation of a written Change Order; preparation of a contractor proposal;

the collection and analysis of cost, schedule, and technical performance impact data; negotiation of the changes in the contract; preparation of supplemental agreements; and the actual amendment of a contract.

Several Government and industry managers told us that the military services do not have enough trained personnel to make any effective analysis of the impact of a proposed change. The following comments reflect that point of view.

- Senior military procurement officer: "It often takes a long time to appraise the impact of changes because the required information is not available and letters must be written back and forth to the contractor to obtain the information."
- Industry program manager: "We have many problems in the area of contract changes. A general writes a letter and tells us to go ahead with a change in the program. Then we tell him what we need in the way of funds for the next three months to carry out the change, and he makes the funds available. The preparation of the statement of work for the Engineering Change Proposal may take one or more months evolving before it is ready for estimating. Then it may be another month or more before the change is negotiated. By then, we may have completed the work on the change."
- Government program manager: "Our project office does not conduct what we consider to be a proper review and evaluation of all changes because of a lack of qualified personnel."
- Government program manager: "If we were to evaluate the reasonableness of the contractor's proposed cost of changes, we would need many more people of higher technical capability than we have. Most Government program offices have never had individuals with the capability for appraising the reasonableness of the proposed cost of changes."

In the fall of 1969 the Army Audit Agency issued a report resulting from a comprehensive analysis of contract changes on Army programs. The report contained the following observation on Government activities in the management of changes.

In several instances, the reasonableness of prices was not readily determinable by reference to the contract administration files and records of negotiation. Examination of contract files disclosed that (i) contractors had not been requested to submit required certificates showing accurate, complete, and current data, (ii) contractor proposals did not provide sufficient details to permit a meaningful analysis or comparison with Government estimates, (iii) Government estimates were either not prepared or lacked sufficient depth, (iv) Government price analyses were either not performed or were too restrictive, and (v) technical and professional assistance was either not requested or not given consideration in reaching procurement pricing decisions.[12]

Further evidence of the Government's inability to analyze the impact of contract changes is contained in an internal report made by one military service. Here is an excerpt from that report:

> The lack of a total impact evaluation of contract changes is obvious. In one project, three of the five engineering change proposals sampled were approved on the same day they were submitted, or the next day (although they were not to correct emergency conditions); one of the engineering change proposals was not submitted to a configuration control board until 74 days after it was approved. Another engineering change was implemented 124 days before it received official approval.
>
> At another command, three of the sample engineering change proposals were approved on the spot, at the contractor's plant, by a representative of the development engineering division of the Government project office, without the benefit of inputs from any other impacted organizations.
>
> At still another command, the configuration management organization had no idea whether or not any of the engineering change proposals we sampled had an impact on repair parts or publications, or even if modification kits were required.

NEGOTIATING CONTRACT CHANGES

Every negotiation for a Change Order occurs in a sole-source environment. In most cases the work has already been committed to the contractor's plant in the original contract, and it is rarely feasible to transfer the work to another contractor for implementation of the change. Thus, the contractor is in a particularly strong position to negotiate. A contractor may have special motives for taking advantage of his negotiating strength. If, for example, a contractor has "bought in" on a new and potentially profitable area of Government work by submitting an unrealistically low bid or proposal, he may try to recoup some of his losses by obtaining a high price for subsequent contract changes.

Contract changes are frequently negotiated about three to six months or more after a change proposal is submitted by a contractor. For large changes, these negotiations take place at the Government program office. For small changes, the Government program manager delegates the negotiations to the Government representative at the contractor's plant, usually an employee of the Defense Contract Administration Service (DCAS). During the long time span between the approval of a change and the actual negotiation of the change into the contract, the contractor's cost proposal is often revised one or more times.

Again because of the long time span between change approval and change negotiation, the work required by the change has often begun, and may even be completed at the time of the negotiations. One contractor estimated that during his experience with hundreds of contract changes, the work required by the change had started prior to the negotiations in 99% of the cases, was half finished 50% of the time, and was fully completed 20% of the time. Senior officers from one Government buying agency estimated that more than 50% of the contract changes they had experienced over the past year were negotiated after the fact, from *actual costs*. Many procurement officials realize that the contractor has no incentive to control costs of changes when work is partially or fully completed before negotiations take place. A contractor's negotiation position is strongest when he negotiates on the basis of actual costs instead of estimates. Such a negotiation then focuses on allowability of costs (i.e., have the costs been charged to the allowable cost categories specified in Section 15 of ASPR) rather than reasonableness of costs. It is difficult for Government negotiators to prove that costs already incurred for changes should have been lower. (A 1963 court decision held that there is no better proof of the cost of a change than actual costs.[13])

If by delaying a negotiation until the work required by a Change Order is well under way a contractor can assure coverage of all his actual costs, he gains nothing by attempting to control or reduce these costs. In fact, such an effort may result in loss of profits, since the profit resulting from a contract change is negotiated as a percentage of costs.

The conduct of negotiations for contract changes varies from case to case, depending on the size and complexity of the change. Large, complex changes are negotiated in terms of work categories (i.e., engineering, tooling, manufacturing, testing); while smaller changes are negotiated on the basis of total costs. A contract change negotiation usually begins by focusing on two cost categories: material and direct labor. When agreement is reached, previously approved direct and indirect cost rates are applied to the material and direct labor amounts to arrive at a total dollar cost for the change. Based on this cost, a profit is then negotiated. Profit is considered as a percentage of target costs rather than an absolute dollar amount. The sum of the costs and the profit then represents the price of the contract change. As mentioned earlier, the negotiation process usually includes several contract changes for a single Supplemental Agreement to the basic contract.

Government personnel from program offices told us that they were often at a disadvantage when negotiating changes. The contractor is able to develop strong supporting data for his negotiation position because he can utilize all necessary personnel. But there are seldom enough Government personnel available to make appropriate analyses. A challenge to the contractor's position without strong supporting arguments would give the contractor reason to appeal to the courts. Such an action would then make it necessary to divert program personnel from normal management activities to the preparation of supporting data for the Government's case in court.

A number of officials from Government program offices told us that the longer the time period between approval of a change and the actual negotiation, the greater the likelihood that the contractor's original cost estimate would be raised.

Contract Change	Initial Estimate and Final Negotiated Price
#1	$15 million to $48 million
#2	$15 million to $62 million
#3	$ 9 million to $20 million

In one case, a Government program engineer told us that he had authorized the prime contractor to make a number of minor changes over a period of time. He claimed that he was assured by the contractor that these were "no-cost" changes. When the contractor later submitted a multimillion dollar contract change proposal to cover the alleged "no-cost" changes, the case went to court. The contractor won the case on the grounds that a Government representative had approved of the changes, and the Government could produce no data to support the alleged "no-cost" agreements.

Sixteen Government program managers were asked how often they were able to negotiate a firm price for a change *before* the contractor was directed to commence work on the change. Three of the program managers answered "always," four answered "never," and nine answered "very seldom." One of the program managers in the survey thought that the answer was so clearly "never" that he wondered whether he had understood the question correctly.

> Maybe I'm wrong—or do not understand the question—but we never negotiate a firm price for a change before the contractor starts working on it. The contractor only estimates the cost and it is negotiated later.[14]

Only five of the 13 program managers who gave negative responses explained why firm prices were not negotiated before the contractor commenced work. Each of the five stressed the need for rigid adherence to the program schedule as the primary factor that prevented negotiation before approval for a contract change was granted. These two comments are typical.

> The reason is that the time utilized in negotiation will cause the change to be effective at a much later production date, resulting in an extended program schedule. In some cases it would be preferable to accept an overstated cost in order to initiate work and be able to incorporate the change at an early date, rather than bear the resultant cost increase that results from delayed negotiations.
>
> The time required to negotiate a firm price and process a definitive contractual document is incompatible with a concurrent development/ production program such as the [name]. If a change is important enough to buy, it's normally desirable to incorporate it in production as soon as possible. Any dollars left at the negotiation table as a result of late pricing are offset by early production incorporation since retrofit is normally more expensive than a production fix.

The situation is quite different for commercial programs. In most commercial development programs (including the automotive business), changes are not made until a signed price agreement has been executed. In an attempt to incorporate such a procedure into the weapons acquisition process, the Defense Department is experimenting with a "not to exceed" clause at the time of initial change approval.[15] Since the introduction of the clause, the number of approved contract changes has declined. This decline might be the result of: (1) factors unrelated to the clause, (2) more careful costing of changes, or (3) the contractors' reluctance to experience the greater risk of the "not to exceed" clause. While full data are not yet available, most Government procurement and program management personnel believe that the clause is responsible for a reduction in the number of contract changes. They believe that the reduction is a result of more accurate pricing of changes and the improved ability of Government personnel to veto costly changes.

IMPACT OF CHANGES ON PROGRAM MANAGEMENT

The most significant impact of contract changes is a substantial increase in the cost of the program. This effect is most clearly observed in the analysis of 52 programs in the GAO report cited earlier.[16] In a separate analysis of 94 Air Force contracts, the RAND Corporation reported in December 1970 that the typical effect of contract changes was to increase contract costs by approximately 40%.[17] On these programs the RAND study reported that cost overruns—i.e., cost growth not attributable to contract changes—came to approximately 6% of the initial contract price.

Contract changes undermine initial contract incentives as well as efforts by program managers to run the program within budget, schedule, and performance specifications. The task of financial management in both Government and industry organizations is frequently complicated by lack of firm knowledge as to the current and projected program scope and budget. Degree of control over contract changes appears to vary considerably from one program to another, and from one organization to another within the same program and contractor organization. Several individuals from both Government and industry program offices told us that the frequency and size of changes on a program were often determined by the availability of funds for additional work.

In a detailed study of a leading contractor's experience with contract changes, Professor Reece found that it was easier to measure and control work performance associated with contract changes in an engineering division than in a manufacturing division.[18] Several reasons were cited for this difference. First, the tasks resulting from contract changes in an engineering organization tended to be relatively short-term, nonrecurring, and thus not so susceptible to further changes as longer duration, repetitive manufacturing tasks. Several industry and Government officials told us that a serious problem posed by changes occurred in those organizations where the changes overlapped, i.e., later changes began to affect earlier changes before the work associated with the earlier changes had been completed.

In industry engineering units, where contract changes are accomplished in a series of short-term tasks, several distinct projects are headed by individual managers responsible for the efficiency of distinct task-oriented groups. In some engineering organizations, however, Professor Reece found that control over individual projects was not effective because management did not evaluate performance in terms of cost control. An engineering manager who succeeded in meeting his budgets received no greater rewards, aside from possible personal satisfaction, than the individual who exceeded his cost targets. What is worse, the latter individual may actually receive the greater rewards in terms of pay increases and promotions. For example, by overrunning budgets, an engineer may be able to achieve a higher level of "engineering excellence" than if he had limited his spending to a level equal to or less than his approved budget.

In manufacturing, Professor Reece found that the longer term, recurring tasks often make it difficult, if not impossible, for a manager to measure or control the cost of work required by a change, separate from the ongoing manufacturing task. In this type of situation, the budget and schedule impact of a change loses its identity as a separate work order, and merely serves to adjust the budget and schedule for the basic manufacturing task. As a result of this submergence of change impact visibility, a foreman can blame unfavorable variances (i.e., schedule slippage and cost growth) on changes. In discussions with contractor engineers who were analyzing manufacturing costs and schedule variances, we heard at least six change-related explanations for unfavorable performance from foremen. These were:

1. *Parts shortages*—A new part required by a change was not available when the task was scheduled for completion.
2. *Out-of-station work*—The original task, scheduled in-station, had to be accomplished out-of-station as a result of a contract change. This reduced efficiency because of:
   —Time needed to travel to another station, including moving tools and fixtures;
   —Interference from workers in the new station who were performing their assigned tasks;
   —More difficult access to the affected area because of installations subsequent to the in-station location.
3. *Inspection time*—Too much time was required to "sell" change tasks to Government and contractor quality assurance inspectors.
4. *Crewload chart deficiencies*—Not enough "added task" blocks were included to cover the actual tasks added by contract changes.
5. *"Bugs" in new task*—New parts did not fit, or a new assembly tool was faulty (i.e., parts did not fit the tool or the tool did not fit the aircraft).
6. *"Inherited" problems*—Related change tasks in previous work stations were accomplished late, were not finished, or were handled incorrectly.

Industrial engineers and general foremen find it difficult to determine whether these reasons are valid explanations for poor performance, or simply excuses. Although contract changes certainly do not explain all management difficulties, they do exacerbate control problems to the point that both the original and the changed tasks are beyond control. The high frequency of changes tends to dilute any existing capability in the Government program office to control program costs, schedules, and technical performance. Many Government program managers describe themselves as "fire fighters," with little time to measure performance and identify problems early enough to take preventive action. It also seems clear that Government program offices do not have the number of trained personnel required to review and evaluate even major program changes properly. If the Department of Defense is ever to achieve better control over contract changes, Government engineers must be trained to maximize return for a given budget level, rather than to pursue engineering excellence with little regard to cost management.

The problem of contract changes is discussed at length in *The Weapons Acquisition Process*.[19] In June 1952 the Operational Engineering Section at MacDill Air Force Base included the following statements in its "Specific Item Report #52" to the Wright Air Development Center, Wright-Patterson Air Force Base, Ohio:

> Almost all Air Force agencies involved with the B-47 are recommending addition of equipment to the aircraft. Everybody feels the small weight increase desired by himself is justified and is so minor it cannot possibly affect the B-47 performance capability. However, when all these items are assembled on one list and totaled, it is apparent the aircraft's basic weight is snow-balling at an alarming rate. People are getting carried away with making this a perfect airplane that incorporates every conceivable piece of equipment desired for aircraft reliability and tactical suitability. These little items from three pounds of nine hundred pounds are rapidly adding up to an extent that the range loss being paid is measured in hundreds of miles. Also, the bombing altitude over target is becoming lower and lower with each pound added; the B-47 mission profile is not only settling down to an altitude enemy fighters enjoy, but also into a zone of accurate anti-aircraft gun fire. Instead of improving ground handling equipment and operating procedures, the tendency is to add equipment to the airplane to overcome each difficulty encountered. Instead of building runways of sufficient length to permit heavy-weight take-offs, assist equipment is installed in the aircraft. All this equipment must be carried to the target and back. Too many items are being added to take care of every possible emergency. Some of these pieces of equipment will be of aid to a pilot in possibly one flight out of every several thousand, yet all the remaining flights suffer range loss by carrying the same equipment to the target and back. The airplane is approaching the stage at which it is not only possessing an emergency system for each primary system, but in several cases, it is acquiring an emergency system. The basic weight of the B-47 is scheduled to keep on increasing with each additional block programmed for production during the next few years. We will soon have hundreds of efficient flying machines that can take off on short runways at heavy weight, dispense chaff, employ ECM, navigate with several different types of electronic and radio equipment, withstand enemy fire, communicate thousands of miles by radio, cope with almost any emergency by rise of duplicate systems, and boast every other feature developed by modern science for crew efficiency and convenience. There is one thing wrong with these B-47's—they can't fly far enough to reach the target.

More than twenty years later, contract changes continue to undermine program management efficiency.

NOTES TO CHAPTER XIX

1. In September 1863 the Navy Department awarded a contract for the construction of the ETLAH, a sister ship to the MONITOR. The contract contained a "changes" clause that was considered in *McCord v. United States*, 9 Ct. Cl. 155, affirmed subnomine, *Chouteau v. United States*, 95 U.S. 61.
2. Armed Services Procurement Regulation, Section 7-130.2.
3. Appeal of Rainier Co., Inc., ASBCA 3536, ASBCA 57-1 BCA 1231 (1957); Spector, *An Analysis of the Standard Changes Clause*, 25 Fed. B.J. 177 (1965).
4. Office of the Secretary of Defense, *Defense Industry Bulletin*, April 1967, p. 41.
5. Office of the Assistant Secretary of Defense (Comptroller), Directorate of Information Operations, *Change Orders and Letter Contracts, 1966–1970*.
6. Logistics Management Institute, Interim Report, Project 2B, *Change Management Control of Engineering and Design Changes*, January 1964.
7. James S. Reece, "The Effects of Contract Changes on the Control of a Major Defense Weapon System Program" (Boston: unpublished doctoral dissertation, Harvard Business School, 1970), p. 18.
8. Ibid., pp. 2–24.
9. For a description of the training and experience of Government program managers, see Chapter IX.
10. U.S. Army Audit Agency Headquarters, *Summary Analysis of Audit Findings—Fiscal Year 1969*, Washington, D.C., October 1969.
11. An interview with Dr. Thomas A. Cheatham, Jr., vice president of Grumman Aircraft Engineering Corporation and a former deputy director of Tactical Warfare Programs in the Department of Defense, Office of the Directorate of Defense Research and Engineering. Reported in *Electronic News*, October 9, 1967.
12. U.S. Army Audit Agency, *Summary Analysis of Audit Findings*.
13. *Bruce v. United States*, 163 Ct. Cl. 97 (1963). In *Watts Construction Co.*, ASBCA 9454, 64 BCA 4171 (1964), the Government specifically rejected the contention that the use of actual costs violated the prohibition against cost-plus-a-percentage-of-cost contracting.
14. Richard J. Lorette, "The Relationship Between the Pressures on the System Program Director and the Growth of Weapon System Cost Estimates" (Boston: unpublished doctoral dissertation, Harvard Business School, 1967), p. 421.
15. Interview with representatives from the Office of the Assistant Secretary of Defense (Installations and Logistics), 1972.
16. Comptroller General of the United States, Report to the Congress on the *Acquisition of Major Weapon Systems*, March 18, 1971, p. 61.
17. RAND Report WN7117, *A Preliminary Analysis of Contractual Outcomes for 94 Air Force Systems Command Contracts*, December 1970, p. 28.
18. Reece, op. cit., Chapter VII, p. 27.
19. Merton J. Peck and Frederic M. Scherer, *The Weapons Acquisition Process: An Economic Analysis* (Boston: Division of Research, Harvard Business School, 1962), Chapter 16.

CHAPTER XX

Program Control—Part I

An Overview

THE TERM "CONTROL" as it is used throughout this book refers to the process by which Government and industry managers maintain an effective and efficient utilization of resources as program objectives are realized.[1] Under the terms of a cost-reimbursement contract, the Defense Department retains the management responsibility for the acquisition program. The contractor assumes only slight risk. Under a fixed-price contract, management responsibility for an acquisition program is transferred to the contractor. This may change, however, if the Government actively or passively agrees to assume more management responsibility when contract changes are negotiated. In practice, Government managers need to maintain some form of control over all major development and production programs, regardless of the type of contract that is negotiated. This is increasingly true as more and more contractors fail to perform according to contract terms.

When Deputy Secretary of Defense David Packard accepted his Pentagon appointment in 1969, he strongly advocated Defense Department disengagement from industry operations and a reduction in the requirements for cost and technical performance reports from defense contractors. During his first two years in office, he was again and again confronted with the problems resulting from industry failure to fulfill contract terms. Reluctantly he concluded that the Defense Department must become involved in the management of large development and production programs. He ordered that cost-reimbursement contracts be used for major development programs and that Defense Department managers exercise increased control over aspects of program activity that contribute to cost growth and technical performance degradation. On March 19, 1971, he told the House Subcommittee on Department of Defense Appropriations:

. . . Managers must understand cost control and management systems. And contractors who accept [cost-incentive] contracts must be willing to accept detailed management by the [military] Services.

I wish I could recommend some other approach to you, because I have great faith in the competitive free enterprise system. I believe it to be generally more efficient than government control or government management. But I have reluctantly concluded that where we have complex, expensive military weapons and military systems, and where only one customer exists, the leveling actions of a free market economy simply do not work. As a former and future businessman I am prepared to tell you candidly that we might as well accept this fact and get on with the job of national defense.[2]

One reason that companies are lax in maintaining adequate control activity is that the Defense Department has been unwilling to penalize them for contract default. For most large programs, the Defense Department feels compelled to continue with the initial contractor no matter how inefficiently resources are utilized. The rationale is that most programs are too "urgent" to reassign, and that a substantial investment has already been made with the current contractor. Thus, major contracts are seldom canceled, nor are other alternatives considered for accomplishing mission objectives when a contractor does not satisfy contract specifications. In the last few years, the Government has modified fixed-price contract terms for a number of major defense programs, including the C-5A aircraft, the AH-56A Cheyenne Helicopter, the Main Battle Tank, and the F-111 aircraft. In all cases, performance specifications were relaxed. Holding the contractors to original contract specifications and/or canceling the contracts for default were not considered realistic alternatives.

The degree of Government involvement in the control of ongoing programs varies from program to program. A production program involving little or no risk, operating under a firm fixed-price contract, and requiring no contract changes, may need little or no control activity by Defense Department managers. A development program operating under a cost-reimbursement contract, or a program experiencing frequent contract changes (regardless of the type of contract), may require substantial Defense Department involvement in order to insure that the Government's best interests are protected as program decisions are made.

To control an ongoing program, managers must anticipate deviations from approved program plans and must understand the impact of contract changes on the program's budget and schedule and the weapon system's technical performance. The sooner a manager knows that a problem is developing, the wider are his options for dealing with it.

As discussed in earlier sections of this book, building a technologically sophisticated weapon system is not like producing an ordinary commercial product where past experience can be used as a standard for measuring progress. Advanced technological development programs, by their very nature, include a number of new activities. One method for identifying actual or possible problems in the areas of cost, schedule, or technical performance is to compare actual performance with planned performance, and to identify significant deviations.

The factors that cause program deviations include: (1) inadequate planning by the Defense Department or the contractor; (2) inadequate control by the contractor; or (3) technological difficulties unforeseen by the Defense Department or the contractor.

Given the limitations in contract mechanisms and the frequency of changes in major defense programs, Government control activities should be geared to the following goals:

1. Reviewing contractors' internal planning and control systems. The Government should be able to identify deviations from weapon system specifications or program plans early enough to work out solutions *other than* increasing the budget, or making arbitrary reductions in program activity or in the number of weapons to be produced.
2. Establishing limits on the number of contract changes that can be made by military or industry officials after a program has been approved by Congress and a contract negotiated.
3. Maintaining the option of canceling a contract when a contractor fails to meet contract terms.

At the present time, Defense Department managers rarely respond to cost growth by reducing contractor costs, by modifying technical approaches, or by calling for changes in the contractor's supervisory personnel. Clearly, it is not an easy matter to impose any one of these controls. Reducing costs usually means establishing more stringent work standards or removing personnel from the contractor's payroll. Changing a technical approach means challenging Defense Department and industry engineers and their supervisors, most of whom are committed to proving the value of the original approach. A change in supervisors amounts to an admission that company managers, Government plant representatives, and Government program managers have failed to detect program weaknesses early enough to correct them. In the face of these deterrents, Government and contractor personnel often continue "business as usual" when problems arise. A popular manual for defense industry managers—*A Guide to Aerospace-Defense Contracts,* by Emerson Clark[3]— reflects current practice. If a contract is behind schedule and is experiencing cost overruns, Mr. Clark advises managers to (a) extend the schedule; (b) increase the level of effort; (c) reduce weapon system requirement; and/or (d) increase funding. These recommendations all involve contract changes that will reflect actual program performance. This is exactly the reverse of normal commercial practice. When commercial development programs run into difficulty, technical goals and planned approaches are usually modified so that contract objectives can be met.

Military and industry program managers, and their superiors, use several techniques to avoid the necessity of imposing stringent program controls. They may simply fail to report problems to higher levels of the Defense Department. Their rationale is that officials at higher levels will "misunderstand the problem," or "fail to appreciate the complexity of the program," or "overreact to problems that are transitory." Since most of them do not institute corrective action themselves, problems often grow into full-scale crises. Several junior military officers assigned to program offices told us that their superiors changed data in progress reports to forestall the identification of problem areas. A management consultant who had designed and implemented a formal management information system for ten defense procurement programs reported that he no longer accepted such assignments from the Defense Department: "Time after time, I have seen program managers who discard the information in the formal management information system, and report to higher levels only what they perceive as most likely to help the program."

An industry manager told us that the military manager on his program had instructed him to report overruns only when given specific directions to do so. The Defense Department manager made it clear that *he* would control the flow of information to higher levels of the Department (an interesting perversion of the meaning of management control).

Senior Pentagon officials hold frequent progress meetings to review the critical issues affecting acquisition programs under their jurisdiction. Usually, program managers use these occasions to "sell" their programs to their Pentagon superiors. I attended one such meeting in November 1970 to discuss an acquisition program that was experiencing alarming cost growth. The program manager's presentation included a few photographs, a 15-minute movie, and a discussion of minor technical problems. His report was studded with such phrases as:

> "We have great confidence. . . ."
> "Great progress has been made. . . ."
> "Here are some of the interesting things we have been doing lately. . . ."

"We want to show you the great complexities in our program. . . ."
"It is a very important program. . . ."
"Progress in the past six months has been gratifying. . . ."

A brief portion of the meeting was devoted to a discussion of the program's funding requirements. There was no mention of cost performance or problems of cost control. Within two months, it was revealed that this program had been experiencing technical and cost problems for over a year.

CHANGES IN GOVERNMENT MANAGEMENT TECHNIQUES

During the past 15 years, the changing nature of the defense and aerospace industry, coupled with the increasing size and complexity of weapon systems, has brought about a change in traditional management techniques. Effective Government control of contractor costs was originally thought to be the result of close monitoring and detailed analysis of contractor expenses. Reporting systems were built in terms of time periods, usually months. The Office of the Secretary of Defense would "wholesale" procurement funds to the Army, Navy, and Air Force. The task of management control was to match estimated contractor billings and expenses with actual expenses as they were incurred each month, rather than to relate billings and expenses to the actual work performed. At the same time, contractors geared their efforts toward meeting technical and schedule requirements. The major task for financial managers in the Defense Department was simply to acquire funds from Congress.[4]

In the first half of the 1960s Charles Hitch, then Assistant Secretary of Defense, was engaged in implementing a new Planning, Programming, and Budgeting system. At the same time the Office of the Secretary of Defense made funds available to the military services for specific weapon system acquisition programs. This effort marked a continuation of the transition from "wholesale" to "retail" decision making within the Office of the Secretary of Defense. Budgets were approved for specific weapon systems rather than for a total procurement effort. As this change occurred, however, neither the military services nor their contractors were prepared to apply new methods of financial control. During the period of transition, the military departments designed a variety of management information systems for use in controlling major acquisition programs. Each military program manager devised his own system for describing his plans and for measuring and controlling progress. By 1965 a large number of different cost control systems had been developed. Contractors working on several programs might be required to use one cost planning and control system for Program X with the Army, another for Program Y with the Navy, and a third for Program Z with the Air Force.

Not surprisingly, there were conflicts over the use of the information generated by the new planning and control systems. Contractors were frequently confronted with information requirements from the Defense Department that were not compatible with their internal control systems. When a contractor translated his internal data to conform to Defense Department requirements, the information frequently lost credibility. In some cases, contractors' data were so inaccurate that it was impossible to relate schedule and technical progress to actual and projected costs. Some of the difficulties were caused by the translation of information from one cost reporting system to another. Further complications arose because contractors often assigned resources to functional units (e.g., engineering, manufacturing, testing) without relating these resources directly to the specific work performed by the units.

When Government program managers and procurement officers attempted to identify and solve ongoing problems, they were often hampered by invalid information. It soon became apparent to them that the most useful and valid information on program status was provided by contractors' internal planning and control systems, not by external reporting systems designed by Defense Department managers. Consequently, the Department of Defense made attempts to retrieve data from defense contractors' internal planning and control systems.

Management decisions for development and production programs are based on data pertaining to current and projected schedules, costs, and technical performance. The objective of most reporting techniques is to produce maximum program "visibility." The Defense Department attempts to keep abreast of contractor performance by requiring specific data in five areas:

1. A description of the *work accomplished* to date and the work that remains to be accomplished.

2. A description of *program schedules*—planned, actual, and projected. This includes answers to the following questions:
   a. What parts of the program are ahead of schedule, on schedule, behind schedule?
   b. For those parts of the program behind schedule, how critical is the problem? What other parts of the program depend on the completion of the work that is behind schedule? What is the cause of the problem—technical barriers, unavailability of personnel or facilities, or limitations in the qualifications of personnel assigned to the program?

    c. What can be done to correct the problem? How long will it take
       to correct the problem? What is the impact of the schedule delay
       on the program's cost and technical performance parameters?

3. A description of the program's planned, actual, and projected *funding
   status*. This includes answers to the following questions:
    a. What are the planned and actual funding levels required for the
       program, by year and by Congressional appropriation category?
       Where do variances exist between planned and actual funding
       levels? What can be done to correct these variances?
       (e.g., accelerate the program, slow down the program, reduce the
       amount of work planned for the program)
    b. What is the impact of the program's funding status on the schedule
       and technical performance requirements?

4. A description of the planned, actual, and projected *cost status* of the
   program. This includes answers to the following questions:
    a. What are the planned and actual costs for the amount of work that
       has been accomplished? Where do variances exist in these compari-
       sons? What can be done to correct these variances?
       (e.g., reduce overhead costs; improve internal standards of per-
       formance; pursue alternative technical approaches)
    b. What is the impact of the cost status of the program on the schedule
       and technical performance requirements?
    c. What is the projection of planned and actual cost performance,
       based on experience gained on the program to date?

5. A description of the planned, actual, and projected *technical performance* of the weapon system. This includes answers to the following
   questions:
    a. What problems are being experienced in the technology of the
       program?
    b. What major technical milestones have been scheduled to occur in
       the program to date? What has been the actual experience in re-
       spect to these milestones?
    c. What are the areas of high and low technical risk in the program?
       What steps can be taken to rescue the high risk areas?
    d. What is the schedule for resolution of the high risk areas of the
       program?
    e. What is the actual and projected impact of the program's technical
       problems on the schedule, costs, and funding requirements?

    Each level of Government management that oversees the acquisition
process—the program management office, the service headquarters, the Office
of the Secretary of Defense, Congress—has different requirements for program

visibility. Thoretically, each level of Government management should have access to the information gathered at other levels. In practice, however, each level of management frequently requests information solely for its own use.

Although Government managers may know that problems exist without recourse to formal reporting systems, they often do not know the full impact of these problems on costs, schedules, and technical performance. A formal information system can expose the magnitude of problems, as well as particular performance patterns. Managers can then make decisions that will affect future program performance. They may cancel work or add to the budget. They may cut out less essential parts of the program, pursue alternate approaches to upcoming program activity, change personnel, establish stricter standards for work performance, or make plans to monitor work more closely.

Higher levels of Government management depend on program visibility in order to respond to inquiries from Congress, the General Accounting Office, other governmental organizations, and the media. Above the program management level, Defense Department officials are particularly anxious to avoid "surprises." They want to be able to consider alternatives when problems arise. They do not want to learn about program decisions after the fact. Since the military program manager has the primary Government responsibility for supervising his program, he must see that optimum visibility is maintained. He receives information from three sources:

1. From routine reports prepared by the contractor, as specified in the contract or in special directives;
2. From Government plant representatives;
3. From direct contact with contractor personnel.

Subsequent chapters in this book deal with several problems that inhibit adequate measurement and control of contractor performance. The Air Force F-111 program has probably raised more questions about the effectiveness of program controls than any other acquisition program. The May 11, 1970, issue of *Barron's* magazine contained the last of a series of six articles on the program. Excerpts from the article give insights into the kind of problems that hamper performance on most major acquisition programs:

> Mr. Walsh's years of investigation deserve far more than a brief summary.* Here are his major conclusions in testimony last month before the McClellan Committee and in devastating detail:

---

* Mr. Walsh had been a staff investigator for the McClellan Senate Investigating Committee since 1963.

1. The record clearly shows that when the [F-111] R&D contract was definitized in 1964, there was strong evidence that the design of both the Air Force and Navy F-111 planes would likely fail to produce an acceptable aircraft. Aeronautical experts were giving clear warnings that performance set out in the specifications could not be met without major redesign of the airframe.

2. The performance items in the specifications were stated to be "guaranteed" but the "guarantee" was little more than window dressing. The penalties for failure to meet these "guarantees" were negligible in amount compared with the total cost of the program. Many of the "guarantees" did not call for any penalty at all. Moreover, the "guarantees" contained built-in contingencies and there was no time schedule in which they had to be met. This, for all practical purposes, resulted in the unenforceability of the "guarantees."

3. The R&D contract was written in such a way as to make termination for default for performance deficiency a practical impossibility. . . .

* * * * *

6. The Government approved first a letter contract and then a definitive contract for production quantities of F-111 airplanes without binding performance specifications. General Dynamics was authorized to manufacture planes and has, in fact, delivered 207 aircraft and has 226 planes in production. By failing to include a binding performance specification, the Government is precluded from terminating the production contract for default for performance failure.

7. The production aircraft delivered have been accepted by the Government contingent on their meeting performance specifications which will "evolve" from the R&D contract. After more than seven years of effort under the R&D contract, this "evolution" has not taken place nor can any date be set in the foreseeable future when it will take place.

8. The "evolution" requires, among other things, a detailed negotiation on thousands of engineering changes. . . .

9. Once this is done, the Government will downgrade the basic performance specifications in the contract. It then must be determined whether the hundreds of aircraft delivered meet this downgraded specification. If they do not, then the Government will have to determine on each plane the extent of and the reason for the deficiency. The Government will then attempt to negotiate an "equitable" reduction in the price. The difficulties in this process are obvious.

10. The Government now finds itself with 141 F-111's which are permanently limited in use because of the inlet and an underpowered engine. Further, all the planes delivered to date face the possibility of structural defects in the carry-through structure and the wings. The

Government may be saddled with a multimillion dollar retrofit program to make the planes delivered to date safe to fly.

11. None of the 493 production planes delivered or on order will meet the performance required in the specifications. . . . "Mission requirements," however, are undefined and will apparently be tailored to meet the actual performance of the F-111's on delivery. In any event, the "mission requirements" will be severely downgraded from that promised in 1962. For an expenditure of about $9 billion the Government will receive at best 210 usable planes with a capability greatly scaled down from the original specifications.

The incredible part, to sum up, is that the U.S. evidently has no recourse. "The actual situation," Walsh concluded, "is that General Dynamics has manufactured and delivered hundreds of production airplanes without a binding performance specification. . . . The possibility of protecting the Government's interests in such a negotiation (which has not even started yet) appears to be exceedingly remote. . . . The responsibility for this failure extends to the highest level in the Department of Defense." [5]

In 1966 Robert Charles, Assistant Secretary of the Air Force and former defense industry executive, made the following comments in a speech to the Defense Industry Advisory Council:

On one program, involving an airplane already in production, actual costs today exceed the sales proposal by 27%. On another, a new program which did not stretch the state-of-the-art, the difference is 39%. On still another, it is 41%. Now you would suppose that such excessive costs were to improve performance, or at least to correct deficiencies. Not entirely so. On one of these, various performance requirements are degraded to 43% and the average degradation for ten performance requirements is 13½%. . . .[6]

In the management of development or production programs, reports of actual and anticipated costs are submitted regularly by the contractor to the Defense Department. Unfortunately, some Government managers believe that cost control requirements are met when these reports are received. They have little idea that an effective control system must include provisions for comparing actual costs to meaningful benchmarks, as well as analyses of deviations from program plans and timely corrective actions by Government and contractor personnel.

It is clear from our interviews with contractor personnel that control problems begin when standards are not set at the level where work is performed. One senior Pentagon official told us that there is often a serious communication problem between the technical personnel and the costing personnel in the defense and aerospace business. Possibly, this problem exists because the approved schedule for a defense program places individuals responsible for production under continual pressure. They respond by accepting inadequate work from R&D personnel. A senior general in the Pentagon commented:

> The most serious mistakes in the weapons acquisition process that I have observed have not occurred in the areas of procurement or contract administration. Rather, they have simply been mistakes made by engineers in Government and industry. In the face of these mistakes, there is continuing pressure by the users to accept a product that is less than satisfactory. Examples of this situation are the F-111 program, the Main Battle Tank, the C-5A, the TACFIRE program, the Kinetic Energy Round, and the Cheyenne Helicopter.

During our interviews, a number of additional control problems were identified. One Pentagon official pointed out that Defense Department program managers usually have no control over contractors' overhead costs. These are generated on a division-wide or company-wide basis, collected in pools, and allocated to specific products or contracts. The Government program manager pays attention to direct costs, on the assumption that his control can be most effective in this area. Direct costs, however, may constitute less than 50% of a program's total costs.

To most Government personnel, financial management consists of controlling the rate of the obligation of funds by periods of time. They are encouraged in this view because Congress appropriates funds on a yearly basis rather than by total programs, and because it is easier to control expenditures by time periods (e.g., months, quarters) than by a unit of work. In our interviews with Government program personnel, we observed that in most program offices, financial management consists of two activities:

1. Preparing budget estimates for annual periods and for Congressional appropriation categories;
2. Monitoring the time-phased spending plan in terms of obligations, commitments, and expenditures of funds.

A contractor is seldom authorized to spend the full amount specified in a contract. He is first authorized to spend only a relatively small part of the total budget. Then, from time to time, funding is incrementally increased. Since few Government management personnel have been trained to correlate contractor costs with specific work performed, they manage costs by limiting the amount of funds that can actually be spent in a particular time period.

Actual program costs often exceed estimates because the negotiated contract price is not subdivided according to work performed. On three of the programs we studied, we found that the sum of budgets prepared by functional units within the defense firm exceeded the total contract price. This situation was not uncommon. A contractor's bid is often based on one form of program definition (e.g., a description of the total weapon system), while the contractor's internal budgeting may be based on different definitions (e.g., functional definitions, such as electrical engineering, mechanical engineering, tooling, manufacturing). When the various functional groups assign costs to their work, the budget may not equal the estimate prepared for the total cost of the program. Cost estimates prepared on the highest company levels are not effectively transmitted to the functional units within the company. This may explain why incentive contracts fail. The vice president of a major defense firm commented: "Our factory workers on the floor simply don't know what kind of a contract they are working on."

A number of additional control problems were cited by the General Accounting Office in its report entitled *The Feasibility of Applying Uniform Cost Accounting Standards to Negotiated Defense Contracts.*[7]

> The basic problem as we see it, on the basis of the cases we reviewed, is one of inconsistency by contractors in the assignment of Government contract costs. We believe that, to assist in overcoming this difficulty, a standard of consistency is needed in cost accounting practices as they relate to Government contracts. . . .
>
> Contractors sometimes charge indirectly costs which should be charged directly, because the costs are specifically identifiable with either Government or commercial work. Conversely, costs are sometimes charged directly even though no specific identification to a cost objective exists. . . .
>
> In some cases, costs normally handled as direct charges were handled as indirect charges because they would not be acceptable as direct charges due to ceilings or other limitations on charges to the contracts to which they were directly related. By handling these costs as indirect costs, they were charged, in part, indirectly to the contractors' other business, including other Government contracts. . . .
>
> A. Indirect Costs Charged Directly
>
> . . . . .
>
> 1. A Government firm fixed-price subcontractor proposal included as direct costs, salaries and related expenses of the project manager, quality control engineer, financial manager, etc., totaling $150,000, which the contractor normally charges to overhead. Indirect costs of leasing quarters and expenses related to new hire, such as agency fees, moving expenses,

etc., amounting to $41,000, were similarly proposed as direct costs. The contractor did not adjust the overhead rate for similar costs included therein.

. . . . .

7. In its proposal to definitize two letter contracts, the contractor treated temporary duty costs (labor, related fringe benefits, and travel and living expenses) totaling $504,000 as "other direct costs." The contractor's normal accounting treatment is to include the labor portion of such costs as direct labor and to charge the remaining costs to overhead.

. . . . .

11. The contractor included in its proposed direct labor hours, normally indirect functions such as production support, packaging, shipping, shipping inspection, and test acceptance. The proposed overhead rate was not adjusted. Accordingly, the proposing of these functions as direct charges would result in the contractor's duplicate recovery of the costs involved.

. . . . .

15. The contractor duplicated overtime premiums of $18,000 by treating them as part of its proposed direct manufacturing labor. Consistent with the contractor's policy, however, such premiums were also charged to overhead.

. . . . .

23. The contractor charged most of its product engineering expenses to overhead and then allocated them among Government and commercial contracts on the basis of the estimated costs of production. In some cases, however, product engineering costs were charged directly to the Government while at the same time these contracts also apparently absorbed their proportionate share of such costs through overhead.

. . . . .

B. Direct Costs Charged Indirectly

. . . . .

4. The contractor departed from its normal practices or changed its procedures. As a result, travel costs of $390,000 were charged to overhead which should have been charged directly to fixed-price contracts. This resulted in excess costs being allocated to Government cost-type contracts.

5. The contractor had a $60 million research and development contract calling for cost-sharing on a 75/25 basis. This contract was to form the basis for a follow-on contract for a prototype program. The contractor, however, had overrun the contract amount by $1 million and failed in its bid to secure the follow-on contract. Direct labor costs aggregating to $381,000 of normally direct personnel were charged to overhead. The contractor also charged to overhead $911,000 of labor costs of normally indirect personnel who worked directly on the contract on the premise

that the treatment was proper since the personnel usually performed indirect functions. The costs, however, were properly chargeable to the contract in question because the contractor's policy contemplated charging these costs directly under the particular circumstances of the research and development contract.

6. The contractor included premiums for product liability insurance in a pool of G&A expenses which were apportioned among Government and commercial work on the basis of the costs of production and development. Actual premium costs and rates (which were much lower for Government as opposed to commercial work) were readily identifiable and the premiums should thus have been directly charged. The method employed by the contractor resulted in a $2.2 million overcharge to the Government over a seven-year period. The overcharge was not recoverable by the Government. . . .

A contractor with preponderantly commercial business had completely changed the method of indirect cost allocation for the purpose of a Government firm fixed-price contract proposal. The contractor's manufacturing overhead rate is normally developed on a plant-wide basis only and the books are kept accordingly. In its proposal, however, the contractor had developed an overhead rate for each of the plant's 15 product lines. The amount of indirect costs proposed was about $130,000 higher than that computed on the basis of the contractor's consistent basis of allocation. It is also significant that the contractor stated that it had no intention of changing its accounting system to record costs by product lines. . . .

The contractor had eight plants in one metropolitan area with varying levels of Government work. Instead of using individual plant rates for use and occupancy expenses (e.g., depreciation, real estate taxes, maintenance), the contractor lumped all expenses and used an average rate for all plants, based on square footage. This resulted in charging the Government $146,250 more in one year than had individual rates for each plant been used. The principal reason for the overcharge was that one plant with about 83% Government business was a rent-free Government-owned facility, and thus did not have any applicable depreciation, real estate taxes, and similar expenses chargeable to its operations. By commingling the dissimilar costs of the eight plants, this one particular plant absorbed a disproportionately high share of the total use and occupancy expenses of all eight plants. . . .

A survey of 20 contractors on the East Coast disclosed variances in the capitalization policies of these contractors, the low dollar value limit for capitalizing ranging from $0 to $1,000, with 18 contractors at $250 or less. One problem is the expensing of quantity purchases of low value assets. At one plant with a $200 minimum capitalization policy, about $3.3 million in low value items were expensed in two years. Our tests showed that roughly two-thirds of the low-cost items expensed were for

Arming America: How the U.S. Buys Weapons

purchases in quantity. The variation in practices, and the substantial values involved, indicate a need for consideration of capitalization policies in the formulation of cost standards.

A similar need was observed in a survey conducted of four West Coast contractors (with virtually 100% Government sales) which showed minimum capitalization policies ranging from $100 to $500. Differences in depreciating capital assets were also noted including, for similar classes of assets, the use of different useful lives and depreciation methods. The expensing of large quantity buys of low value assets was also noted. . . .

In 1962 Peck and Scherer concluded that lack of timely decision making appeared to be a contributing cause to inadequate program controls.

Rapid progress through the many steps of a development program depends upon timely decision making. Decision making takes on particular importance if one accepts the hypothesis that scientists and engineers would tend to continue exploring interesting technical problems indefinitely were it not for management's decisions to stop searching for better answers and to begin finalizing hardware designs. But good project management, like knowledge, is often an imperfectly expandable commodity. Adding to a project more and more people and technical approaches could conceivably increase the time required for management to render decisions. This is so for at least three reasons: (1) It becomes increasingly difficult to ensure that peripheral projects do not divert attention from the really important problems. (2) With more people and more technical approaches, there are more different points of view to weigh in making decisions. This demands either more management time per decision or less careful consideration of each single alternative. (3) Project management may be required to spend an undue amount of time on personnel administration at the expense of technical direction and decision making. As a result, there may very well be a tendency for development time to increase with the amount of resources employed.[8]

In 1970 the problem of delayed decision making remained a problem in defense procurement. According to the Blue Ribbon Panel:

. . . Typically, for major weapons systems, the head of this project office or program manager reports to the Deputy Commander for Systems Management of the procuring command, some five or six levels below that of the Secretary of the Military Services. . . .

In vertical organizations, the management system maze and the extensive reporting requirements often result in an excessively large staff for the program manager. A Program Management Office on a major system can include more than 200 people, adding significantly to the overall management cost of the project.[9]

One year later the General Accounting Office made its own study. That report included the following:

One of the most troublesome features of the present program management structure is difficulty in obtaining decisions. It seems to us that the most likely cause of this problem is that decision-making layering is not commensurate with organizational layering. In general, the military services have not deemed it wise to place the project manager high in the organization because of some practical considerations, such as the large number of project managers and the need for them to work directly at lower levels of the organizations. However, the effect has been to preserve levels of review authority which do not have clear roles in the process of formulating decisions.

Most of the decisions that the project manager does not make himself are made at the highest levels of the service or by OSD. Between the project manager and top management are a large group of organizational units whose commanders attempt to keep themselves informed about a particular weapon system and study and deliberate on pending programs to recommend some course of action. As a rule, they have no direct approval powers. They can delay or stop a project but cannot make decisions to proceed, change direction, provide money, or take other positive action.

Military service organization charts frequently do not show the many subdivisions that become involved or the special *ad hoc* panels and committees which inevitably arise in the weapon system acquisition process. All these organizational units, panels, and committees impact heavily on the project manager. His program may be delayed or stopped while matters are being studied or while decisions are being made, or his program may proceed without timely decisions.

In the Army, for instance, any significant decision that the project manager cannot make usually is made at the highest levels of the Department or in OSD. With respect to these decisions, the primary role of the project manager is to make recommendations or to work with other groups that make recommendations. Recommendations go through the normal chain of command, to the Commanding General of the Commodity Command, to the Commanding General of the Army Materiel Command (AMC), to the Army staff. To formulate recommendations, though, it is necessary to coordinate a number of functional groups. These include functional groups within the project managers' organizations (i.e., the Commodity Command) as well as organizations outside the Command, such as Conarc and the Combat Development Command. The essential task of these groups is to help formulate a recommendation, but their decision-making function is limited to agreeing or disagreeing with it. Once the recommendation is made, there are a number of functional groups at the AMC and Army headquarters staff levels (about a dozen at Headquarters staff alone) who can influence the decision. The contribution of all these groups is much the same. They can either agree or disagree with the recommendation made.

The inevitable result of this process is the scheduling of repetitive meetings, briefings, and studies in an attempt to reach agreement on the recommendation to be made. Supplying information to numerous groups can be almost a full-time job for the project manager. During 1969, one project manager spent about two-thirds of his time conducting 166 briefings and from January to August 1970 participated in 62 additional briefings. From January 1969 through July 1970, another project manager participated in 124 briefings. Many of the briefings involved levels below the top Headquarters staff, but the most important function of those participating was to recommend.

In another instance of extensive layering, several reviews of a program were conducted between September 1969 and April 1970, including an in-depth review by several boards and committees at all levels. Of particular importance was the requirement that briefings for decision-making groups be previewed as many as 20 to 30 times before presentation to an action-taking body. The project manager spent a large part of his time participating in these reviews.[10]

Despite the many problems of program control, hundreds of reports are submitted by contractors to the Defense Department during the course of a major development or production program. A study group from the Office of the Secretary of Defense reported in 1970 that the Defense Department was spending between $225 and $450 million for data and management systems. The study included a detailed examination of three major defense programs. On a $33 million contract, the cost of submitting data to the Government was priced by the contractor at $1.3 million. On a second, $143 million, contract, the cost of data submitted by the contractor to the Government was $3.4 million. On a third contract, for $388 million, the cost of data was $4.6 million. The study group found that the majority of data submitted to the Government program office was prepared in response to instructions and regulations from offices at higher levels in the Pentagon. Much of the information was never used by Government program office personnel. Either the data were not needed, or program management personnel did not understand how to use the information.

To examine specific data requirements, we interviewed ten contractors.

We found that more than 80% of the information required by the Defense Department was technical engineering data. In all cases, substantially less than 20% of the data pertained to financial information. In one typical defense company, we found that the following reports satisfied the bulk of reporting requirements:

Monthly
- A quality assurance report (300 pages)
- A functional-hour report (23 pages)
- An Engineering Accomplishment Report (150 pages)
- A Preliminary Maintenance Allocation Report (55 pages)

Quarterly
- A list of special tools and equipment (100 pages)
- A configuration status tape (300 pages)
- An engineering data list (70 pages)

In 1970 the Office of the Secretary of Defense directed a major effort to reduce the data requirements placed on contractors. A major part of this effort involved a review of Defense Department directives. By the end of the year 1,200 defense directives had been analyzed and 35% had been deleted. Another 35% were being revised because of obsolete requirements. Most defense officials admit, however, that much remains to be done to reduce unnecessary data requirements.

To make change meaningful, military and civilian personnel assigned to program offices must be trained how to use the data prepared by contractors to make their own analyses, as the basis of informed decision making. Both military and industry managers must improve the quality of control efforts. Without appropriate controls, managers will continue to miss schedule, cost, and performance objectives.

One industry manager described his management technique:

> Design engineers will fiddle and tinker forever. If you let them alone, you are guaranteed to have schedule slippages and cost problems. Nothing will come out of the end of the pipe unless you push it out.
>
> One technique that works for me when I see them at the fiddling stage—making things a little better and not worrying about the schedule—is to shove an absolute deadline on them and tell them that we will just have to go with what is available then. As a matter of fact, it is often surprising how much they squeeze out of the last few weeks. They just don't like the idea of your going with less than the best.

In testimony before the Senate Armed Services Committee, Admiral Hyman Rickover talked of the same problem:

There ought to be a "chopper-off-er" in every research and development organization who chops off complete developments or parts of them.[11]

In the next three chapters some of the basic inconsistencies in the present control systems and incentive systems will be described.

NOTES TO CHAPTER XX

1. Robert N. Anthony, *Planning and Control Systems: A Framework for Analysis* (Boston: Division of Research, Harvard Business School, 1965), p. 17.
2. Statement of Deputy Secretary of Defense David Packard before the U.S. House of Representatives Subcommittee on Department of Defense Appropriations on *Selected Aspects of the Fiscal Year 1972–1976 Defense Program*, April 19, 1971.
3. Emerson Clark, *A Guide to Aerospace-Defense Contracts* (New York: Industrial Press, 1970), p. 104.
4. This interpretation of "control" is described at length in Merton J. Peck and Frederic M. Scherer, *The Weapons Acquisition Process: An Economic Analysis* (Boston: Division of Research, Harvard Business School, 1962).
5. "Incredible Contract: General Dynamic's Gain Is the Nation's Loss," *Barron's*, May 11, 1970.
6. Address by the Honorable Robert Charles to the Defense Industry Advisory Council, Washington, D.C., February 18, 1966.
7. Comptroller General of the United States, Report to the Congress on *The Feasibility of Applying Uniform Cost Accounting Standards to Negotiated Defense Contracts*, January 1970.
8. Peck and Scherer, op. cit., pp. 263–264.
9. Report by the Blue Ribbon Panel to the President and the Secretary of Defense on the Department of Defense, July 1, 1970.
10. Comptroller General of the United States, Report to the Congress on *The Acquisition of Major Weapons Systems*, March 18, 1971, pp. 52–53.
11. U.S. Senate, Hearings before the Preparedness Investigating Subcommittee of the Committee on Armed Services, *Inquiry into Satellite and Missile Programs*, Part 2, 1958, p. 1435.

CHAPTER **XXI**

Program Control—Part II

Measuring the Defense Contractor's Performance

IN 1960 THE NAVY'S POLARIS program management office was in the process of developing a management information system that could be used to measure contractor performance throughout the course of the program. Senior Government managers recognized that contractor cost reports usually provided little or no warning of cost problems. Therefore, they were frequently unaware of cost growth until long after problems occurred. They believed that no existing reporting systems could solve the problem, since preliminary investigations had revealed that their contractors did not have adequate information on planned-versus-actual cost of work.

PERT COST SYSTEM

During 1961 and 1962 I served as project manager for the design and pilot testing of a Polaris management information system, subsequently to be called the PERT COST system. The PERT COST design team first studied the planning, control, and reporting systems used by 40 defense and aerospace firms under contract for acquisition programs with the Army, Navy, Air Force, and NASA. The study enabled the team to assess the strengths and weaknesses of existing planning and control systems. We learned three basic facts about records kept by defense contractors.

1. Most contractors did not maintain records for the planned, or budgeted, value of work performed. (This type of report was routine for commercial programs.)
2. Contractors usually kept one set of internal cost records and another

set for use in preparing financial reports for the Defense Department. These two sets of reports frequently gave significantly different pictures of current program status.

3. Contractors were able to provide records of planned-versus-actual costs of work performed if the Defense Department required them to do so.

In several programs studied, defense contractors expressed more interest in future sales, and in the Government's contribution to their overhead, than in the amount of profit derived from the current contract. This was easy to understand, since profit as a percentage of sales frequently amounted to 6% or less, whereas Government contributions to contractor overhead frequently approached 50% of the total cost of a program.

The PERT COST team began the initial design and pilot test of the new cost information system at the Lockheed Missiles and Space Company at Sunnyvale, California, and the General Electric Ordnance Department in Pittsfield, Massachusetts. The team learned that it was impractical for contractors to budget and report costs by PERT network activities. Since the purpose of a PERT network was to identify significant relationships among all the work elements in a program, it could not readily be used to identify work units specifically relevant to cost planning and control. On the other hand, if a PERT network were to focus solely on cost planning and control, it would not be useful in determining schedule planning and control.

It became clear from the PERT COST pilot tests that cost planning and control could be based on a system that was used on most large commercial development and production programs. This cost information system could be based on a work breakdown structure that subdivided the program according to the manner in which work responsibility was assigned. Program work was traced down through several levels of work definition to the point where short-term work packages could be identified as the basis for planning and controlling manpower. Budgets were then established for each short-term work package. Costs were estimated at every level of the work breakdown structure, to arrive at a total cost estimate for the program. As a contractor began a development program, actual manhours and costs were assigned to the work packages. As work was completed in the development program, the contractor could compare estimates of cost for short-term work packages with the actual manhours and costs required to accomplish the work. Thus, the contractor could keep a constant check on whether work was costing more or less than was estimated.

In preparing a description of PERT COST for the Polaris program and, subsequently, for the *DOD and NASA PERT COST Guide,* the design group intended to make clear that the work breakdown structure, not the network, was the basis for cost planning and control. In retrospect, this distinction was far from clear. Confusion arose because many defense contractors, as well as other Governmental agencies (e.g., the Army, Air Force, and NASA), were developing their own versions of PERT COST. Several of these versions called for the use of PERT networks in the budgeting and reporting of costs by network activities, a requirement that resulted in the collection of vast amounts of very detailed cost information.

EARNED VALUE SYSTEM

In 1963 the Air Force Minuteman Missile program office, in conjunction with a group that later became known as Performance Technology Corporation (PTC), initiated a project to design a contractor performance measurement system. This team built on the lessons learned by the Polaris PERT COST group. The Minuteman Contractor Performance Measurement System employed the work-package concept of PERT COST with several improvements and was labeled the "Earned Value" system.

By 1964 more than ten variations of PERT COST existed throughout the Defense Department and NASA, most of which called for separate costing of PERT network activities and the submission of detailed cost information on a monthly basis. Contractors recognized the impracticality of these systems and created their own PERT COST groups to prepare reports for the Defense Department. These groups operated separately from management teams responsible for actual planning, scheduling, budgeting, and program performance measurement. Government auditors decided that PERT COST groups were a legitimate overhead expense that could be charged to the Government. Many contractors considered PERT COST a "make work" operation. Some used PERT COST as the basis for negotiating higher overhead rates and were then able to produce a larger base for profit negotiations.

Since there was so much confusion over PERT COST throughout the defense industry in 1964, the Office of the Secretary of the Air Force defined a simplified standard by which to measure a contractor's internal cost management system before the company could qualify for defense work. The specifications contained the essential elements of the PERT COST and Earned Value systems, but did not include detailed reporting of cost information from PERT networks.

During 1964 and 1965, the Air Force Systems Command engaged a management consulting firm (McKinsey & Co.) to develop and pilot test the "Specification Approach" to contractor cost planning and control, as part of a larger management information system project. The efforts by McKinsey & Co. and Air Force personnel achieved some success, and resulted in an improved specification and implementation manual for contractor performance measurement, incorporating the most effective points of the PERT COST and Earned Value systems.

Throughout this period, the Minuteman Program continued to extend and improve its Earned Value system. One of its major contributions was the recognition that a realistic appraisal of a contractor's cost performance measurement system must include a detailed study of the contractor's internal reporting system. Thus, the concept of "systems demonstration" was adopted, a concept calling for the examination and validation of a contractor's internal planning and control systems.

COST CONTROL VERSUS FUNDS CONTROL

During the development of the PERT COST and Earned Value systems, the design teams noted that Government program managers were repeatedly faced with four questions about the financial status of their programs:

1. Are sufficient funds available for the program work scheduled during the next few months, and does the budget in the five-year defense plan contain the funds required for the entire program?
2. Are funds being obligated at the budgeted rate, by months and quarters?
3. Is progress being achieved at a cost higher, or lower, than budgeted?
4. Are the present and projected deviations from the program plan identified soon enough to consider alternatives other than providing additional funds or making major reductions in the size of the program?

The first two questions pertain to funds control; the remaining two, to cost control.

Since programs are authorized and funds appropriated annually, Government program managers had developed a unique series of funds-control techniques during the 1950s. In brief, the managers required monthly financial reports from contractors, continuing a comparison of budgeted-versus-actual rate of obligation and expenditure. The traditional funds-control display was a chart (Figure XXI-1) showing budgeted and actual cumulative obligations or expenditures, by month. In most cases, military program managers prepared one chart for the total program and one for each contractor working on the program. Some military program managers required their contractors to sub-

FIGURE XXI-1. MILESTONE CHART AND EXPENDITURE CURVE—1

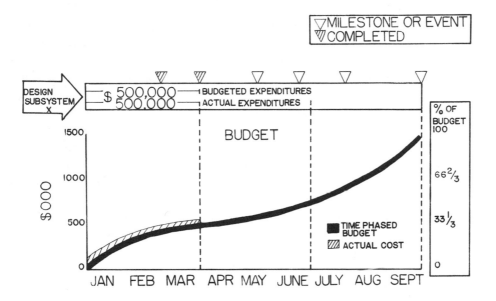

mit this type of chart for each functional category (e.g., electrical engineering, mechanical engineering, manufacturing, testing).

While the program manager's attention to funding is essential, this represents only a small part of his financial management responsibilities. The difference between funds control and cost control is significant. For funds control, reports and activity are geared toward spending funds at a rate no faster or slower than budgeted. Cost control, on the other hand, relates funds flow to work. It requires an analysis of the planned and actual cost of work performed, to ascertain whether progress is being achieved at a cost higher or lower than planned. Program managers obtain funds-control information by comparing program milestone charts to charts showing planned-versus-actual expenditures, by month. This information is supplemented with engineering estimates of "percentage of the total work completed" to date. In some cases, program managers also attempt to answer cost-control questions by correlating schedule performance (derived from a PERT network) with the funds-control report. If a program is using funds at the planned monthly rate, and the PERT network shows no significant schedule slippage, most program managers believe that work is proceeding in a satisfactory manner.

Such a belief may or may not be well founded. A program may be on schedule according to a PERT network analysis, yet be substantially behind schedule in terms of the total work to be accomplished, if noncritical path work has been scheduled but not performed. In such a situation, programs may be building in significant cost overruns that may not be identified until late in the program, when few options are available to the program manager. An illustration will clarify this problem. Figure XXI-1, in simplified terms, depicts a program that will last for nine months. It will require a total expenditure of $1,500,000. Six "milestones" will be achieved. The Government program manager seeks to correlate cost with progress by comparing the budgeted and actual rate of expenditure with the planned-versus-actual accomplishment of milestones. The chart shows that at the end of the first three months, $500,000 has been spent, as budgeted. Two major milestones have been accomplished on schedule. The program manager is satisfied that funds are not being spent any faster or slower than budgeted. He may even assume that work is being accomplished according to plan, since money is being spent at the planned monthly rate.

An examination of the work actually performed, however, reveals that the work does not match the flow of funds, in terms of budget plans. Significant cost overruns are actually being incurred, without the knowledge of the military program manager. To observe how this happens, examine Figure XXI-2.

The figure shows that four tasks are involved in the design of subsystem X

FIGURE XXI-2. MILESTONE CHART AND EXPENDITURE CURVE—2

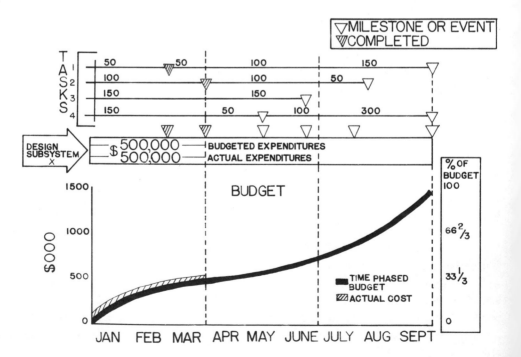

and gives their budgets. For the first task, $50,000 was budgeted to accomplish the first milestone, and $50,000 was budgeted for the work remaining beyond the milestone in the first three-month period. For the second task, $100,000 was budgeted to accomplish the three months of work leading to the first milestone. For both the third and the fourth tasks, $150,000 was budgeted for work accomplished during the first three months, but no milestones were scheduled during that time.

FIGURE XXI-3. MILESTONE CHART AND EXPENDITURE CURVE—3

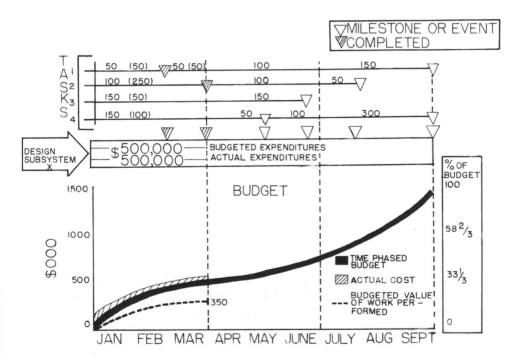

Figure XXI-3 shows how resources were actually applied to the program. For the first task, $50,000 was spent for the first milestone, as budgeted, and $50,000 was spent, as budgeted, during the remainder of the first quarter. For the second task, however, problems were encountered. To accomplish the first milestone on schedule, $250,000 was spent, rather than the budgeted $100,-000. To solve the problems encountered in the second task, manpower was applied that had been planned for the third and fourth tasks. This meant that only $50,000 was used for the third task, and only $100,000 for the fourth task—rather than the $150,000 planned for each of these tasks.

In total, then, $50,000 was spent during the first three months, as planned, despite the changes in the application of funds. But the *budgeted value* of the total work performed was only $350,000. (Although the second task actually cost $250,000, its *budgeted value* was only $100,000.)

Other changes in the application of resources may occur during the second quarter and still go undetected if the program manager is only correlating milestones with the rate-of-expenditure curve. At the end of the second quarter, a total of $1,000,000 will be spent, as budgeted, and the milestones will have been achieved. If the military program manager is not aware of the *budgeted value* of the work actually performed, however, he will not be aware of significant deviations from the budget during the first half of the program. He may not learn that additional funds are needed to complete the program until long after the problems have occurred. Only when the program is in the midst of its third quarter will it become clear that there are not enough funds available to complete the required work. By this time resources can no longer be shifted among the tasks. The program manager will probably have no alternative except to seek additional funds, or to make arbitrary reductions in the work to be performed in the last part of the program.

The military program manager could have learned of the "$150,000 problem" that occurred during the first quarter if one additional piece of information had been provided in the contractor's financial report; namely, a summary of the *budgeted value of work performed*. Had this information been available, the manager would have seen that although $500,000 had been spent as planned, the budgeted value of the work performed was only $350,000. In other words, work valued at $150,000 was yet to be accomplished, although the money to pay for it had already been spent.

This illustrates a problem that continually confronts military program managers on large development programs. For the sake of simplicity, the program depicted in Figures XXI-1, 2, and 3 lasted for only nine months, and required only $1.5 million in funds. On such a small program, it is quite possible that the program manager could have identified the problems and their impact on the program budget without a formal reporting system. On larger programs, involving hundreds or thousands of concurrent tasks over a much longer period of time, it is impossible for a program manager to identify problems and their impact on the budget without the help of a formal cost reporting system.

Unexpected cost growth occurs on many defense programs. It is obvious that Government managers on large complex programs find it difficult, or impossible, to make reasonable informal estimates of the percentage of work completed, or the budgeted value of work performed. Inevitably, some parts of the program have been accomplished ahead of schedule, some behind schedule, and some on schedule. In such a situation, the Government manager is usually unable to appraise the net cost effect on the program of any of these occurrences.

The basic information needed to identify the budgeted value of work performed is available at the functional working level in the contractor's plant. On commercial development programs, this information is collected and summarized at the functional working level for the benefit of higher levels of management. On most defense programs, however, contractors have not been required to collect or summarize this information for Government managers. Therefore the information usually remains in the contractor's plant at the working level as unsummarized data.

No changes are necessary in a contractor's accounting system to enable a firm to collect and summarize the budgeted value of work performed. A change in the firm's budgeting system may be necessary, however, if the firm does not already prepare budgets for tasks to be performed at the working level, and if budget summaries are not prepared periodically as work is performed.

Most Government program managers have not been trained to understand the concept of "budgeted value of work performed," nor the need to collect and use this information. And this lack of training is not limited to Government program managers. Although defense industry program managers usually have had extensive technical training and experience, they have often had little or no commercial business experience. As a result, they often have little or no greater skill in the collection and use of cost performance information than their military counterparts.

Several defense industry program managers told us that they were unfamiliar with the concepts of "earned value" and "budgeted value of work performed." One industry manager told us: "I have a simple way of determining whether the program is proceeding as planned. I review the rate of spending funds on the program and I correlate the rate-of-expenditure curve with a set of milestones."

More than 85% of the Government program managers in our sample did not use a formal system to identify the budgeted value of work performed on their programs. Approximately one-third of them indicated that this task was the responsibility of the Government plant representatives. At the same time, however, none of the Government plant representatives in the more than 20 defense plants we visited included this responsibility in their job descriptions.

The term "cost performance measurement" or "contractor cost performance measurement," is often misunderstood by Government program management personnel. The term is often used to represent no more than an appraisal of whether funds are being spent too fast or too slowly during specific time periods. For example, three defense buying commands used formal cost performance indicators for each major program, described as follows:

COST PERFORMANCE

1st SYMBOL SERIES

O = ON SCHEDULE—The planned-versus-actual rate of total costs is within rea-
    sonable tolerance.
− = OVERRUN POSSIBILITY—The actual costs have exceeded the planned *rate*.
    [italics added]

2nd SYMBOL SERIES

X = Additional funds are being requested *for this fiscal year*. [italics added]
R = Excess of funds *for this fiscal year* is forecast. [italics added]

As shown by these reporting symbols, the major, and often the exclusive,
emphasis in financial reporting is the determination of whether funds are being
used at a reasonable rate for specific time periods, and whether additional
funds will be needed during the fiscal year.

Colonel Albert W. Buesking (USAF, Ret.) was the individual responsible
for financial management on the billion dollar Air Force Minuteman Missile
program during the mid-1960s. In 1968 he made the following comments
before the U.S. Congress Joint Economic Committee:

> After apportionment of funds to the military departments, the financial
> management task was primarily one of matching funds against contractor
> expenditures rather than relating requirements to work content and
> progress. Even though major programs and contracts ran over extended
> periods of time, management attention focused primarily on the costs
> associated with the specific fiscal year involved and the funds required to
> cover expenditures. In turn, under cost-plus contracting and schedule
> urgency, contractors viewed their performance responsibility as meeting
> technical and schedule requirements. Their financial management task
> was primarily to secure contract financing rather than control of costs.[1]

The deficiencies in program management cited above, coupled with the
absence of the competitive pricing forces of the free market place, foster practices rarely tolerated in commercial activities. For example, in our review of
major defense programs, we frequently observed that retroactive changes were
made in programs' financial plans. That is, the financial plan for work performed to date was changed retroactively throughout the course of a program
to conform to actual experience. This practice effectively prevents identification of cost problems at the time when corrective actions can still be taken.

In a review of management control practices in ten major defense contractor plants, a team of Pentagon analysts noted this problem in a report entitled "Capricious Changing of Plans":

This problem has been common enough to acquire the esoteric but descriptive label, "the rubber baseline." Translated, this means that contractor managers would periodically make retroactive adjustments to cost estimates and schedules so that plans would equal actuals. A variation of this practice was to denude distant future budgets to provide "get well" budgets for the immediate future. Both these practices, with many variations and combinations, tend to obscure true program status. Obscuring overruns in this fashion contributed to our being caught short on funding for two major programs last fiscal year.

In an interview with the financial manager from one large plant, we learned that the contractor's internal budgets were developed by allocating all unassigned personnel to the program, rather than by estimating the effort required for an individual task or set of tasks.

The Government doesn't seem to realize that we don't build up the task to come up with the total planned value of work accomplished. Rather, we start with a level of personnel on the payroll, and fill in whatever work packages we have actually accomplished.

Several contractors in our sample employ a practice still acceptable to the Department of Defense: they maintain two sets of cost records. One set of records is maintained at a summary level in terms of dollars, subject to Government audit. The other set is maintained in manhours and material dollars, usually at the level of first-line managers. These records are rarely reviewed by Government audit. Frequently, these two sets of records portray widely divergent program status. A Department of Defense Instruction, now being implemented on major acquisition programs, is intended to prohibit this practice.

Another management problem results from contractor use of nonintegrated work breakdown structures and nonintegrated charts of cost accounts. In these situations, the sum total of budget dollars on one level of the work breakdown structure may exceed the dollars assigned to the summary item at the next higher level. This means that substantial cost overruns can be built into programs from the beginning, without the knowledge of the Government program manager and, at times, even without the knowledge of the industry program manager. On one missile program we found that contractor internal budgets for work performed had not been summarized for comparison with the contract value. On a large development program, a summary of the contractor's internal budgets for work planned exceeded the amount budgeted by the Government by $100 million. On a major aircraft program, the contractor's internal budgets exceeded the contract value by more than $50 million. On a major radar program, the contractor's budgets had not been summarized for comparison with the contract value. The Government plant representative readily admitted that he did not know whether the work planned and budgeted exceeded the contract value.

We observed that some defense contractors did not develop or maintain plans or budgets for specific short-term work packages at the working level in their plants. The practice of budgeting for long-term work packages (a year or more) encourages optimism in predicting the amount of work to be accomplished. Without budgets for short-term work packages and summarized information on the budgeted value of work completed, Government program managers must often rely on informal estimates of "percentage of program completed." These are supplied by contractors as an indicator of whether work is being accomplished for the planned cost. Unfortunately, the industry managers who prepare the estimates of percentage of program completed often do not have information on the budgeted value of work completed. Their estimates of percentage of work completed are usually determined by dividing the amount spent on the program to date by the total contract price. The resulting figure is of little or no use for purposes of identifying any significant deviations from plan. We met with one contractor who had even prepared a computer program to calculate percentage of program completed, for Government reports, in the manner described above.

Even when industry managers totally familiar with a program prepare estimates of the percentage of work completed, they tend to be optimistic about their own performance. The fact that estimates of percentage of work completed are often reported to higher levels of management for purposes of program appraisal understandably influences managers to present favorable data. Managers want as much time as possible to work out their own problems without inquiries and "interference" from higher levels of management.

CONTRACTOR PERFORMANCE MEASUREMENT PROGRAM

In order to correct the problems described above, the Department of Defense initiated a two-part Contractor Performance Measurement program:

> Part One of the program requires that contractors use internal planning and control systems that meet minimum Government criteria. These criteria are called the "Cost and Schedule Control System Criteria" (CSCSC).
>
> Part Two of the program requires that contractors regularly submit

Cost Performance Reports which contain information on the budgeted value of work performed to date. (The criteria themselves do not require the submission of any reports to the Government, but specify the reporting capabilities which contractors' internal systems must have, and the types of data which the systems should be able to produce.) The contractor is free to design his internal planning and control systems to correspond to the manner in which he organizes his work units and assigns responsibility for performing work.

The monthly Cost Performance Report required from contractors on major programs need include no more than from 3 to 10 pages of cost information. Only summary level cost information is required from a contractor as long as the program is proceeding according to plan. When deviations from plan occur, the contractor's system must be able to provide information on the problem areas and their impact on program costs.

The performance measurement program can be abused by any contractor who decides to change information in the Cost Performance Report before it is submitted to the Defense Department. But the new Department requirement for performance measurement at least makes clear that such an act is a violation of the contract agreement. In the past, there has been no requirement that contractors' cost reports be a direct summary of the budgets for work actually performed.

The Government's criteria for defense companies' internal planning and control systems are summarized below.

Contractor planning and control systems for budgeting, scheduling, and authorizing work, and for accumulating costs, must be constructed according to a common framework. This simply means that a work authorization document should contain an appropriate budget and schedule, and that costs should be accumulated on the same basis as the budgets. This will facilitate comparisons of planned-versus-actual costs as work proceeds on the program. The work breakdown structure provides the framework for carrying out these activities and for accumulating actual cost and schedule performance information for reporting to higher levels of contractor and Government management.

Probably the most important concept in the reporting criteria is that contract cost status reports must be based strictly on the number of jobs completed to date. The lowest-level job assignment in most contractors' plants is called a "shop order," an "engineering work order," or a "task authorization." In the reporting criteria, these first-level jobs are referred to as "work packages." Since work packages must normally be limited in duration to no more than a few weeks, the number of work packages in process at any point in time is small. By adding the budgets for completed work packages to estimated budgets for short-term, in-process work packages, the contractor can arrive at a reasonably objective estimate of the budgeted value of work accomplished to date. A comparison of actual costs incurred with the budgeted value of work accomplished will then provide a measurement of contractor cost performance for successive time periods. Over time, cost performance trends can be analyzed to ascertain whether contractor performance in meeting budgets is improving or deteriorating. Subjective evaluation of "percentage of work completed" is limited to that small portion of the program made up of short-term, in-process work packages.

By January 1972, six years after the development of the Department of Defense Cost and Schedule Criteria, only 36 defense contractors had complied with the criteria. One encouraging sign was that 20 of the 36 had been validated during 1971. Initially, there had been indifference or resistance to the concept of criteria in the Army and the Navy. By 1972, however, all three services were actively implementing the program.

A number of factors contributed to the slow and often ineffective implementation of the new reporting standards: (1) the imposition of unreasonable or improper reporting requirements by the military services; (2) lack of a clear consensus in the Defense Department on the need for the criteria; and (3) lack of clear enforcement procedures, including penalties, for failure to comply.

During our interviews, a number of instances were identified in which excessively detailed reporting requirements were imposed on contractors by Government program offices. In other cases, as cited earlier, contractors were allowed to maintain a separate set of books for reporting to the Government. These problems occurred as the result of ineffective training of Government personnel. The fact that by 1971 the military services had established basic training programs relating to the use of the criteria, and were sending increasing numbers of their people to these schools, provides some hope that the problems of implementation may diminish.

With respect to developing a consensus within the Defense Department, serious problems remain. While some senior officials support the criteria, there is little active support for the concept at other levels. Since the establishment of the criteria in 1965, their primary sponsors have been the Comptrollers in each service. On the other hand, the Assistant Secretaries for Research and Development for at least two services, and the Office of the Director of Defense Research and Engineering, have opposed the use of contractor performance measurement systems and have only reluctantly accepted the actions of other Pentagon officials to implement the systems. One Assistant Secretary for Research and Development expressed his reason for strong resistance to any performance measurement on development programs: measurement systems would strengthen the hand of Pentagon critics.

Unfortunately for those Government personnel seeking to implement the criteria, a number of senior defense officials who are opposed often express their views to defense contractors. The vice president of finance of one defense firm had worked with the vice presidents of engineering and manufacturing to implement the criteria. Soon after procedures had been developed to collect information on the budgeted value of work performed, an Assistant Secretary for Research and Development visited the plant. He asked the vice president of engineering why he was bothering to collect performance measurement information. This visit seriously damaged the financial vice president's efforts.

In another case, four months after one contractor had begun to report performance measurement information to a Government program office, a newly assigned supervisor from the program office called the contractor and asked why the information was being submitted. The new Government supervisor had not been trained to use the information and indicated to the contractor that he saw no need for it to be submitted to him.

Contractors who do not comply with the criteria are seldom penalized. It is often impractical to terminate a contract solely because a contractor has not submitted information as stipulated in the contract. Contractor compliance is often delayed for months or years while the contractor calls meetings to discuss various interpretations of the criteria. In addition, months can pass before a contractor reacts to Government requests for specific information.

A sizable number of defense contractors are uncertain whether to establish the procedures necessary to comply with the criteria. They wonder if the requirement to comply will disappear with the next change in Pentagon personnel. Several contractors who indicated a serious desire to comply with the reporting criteria were confused and frustrated by the lack of clear support from the Pentagon. Others who opposed the criteria cited the lack of Pentagon unanimity as a reason for delay.

Resistance to reporting criteria assumes many forms. Contractors commonly cite one or more of the following eight reasons for failure to comply.

1. Government action to make me comply with the criteria represents unwarranted interference with internal company affairs.
2. If I comply with the criteria, information I provide will be used against me during future negotiations.
3. It will cost the Government "X" million dollars if I alter company procedures in order to comply with the criteria.
4. Why should I respond to the criteria when I am being paid to manage

> the work on this program? There is, after all, a specific task entitled "Program Management" in the contract.
> 5. The work on this program is too dynamic to submit to cost performance measurement.
> 6. Compliance with the criteria will mean that the company will need two reporting systems—one to satisfy Government requirements and one for "the real world."
> 7. Complying with the criteria means changing my cost collection, accounting, work authorization, and other internal systems.
> 8. Complying with the criteria is not cost-effective. I have to get into too much detail.

Discussions related to these arguments have revealed several more problems. First, contractors have often misunderstood what is required by the criteria. Second, incompetent implementation efforts by the Government personnel have given substance to some of the concerns expressed by contractors. Third, in some cases, contractors exaggerate problems to test the resolve of Government personnel. A high cost figure is frequently cited by defense contractors, for example. In two cases, we found that contractors had obtained new computer equipment and new computer programs, at Government expense, to handle their regular planning and control systems. Personnel in the financial office of another firm were pleased to comply with the criteria because it provided them with the opportunity to improve their own planning and control systems at Government expense. A third contractor cited a cost of several million dollars to comply with reporting criteria. When a trained Government representative visited the plant to analyze the figure, he found that new systems, procedures, and equipment which were unrelated to the criteria were included in the cost estimate. When this was pointed out to the systems and procedures supervisor, he commented: "OK, so we went a little overboard, but that's the only way we can get something done around here." He strongly criticized the military officer for "pulling the rug out from under my improvement program."

At another contractor plant an estimate of $2.5 million was submitted to the Defense Department as the expense for compliance with the reporting criteria. A subsequent Government audit found that only one additional person had been hired. The $2.5 million figure was the total cost for operating the company's entire program office.

Another contractor proposed $9 million as the cost of compliance. Subsequent negotiations reduced the figure to less than $1 million. In addition it was discovered at this plant that compliance with the criteria had enabled the company to consolidate many internal reports at a great saving.

Most contractors did not want to submit information that would enable the

Defense Department to piece together an accurate picture of planned-versus-actual costs for work performed. They feared that untrained Government personnel would misuse the information. It would be, according to one company executive, "like giving razor blades to a baby."

Problems of implementing Government reporting criteria do not end when contractors agree to comply. Implementation efforts usually include two or more negotiation sessions, during which specific parts of the criteria are clarified. Once the contractor indicates that his system complies with the criteria, a team of Government personnel visits the plant to review the system. During these review periods, deficiencies are frequently found in the contractor internal reporting systems. Some problems observed during review periods are described below:

- Departmental budgets exceed higher level budgets.
- The system provides cost information relating to time-phased spending plans but not work that has been accomplished.
- The contractor's reporting system does not summarize the budgeted value of work accomplished on the work-package level.
- The contractor defines work packages as he goes along, drawing funds from future budgets.
- Work packages are poorly defined, and budgeted value of work packages is changed upon completion of the actual work.

During a review of the internal systems at ten defense plants, one Government team found the most frequent problem to be lack of contractor control over work authorization. Additional work was often authorized within functional organizations without an upward adjustment in the total program budget. In eight of the ten defense companies, this practice caused the total internal budget to exceed the full contract price.

To illustrate: an industry program manager might authorize the manager of his engineering department to spend $50 million to carry out the total work described in the contract work statement. The engineering manager might then authorize his immediate subordinate managers to accomplish work estimated to cost $55 million. The third-level managers would then authorize their personnel to accomplish work estimated to cost $65 million. Each authorization is made on the assumption that additional funds will be made available, as they have in the past. This practice obviously builds cost overruns into the program budget at the time work is authorized. Once a budget is established for work packages at the lowest functional levels, it is extremely rare that work is accomplished for less money.

Several persons working in comptrollers' offices in defense plants told us that their biggest difficulty in complying with Government reporting criteria had little to do with accounting procedures. Rather, their primary problem in calculating the planned value of work to be accomplished was the difficulty of getting their engineers to plan and budget ahead. "We have problems getting them to budget for packages of work a week or two ahead, to say nothing of planning six months ahead." (The criteria require that work packages be planned ahead in detail for periods of at least six months.) A senior vice president told us that "the engineers would like to have a bucket of money for engineering for the total program and then have us go away and leave them alone." An engineering manager told us: "We do not think that an engineer should be required to explain to the Government where he has been and how far he is off plan. In his own mind, he is trying to do the best job."

The resistance of engineering organizations to the discipline of planning or measuring performance occurs in other countries as well as in the United States. In a study of British engineers, H. A. Collinson observed:

> When planning is first introduced, there is often resistance and opposition to it, on the grounds that scientific research does not lend itself to this type of organization: "We are chemists, not astrologers—this sort of thing needs crystal balls, not test tubes." This attitude derives largely from the impression that an agreed plan is rigid and that deviation from it will be considered to be failure.[2]

By mid-1971 Defense Department efforts to implement the criteria had come to the attention of the Senate Armed Services Committee. In its report authorizing defense appropriations for fiscal year 1972, the committee included the following comments:

Cost/performance management
   The committee is particularly interested in the cost performance measurement system that has evolved to better manage and control the cost and performance of these weapon programs. The committee understands that this system is not a panacea that will prevent cost overruns or improve performance of the weapon systems. The committee believes, however, that if properly used, this system under a Defense Department policy directive entitled "Performance Measurement for Selected Acquisitions" should provide early identification of any problems related to the cost and progress of a program that could enable alternate or corrective action to be taken. For example, the committee understands that one of the features of this new system is employment of a firm baseline position tied to an established work and expenditure plan that enables the program director to measure the cost and performance progress.

Cooperative effort needed

The committee also understands that one of the purposes of establishing this system and the implementing criteria which have been agreed to by all the service agencies was to reduce the proliferation of costly management reporting requirements at contractor locations. The committee, therefore, is somewhat disturbed to find that the Navy is not in agreement with the implementing procedures employed by the other services even after over two years of the Defense Department attempting to achieve a common position and agreement on implementation of the governing directive. As with other directives and implementing regulations governing the procurement and management process, the committee is aware that a major step toward fruition is the sincere and cooperative effort and understanding of those involved in carrying out the policy. The committee has noted that the system criteria for implementation are being introduced into many programs. However, the committee also is concerned that some major programs, such as the Army Safeguard program, appear to be quite slow in implementing this policy for cost and performance management and validating the systems at contractor locations.

The committee's concern for the procurement and management improvements in the weapon system process is directly related to the committee's concern with the increased cost of these weapon programs. The committee plans during the coming year to continue monitoring and reviewing selected activities in the procurement and management process.[3]

Chapters XXII and XXIII are devoted to Government and industry managers' performance and the incentives which influence their activities in the area of program controls.

NOTES TO CHAPTER XXI

1. Statement of Colonel Albert W. Buesking (Ret.) at the Hearings of the Subcommittee on Economy in Government of the U.S. Congress Joint Economic Committee, November 13, 1968.
2. H. A. Collinson, *Management for Research and Development* (London: Sir Isaac Pitman and Sons, 1964), pp. 8–9.
3. U.S. Senate, Armed Services Committee, Report 92-359, *Authorizing Defense Appropriations for Fiscal Year 1972*.

CHAPTER XXII

Program Control—Part III

Defense Department Managers: Performance and Incentives

IN PRIVATE INDUSTRY the responsibilities of business managers and program managers normally include marketing, planning, scheduling, and supervision of personnel. In addition, cost control activities are a major responsibility. Government program managers, like their industry counterparts, also list marketing (obtaining funds for their programs), planning, scheduling, and supervision of personnel as their primary responsibilities. Relatively few, however, believe that cost control on programs under contract with industry is something they can do much about. A military officer assigned to a buying command headquarters told us: "Many of our people believe that a program will end up taking a specific amount of time and all the funds obtainable, regardless of any action they might take. When individuals hold such a belief, they often lose control of their programs."

Government managers told us that strict cost management could effect a savings of only 5% to 10% of their total program budget. Although Should-Cost analysts have been able to identify up to 30% in excess costs on a number of acquisition programs, many Government managers think that contractor cost figures are immutable. They assume that once a program price has been set, there are few ways to lower it. It must be accepted in full or rejected outright. Furthermore, when cost overruns are reported by contractors, Government managers believe that they are inevitable—not the result of poor planning or mismanagement, but "facts of life." The Government program manager faced with cost overruns usually turns, not to the contractor, to demand accountability, but to his Defense Department superiors, to find more money. He sees no other alternative. He then finds himself in competition with every other Government program manager within his service for a larger slice of the budget. If additional funds are obtained, his "problem" disappears. If funds are not available, the program schedule is extended and the work level for the current year is reduced. In other words, when contractor costs are higher than the approved budget, most military managers do not think that costs are too high, but that the budget is too low. During our interviews, at least 15 program managers told us that their "most serious problem" was insufficient funding. Two senior Pentagon officials told us that over a three-year period they had never heard a program manager propose cost reduction as a solution to a "funding problem."

Late in 1970 the Office of the Secretary of Defense conducted a comprehensive study of cost analysis capabilities within military buying commands. In its report on a particular buying organization, the study team stated:

> No current effort appears to exist at [organization] to analyze the cost of programs after acquisition has been started or to determine how the actual costs compare with the estimates. We saw no evidence of a systematic effort to identify the source or basic cause for significant differences. Similarly, when configurations are changed to accommodate procurement within funds available, cost estimates are not made to the changed configurations.

Government managers assume that if contractor costs have been approved by Defense Department auditors, they must be reasonable and accurate. In fact, however, our interviews with Government auditors revealed that audits are normally limited to questions of "allowability" for contractor cost categories (e.g., engineering, manufacturing, management). Government auditors do not rule on the accuracy of cost estimates within these categories. They determine whether a contractor is including costs for any activities prohibited by the ASPR, such as advertising, interest, or entertainment. Government auditors readily admit that they do not have enough time or skill to judge whether the costs cited by the contractor are reasonable. Under these circumstances, the expectations of Government procurement personnel relying on a Government audit are unrealistic. Nevertheless, a senior procurement official in a military buying organization told us:

> The Defense Contract Audit Agency has the responsibility for controlling the reasonableness of costs. The reason that *we* forecast the trend of dollar cost increases on a contract is to determine what additional funds we will need.

One of the reasons Government program managers shy away from control of program costs is because they lack training and experience in the analysis and use of financial information. Early in 1970 the Office of the Secretary of

Defense studied the management control reports required of defense contractors. A study team found that contractor reports costing several million dollars were not being used by the Defense Department program officials who had required them. One of the most frequently cited reasons for having such reports prepared is the "warm feeling" syndrome. Extensive contractor data are collected in case someone higher up in the Defense Department hierarchy should ask for any kind of information. Since it is impossible to know ahead of time what questions might be asked, managers told us that they have a "warm feeling" when their files are full of lengthy reports.

When we asked other officials in the program office why contractors' reports are not used, we were given these explanations:

- I don't know why I received this report.
- I can't recall how this report is used.
- I wouldn't know what to do with this report without going to school.

In one Government program office that we visited, cost growth of more than $100 million had recently been identified. Supervisory personnel told us that there was nothing they could do to halt continuing cost growth. They admitted, however, that they had not considered examining contractor overhead cost figures or internal cost performance standards, nor did they know how to measure either of them. Two years prior to the identification of cost growth on this program, I had visited the same office and reviewed the activities of the program control division. I learned that the colonel in charge of program control received hundreds of pages of detailed cost information from contractors each month. Many reports contained substantial duplication of cost information. When this was pointed out to him, he stated that he wanted to have contractor cost information available in a variety of forms in case someone from a higher level asked him for information in a specific format.

The senior vice president of a defense company expressed a concern that was repeated many times during our interviews. He pointed out that "people at lower levels in Government contract administration often do not understand the theory and the 'how' to implement the new procedures, where to exercise judgment, and where to exercise specific decision rules."

In our interviews with military program managers, we learned that most did not understand the need for obtaining cost performance information of any kind from the contractor, and did not know what kinds of information would be needed to measure cost performance. They recognized the need for early "visibility" of developing cost problems, but they did not know how to get such information in any systematic way. When we asked how they monitored contractor performance, the Government program managers described a variety of techniques.

1. They assigned someone to the defense plant to witness tests and inspections, and to "get into the details"—a commonly used phrase meaning: to watch, listen, and talk to plant personnel.
2. They related technical milestones to manhours on a weekly or monthly basis.
3. They required the contractor to describe program progress, technical approaches, and testing plans on a regular basis, for their approval.
4. They talked with men "on the floor" in the plants.

An industry vice president told us that his monthly program reports were often so voluminous that it would be a major undertaking for anyone in the Government program office to read them. In fact, the reports were so complex that no one in the Government program office did understand them. Regularly, 10 to 20 Government program office personnel visited the contractor's plant to discuss the reports. The company vice president stated that in his opinion these visits prevented his personnel from accomplishing their "real" jobs. He told us that in addition to visits from Government program office personnel, his company had received visitors in the past five months from the Tactical Air Command, the Office of the Secretary of Defense, the Air Force Supply Depot, the Air Training Command, Air Force Headquarters, the Air Force Logistics Command, Air Force Systems Command Headquarters, and the Air Force Test Center. In addition, company personnel met regularly with the more than 100 personnel assigned to the Government plant representative office.

Since they lack the ability to measure contractor performance and to determine whether work costs are reasonable, most Government managers exercise control by regulating the amount of money given to the contractor each month or each quarter. As one military program manager commented, "The best control I have is to simply tell the contractor how much he can spend on a monthly basis." On the same subject, the director of contracting and pricing for a defense firm told us: "I have encountered a number of Government program managers who tell me that I can spend just so much in the next six months. They seem to be much less concerned about what we accomplish in the next six months than they are that we spend a specified amount of money, no more or less."

Several further observations can be made about Government program management. First, program managers and their subordinates often try to explain problems rather than to solve them. This may be a result of the requirement placed on them to make frequent briefings to higher level supervisors. One program manager told us: "We spend so much time justifying what we are going to do that we never have time to do it." Another said: "If I report problems, I won't have a chance to solve them. I'll be writing position papers and explaining the problems to higher levels of Government management instead." A third official told us: "A program manager needs to be careful about exposing problems on his program, or else he will be deluged by visitors from higher levels of Government management. So, he hides those problems that he has any significant probability of solving." In examining the records of visits to program offices and plant representative offices cited earlier in Chapters IX and X, it appears that there is substantial credibility to the claims of these program managers.

Second, information presented to Government program managers by contractors is not always reliable. Much of the "information" passed on by industry and Government program management to higher levels in the Defense Department is designed to create a good impression, rather than to present an objective picture of the current and projected status of a program. Progress review meetings are attended by Government personnel who are interested in solving problems, but they may not receive unbiased information. In effect, a high percentage of progress review meetings are devoted to discussions of how to obtain additional funds for programs experiencing cost overruns.

Third, Government program managers often do not understand how industrial plants operate. Program managers often admit that they have to accept what a contractor tells them about program activity because they are not qualified to challenge the data they receive.

Another reason for Government managers' limited control activity is the vast scope of the work they are expected to perform. They are often simultaneously responsible for several contracts and several contractors. One program official we interviewed was in charge of the production portion of seven different contracts with seven different contractors. He recognized that he was at a disadvantage in administering his contracts, since each of his seven industry counterparts dealt exclusively with single contracts. Furthermore, each industry manager had substantially more experience than he in the field of Government contracting and business management. It was not uncommon to hear that Government managers were unable to understand points raised by industry managers because of their own limited training and experience.

To alleviate the management problems experienced on acquisition programs, Gordon W. Rule, then the Navy's chief contract negotiator, summarized many of these problems and made a number of recommendations to

Congress in 1969, during the Joint Economic Committee's hearings on military procurement.

> I have recommended, Senator, that the Department of Defense ought to have a group, a highly professional full-time group, of industrial engineers and cost analysts to go into these plants periodically. Each service now has a group that can go in and scratch the surface but I think that the Department of Defense would be well advised to have a highly professional group to make periodic checks of our big procurements, and bear in mind that you don't have to do this really if you are in a real competitive environment. We have always thought, and I think rightly so, that where you have got genuine competition, and I am not talking about phony competition, you rely on the forces of the marketplace to get you a reasonable price. But such a group could go into our large sole-source producers periodically, not in connection with any one contract but in connection with just checking over the overall efficiency of that plant.[1]

REWARDS AND PENALTIES FOR GOVERNMENT MANAGERS

In commercial business, managers are evaluated and rewarded by their superiors on the basis of their ability to generate sales, and on profit return on net worth, profit return on total capital invested, and total profit generated. For Government managers, on the other hand, profit is not and cannot be used as a measure of performance. Nonetheless, rewards and penalties for management performance are as important within the Defense Department as in private enterprise. Although it is difficult to attribute behavior in a particular situation to any single incentive, a clear understanding of acquisition management requires an appreciation of the rewards and penalties for "good" and "bad" performance by Government program managers.

There are six "reward" categories:

1. The personal satisfaction that comes from contributing to national security or to the well-being of the manager's own military service;
2. The personal satisfaction of a job well done;
3. A favorable personal performance rating from a superior and/or promotion to a higher position or rank;
4. Recognition and praise from peers and superiors;
5. Cooperation and assistance from industry personnel in the management of the program or the preparation of progress reports for higher level Government superiors;

6. The friendship of industry personnel for social purposes; references from industry executives for future employment.

There are seven "penalty" categories:

1. Personal dissatisfaction when a weapon system perceived as needed "for the good of the nation" is canceled, reduced in scope, or not delivered on schedule.
2. Personal dissatisfaction with a job poorly done;
3. Dismissal from the job, or transfer to a less desirable assignment;
4. An unfavorable personal performance rating that will make future promotions unlikely;
5. Criticism from peers, superiors, the press, the General Accounting Office, or the Congress;
6. Lack of cooperation, and sometimes active obstruction, from industry personnel in management of the program and/or preparation of progress reports for higher level Government managers;
7. Hostility from contractor personnel; obstruction in attempts to gain future employment in industry.

These rewards and penalties often produce conflicting incentives. For example, warm personal relationships with company personnel may be jeopardized by a Government manager's aggressive control activity. Or a Government manager may impose careful cost controls only to have his military superiors blame him for delays in the acquisition schedule.

One Government plant representative told us that he was simply not interested in cost control. His primary interest was in "keeping this vital resource (the defense plant) available to our country." In another case, a military officer with extensive experience in program management told us that "program managers are not rated on the cost of a program, but rather on its performance and its timely completion for use by a military service." All the military program managers he knew "believed that their programs should receive more funds because of their major importance to their military service." A Pentagon official described his program management associates: "These men believe that their job is to get the most technically sophisticated hardware in the shortest time frame. Their point of view is supported by contractors' interest in maximizing reimbursed costs to build and retain their technical base."

On large programs it is easy for Government personnel to rationalize that cost overruns should be ignored and that it is all right for the contractor to use more than the necessary number of personnel. In hearings conducted on the cost of the C-5A aircraft, Congressman Mendel Rivers, then chairman of the House Armed Services Committee, assured Lockheed president Dan Haughton that the Air Force would definitely buy all 115 airplanes authorized for the C-5A program. "Regardless of what this plane costs," Congressman Rivers stated, "we need it, and we must have it." [2] Secretary of the Treasury John Connally expressed similar feelings in testimony before the Senate Banking, Housing, and Urban Affairs Committee. In June 1971 the following exchange took place between Secretary Connally and Senator William Proxmire:

> SENATOR PROXMIRE: Lockheed's bail-out, I would agree with Senator Tower, is not a subsidy; it is different from a subsidy; it is the beginning of a welfare program for large corporations.
>
> I would remind you in a subsidy program it is different: there is a *quid pro quo*. You make a payment to a railroad and in return they build trackage; you make a payment to an airline and they provide a certain amount of service for it.
>
> In welfare, of course, you make a payment and there is no return. In this case, we have a guarantee and there is no requirement on the part of Lockheed to perform under that guarantee. A guarantee of $250 million and no benefit, no *quid* for the *quo*.
>
> SECRETARY CONNALLY: What do you mean "no benefit"?
>
> SENATOR PROXMIRE: Well, they don't have to perform.
>
> SECRETARY CONNALLY: *What do we care whether they perform?* [italics added] We are guaranteeing them basically a $250 million loan. What for? Basically so they can hopefully minimize their losses, so they can provide employment for 31,000 people throughout the country at a time when we desperately need that type of employment. That is basically the rationale and justification.[3]

ment procurement. After World War I, the House of Representatives conducted hearings into charges of mismanagement of funds in the procurement of war supplies. Charles G. Dawes, head of a U.S. military supply group during World War I, told the House committee:

> Sure we paid. We didn't dicker. Why, man alive, we had to win the the war. We would have paid horse prices for sheep if sheep could have pulled artillery to the front. Oh, it's all right now to say we bought too much vinegar and too many chisels, but we saved the civilization of the world. Damn it all, the business of an Army is to win the war, not to quibble around with a lot of cheap buying. Hell and Maria, we weren't trying to keep a set of books, we were trying to win the war! [4]

Many Government program managers feel that one of their primary tasks is to identify and promote possibilities for program additions and improvements. One military service director of research and development told us that he instructed program managers to devote their time to promoting program expansion. In his view, the official who was responsible for contracting and procurement on a program (a subordinate to the program manager), rather than the program manager himself, should administer cost control and the "fine print of the contract."

During our interviews, Government program managers told us that their major goal was to keep their programs "alive" despite technical problems and cost overruns. To this end, they postponed problem identification. During hearings of the Senate Armed Services Committee in June 1969, Senator Howard Cannon asked Air Force officials if they had received "timely notice that there were going to be cost overruns on this [C-5A] contract." The Air Force officers indicated that they had received "timely notice." When no further explanation was forthcoming, Senator Cannon asked: "Is that the end of your answer?" The Senator pointed out that the Air Force had concealed cost problems in annual funding requests for the C-5A. The Air Force representatives explained that although they had had "indications" of a cost overrun, the indications had not been "conclusive." Senator Cannon replied: "You say you had indications in 1966 and 1967 that you were going to have these cost overruns [but] apparently all you did is question the estimates and make more studies." [5]

Similar questions were addressed to Colonel Beckman, program manager for the C-5A during the House Military Operations Subcommittee hearings in April 1969. At that time, the subcommittee was trying to find out why cost overruns had not been reported at earlier C-5A hearings. Subcommittee counsel Herbert Roback asked Colonel Beckman why cost overrun estimates had been left out of the official reports. Colonel Beckman responded: "Because of the nature of the overrun, we felt . . . that the projections we were making were actually estimates, subject to actual proof later on, and that the nature of the estimates was such that if publicly disclosed, they might put Lockheed's position in the common market in jeopardy."

To most procurement personnel, a "successful" program is one that is completed without having limitations imposed by Defense Department officials above the program management level, or by Congress. One military manager told us that to achieve this kind of success it is necessary to have strong program support both inside and outside the Government. He cited the Polaris and Atlas programs as examples: both had such broad support that they were able to move ahead despite substantial cost growth.

In order to maintain support for their programs it is common for Government managers to attempt to amend contracts, to relieve contractors of contractual commitments. Gordon Rule discussed this kind of activity in testimony before the Joint Economic Committee in May 1971.

> MR. RULE: Well, I don't think we do that in the Navy. I really don't. I sat in a meeting with an Admiral once who was just about to do that. He made a statement, the company had come in and was crying about losing money, and he said, "I am going to reform the contract." And I said in front of the whole group, "Over my dead body you will reform that contract."
>
> SENATOR PROXMIRE: That is exactly the kind of response that is the most helpful because it indicates that if the Navy doesn't do it, why in the world should the Air Force have to do it.
>
> MR. RULE: This Admiral would have done it just like that, he would have done it that afternoon. So I say, there are problems in-house, but I really did say, "Over my dead body you will reform that contract."

Government buying organizations and program offices are usually limited to making the best of their own limited management capabilities and performance. During the course of a program, technical consultants are often hired to review technical plans, to interpret test results, or to appraise risk. In only a few cases are management consultants employed to review contractor cost information or to identify cost problem areas and opportunities for cost reduction. Government managers are hesitant to employ management consultants because a request for such assistance has to be reviewed, justified, and approved by each level of management above the program office, including the Office of the Assistant Secretary of the service concerned. Such a request has to state that the specific management capability is not available within the program office or elsewhere in the Defense Department. The individuals we interviewed were concerned that such a statement might be interpreted to mean that they were not qualified to do their own jobs.

Not only is cost control not always encouraged within the Defense Department, but in some cases vigorous cost control activity may actually be penalized. During our research we learned of three Defense Department personnel who claimed that they had been removed from their jobs because of their attempts to control or reduce costs. In all three cases, we found it difficult to determine whether these claims were wholly or partially justified. Each official so affected claimed that his work in identifying cost problems embarrassed higher level Government officials who did not want cost overruns to be revealed. On the other hand, their supervisors maintained that the dismissed or transferred manager had been a "troublemaker," had a "personality conflict," or was "not suited" for his assignment. The individual cases are described below:

    Case #1: A military officer was unexpectedly transferred to the Middle East. He had predicted that cost growth would occur on his program and that part of this cost growth could be avoided by an aggressive cost reduction program. His orders for the Middle East were subsequently revoked and he was assigned to another Washington, D.C., office at the request of the Office of the Secretary of Defense. His prediction of cost growth proved to be correct.

    Case #2: An officer who had been the focal point for all cost information on his program was removed from his duties. He had insisted that cost estimates from the field revealed that program costs would be much higher than the service headquarters had reported in official estimates to the Office of the Secretary of Defense. The higher costs subsequently occurred.

    Case #3: An official was removed from his program office. He alleged that significant cost growth was occurring on a program, contrary to official reports submitted to the Office of the Secretary of Defense and to Congress. His allegations subsequently proved to be correct.

In another case, a Government plant representative was threatened with transfer if he persisted in questioning the contractor's overhead rate. The threat was made by a military officer from the service headquarters, who had stated publicly that the program budget was "austere." The plant representative stopped questioning contractor costs and the transfer never took place.

It may be impossible to verify the actual reasons for the transfers and dismissals in the cases described above. But it is a fact that if Government personnel *believe* that vigorous efforts to control costs will result in transfer or dismissal, they are not likely to enforce controls. Government program management personnel are at all times impressed with the need to present a "united front" to Congress and the press. Officials at each level of management, from the program office to the Office of the Secretary of Defense, talk about the need for "team players." Individuals who challenge official briefings are unlikely to receive positions of responsibility on "the team."

One of the most pervasive deterrents to cost control has already been discussed in Chapter VII. Since Congress provides funds annually, program managers are warned by their superiors that they must have a "zero balance" at the end of each fiscal year. Congress may otherwise reduce program budgets, if the Office of the Secretary of Defense or the service headquarters has not already done so. Both Defense Department and industry managers are therefore eager to find opportunities to spend available money.

Government managers' need for industry cooperation can also soften their approach to control activity. Program managers attempt to work with contractors to present a single, coordinated position to higher Pentagon levels and to the Congress when funds are needed. Differences between the Government program office and the contractor would quickly be exploited by other Government personnel competing for the same funds. As one program manager stated: "There are always people around sniping at you, who have other uses for the funds. At the first sign of a problem, they are standing there with their hatchet." This need to maintain a unified approach means that there is little incentive to challenge a contractor's cost figures or to convince industry managers to remove personnel from the payroll when they are no longer needed.

Throughout our interviews, we were told by Government program personnel that it is easier to request additional funds to cover cost growth than to motivate a contractor to undertake an aggressive cost reduction program. Prolonged attempts to reduce costs result in diminishing cooperation from the contractor, as well as criticism from peers and superiors. On the other hand, it is relatively easy to justify requests for additional funds. If funds are not granted, program problems can be attributed to the Government officials who deny funding requests.

Government technical specialists are especially likely to identify with their industry counterparts. In most cases, there is a friendly, first-name-basis relationship between these personnel in Government and industry. They also share an interest in the successful development and production of a weapon system. Government technical specialists believe that their advice and direction to contractors is at least partially responsible for the successful performance of a program. Most of them are thoroughly familiar with the virtues of the program and display in their offices scale models of the finished product given to them by the contractor. In most cases, they spend a great deal of time extolling the technical capabilities of the program and very little time discussing management problems.

After many interviews with Defense Department managers, and examination of the rewards and penalties attached to various types of performance, we concluded that Government program managers are most consistently motivated to maintain the cooperation of their contractors, to avoid problem identification, and to be cautious in their attempts to impose efficient program controls. A military officer who had been a legal counsel for a major development program for three years told us that officers who are hoping for military promotions pay little attention to policy statements issued by senior Pentagon officials on the need for better controls and cost reductions. "Regardless of the policy at the top, the informal word that gets passed down to the men at the working level is: don't let the contractor get into trouble. Change the contract or provide financial relief for the contractor if necessary, but don't let him get into trouble."

Several junior military officers assigned to program offices expressed disappointment in the performance 'of their senior officers. One graduate of a military academy, who had spent the last two of his six years in the service in a program office, told us that he had been instructed by senior officers to "misrepresent the facts on the program, to improve the likelihood of obtaining the required additional funds from the Congress." He told us that he had been thoroughly trained in the code of "duty, honor, and country," but that the code did not seem to apply to the acquisition of arms. Another military academy graduate talked to us of his surprise and disappointment at being told by military program managers not to identify or report cost growth. Each of these two officers discussed his experiences in the presence of several other junior military officers assigned to other program offices. All had witnessed instances when reports to high-level Government managers had been falsified in order to obtain funds or to avoid criticism of management performance.

Perhaps the most significant reason for inefficient cost control activity is the lack of clear responsibility for managing cost performance. At the present time, this responsibility is shared by several divisions within Government program offices and Government plant representative offices. The managers of each of these offices report to different supervisors. There is no official who coordinates their separate activities below the level of the Office of the Secretary of Defense. The responsibility within each service is shared by the Assistant Secretaries for Research and Development, Installations and Logistics, and Financial Management (Comptroller).

In summary, our findings corroborate a report issued by the Joint Economic Committee following hearings on defense procurement in 1969.

Cost Control as an Antisocial Activity

Considerable testimony was received on the need to protect and encourage Government personnel attempting to keep the costs of procurement down. But cost control had been interpreted by many within and outside of Government as antisocial activity. The phenomenon of officials in the bureaucracy pushing for ever-enlarged programs is widely known. To such bureaucrats, any employee who wants to cut costs, and possibly reduce the size of the program, is stepping out of line.

The problems encountered by Fitzgerald in connection with the C-5A were underlined by Admiral Rickover. According to the Admiral, subordinates in DOD are supposed to "hew to the party line." Personnel who speak out against excessive costs may be subjected to disciplinary action. Rickover testified: "We have all heard of cases where Government personnel were apparently 'punished' for speaking out against the policies of their superiors. I do not mean the spectacular punishments that might be meted out to a dissenter in other countries; but there are subtle methods of reprisal that have been brought to bear against subordinates who publicly refuse to toe the agency line."

Colonel Buesking similarly observed that the sanctions have been imposed on those who have attempted to bring about major improvements in reducing costs. He testified: "It has been my personal observation that a number of competent people who did attempt to stimulate major change in the cost environment are no longer involved in working in that particular environment."

In a written statement submitted for the record by Fitzgerald, a civilian employee of the Navy, Mr. Gordon Rule, cautioned his fellow employees engaged in controlling costs to expect resistance not only from the contractor but from people in the Government as well. Mr. Rule stated: "This 'homefront' resistance can be much more brutal than that from a contractor." The subcommittee is deeply disturbed over the evidence of the lack of support for those conscientious individuals in DOD who want to reduce procurement costs. The negative attitude toward cost control and the apparent hostility against those who try to perform this function, is another example of "reverse incentives" in military procurement.[6]

It is important to point out that the effect of an incentive depends on how it is perceived, not on its intention. Senior Pentagon officials may talk of rewards for efficient management and penalties for inefficiency, but if this policy is not accepted by the supervisors who actually control rewards and penalties, or if other incentives are stronger, the policy has no effect on management performance.

Notes to Chapter XXII

1. Testimony of Gorden W. Rule at the Hearings of the Subcommittee on Economy in Government of the U.S. Congress Joint Economic Committee, *Military Procurement,* December 30, 1969.
2. U.S. House of Representatives, Armed Services Committee, Hearings on *Military Procurement for Fiscal Year 1970,* Part 2, June 17, 1969.
3. U.S. Senate, Committee on Banking, Housing, and Urban Affairs, Hearings on the *Lockheed Guaranteed $250 Million Loan,* June 8, 1971.
4. Testimony of Charles G. Dawes, Head of Defense Supply Procurement Division in France, World War I, before the U.S. House of Representatives; quoted in Mark Sullivan, *Our Times* (New York: Charles Scribner's Sons, Volume VI, 1935), p. 204.
5. U.S. Senate, Armed Services Committee, Hearings on *Military Procurement for Fiscal Year 1970,* Part 2, June 3, 1969.
6. U.S. Congress, Joint Economic Committee, Subcommittee on Economy in Government, Report on *The Economics of Military Procurement,* May 1969.

CHAPTER **XXIII**

Program Control—Part IV

Industry Managers: Performance and Incentives

OUR ANALYSIS of the defense procurement process and our interviews with industry personnel involved in the process have provided a number of insights into the industry's incentive system. As is true for Government managers, the significance of particular rewards and penalties to any one individual is difficult to evaluate, although several general observations can be made.

REWARDS AND PENALTIES

Five "reward" categories are relevant to contractor personnel:

1. The personal satisfaction of contributing to national security;
2. Personal satisfaction from a job well done;
3. A favorable performance rating from supervisors, and promotion to a better job;
4. Cooperation and assistance from Government personnel in the management of the program;
5. Recognition and praise from peers and superiors. Peers and superiors approve of managers who are able to:
   - Maintain, continue, or increase sales;
   - Develop a technologically sophisticated weapon system;
   - Increase Government contributions to company overhead;
   - Maximize long-term profits.

There are nine "penalty" categories for industry managers. The first six are shared in common with Government managers.

1. Personal dissatisfaction when a weapon system perceived as needed "for the good of the nation" is canceled, reduced in scope, or not delivered on schedule;
2. Personal dissatisfaction when a job is poorly done;
3. Dismissal from the job, or transfer to a less desirable assignment;
4. An unfavorable performance rating, likely to have an adverse effect on future promotions within the firm;
5. Criticism from peers, superiors, the press, the General Accounting Office, or Congress;
6. Lack of cooperation and assistance, and possible obstruction, from Government personnel;
7. Financial loss for the company;
8. Reduction in the Government's contribution to company overhead costs;
9. Reduction in future sales to the Government.

As with Government personnel, rewards and penalties often have conflicting effects on behavior. Completing a job for the lowest reasonable cost, or in the shortest period of time, may give personal satisfaction, but may reduce the Federal Government's contribution to overhead expenses, or may reduce total sales for the year.

In the second volume of *The Weapons Acquisition Process,* Scherer discussed incentives at length. He quoted from the testimony of William Allen, President of Boeing Company, to the Senate Armed Services Committee during its inquiry into satellite and missile programs.

> No one, certainly I do not, want to earn earnings beyond what are reasonable and proper. But this matter of incentive is all-important, and I only cite it as an example. We must have it. We must have that incentive. We must preserve competition. That is the American way. And it is not being done.[1]

Industry managers give at least one reason for this ineffectiveness of Defense Department efforts to obtain cost performance information: no penalties are inflicted when contractors do not fulfill reporting requirements. Contractors will not provide early visibility of problem areas unless they are rewarded for doing so, and unless some penalty is associated with the failure to report problems.

A senior industry vice president commented on incentives:

> It makes no matter what kinds of orders emanate from the top, or how strong the top manager is. Unless the men in the organization can see

how they can advance or receive greater pay or be able to do their jobs with less effort by behaving in the way you want, they will not respond in the desired way to an order from the top.

Government managers stressed that they had learned to obtain written agreements from contractors covering all reporting procedures *before* a contract was signed. They had learned that contractors undergo a dramatic change in their willingness to respond to Government requests after the contract is signed.

> All the words in the contractor's proposal don't mean a thing until they appear in a signed contract. Many of the promises and approaches in the contractor's proposal are written by cultists or hired consultants, and in some cases contractor personnel apparently don't even understand what is meant by the words. Once the contract is signed, the honeymoon is over and it is like pulling teeth to have contractors provide us with visibility if it is not clearly specified in the contract.

During our interviews, industry executives repeatedly stated that the present system of rewards and penalties in defense procurement discourages cost control and cost reduction. Many expressed their disapproval of the Government's conversion of Lockheed Corporation's fixed-price contracts for the C-5A aircraft and the Cheyenne Helicopter to cost reimbursement contracts, with a guarantee of a $250 million loan. A typical comment was: "If the Government doesn't hold us to our contractual commitments, what will they hold us to?" On the other hand, some executives stated that because of the Defense Department's emphasis on fixed-price contracts during the 1960s, Lockheed was forced to accept this type of contract to maintain its work force. They did not consider it unreasonable for the Defense Department to rectify the situation at a later date.

Scherer drew the following conclusions from his research during the late 1950s, with regard to industry's efforts to avoid losses.

> A similar propensity appears to affect actual contract performance once cost targets and sharing provisions have been negotiated. For corporate executives, there is something especially repugnant about financial losses. A $1 million loss is disliked and feared not only because it entails, e.g., $2 million less profit than a $1 million net profit, but also because it is a loss *per se*. One reason for this aversion to losses is undoubtedly the fact that losses are a symptom of managerial failure. Executives responsible for losing money on a particular contract are liable also to forfeit their opportunities for promotion and perhaps even their jobs.[2]

Ten years later, three researchers from the State University of Buffalo studied seven defense firms and presented findings on risk aversion that were similar to Scherer's. Hunt, Rubin, and Perry found that contractors were intent on maintaining a strong bargaining position on Government programs, were motivated to maintain a high level of technical performance, and were not primarily concerned about controlling or reducing costs or maximizing profits.[3]

Our interviews with defense contractors support the conclusions of Scherer as well as those of the Hunt, Rubin, and Perry study. Industry executives repeatedly expressed concern over the possibility of experiencing losses on defense contracts. One summarized this feeling by stating: "We want to minimize the possibility of severe loss. There is no likelihood of a cost underrun; there is always something we can do to make the hardware that much better."

Contractors also told us that cost underruns are as likely to be penalized as cost overruns.

> The only thing worse than a serious cost overrun is a cost underrun of 15% or more. If such an underrun occurred, we would make the Government contracting officer look bad. This in turn would endanger our relationship with him and motivate him to negotiate a lower target price with us on the next contract.

It is paradoxical that a defense company should worry about losses but do little to control or reduce costs.

In 1969 Professor James S. Reece of the Harvard Business School studied evaluation procedures for management personnel in two large defense plants. One program manager told him:

> We are an integrative function, making sure that the various departmental plans are consistent and properly dovetail. The premium (in the Program Office) is on "expediting" rather than control—that is, problem solving rather than planning and control.
>
> My personal effectiveness, as measured by my superiors, is not at all based on financial results. Rather, it is based on three things: (1) my acceptance by the customer; (2) my responsiveness to acute customer problems; and (3) my ability to resolve interdepartmental hang-ups on the program.[4]

Professor Reece further observed:

> Rather than managing the program *per se,* a program director seems more involved with managing contractor-customer relations and managing intra-divisional conflict. While these are important aspects of manage-

ment, one is left with the impression that the program directors are essentially "fire fighters," who are seemingly not involved in planning and controlling the major program tasks, and certainly not involved in controlling the costs expended in accomplishing the contractual tasks. Who at the division level, if not the program directors, is concerned with controlling program costs? As nearly as I was able to determine during my field research, the answer is "no one." There is great concern about costs in the Controller and Plans and Contracts areas, but neither of these departments can control costs because neither is involved in controlling the tasks which generate the costs. As one Plans and Contracts executive succinctly put it, "I know what causes excess costs in the factory. . . . Our job is to see how we can accommodate these costs in the future."

Thus, at the division level, cost problems are not control problems—rather, they are funding (accommodation of costs) problems. That is, the question asked seems to be—How can we get enough money added to the contract so we don't lose anything and protect the corporate financial position? rather than—How can we control our costs so we will be within our target costs and thus earn a profit?

In sum, at the division level the control "mentality" seems to be a carry-over from the years of operation in a "cost-plus" environment: i.e. "funds control" as opposed to "cost control." Yet the contractor alone cannot be faulted for this low priority put on cost control. If one believed that a company cannot long survive without adapting to its environment, then one must attribute the survival of major defense firms to a lack of real concern over cost control within the Government program management organizations.[5]

Since 1962 little has changed in industry attitudes toward profit. We were told by industry executives: "Profit has little to do with contractor motivation in the management of the acquisition process"; "The average stockholder doesn't care about how much profit we make"; "I don't care about profits; the important thing is getting more sales to cover our costs." In short, contractors were virtually unanimous in their willingness to sacrifice short-run profit for the sake of (1) company growth; (2) an increased share of the defense market; (3) a better public image; (4) organizational prestige; (5) carry-over benefits to commercial business; (6) opportunities for follow-on business; (7) greater expectations for future growth and profit.

Industry executives described techniques for increasing sales and profit. Follow-on contracts are negotiated to prolong a program long after its original scheduled completion date. The contractor often adds as many personnel as possible to a program. An industry manager told us why.

When we went from program (X) to program (Y) it was a big step forward and we needed 1,500 engineers, or at least that is the number we had on the payroll. When we went from program (Y) to our current program we employed 3,000–3,800 engineers to translate the conceptual model to a prototype and production model. Most people don't know that it took no more than 100–200 engineers to do the entire conceptual design and build the mockup for the current program. You see, we are still living in the times when the companies, in this business, that survived and got the business were those who had the engineers on the payroll. So we hired every man we could find.

During 1970 and early 1971 I served as chairman of a joint Government-industry study group investigating defense profit policy. The study team concluded that current defense profit policy provides contractors with a negative incentive for cost reduction.[6] (The results of the study are discussed at length in Chapter XV.) From his study of the relationship between industry operations and profit policy, Professor Reece drew similar conclusions:

> For the moment, then, assume that the contractor's top management does wish to motivate the heads of the cost-responsible engineering organization (i.e., department directors, section managers or chiefs, and group supervisors) to accomplish their assigned tasks within the allotted task budgets. What evidence is there that this objective is transmitted to the engineering department, and that engineering managers are rewarded for attaining this objective?
>
> As nearly as I could determine, in the engineering organizations at both contractors studied, the answer to this question is:
>
> > Either the cost control objective is not transmitted to engineering or, if it is transmitted, it does not appear to be because of the lack of rewards for managers who accomplish tasks within the assigned budgets.
>
> To support this statement, I can only state that not one of the many people interviewed in both of these contractors' organizations denied that their engineering managers were not evaluated in any significant way on the basis of their cost performance. Typical of the comments collected were these:
>
> 1. What if an engineer overruns his budget? Nothing. He gets more money, and gives fifteen reasons why someone else caused the overrun. The top (division) management's motivation to maximize return on investment simply isn't translated down the line to our engineers.
> 2. The incentives in the contract don't get transmitted down through the organization to either the factory or engineering personnel.
> 3. I don't feel budget performance is a significant factor in (engineering) personnel evaluation, from the manager clear

up through the V.P. and it definitely is not a consideration in evaluating supervisors.

4. People pay a lot of attention to budgets when they are in or approaching an overrun position, but they are not really a factor in personnel evaluation. Budgets here are a group issue, but not a personal issue.
5. Never has an engineer been fired for consistently poor budget performance.

Thus, there was general agreement regarding the absence of cost performance as a factor in personnel evaluation.

Several explanations were given for this absence. Among the problems these contractors' personnel mentioned in trying to reward cost performance were these:

One problem is that most engineers in this (defense/aerospace) business "grew up" in a CPFF (cost plus fixed fee) environment. In four years' time our business went from 20% to 80% fixed-price, and these guys just haven't been able to adjust that fast.

In other words, it is not measuring the manager's cost performance since this is a factor beyond his ability because of his past "conditioning."

A problem in rewarding our engineers is that apparent good performance may really be good justification of a high initial estimate.

Recall that these estimates come back (less negotiating losses) as budgets.

Engineers' and businessmen's viewpoints often conflict. Since an engineer's supervisor, regardless of the level in the organization, is also an engineer, this evaluation of an engineer by another engineer tends to reward the kind of performance that may be unsatisfactory to the businessman. For example, overdesign—gold-plating—and studying a problem to death are always a problem in engineering.

That is, by training and experience, engineers are not as cost-conscious as "businessmen," and thus do not hold cost control as important in evaluating each other.

In sum, one must conclude from these explanations that an engineering manager's cost control performance, though measured, is not rewarded because the measurement is considered to be unfair, invalid, or irrelevant. In the third case, the initial assumption that top management holds cost control as an important objective becomes questionable, since engineering top management is apparently not committed to the same objective.

Perhaps the priority placed on cost control is so low in comparison with the priorities for meeting technical specifications and delivery schedules that these latter two completely dominate the attention and efforts of all contractor management. As stated in the previous chapter, this situation results in treating "cost problems" as "funding problems," and is completely in harmony with the Government program office financial control mentality of the past two decades. But if an engineer's cost performance is not rewarded, what is? From the interviews conducted in both companies, two answers emerge: "engineering excellence" and seniority. "Engineering excellence" seems to mean performing an engineering task in a way that is intellectually pleasing to the engineer, his colleagues, and his superiors. This quality is rewarded through pay increases and job promotions. For example, the Vice President of Research and Engineering is held in high esteem by both engineers and non-engineers throughout the company as "our sharpest engineer." Seniority (considered independent of engineering excellence) is rewarded through pay increases.

While a promotion was considered by the engineers to be a very clear reward for past performance, pay increases were not. A typical comment regarding these raises was:

> They seem more like cost-of-living increases than bonuses. Almost everyone gets one, they're not very large, and they can't give them more than once a year.

One problem in this lack of rewards for good performance is the concurrent lack of punishments for poor performance. For example, since there are no monetary incentives which reward the efficient worker, the lack of these rewards cannot constitute a punishment for the poor performer. The ultimate punishment—terminating a worker's employment —is rarely seen, perhaps reflecting the union's adamance in defending a worker against this action. Also, as one manager pointed out:

> The long-term result of poor cost performance is a cutback in the quantity of airplanes the customer will be able to buy. But the long duration of programs in this business make program cutbacks now not reflected in factory layoffs for months, or even years. Thus the workers don't see a cutback as punishment for today's poor performance.

Moreover, even these layoffs are based on seniority, not job performance, as reflected in this extreme example:

> In one case, a new worker was in effect doing the tasks previously done by three men. When a reduction in factory personnel came along, this new person was cut due to low seniority, and three people took over the tasks he had been doing.

In sum, the present reward/punishment system for workers (more accurately, the lack of such a system) for the most part results in the same job situation (i.e., pay and rank) for the good performer as for the poor one. Although performance is measured on a short-term (one week) basis, there are no rewards tied to this short-run behavior. Hence the worker must look to a much longer term and more nebulous incentive—

promotion to management—as his chief tangible motivator for today's good performance.

Unfortunately, this lack of tangible reward for good performance is accompanied by a potential monetary gain from poor performance— overtime. At present, the factory schedule calls for two shifts, five days a week. Having worked in an aerospace factory which also was not scheduled for weekends or holidays, and which similarly paid 150% for Saturdays, 200% for Sundays, and 300% (normal pay plus overtime) for holidays, I can strongly suggest that this potential overtime is a great motivator for poor weekday performance. Even if the individual is not anxious to work weekends, many of his coworkers are, and thus there are group pressures not to accomplish all the week's scheduled tasks during the first five days.[7]

Procurement decisions made by the Defense Department reinforce the attitudes described above. When a company fails to meet the contract schedule and price, it is usually given additional time and money to do the job. These extensions can be interpreted as "rewards" for failure to perform. Managers at several defense firms, as well as several consultants to the defense industry, told us that the Government provides other negative incentives. For example, companies are encouraged to maintain extensive engineering staffs and production facilities. Otherwise, they might be restricted to their current sales levels by a Government "facilities capability review" team. As one manager stated:

> If we want to be in the running for business over the long run, we better have the capability beyond that necessary for our current business level. This business is project-oriented, and projects come to an end. It's either feast or famine, and you better have the men and the facilities when the feast comes along.

In 1971 the Arthur D. Little Company studied ten firms doing both commercial and defense business, in order to identify differences in cost reduction investments. They examined 4,570 capital appropriation requests and found that 27% of the commercial requests were for cost reduction efforts, while only 13% of defense program requests were in this category.[8]

MAINTAINING A FAVORABLE IMAGE OF DEFENSE PROGRAMS

Strong public approval for particular military weapon systems is strenuously courted by industry contractors. Government and industry personnel try to maintain support from the public in order to better their chances to obtain funds and to complete their programs without "interference" from the Pentagon or Congress. There are several ways to build a strong image. Contractors talk with Congressional and civic groups, describing the need for a weapon system and its capabilities in terms of national defense. Since news about technical problems and cost growth spoils the company's and the program's image, such news is delayed as long as possible. Companies hire consultants to promote favorable public relations and to control what is revealed in the media about their programs.

Information control is not limited to the public media. An industry director of financial planning and control described a visit to his plant from two generals. They wanted to know whether the contractor was exercising adequate control over an acquisition program sponsored by their service. The director constructed a matrix chart which listed, on the vertical axis, every important control activity he could think of. On the horizontal axis he listed the names of 20 managers who were working on the program. He then placed "x's" on the chart to indicate that most of the managers were involved in most of the control activities.

> We decided to label the chart "control points" rather than our initial choice, "approval points." The term "control point" seemed sufficiently general to keep us out of trouble, and yet sufficiently worthwhile that it indicated that something was going on that had to do with control. The chart fulfilled its purpose, since the generals sat patiently in the conference room while we went through a long description of how we had the program under control. Fortunately, no one asked for a detailed description of a "control point." Actually we had never used the term around here before. In any event, the generals went back to their headquarters satisfied that they had looked into the "control problem," and that the situation appeared to be well in hand.

In describing the function of the managers listed on the chart, the director told us: "Many of the individuals listed are generally interested in control functions, but are not in the approval cycle for engineering or manufacturing activities. In fact, many of them do not even receive any reports on engineering or manufacturing activities."

A similar incident was cited by a Pentagon Assistant Secretary. On a visit to a defense plant, he listened to a report, requested in advance, on the method for determining the actual cost of work performed and for comparing costs with budgets. A comprehensive system for measuring and controlling costs was described. Five months later, he met a former business associate who had recently worked as a consultant for the same company. The friend told the Assistant Secretary that he had been given a "dog and pony show," a description of what the contractor had been asked to do, not what he was actually doing. The former business associate had been hired to advise the contractor on cost performance measurement and to determine what changes were needed to "maintain a good image" with the Government.

The main reason for building a public image is to convince the Defense Department and Congress that programs are making excellent progress. An industry manager told us that the vice president in charge of his company's engineering department had been disturbed by company reports on the financial status of the program that revealed that work was costing more than planned. The engineering division then took over responsibility for reporting cost status for the program. When the next cost report was issued, all indication of cost overruns had disappeared. Two and a half years later, the engineering office reported a 750,000 manhour overrun. They considered it advantageous to present these data after the fact and as a summary figure, rather than when the overruns were occurring.

In order to verify this situation, we met with representatives from the engineering office. A middle manager who was responsible for cost information told us:

> We knew about the developing 750,000 manhour problem for some time, but we were directed not to reveal the problem until we received the word from the manager of research and engineering. Now that we have revealed the problem, there have been numerous contract changes in the past six months and I really have no idea how much it is going to take us to complete this program.

A military program manager told us that he found it almost impossible to obtain timely and reliable information from the contractors:

> Contractors who have underestimated costs to be selected for a program use every trick in the book to obtain additional funds. Once the program begins, they overstate costs on Government and contractor proposed engineering changes; they cut corners on material and quality, making equipment that barely meets specification requirements; they seek relief from specification requirements that are difficult for them to meet; they argue over interpretations to specifications so as to make their jobs easier; and they may not apply a best effort toward contract performance on a "loss leader"; instead, they may devote their best management talent to those programs where the company stands to gain the most. We have experienced all of these ploys in this program.[9]

As described in Chapter XV, current profit policy provides some explanation for the contractor's lack of interest in cost reduction and cost control.

A decrease in costs means (1) a lower base for negotiating profit as a percentage of costs on future contracts; (2) lower Government payments for overhead expenses (such as bid and proposal expenses, independent research and development, and other technical effort); and (3) lower payments for general and administrative expenses.

In summary, the present defense procurement system provides the industry manager with few rewards, and several penalties, for controlling and reducing costs. It is unreasonable, under these circumstances, to expect managers to press for cost control with the kind of vigor that is demanded on commercial programs. If an industry manager ignores incentives to increase weapon acquisition costs, he may find himself out of the defense business altogether.

Notes to Chapter XXIII

1. Frederic M. Scherer, *The Weapons Acquisition Process: Economic Incentives* (Boston: Division of Research, Harvard Business School, 1964), p. 257. The testimony of William M. Allen, President of Boeing, appeared in the U.S. Senate Hearings before the Preparedness Investigating Subcommittee of the Committee on Armed Services, *Inquiry into Satellite and Missile Programs*, 1958, pp. 1262–63.
2. Scherer, op. cit., p. 231.
3. Raymond G. Hunt, Ira S. Rubin, and Franklyn A. Perry, Jr., "Federal Procurement: A Study of Some Pertinent Properties, Policies, and Practices of a Group of Business Organizations," reported in *National Contract Management Journal*, Fall 1970, pp. 245–299.
4. James S. Reece, "The Effects of Contract Changes on the Control of a Major Defense Weapon System Program" (Boston: unpublished doctoral dissertation, Harvard Business School, 1970), pp. 5–38.
5. Ibid., pp. 5–38, 5–39.
6. Industry Advisory Council, Report to the Secretary of Defense by the Subcommittee to consider *Defense Industry Contract Financing*, June 11, 1971.
7. Reece, op. cit., Chapter 6.
8. Arthur D. Little, Inc., *Final Report to the IAC Subcommittee on Defense Industry Contract Financing*, Phase 1, Cambridge, Mass., May 20, 1971.
9. Richard J. Lorette, "The Relationship Between the Pressures on the System Program Director and the Growth of Weapon System Cost Estimates" (Boston: unpublished doctoral dissertation, Harvard Business School, 1967), p. 420.

CHAPTER XXIV

Conclusions and Recommendations

A BALANCED, REASONABLE, AND WELL-PLANNED schedule of weapons acquisition is the professed goal of every President, every member of Congress, every Secretary of Defense, and every military Chief of Staff. The process by which defense systems are acquired is influenced by several factors: international politics, strategic planning objectives, and the achievements of American technology. It is also influenced by less publicized goals of individual military leaders, private contractors, and politicians. Only occasionally do their goals coincide with national defense needs.

What seldom distinguishes any phase of the acquisition process is a genuine commitment to the most efficient and effective management of resources—people, money, materials, facilities, and time. The current relationships between Congress and the Defense Department, among governmental defense agencies, and between Government and industry, effectively prevent the system from functioning to its best advantage. Although weapons and equipment are, in fact, produced, the United States is paying an inordinate share of its Federal budget to satisfy the needs of an inflexible bureaucracy, an overextended industry, and the desires of the military establishment.

The basic system of acquisition discourages management consistency and stifles reform. Efficiency is penalized; poor management rewarded. A major stumbling block to reform is the Congressional procedure for authorizing and funding defense programs, a procedure so lacking in insight that it encourages deception. Further inhibiting reforms are the narrow objectives of the military, and the counterproductive intra- and interservice rivalries. As each service competes for an increased share of the defense budget, the Secretary of Defense receives only that information that will enhance the service's opportunity to expand its weapons' capability. The goal of communication between ascending levels within the Defense Department, and between the

Defense Department and Congress, is not to inform, but to "sell." Information is proffered or withheld as it best serves a parochial cause; i.e., to win more money, more programs, or both.

Industry receives conflicting signals from the Defense Department. The official message is: control costs. Behind the scenes, contractors hear: spend every available dollar and try to get more. Since the latter is in line with industry goals, this is the message that gets through. Defense contractors have only one way to earn profits comparable to those of the commercial market: increase costs and keep investment at a minimum. Once a company has committed a major portion of its resources to a defense business, it is locked in a life-and-death struggle for bigger programs and more contracts. It, too, begins to dispense information to serve its own needs, and thus finds itself allied with the military establishment.

Reform is not simply a matter, as many believe, of spending less money. The more basic problem is that funds are being spent unwisely. Efficient managers do not cut costs arbitrarily, but they do demand and vigorously enforce an effective utilization of resources. Few members of Congress or the public realize just how inept the present procurement system is. So powerful are the voices of the military and the defense industry that the imperative need for reform is ignored, or more often, simply not given credence.

Perhaps the strongest barrier to change is the difficulty of convincing any defense organization that it stands to gain if the system is reformed. The immediate effect of improved efficiency would probably be a smaller job force for industry and for the Defense Department. This is not attractive to Congress or to defense contractors, and certainly not to men and women—voters —who are dependent on the defense industry for their jobs. So threatened are most segments of the defense community by pressures for reform that critics of the system are labeled "ignorant," "naive," or "traitorous," as parochial concerns are passionately equated with national security.

THE NEED TO DELINEATE RESPONSIBILITIES

The weapons acquisition process has fostered an intimate relationship between the Department of Defense and its major contractors. As a result, it is often impossible to identify responsibility for decisions made during the course of an acquisition program. To improve the system, it is necessary that Government and industry responsibilities be carefully delineated. It is also important that both sides realize that Government management is not an adjunct of private industry, but is charged with independent supervision of the use of public funds.

A defense contractor's objective is to develop or produce a weapon system that performs to the satisfaction of the customer. An equally important objective is to maximize company profits over the long term. Meanwhile, Defense Department program managers and contract administrators must monitor three broad areas of contractor activity: system performance, program scheduling, and programs costs. If the acquisition process is to run smoothly, it should be structured so that contractors have a reasonable opportunity to satisfy their own objectives without undermining Government objectives. On the other hand, when contract terms are not being complied with, Government managers and Government plant representatives must be sufficiently independent of the contractor to report inadequate performance to higher echelons of the Defense Department; to investigate corrective action; and to enforce penalties. Officials at all levels of the Pentagon must be prepared to support this kind of management. Industry managers should also be rewarded by contractors, according to how closely they meet contract terms for schedules, budgets, and weapon performance. Under the present system, however, Government and industry managers are rarely encouraged to adopt such a strict interpretation of their responsibilities.

It is a popular belief that the military-industrial complex is run by dishonest and greedy men who manipulate Government funds for their own gains. This belief is not borne out by the present study. Involved in the production of weapon systems are an understandable coalition of interest groups with an economic, political, or professional stake in defense procurement. The coalition includes military officers, civilian appointees to the Defense Department, members of Congress, and private contractors. Problems develop because each group is primarily interested in enhancing its own growth, and because the "national good" is a concept easily redefined to fit each group's needs.

Most Army, Navy, and Air Force officers consider the acquisition of new and more advanced arms a primary strategic goal. Inherent in the military ethic is the assumption that the United States is in constant potential danger from foreign enemies. Accordingly, servicemen may be called upon at any time to defend their country. It is the responsibility of military leaders to be sure that their services are prepared to fight and to win. The code was described by General Douglas MacArthur in an address to West Point cadets on May 12, 1962.

> Yours is the profession of arms, the will to win, the sure knowledge that in war there is no substitute for victory, that if you lose, the nation will be destroyed, that the very obsession of your public service must be duty, honor, country.

Members of the Congress have a wider spectrum of goals, not the least of which is re-election. Many Congressmen feel that their every vote must be measured for its effect on the electorate, since there is never a long enough time between biannual elections to stop campaigning. Although Senators are not always under this kind of time pressure, neither are they immune from the need to satisfy their constituents. Most voters are, by necessity, interested in steady employment and adequate wages, and they depend on their representatives in Congress to work for these goals. Members of Congress are seldom rewarded for looking beyond local needs to a national goal that most people do not understand, especially if the result is a loss of local jobs.

Private contractors who join the coalition have payrolls to meet and stockholders to satisfy. This means that industry managers must increase sales and must schedule programs that will engage their total work force.

Theoretically, Pentagon leaders appointed by the President are best suited to maintain a balance among the more circumscribed concerns of other groups within the coalition. Unfortunately, by dint of background, preference, or conditioning, many of them support military and industry points of view rather than staking out independent positions based on their analyses and those of their staffs.

If reform is to be achieved, every segment of the defense community must be persuaded that its "constituents" will actually profit from improved management efficiency.

Until the mid-1960s the Defense Department and the defense industry were virtually autonomous. They seldom had difficulty in winning Congressional and administration support for programs they wished to initiate. Since the mid-1960s, however, an increasing number of Congressmen and public citizens have begun to question the continuing need for spiraling defense appropriations. As national priorities are re-examined, attitudes favorable to change begin to emerge. Not since the early 1930s has there been so much pressure for reform.

Unfortunately, trouble occurs at so many stress points throughout the procurement system that it is tempting to treat only the most obvious problems. In the past new contractual approaches and management information systems have been devised to circumvent a few major difficulties, while leaving the fundamental problems unchanged and the acquisition process still complex and unwieldy. The Defense Department undertook several useful short-term improvements during the period 1970–1973. The Should-Cost system for preparing cost estimates is designed to improve contract negotiations. The Performance Measurement system is designed to provide Government and industry managers with cost performance information useful in cost control efforts.

The Value Engineering system encourages Government and contractor personnel to redesign equipment for lower-cost performance. Each of these improvements attacks a crucial problem, but leaves many others unsolved.

Even these piecemeal attempts at reform meet strong resistance from industry. Defense contractors have operated successfully for years by emphasizing technical achievement. They find it difficult to accept cost control as an equally important program activity. In a commercial environment, cost control is a fundamental management concern. But defense contractors have not yet been expected to sustain this type of effort, and many have lost the capability to do so, as they have devoted a major part of their facilities to the defense market. To these contractors, the development of new control techniques by the Government represents unwarranted interference in their internal operations.

Most Government personnel are equally resistant to new management techniques. Many civilian and military managers resent any changes that disturb familiar routines or threaten traditional reward patterns. In addition, they are often unqualified to make use of new approaches to management. Civil service personnel, in particular, are afraid of losing their job security and opportunities for advancement.

Many acquisition problems are rooted in the attempt by Government and industry to foster the illusion that the defense industry fits naturally into the free enterprise system. Most Americans believe that private industry is equipped to handle any kind of development or production. By and large, they also distrust any hint of Government "interference" in the realm of private enterprise. This predisposition has forced the Federal Government to go to great lengths to maintain a myth. In truth, the defense industry is not free enterprise. It never has been.

THE PROBLEM OF THE MARKETPLACE

The free enterprise system is based on the premise that the marketplace is the testing ground for a firm's products and methods of production and management. The well-managed, efficient firm will prosper, and the inefficient, poorly managed firm will fail. Lower costs mean higher profits. Holders of private capital take risks that, if successful, will also be rewarded by higher profits.

In the defense industry there is no public marketplace. Most defense producers depend on Defense Department programs to keep them in business. They develop a large group of engineers, draftsmen, production workers, and managers in order to maintain their capability for defense work. No commercial work would enable them to maintain such a job force. On large defense programs, the Federal Government supplies the major part of a firm's working capital and investment. Once a contract has been signed, a large firm experiences little risk of cancellation for default, since it is difficult to identify responsibility for failure to meet contract terms on a major weapon system. Contractors are further protected because contract cancellation would lengthen the acquisition schedule. Most military planners will accept any program irregularity rather than risk delay.

The Problem of Long-Range Planning

Although planning is a major activity in most types of industry, long-range acquisition planning is not possible as the weapons acquisition process is now structured. A newly elected President and his appointed Secretary of Defense may wish to make plans for a four-year period. They are easily thwarted by members of the House and Senate whose timetable does not coincide with theirs. Since Congress authorizes and funds programs annually, defense officials and contractors must make their plans in one-year segments, although every major program lasts for several years. Each program recommended by the Defense Department will probably outlast the term of the Congress which must approve it, outlast the term of the program manager who will initiate management techniques, and often outlast the current administration. Contractors therefore feel free to express unlimited optimism about future program performance. This optimism is often encouraged and reinforced by civilian and military officials in the Defense Department.

Once a program receives initial authorization, military using commands usually attempt to win approval for additional weapon features. Each service tries to load as many extras as possible into its existing programs since Congressional approval for future programs is unpredictable. Industry exploits this tendency to its own advantage, since program growth adds to profits.

Each service includes several using commands (e.g., submarines, tanks, destroyers, strategic air, naval air, tactical air, helicopters). Traditionally, military personnel rotate from using commands to buying commands, where they serve in program management or procurement positions. Untrained and inexperienced, dependent on officers in the using commands for favorable performance reports, and unsure of how long their present management assignments will last—program managers tend to go the way that maximizes survival. In practice, this often means: don't hold the contractor strictly accountable for costs, schedules, or system performance.

Efforts to Improve Defense Management

Although comprehensive reform of the acquisition process has yet to be achieved, efforts in this direction are initiated from time to time. Any history of reform within the Department of Defense would have to emphasize the Mc-Namara administration. With the creation of the Systems Analysis division in the Office of the Secretary of Defense, and the development of the Planning, Programming, and Budgeting System, McNamara greatly strengthened the formal planning and quantitative analysis part of the acquisition process. Subsequently, the military services initiated or greatly strengthened their own systems analysis organizations. Some saw this as a matter of self-preservation, the only means by which to survive the rigors of an objective system of program evaluation.

McNamara also supported the program management concept as a means of centralizing responsibility for the procurement process. One man was to direct and to be held accountable for the development and/or production of a weapon system.

> I want to look to a point of central control and information in the form of a program manager for each major weapon system. . . . He shall be rewarded in his career for prompt and analytical disclosure of his problems as well as for his successes. This is a key position in our military departments, demanding the best managerial talents on which I want to place full reliance for our future weapons inventories.

These were the words of Robert McNamara in testimony to the House Appropriations Committee in 1964. Although the concept was sound, its implementation has fallen far short of expectations. Deputy Secretary of Defense David Packard told the same committee, seven years later:

> . . . With the long tradition of putting a general in charge of the battle, or putting an admiral in charge of a fleet, one would think it would be easy to get the Services to accept the proposition that you should have one man with authority in charge of a weapon development and acquisition program.
>
> We have been able to get this done in a few isolated cases, but it simply has not been fully accepted as a management must by any of the Services.

The military officers who are assigned to program management positions are poorly trained to negotiate with industrial contractors, and usually fail to have the requisite training and experience in procurement and general business management. Their management assignments are almost always short-term because of the military policy of rotation. As the Government manager furthest removed from the Secretary of Defense, the program manager usually has little effect on major program decisions. And finally, as a military officer, the program manager is rewarded (recommended for promotion) if he complies with regulations and runs a "successful" program. Success is measured by the technical performance of the weapon system and by the manager's ability to maintain and/or enlarge the acquisition program. To do the latter, he is often encouraged by his military superiors to suppress information concerning any budget or schedule problems that occur during the course of his program. In short, his goals as a military officer often run counter to top level management objectives, a factor that cripples the program management concept.

Several other innovations were promoted during the McNamara administration: incentive contracting; formal source selection; techniques for improving cost control, cost estimating, and contract definition; systems engineering; value engineering; total package procurement; contract performance evaluation; and the Program Evaluation and Review Technique (PERT). While each of these innovations was worthwhile in concept, together they did not accomplish the expected rejuvenation of the overall procurement system. There are at least two reasons for this failure. First, there has been no consistent and mandatory training program for Government management personnel, nearly all of whom lack qualifications to cope with the complexities of weapons procurement. Second, military and civilian personnel who adopt new management techniques instituted by officials at the top of the defense hierarchy are not rewarded by their immediate superiors. Below the Office of the Secretary of Defense and the Secretaries and Assistant Secretaries of the services, defense officials discourage the use of new methods and continue to provide rewards for traditional management procedures.

Since McNamara's departure from the Pentagon in 1967, additional management improvements have been instituted, but fundamental problems remain. One promising exception is a profit policy now being tested by the Department. If the policy is actually implemented on a broad scale, contractor profits will no longer be based solely on program costs. For the first time, the contractor's investment in a program will influence the level of his profits.

Since 1969 there have been further attempts to improve other aspects of weapons acquisition management. These include the establishment of "milestones" for major programs (i.e., dates for the accomplishment of crucial program objectives); the synchronization of management personnel changes with program milestones; a reduction in the number of letters of contract; the improvement of training programs for program management officials; and a formal review procedure for each new weapon system's operational specifications. The object of the review would be to insure that program requirements are reasonable and attainable, and that prototype systems are developed and tested *before* a production program is approved. Serious doubts about the successful implementation of this proposal have troubled Defense Department observers, however.

In 1970 the President's Blue Ribbon Panel made a number of recommendations to improve the acquisition process. They suggested that program requirements be simplified, that personnel training be improved, that program managers be granted more actual authority, that the number of reporting levels be cut, and that cost estimating techniques be improved. While the panel successfully identified several problem areas in the procurement process, their report did not explain why previous recommendations along the same lines have never been successfully implemented. Many procurement officials in the Defense Department are, after all, aware that the present system has faults. But despite a steady succession of studies and recommendations, the procurement process has remained impervious to structural reform.

THE ROLE OF CONGRESS

One fundamental problem that cannot be solved without a sweeping change is the need for effective long-term defense planning. The year-by-year Congressional review process limits greatly the value of any long-range planning. In addition, the review process as it now exists lends itself to the most flagrant abuse. Congressmen and their staffs are given too few resources and too little time to make proper evaluations of Defense Department proposals. The long-term effects of short-term proposals are seldom analyzed or understood. And members of the House may not be around to evaluate programs begun with their approval. Thus, accountability from defense contractors, Pentagon officials, and Congress itself is not exacted. Surely it is time to increase the term of members of the House of Representatives to at least four years. Defense (and many other Federal) programs could be funded biannually, allowing more time for more careful analyses of long-term defense objectives, and of individual acquisition proposals.

There can be no doubt that Congress needs substantially more analytical support than it is now receiving. This could be achieved in two ways. First, the General Accounting Office could be authorized to expand the scope of its investigations, in order to provide comprehensive (and independent) background information for members of the House and Senate Armed Services

Committees and Defense Appropriations Subcommittees. Second, the full-time staffs of these four committees could be strengthened by a generous addition of trained analysts.

But no change in Congressional procedures or resources will improve the acquisition process if Congress is not willing to demand accountability from defense officials. As long as the men in the Pentagon know that Congress will routinely provide funds for almost all new and ongoing programs, they have no reason to stop playing time-honored games. When Congress reactivates the concept of civilian control of the military, meaningful and lasting reform can begin. There is no other starting point.

THE PROBLEM OF CIVILIAN CONTROL

Within the Defense Department itself, the role of the Secretary of Defense needs a rigorous re-examination. Each new administration has an opportunity to redefine the decision-making process. Robert McNamara chose to break with tradition by centralizing authority in the Office of the Secretary of Defense, looking to his new Systems Analysis organization to provide a background of expert, independent analysis. The Laird administration returned to more traditional modes of decision making. In 1969 Secretary Laird introduced a plan called "participatory management," a design for "decentralization and delegation of authority under specific guidance" in order to allot to the military "a larger role in making the decisions that affect them." In the process of implementing participatory management, the Systems Analysis division within the Office of the Secretary of Defense was downgraded. Many analysts left the Pentagon for other jobs in Government and industry, since their function was no longer considered as essential in the Defense Department. Much of the job of program evaluation was given back to the individual military departments.

Decentralization of decision-making authority has been successfully achieved in many private businesses. In these firms, however, responsibility for both sales and profits accompanies decision-making authority. Sales and profits then are used to measure performance when decentralization occurs. When decision-making authority resides with the military services, no such easily observable measures of performance are available.

In a private company, a manager might have to decide how to allocate his resources for development of new equipment, personnel, training programs and facilities, logistics support, and operations. Since the Defense Department is organized along service lines with overlapping missions, measures of efficiency in the use of resources are not easily devised. (Missions include strategic defense, tactical defense, defense of the continental United States, etc.)

The fact that the services have a number of overlapping missions is a matter of tradition rather than strategic planning. It was just this tradition, and a corresponding overlap in weapon systems, that caused McNamara to work toward centralized (and independent) decision making in the 1960s.

Four years after the institution of participatory management it is clear that decentralization has meant a return to the military hard-sell. The services are re-emphasizing the practice of reducing ongoing program budgets in order to free funds for new programs, disregarding the effect of service-centered planning on the efficacy of overall defense planning and funding. Only a strong, independent, and informed Secretary of Defense can temper the parochial tendencies of military planners, establish balanced defense priorities, and work toward an effective and efficient use of defense appropriations.

By example, a strong Secretary of Defense can confirm the importance of civilian control within the Defense Department. By example, he can encourage a commitment to cost reductions and to improved management at every level of the defense hierarchy. It is within his jurisdiction to reward civilian and military officials who cooperate with long-term management goals and to penalize those who do not.

A factor that continually thwarts efforts to reform management procedures is the ambiguity of the relationship between Secretaries and Assistant Secretaries and the military officers and civil service personnel who serve under them. Military officers' promotions are controlled by their military service promotion boards. Tenure regulations protect civil servants from dismissal in all but the most flagrant and extreme cases of irresponsibility. Without a viable system of incentives, rewards, and penalties, civilian appointees to senior Pentagon positions have few means at their command to change the direction of procurement management. In fact, they have a great deal to lose if they are at odds with the military and civil service personnel who control the flow of information within the Department.

An additional liability to the management process is the short term of office served by most service Secretaries and Assistant Secretaries. Relatively few have been able to commit themselves for the full term of the Presidential administration during which they were appointed. Thus, procurement policy may shift radically from year to year in several areas of management. One Assistant Secretary may emphasize configuration management; his successor, incentive contracting; a third appointee to the same position, value engineering.

Program Advocates versus Program Managers

Too many officials in the Defense Department have dual roles in the procurement process. They are salesmen for particular programs as well as managers. The roles are not compatible. The dilemma affects officials who serve as Government plant representatives, program managers, service Secretaries and Assistant Secretaries, and all others in positions of leadership within the Department. The problem is compounded by the fact that a promotion (for a military officer) and military cooperation (for a civilian appointee) are largely dependent on competence as a program advocate. Effective management performance—cost and schedule control, strict contract administration—is seldom rewarded. Indeed, if competent management activity exposes an acquisition program to public or Congressional criticism, a defense manager may find himself under strenuous attack from senior officers in his military department.

Program and Procurement Management Career Fields

Military and civil service positions in procurement and program management have few similarities. Military program managers do not usually remain with acquisition programs long enough to develop management expertise; civil servants in positions throughout the department remain in the same jobs for so long that they resist innovation and change. Military and civil service personnel also differ in motivation: most program managers are truly dedicated to their programs and will work 60 hours a week or more if necessary. Civil servants rarely have the same opportunities to win supervisory positions, and are often given routine tasks which demand a minimal commitment. What both these groups do share is an unwillingness to accept procurement/program management as a long-term career. For the career officer, program management is, at best, a temporary detour. The same is true for the ambitious civil servant. With few exceptions, work in this field is not the route to the rank of general, admiral, or GS-18.

A military officer who is a capable manager but who is eventually passed over for promotion to the rank of general or admiral may use his skills after retirement from the service in a position in private industry. Despite the urgent need for competent acquisition managers within the military, there are at present few incentives for qualified officers to remain in the service after 20 years. The defense industry, on the other hand, provides a compelling incentive for a knowledgeable officer to leave the service: rewarding salary scale and career status. The availability of jobs in industry can have a subtle, but debilitating, effect on an officer's performance during his tour of duty in a program management assignment. If he takes too strong a hand in controlling contractor activity, he might be damaging his opportunity for a second career following retirement. Positions are offered to officers who have demonstrated their appreciation for industry's particular problems and commitments.

The military services have at least two options for improving the acquisition process. First, they can offer financial incentives to qualified officers who elect to remain in the service after 20 years to work in procurement and program management. There must be a body of senior procurement officials to rule on the eligibility of officers wishing to choose this option. Otherwise, program management will remain a haven for officers who are not qualified to enter the competitive world of private industry.

A more effective alternative would be the establishment of a separate career field for procurement managers, as has been done in France with considerable success. Advancement would be based strictly on management capability and performance. Assignments and promotions would have to be controlled solely by senior procurement officials, with no interference from officers who command combat operations. In addition, a sufficient number of colonel/captain and general/admiral positions must be created to reward officers in this command for distinguished service.

There are encouraging indications that such a change could be accomplished successfully despite the present military opposition. The Army has one highly respected career field that does not involve combat: the Corps of Engineers. The unit attracts outstanding officers. One reason for its success is that assignments and promotions are largely handled by the Chief of the Corps.

Program managers, however trained and selected, should be given more appropriate incentives for efficient management performance. First of all, marketing responsibility for acquisition programs should be given to using commands or service headquarters. Program managers should be rewarded for: (1) the use of formal analysis and control techniques; (2) early identification of problems affecting cost, schedule, and system performance; and (3) their success in achieving program objectives and decreasing program costs. At the present time, managers who cope with full-scale crises are given high performance ratings. Often, however, timely preventive action could have deactivated problems before they reached the crisis stage. Since preventive action calls for day-to-day attention to management detail, supervisors who control rewards are not likely to notice a good manager's competence. As a result, there is little motivation to attempt systematic control activity. A drastic change of emphasis is needed.

One effective tool for measuring management performance is the use of contingency funds. Such funds could be held in reserve by senior defense officials. Program managers would be rated on the basis of how well they used the budgets specified in program contracts. When they found it necessary to apply for contingency funding, they would be rated negatively unless they were able to prove just cause.

A much expanded practical training program for program managers is needed to prepare officers to deal with the multitude of complex day-to-day problems they will meet in the field. Lectures should be at a minimum. The emphasis should be on real-life case discussions, simulation exercises, role-playing experiences, and other techniques to develop skills in dealing with the fundamental behavioral characteristics of the procurement process. A period of internship should run concurrently with the training program, with select professionals acting as instructors and supervisors.

Lack of professional management training is a serious handicap for civil service as well as military personnel. A comprehensive training program should be established for civil servants who wish to devote their careers to program management and procurement. Only those candidates with the requisite intelligence and ability should be accepted for the program. In addition, a personnel board, composed of senior military and civilian procurement officials, should review applicants for all major management positions, and should be empowered to remove civil servants whose performance is inadequate. The board should also be given the authority to provide financial rewards annually to at least 10% of the procurement and program management force. Bonuses should be given to civil servants who have been responsible for significant program cost reductions. New GS-16, -17, and -18 positions should be authorized, to encourage ambitious and talented personnel to remain in the procurement field.

There are several precedents for changing civil service promotion and tenure rules. The National Security Agency, the Central Intelligence Agency, and the Congress use personnel selection systems that are far less rigid than the system imposed upon the Defense Department by Congress. None of them is hampered by tenure regulations or by an unrealistic restriction on the number of authorized senior civil service positions.

PLANT REPRESENTATIVES

To improve the quality of contract administration in the field, the Defense Department must provide a new set of incentives and rewards for its plant representatives. At present, a Government plant representative is considered successful if he develops a close working relationship with a contractor and if he increases program size. Like the program manager, he is more likely to be penalized than rewarded if his administrative initiatives cause a program to be cut back or canceled. Since he remains at one plant for a good many years, he eventually discovers that his goals parallel those of the contractor. They both have a vested interest in maintaining and/or expanding each acquisition program. To correct this tendency, at least one Government plant representative at each program site should be given responsibility for challenging the contractor's budget figures and for cutting program costs. Rewards should be commensurate with the success of these attempts. In addition, frequent rotation of plant representatives should be mandatory. A Government plant representative who is assigned to a different defense plant every five years, and who is rewarded for reducing program costs, will find it in his own best interests to satisfy his employer rather than the contractor he is supervising.

SPECIFIC AREAS OF MANAGEMENT

In the preceding portion of this chapter, I have discussed broad aspects of procurement policy and planning, emphasizing the special interests of the people who direct the acquisition process. I shall turn now to several more specific areas of management; namely, program definition; cost estimating; source election; contractors, competition among contractors, and types of contracts; and the control of ongoing programs.

Program Definition

Senior officers in using commands, who have no responsibility for managing the budgets for development and production programs, now have considerable influence over the initial determination of program requirements. Traditionally, major acquisition programs are "urgent," and weapon systems "must" have the newest and most technologically sophisticated components. To introduce order and discipline into the acquisition process, the French example might be followed. One or more firms are funded to study components of a new weapon system; e.g., the landing gear, airframe, and/or engine of a fighter aircraft. Every two years, a small development program is authorized and the incremental improvements which have been satisfactorily developed and tested are incorporated into the weapon system. Since new development programs begin at regular intervals, the sense of urgency is minimized and there is no need to pack unnecessary technology into every program.

The outcome of this low-keyed approach to acquisition is a sense of stability and continuity. Since development programs are smaller in scope, fewer contract changes are required. This results in lower budgets and means less risk for the Government and for defense contractors. There are at least two other benefits: development and production programs do not overlap, and design teams remain together beyond the development phase.

Given the lower budgets involved in this approach to weapons acquisition, the Congress would probably find it feasible to provide funds for competitive prototype development. At present, the funding of one prototype demands such a major outlay of funds that competitive development programs are usually beyond reach.

On March 12, 1970, Dr. John Foster, Director of Defense Research and Engineering, described his standards for system development in a speech to the National Security Industrial Association.

> We shall insist relentlessly—as a point without peer in our management—that price has as much priority as performance. This does not rule out vigorous pursuit of new technology where that technology is required or can pay its way. And frequently, new technology can be used to reduce costs. Yet we must design to a price, a much lower price, or else we will not be able to afford what we need. . . .
>
> We must revamp, and thoroughly, the design philosophy in every corner of the Defense Department and defense industry. This task falls within my responsibilities and there is no other matter about which I feel more strongly. We shall not in the future indulge the present syndrome of incorporating into every system the most advanced technology as soon as it seems to be available or merely because it is advanced. We shall ask only for what we really need—the minimum necessary performance—and we shall match, wherever possible, proven technology to that essential, realistic need.

To achieve these goals, the Secretary of Defense would have to give his unqualified support. The Director of Defense Research and Engineering and his staff would be required to make independent evaluations of all recommended system specifications, and to exercise strict control over program planning.

Early in 1972 one hopeful step was taken: potential bidders on four new programs—the XM-800 armored reconnaissance vehicle; the STOL replacement for the C-130 cargo aircraft; the replacement for the Bell UH-1 ("Huey") helicopter; and the A-X close air support aircraft—were all given target budgets. As of 1973, however, there are few signs of the comprehensive reform described by Dr. Foster in 1970.

Cost Estimating

There is no single agency within each military service that is responsible for developing and tracking a cost estimate for each program as it matures from conceptual effort to development to production. Before any meaningful cost control effort can begin, responsibility for the cost estimating function must be centralized, possibly in the office of the Comptroller for each service.

The type of cost estimate that will provide the most useful and accurate information has not been easy to find. Both parametric and learning curve estimates, used extensively by the Defense Department, are based on cost histories of earlier programs. Little or no allowance is made for the inefficient management and the false starts that added unnecessary costs to previous programs. Thus, built into these estimates are the overruns that should have been avoided. This works to the serious detriment of the Government. For, once contractors discover what estimates have been made for a new program, they plan program activities that will use up the entire amount. New problems inevitably arise during the course of each new program and cost overruns must be added to the initial estimates. In the future, the data base on which a cost estimate is founded must be purged of unnecessary and avoidable expense.

The Should-Cost estimate is being used in some sections of the Defense Department. This is a far more rigorous type of estimate than any other now in use. To prepare a Should-Cost estimate, an independent team of specialists analyzes a contractor's cost proposal for a new program. Should-Cost estimates have already saved the Government considerable expense. They are opposed by many defense contractors and by the numerous Defense Department officials and other program advocates who resist any efforts to reduce the size of military programs.

The success of each Should-Cost estimate depends on the team of specialists who develop it. Each team must devote several weeks of intense effort at the defense plant whose proposal is under review. The team leader is the key figure in each group, and he must be chosen carefully on the basis of training, experience, and ability. He should have worked on at least one previous Should-Cost estimating team.

To assure quality performance in this arduous and crucial task, Should-Cost teams should be given substantial backing and generous rewards. The Defense Department should make Should-Cost estimates mandatory for every major new acquisition program in order to discover when contractors have proposed costs that are unnecessarily high or unreasonably low. Should-Cost teams should continue to provide documented evidence to support the level of costs they consider reasonable for new acquisition programs. They now provide expert back-up material for Government contract negotiators. To realize the fullest value of Should-Cost estimates, the Defense Department should establish and maintain cost control activity throughout the life of an acquisition program. Should-Cost estimates should be used by program management personnel as a guide in preventing overruns and unreasonable contract changes.

Source Selection

The source selection process should require less time and less paperwork. Government and industry personnel are now involved for too many months preparing Requests for Proposals, proposals, and evaluations of proposals. Although the process is essential, efficiency in all three phases could be improved dramatically.

1. The Defense Department should distribute to prospective contractors a preliminary draft of its Request for Proposal for each major new program. Contractors should be invited to recommend changes in program specifications that would streamline the process of documentation and evaluation.
2. The Department should establish a board to review final Requests for Proposals. Before RFP's are distributed to industry, the board should ascertain whether system specifications are essential, reasonable, and attainable.
3. The Department should set a page limit for most contractor proposals thereby forcing defense firms to edit their own material, excluding nonessential detail. This would reduce the time needed for the Defense Department's evaluation effort, and would also release contractor personnel for other essential tasks.
4. A target budget should be provided for prospective bidders. Companies now seek out information on defense appropriations and budgets through private intelligence channels, and design their proposals accordingly.
5. There should be a formal procedure for reviewing contractors' past performance on Government programs. Bidders on new programs would be penalized for failure to cooperate in the preparation of Should-Cost estimates by the Defense Department, for failure to meet contract terms on previous programs, and for failure to use adequate management controls on previous programs. Defense contractors are not now formally rated by Government program management personnel. By the time established defense firms bid on new programs, the Government officials who are familiar with their past work are located in widely scattered assignments. If the Department were to establish a corps of procurement and program management specialists, a formal system of contractor performance evaluation would be feasible. This would add needed depth to the source selection process.

Contractors and Competition

Profit is not a defense contractor's only concern when bidding on or conducting a development or production program. Defense contracts are sought to cover payroll and overhead costs, and to provide company personnel with the opportunity to develop technical and managerial skills useful in future commercial and defense business. Once a contract is won, a company seeks every opportunity to add work and funds to the program. The need for follow-on work is crucial, since (1) the initial effort to secure a contract involves a large outlay of money, and (2) there is usually a long time lapse between contracts for the same weapon system. Over the course of a program, the contractor builds up a large, skilled work force and constantly promotes Government funded contract additions, in order to keep these employees on the payroll.

Once a company has committed its work force and facilities to defense programs, the need for continuing defense work becomes a matter of survival. Established defense companies compete fiercely for new contracts. They inevitably promise maximum performance for a minimum price, knowing from experience that once a contract is won, they can negotiate contract changes to cover cost overruns, schedule delays, and reductions in weapon performance. Traditionally, companies have been relieved of contract obligations by the Defense Department when unable to meet them.

Given the industry's dependence on Government business, an outsider might suppose that the Federal Government could exact unusually competent performance from its contractors. This has obviously not happened. The military services have been preoccupied with their own growth, and the Defense Department has not developed a unified, independent approach to the management of the acquisition process. Many layers of Defense Department bureaucracy are involved in procurement, each with its own interests to protect. In comparison, defense companies have relatively uncomplicated needs and goals.

It would be inaccurate to give the impression that all defense companies have equal negotiating strength. Small contractors are often unable to win the benefits that have become standard on large contracts; i.e., special progress payments, contract changes to avoid terminations for default, and payment for marketing costs, independent research and development, and other technical effort. In the future, the size of the contract should influence the stringency of management controls. Small companies should be allowed the same benefits as large companies, but should not be hamstrung by unsuitably complex regulations. On the other hand, large companies, as well as small, should be expected to cooperate with Governmental efforts to obtain maximum management efficiency.

If the Federal Government is ever to achieve a fair return on its investment in defense procurement, it must convince contractors that they will be penalized for failure to meet contractual commitments. Penalties must include cancellation of contracts when the default goes beyond a pre-established threshold.

Competition in the defense industry bears little resemblance to the competition of the open marketplace. In the commercial market, price is usually a major factor in competition. A producer attempts (1) to lower its price on an established product, or (2) to produce a better product for a competitive price. In both cases, the characteristics of the product are usually known and judged by the customer before a purchase is made. In the defense industry, companies compete by predicting performance and costs for a product whose performance will not be tested for several years. In ordinary business, if a company has achieved financial stability, it can usually withstand the loss of a segment of its market, and will search for new customers elsewhere. In the defense industry, companies become totally dependent on Federal contracts. Winning contractors are assured of financial health for a number of years. Losers face the possibility of going out of business altogether.

Competition in the defense industry was accurately described by Robert S. Tucker, formerly an official in the Office of the Secretary of Defense and now a defense industry manager. In an interview in 1969 with a National Security Industrial Association team investigating the acquisition process, he made the following remarks:

No description of the weapon system acquisition process can be realistic or helpful, without acknowledging the pervasive element of grinding competition which is present in every phase of the process, in Government as well as industry. Within the Department of Defense, competition is an active force:

1. In its drive to stay ahead of our potential enemies by fielding weapons which incorporate the latest possible technology,
2. In its relationship with other Government departments,
3. In the efforts of our military departments to protect and extend their respective roles and missions and to obtain an increased share of the defense budget,
4. In the relationship between the military departments and the Office of the Secretary of Defense,
5. Among the branches, commands, arsenals, yards, centers and laboratories of our military services.

Outside the Federal Government itself, the monopsonistic character of the defense business forces companies into a continuous life or death struggle to obtain defense contracts, the overall total of which is seldom adequate to support the available capacity of even the hard core defense contractors. This competition takes on state and national proportions as industry's salesmen, admen, public relations experts, engineers and executives are joined by state representatives anxious to obtain Government dollars to support their local economies. . . .

Competition to produce and field advanced weapons encourages excessive optimism by the military services and their contractors in regard to the extent of technical advance which may be reasonably expected in new weapon programs. To begin with, a sizable step forward must be offered in order to justify the great cost of creating a new generation of weapon systems, especially when the cost of related training, spares, and support equipment is taken into account. Defense policy contemplates an orderly evolution of technology from research through exploratory development, advanced development, i.e., the "building block" concept. Undue optimism, however, often results in hurrying through or even skipping work in the early phases of development, thus bringing about the all too familiar pattern of production and operational difficulties, delays, changes and cost escalation. The demand for large dollar amounts to rectify such unforeseen problems in operational programs is particularly insidious, since the funds required to salvage these programs reduce the amounts available to support exploratory and advanced developments on components and subsystems required for the next generation of systems, thus perpetuating the cycle and the certain consequences of inadequate development. . . .

Competition among the military services for available budget dollars increases still further the bias which works against cost and schedule realism. Since it is the responsibility of the Office of the Secretary of Defense, and particularly the Director of Defense Research and Engineering, to both supervise research and development carried out by the military departments and to decide the allocation of resources, the services are naturally inclined toward spirited promotion of their own parochial position, leaving the Office of the Secretary of Defense to ferret out soft spots, to weigh risks, to perform trade-off studies, and to estimate cost effectiveness. While the Office of the Secretary of Defense thus provides an essential check-and-balance capability, its work is obviously made more difficult by the highly subjective environment in which it must be carried out. . . .

This study corroborates Mr. Tucker's analysis. Despite the Defense Department's efforts to simulate a free enterprise environment, the uncertainties of weapons development and production preclude normal competition. In its own way, the Government acknowledges the singularity of the defense industry. When large companies fail to meet the requirements of a major contract, the Government may intervene to prevent bankruptcy. This was the case when the Lockheed Aircraft Corporation failed to achieve contract requirements on the Army's Cheyenne Helicopter program and the Air Force C-5A aircraft program.

There is no sensible reason to deny the obvious: the defense industry is unique. The basic tenets of the free enterprise system do not apply. To insure adequate weapon production, the Government must involve itself in every aspect of the acquisition process. European governments reached this conclusion long ago, probably because their economies could not sustain the enormous price of simulated competition as practiced in the United States. We have seen the results of maintaining a myth: overcapacity, cost overruns, expensive contract changes, schedule slippage, performance shortfalls.

For its part, industry has no choice but to play the game as defined by its military customers. If contracts are awarded on the basis of cost estimates and technical promises, no matter how unrealistic this kind of competition is, companies will continue to make optimistic and unrealistic bids. To do otherwise would be too risky. As Mr. Tucker told the NSIA in 1969:

> A company which does a thorough and factual job of analyzing and pricing the risks attending its proposed approach to system development will more likely than not find itself the loser to a more optimistic competitor. With too little business to go around, survival is inevitably more compelling than objectivity.

It is time to admit that price competition is not a feasible concept in selecting contractors for multimillion dollar defense development programs. To encourage the industry to prepare for reduced Government spending, the Government should introduce a new form of competition. First, the Government should project its plans for acquiring various types of weapon systems over a five-year period. Second, the Government should initiate a formal design and capabilities competition on major programs to determine which two producers will develop prototypes for selected parts of each new weapon system. The contractors will then engage in competitive prototype development. The company which develops the winning prototype will be awarded the production contract for the weapon system. In addition, both contractors will be retained for research and development leading to the next generation of prototypes. New development and production programs should begin every two to four years.

To make the system work, the Government must begin to hold contractors responsible for meeting contract terms. If and when a contract is canceled because a contractor has defaulted, the Government should provide help for unemployed defense workers in the form of financial relief, job counseling, and technical training for new jobs. If the defaulting contractor can no longer maintain his plant, the Government could provide guaranteed loans to a new buyer, or could purchase the plant and equipment for leasing to another company. Thus, if contract termination were to force a defaulting contractor into bankruptcy or if a firm had to reorganize, only its stockholders and creditors would feel the effects. The Government would have little trouble in making arrangements for another firm to operate most such facilities.

The acquisition process and the defense industry as a whole would be well served if defense companies would begin to diversify. The Government could assist them by instituting training programs to prepare employees for nondefense work. Some firms—including Raytheon, Texas Instruments, Boeing Aircraft, Litton Industries—have already begun. But it is not easily done. One New England defense company found that its engineers were unable to fulfill specifications for commercial display equipment for computers on a price competitive basis. The chief executive of another company, a large electrical manufacturing firm, explained:

> We have never been able to take a large group of people who had been involved in defense work and form a commercial business. Few other companies have been able to do so. This problem results from the large overhead costs that engineers and managers become accustomed to in defense work.

During discussions with senior managers at several defense firms on the West Coast, it became obvious that although they recognized that U.S. defense spending would eventually be reduced, each believed that only his competitors would suffer. They all hoped there would be no need to diversify or to reduce their work force.

Contracts

There are several reasons for the failure of contract incentives to influence the industry's attitude toward cost control. (1) A cost-based profit policy encourages contractors to boost costs. (2) Frequent contract changes during ongoing programs make cost reduction incentives negotiated at the beginning of a program meaningless. With each contract change, the contract price and other provisions are renegotiated. (3) The Government usually agrees to subsidize contractors' overhead expenses. (4) Contractors negotiate follow-on contracts. (5) The Government does not enforce contract provisions.

Government contract negotiators work under several handicaps. They have smaller and less experienced staffs than those available to their industry counterparts. They themselves, however dedicated, are relatively inexperienced in dealing with major corporations. The information available to them is often inadequate. Rewards for resourceful bargaining are not provided by the Defense Department. In contrast, large company negotiators are highly trained and are supported by expert staffs, who provide comprehensive background information. Industry negotiators receive generous rewards for successful bargaining. Often, effective Government negotiators are offered positions in defense firms at substantially higher salaries than are available to military or civil service procurement personnel.

Should-Cost estimates go a long way toward strengthening a Government negotiator's bargaining position. For the first time he is able to challenge a contractor's cost estimates with authority. On those contracts for which Should-Cost estimates have been prepared, Government negotiators have been able to reduce contractors' initial proposals by from 30% to 50%. At the present time, however, the use of Should-Cost estimates does not have widespread Defense Department backing. There are too few qualified analysts and too few rewards for personnel involved in the rigorous work required. Were the Department to provide generous incentives for Should-Cost analysis, most major defense programs could experience cost reduction.

Once defense contracts are negotiated, Defense Department managers should keep a tight rein on contract changes. This is only possible if the original contract is reasonable and enforceable—an argument for the use of Should-Cost estimates. Formal change boards, staffed by cost specialists, should withhold approval of each recommended contract modification until the contractor has prepared a revised cost estimate. In addition, the issuance of letter contracts should be held to a minimum. In 1970 and 1971 the Army Materiel Command reduced the number of letter contracts by 80%. Similar reductions can be achieved on other defense programs with an increased efficiency in management planning. Each request for a letter contract should be vigorously challenged.

Controlling Ongoing Programs

Successful program control—the disciplined management of Government and industry resources—will depend on several Defense Department reforms: the establishment of a professional career category for procurement and program management; the institution of a professional training program for acquisition managers; longer assignments for military personnel; improvements in cost estimating and contract negotiations; a reduction in the number of reporting levels; and the re-introduction of a strong system analysis organization in the Office of the Secretary of Defense. The recommendations made throughout this chapter are all pointed toward the improvement of ongoing program control. In addition, another weakness in the system must be addressed. Responsibility for the management and control of ongoing development and production programs must be clarified.

Cost control responsibility is often shared by personnel in three functional areas: research and development; financial management; installations and logistics. Too often, this dispersal of authority results in a total breakdown of efficiency. To clarify responsibility, a single position should be created within the Office of the Secretary of Defense and within each of the three military departments: an Assistant Secretary for Material Acquisition. In each service, this official would absorb responsibility for all the tasks involved in the acquisition process, tasks now directed by the Assistant Secretaries for Research and Development and the Assistant Secretaries for Installations and Logistics. Such a consolidation would reflect the present relationship between research and development and production programs. As research and development costs have increased, production costs have been correspondingly lowered by decreasing the number of weapon systems to be acquired. Trade-off decisions between development and production programs could be more efficiently handled if one official had responsibility for the entire acquisition process.

At the other end of the spectrum, it cannot be too strongly emphasized that program managers must be shielded from the pressures imposed by senior officers in their using commands. This will only happen when procurement/program management is defined as a separate career field within the military, with promotion and assignments beyond the influence of officers in using commands.

It is vividly clear that better information and reporting systems may easily be subverted by groups influenced by the powerful pressures and incentives analyzed throughout the earlier chapters of this book. Unless there is an enormous improvement in the quality of the people who manage military procurement agencies, and unless there can be radical changes in incentives, other changes in management techniques will have little or no positive effect.

To obtain objective appraisals of initial program proposals, as well as subsequent program progress reports, the Defense Department should hire one or more independent organizations to conduct periodic audits of program performance. These private organizations should have no vested interest in the continuation or expansion of any defense program. Their findings should also be available to members of Congressional authorization and appropriations committees, for use in evaluating proposed defense budgets.

Many Government and industry managers have yet to learn the distinction between controlling funds ("funds control") and controlling the cost of work ("cost control"). Funds control means monitoring and controlling the monthly rate at which funds are expended, regardless of the work accomplished. Cost control means monitoring and controlling the cost of specific work, regardless of the month in which it is performed. In most Government program offices, funds control is the prevalent management technique. Gearing their control systems to Government techniques, contractors also emphasize funds control rather than cost control. As a result, few program management officials measure cost performance, and there is no way short of the end of a long program to tell whether work is costing more or less than estimated.

DOD Directive 7000.2 gives systematic instructions concerning cost performance measurement on acquisition programs. Its use and implementation would familiarize management officials with the types of controls that are standard for commercial programs. Unfortunately, however, many senior defense officials simply do not understand how or why cost performance is measured. Some Secretaries, Assistant Secretaries, generals, and admirals support the techniques described in the directive; others neither understand nor condone them.

Since defense companies are hostile to any form of governmental control, they also resist implementation of Directive 7000.2. Many of the reasons for their antagonism make good sense. Since Government managers are not trained to use complex cost control tools, they often require contractors to prepare reports containing useless detail. In addition, they often misinterpret and misuse data supplied by contractors. Obviously, any control system is only as efficient as the administrators who use it.

Industry and Government managers share the responsibility for mismanagement of defense programs. Industry management is adversely affected by the practice of rewarding outstanding engineers with promotions to management positions. Engineer/managers consistently emphasize technological achievement with minor attention to planning, budgeting, and control activities. The Government's willingness to overlook cost growth and schedule slippage reinforces this inclination.

Robert Tucker's description of industry program control to the National Security Industrial Association team, already cited, emphasizes this problem.

> During the decade of the '50's, the defense business was characterized by advanced technology, concurrency and cost-type contracts. Many of the scientists, engineers and managers who shape the industry today were "brought up" in that unique environment. It is hardly surprising that the transitional '60's were traumatic years for both industry and Government.
>
> With the emphasis of the '50's on developing and producing weapons incorporating the latest in the state of the art, there was created an almost insatiable demand for scientific and engineering personnel capable of

major technical innovation. Since both development and production were carried out under cost reimbursement contracts, production cost was not a major constraint on engineering design. Factory personnel were often not required to advise engineers regarding cost implications of various design alternatives, as money was made available to produce whatever was designed, so long as it promised a performance advantage over counterpart equipment thought to be in the hands of unfriendly nations. Those designs found impracticable in production or inoperative in the field were simply modified by Government-funded engineering changes.

It is small wonder that when faced with this environment, the engineering schools of the country responded by producing engineers superbly trained in advanced technology, with many of the scientific skills previously available only in those having graduate training in mathematics and physics. Unfortunately, one cannot be all things simultaneously, and classical engineers, industry's cost conscious, applied science practitioners, decreased in number and influence in the defense community.

A parallel evolution occurred among those who managed engineering organizations. It is well known that a permissive semi-academic environment is most conducive to scientific accomplishment. One cannot "invent on schedule" or within a predetermined cost. Since most new weapons depended heavily on scientific breakthrough, many engineering departments were forced to emulate research laboratories, with similarly laissez-faire managements. New managers were selected primarily for their technical expertise rather than for skill and interest in the management disciplines.

Effective program control depends on the constant watchfulness of a "chopper-off-er," to use Admiral Rickover's term—someone who calls a halt to engineering refinements. It is up to the Defense Department to define this as a basic management task, as well as to establish specific cost control objectives and to insure adequate management training directed toward the realization of these goals.

As more and more of its budget is used for the development of new kinds of weapon systems, the Defense Department has had to cut costs elsewhere. Sometimes fewer weapon systems are acquired than originally planned because development costs are excessive. This was true for the C-5A, the F-111, the Cheyenne Helicopter, and the Main Battle Tank. Fewer quantities of items are purchased to replace outdated vehicles and other equipment. Even the living quarters for military personnel are affected. On many bases around the world, barracks are in disrepair because available funds are directed to weapons development. In its report for Fiscal Year 1972, the Senate Armed Services Committee took note of the effect of increased defense spending on the nation's total defense capability.

The foregoing tendencies are deeply troubling. If the geometric cost increase for weapon systems is not sharply reversed, then even significant increases in the defense budget may not insure the force levels required for our national security. In the more likely case the share of our national resources taken by defense will stabilize or continue to decline, and it will thus soon become clear that the present system cannot provide sufficient forces to protect our security. If we can afford a permanent force structure of only one-fifth as many fighter aircraft or tanks as our potential adversaries—because our systems are about five times more expensive than theirs—then a future crisis may find us at a sharp numerical disadvantage, since the lead times required to develop and produce modern weapons systems are now measured in years, deficiencies cannot be corrected after a crisis begins.

Management standards for defense programs are so much lower than for commercial programs that the capabilities of workers to perform other jobs is affected. Government Should-Cost studies conducted in 1972 for more than 20 acquisition programs revealed that thousands of workers in the defense industry were becoming accustomed to low work standards. Managers have grown used to stretching programs for as long as customers will tolerate delay. This slackness affects program budgets. Should-Cost estimates have shown that 30% to 50% of program costs can be cut with the introduction of business practices and standards developed for large commercial programs (e.g., large commercial aircraft, ships, and custom turbines). This amounts to a potential cost savings of $8 to $12 billion per year—the cost of building more than 1,000 schools and operating them for 30 years, or the cost of building 2,000 electric power plants, each servicing a town of 60,000 people. F. Trowbridge VomBauer, former General Counsel of the Navy Department, talked about the savings that would result from acquisition reforms in testimony in 1970 before the Joint Economic Committee.

> . . . there are simply great quantities of mistakes and errors which are made by people in the business side of DOD today, which are tremendously expensive for the Department of Defense, which delay the delivery of ships and other hardware, but which simply do not have to be made. In my judgment these unnecessary mistakes cost the Government and the taxpayer something like 25–30% of the procurement budget. The procurement budget is now about $40 billion, meaning that, in my opinion, some $10–12 billion a year is wasted through this downgrading of the business side of the Department of Defense.

Unfortunately, many Government and industry officials believe that the only problem to be solved in defense procurement is how to silence critics. There are only a few officials who understand what changes need to be made and how to make them, and who are willing to endure hostility from supporters of the status quo. Some of the most vocal critics of the system have been motivated by their opposition to the war in Vietnam. With the ending of the war, the mounting pressure for reform may be dissipated. There is no indication from within the Pentagon that defense budgets are about to experience major reductions. Indeed, many officials have voiced their enthusiasm about the opportunity the Vietnam war afforded as a testing ground for new weapon systems.

Pressures for reform may grow as a result of continuing contractor defaults. Domestic needs in areas such as health and education may lead to cuts in the defense budget. But unless there is a sustained sense of urgency, such imperatives will wither under the assault of military and industry advocacy of increased weapons development. The hidden Government subsidies represented by negotiated overhead costs have been a boon to industry. But the Government and the ordinary taxpayer have received little in return for their generosity. Only with an integrated, across-the-board approach to reform will the direction of acquisition spending change.

What is the solution? In an address to the NSIA after receiving the Forrestal Award for dedicated public service (March 9, 1972), David Packard tried to answer this question.

> What is the solution? We are going to have to stop this problem of people playing games with each other. Games that will destroy us if we do not bring them to a halt.
>
> Let's take the case of the F-14. The only sensible course is to hold the contractor to his contract. Although some companies may be forced to suffer financially because of this concept, it will not be a major disaster to the country. It will be a major disaster to the country if we cannot get the military industrial complex to play the game straight. Until and unless we can stop this attitude, we are going to continue to waste the taxpayer's dollars—get less defense for the dollars we spend.
>
> Quite simply it means the Army, the Navy, the Air Force and the Marines must put the welfare of America ahead of the welfare of their respective service in peacetime as well as in war. It means the great industrial corporations that forge the seams of our military strength must put the long-term gains of America ahead of the short-term gains of their respective organizations. It means that Congress should address America's security policy, stay out of day-to-day administrative problems, and discourage game-playing between the services and the business community.

In 1969 Mr. Packard had resigned from his position as chief executive of the Hewlett Packard Corporation to serve as Deputy Secretary of Defense.

After three years of sustained effort to reform the procurement system, he left the Pentagon in 1972—disappointed at the bureaucracy's successful resistance to change.

The imperative for reform in the acquisition process must come from ordinary voters who want their tax money used to solve their own domestic problems, from a Congress alive to the need for vigorous control of defense activity, from a military establishment which puts national defense needs before parochial concerns, and, finally, from a Secretary of Defense whose vision transcends the goals of narrow interest groups. Such a coalition could bring stability and discipline to a system long out of control.

Index

Advanced production engineering (APE), 142

Advertising: formal, 250–251; role of, in commercial industrial versus defense marketing, 304

Aerospace Industries Association (AIA), 5, 66, 67, 266

Air Force, research, development, and procurement budget for, 35–37

Air Force Magazine, 5

Allen, William, 438

Anthony, Robert N., 86, 333

Appropriations Committees, 117–118, 123–124. *See also* Congress

Armed Services Committees (Senate and House), 19–20, 117–118, 130; on cost/performance management, 420–421; on defense budget, 28–29; on effect of increased defense spending, 475–476; hearings on authorization, 121–122; on increasing cost of weapon systems, 22–23

Armed Services Procurement Regulations (ASPR), 14, 110–111, 174, 194, 214–215; on contract types, 225–226, 230–231; on cost or pricing data, 226–227; on defense profit policy, 307; on Government cost analysis, 333; and methods of Government procurement, 253

Army, research, development, and procurement budget for, 34–35

Arthur D. Little Company, 445

ASPR, *see* Armed Services Procurement Regulations

Atlantic Monthly, The, 99

Atomic Energy Commission (AEC), 10

Authorization hearings, 121–122

AWACS (airborne warning and control system), 21

Barron's magazine, 391

Battelle Memorial Institute, 256

Bell Aircraft Company, 125

Benson, Robert, 3

Betts, A. W., 102

Blue Ribbon Panel, President's, 5; on Contract Definition phase of acquisition process, 17–18; on defense marketing, 302–303; on improving acquisition process, 457; on negotiating contracts, 358; on policy of rotation, 191–192; on program control, 398–399; on program management, 171–172; on role of Defense Secretary, 90–91; on service parochialism, 99; on source selection process, 269–270; study of careers of military officers by, 77, 191

B-1 bomber, Air Force manned, 21

Budget, defense: and buying organizations, 34–37; categories of, 22–24; by major industry groupings, 33–34; nature of Federal, 119–121; 1940–1972, 26, 27, 28, 29; and nondefense budget trends, 28, 30; as percentage of GNP, 28–30, 31; as percentage of total budget, 28, 31; for R&D and procurement, 26–27, 32–33, 34–37; wartime trends in, 27–28

Buesking, Albert W., 412, 435

Burns, Arthur F., 30

Calvert, James, 206

Cannon, Howard, 430

tractor proposals, 300; on defense management, 455; and F-14 cost coverup, 289–290; on reform of procurement system, 477–478; on state of defense procurement, 1, 6–7; on unqualified procurement personnel, 200
Parametric cost estimates, 156–157, 158, 161, 164–165
Patman, Wright, 117
Patton, Arch, 297–298
PDM's (Program Decision Memoranda), 96–97
Peck, Merton J., *The Weapons Acquisition Process,* 1–2, 9, 10, 14, 34; on contract changes, 382; on cost estimates, 161; on defense contractors, 42–43, 53; on defense market, 26, 37; on Government pricing techniques, 333; on initiation of defense programs, 101–102; on personnel instability, 193–194; on productivity of engineers in weapons industry, 332; on profit maximization, 298; on program controls, 398
Pentagon, 20; and cost control, 74–77; personnel of, 70–73; relationship between civilian and military personnel in, 82–83; relations between Congress and, 83–84; relations between defense contractors and, 84–86; reporting progress to, 86–92; responsibility for weapons acquisition within, 73–86
Perry, Franklyn A., Jr., 440
PERT COST system, 2, 7, 403–405, 406, 407
Planning, problem of long-range, in weapons acquisition process, 454
Plant representatives, 215–223, 462–463
Polaris project, 7, 403–405
POM (Program Objective Memorandum), 96–97
Power, Thomas S., 83
Pownall, Thomas G., 41, 66
Pricing techniques, Government, 331–333. *See also* Should-Cost
Procurement personnel (military and civilian): age distribution of, 186–187; educational attainment of, 187–188; evaluating and rewarding performance

of, 197–199; importance of civil service, 202–205; need for career field in management of, 201–202, 460–462; number of civilian, 185–186; number of military officers in, 186; policy of rotation for, 191–194, 200–201; problem of unqualified, 194–195, 199–200; problems of, 180–184; promotions for, 195–197; rating systems for, 189–190; recommended reforms for, 455–457, 458–459, 460–462; training program for, 205–206
Profit(s), in defense industry, 306–309; and cost reduction investments, 317–318; and defense contractor investments, 318–319; GAO study on, 310–316; measures of, 309–310; negotiation and defense contracting, European, 322–324; proposal for improved policy for, 319–322
Program control, 384–388, 472–478. *See also* Management techniques, changes in Government
Program definition, 463–464
Program managers, 109, 169, 171; Government, performance of, 422–427; Government, rewards and penalties for, 427–435; industry, rewards and penalties for, 437–445; private industry, 207–213; program advocates versus, 460; role and responsibilities of, 173–180
Program offices, 169, 170–172, 173; personnel problems in, 180–182
Proposals, *see* Contractor proposals; Request for proposal
Proxmire, William, 6, 30, 135, 199, 429, 431

RAND Corporation, 241–242, 256, 379
Reece, James S., 8, 370, 380, 440–441, 442–445
Request for Proposal (RFP), 16, 17–18, 163, 252, 264–265, 266; Blue Ribbon Panel on, 270; and defense marketing, 290, 293–294
Research and development, defense, budget for, 21